Divided Hearts

Divided Hearts

Britain and the American Civil War

R. J. M. BLACKETT

LOUISIANA STATE UNIVERSITY PRESS
Baton Rouge

Designer: Melanie O'Quinn Samaha
Typeface: Goudy
Typesetter: Crane Composition, Inc.
Printer and binder: Thomson-Shore, Inc.

Library of Congress Cataloging-in-Publication Data:
Blackett, R. J. M., 1943–
  Divided hearts : Britain and the American Civil War / R. J. M. Blackett.
    p. cm.
Includes bibliographical references and index.
  ISBN 0-8071-2595-4
1. United States—History—Civil War, 1861–1865—Foreign public
opinion, British. 2. United States—Foreign relations—Great Britain.
3. Great Britain—Foreign relations—United States. 4. Public
opinion—Great Britain—History—19th century. 5. United
States—Foreign relations—1861–1865. 6. Great Britain—Politics and
government—1837–1901. 7. Confederate States of America—Foreign public
opinion, British. I. Title.
  E469.8 .B66 2000
  973.7—dc21

                              00-009794

In memory of my mother, Philomena Blackett,
and brother-in-law, Assafa Fre-Hiwet

Contents

Illustrations

Acknowledgments

This study was so long in the making that the research was begun at one university, Indiana University, and the writing completed at another, the University of Houston. A summer stipend from Research and University Graduate School at Indiana University seeded the project, and a generous grant from the American Council of Learned Societies saw me through at a very critical stage.

If it is true that music is the food of life, then food and wine are the life of research. I had more than my fair share from Martin Crawford and Christine Turner, who welcomed me to their home in the beautiful Staffordshire village of Betley. From there I sortied out to libraries, comforted by the thought that there was always a warm meal and a glass of "plonk" when I returned at the end of the day. Other friends filled these vital needs when I visited libraries beyond the easy reach of Betley. Gad and Ruth Heuman in London, Jim and Jenny Walvin in York, and my cousins Joan and Louis Songui in Carshalton were sources of comfort and food. Gordon Batchelor welcomed me to his Kent home in the village of Goudhurst and gave me a tour of Bedgebury Park, the ancestral home of Beresford-Hope, a major supporter of the Confederacy. At the end of the day we swapped stories about English and West Indian cricket over a glass of his wife Betty's gooseberry champagne. Other researchers should be so lucky.

Archivists and librarians never fail to surprise me with the ease and enthusiasms they bring to any obscure request for assistance. When I wrote the librarian at Dundee requesting biographical information on a number of local figures, I got what she had and more: a copy of the pages from the diary of a local who reported on news from his family in America. Rather than keep me waiting, the librarian at Rawtenstall took home the microfilm copy of a local newspaper so she could locate information for me. In response to a request for biographical information on John Donald, a radical and local supporter of the Union, the librarian at Newmilns, Scotland, passed on my letter to Mrs. J. Murray, Donald's great-granddaughter, who promptly got in touch with her local newspaper to let its readers know that I was doing this study and ask for their support. After trying for months to figure out why there were so many Confederate supporters in Peterhead, Scotland, a port city with no apparent trading connections with the South, I called Roderick McDonald, an old friend who teaches at Rider College. He put me in touch with Jim Buchan, a local historian who just happened to live across the street from Roderick's brother in Peterhead. Buchan set me straight. Alice Lock at Tameside promptly responded to every one of my queries and pointed out additional information. So did David Taylor at Manchester and Rita Hurst at Bury. Anne Young at John Rylands Library, Manchester, was sympathetic and worried whether I would survive working in what must be the coldest reading room in the world! David Webb of the Bishopgate Institute had an answer for every question I lobbed at him.

Others were equally helpful. Owen Ashton showed me why W. E. Adams was so important to the Union's cause. Clare Midgley sent along information about the women officers of the Preston Anti Slavery Society. Robert Reinders, who has long been interested in my work, stayed engaged. Brian Jenkins pointed me to sources he had used in his splendid study of British reactions to the Civil War. Janet Toole showed me around Liverpool and provided information on Ashton and Stalybridge, as did Robert Hall, who shared with me his notes on leading working-class figures in the towns and later read the entire manuscript. W. H. Fraser helped piece together information on Scots working-class leaders. Fernand Garlington, a graduate student at the University of Houston, spent many hours ploughing through the London *Times*.

It is customary to thank those who read a manuscript and then absolve them from all responsibility for any shortcomings. It is an outdated custom; it seems to me perfectly reasonable for an author to take credit for all that is commendable and place the blame for all that is questionable at the feet of readers. Friends will understand this need to buck tradition. Martin Crawford read each chapter hot off the press and offered invaluable comments. Jim Epstein and Seymour Drescher read the two sociological chapters, as did Betty Fladeland, an old friend and an inspiration. Steve Mintz and Karl Ittmann, colleagues at Houston, commented on one of the chapters. Another colleague, Joe Glatthaar, read a later version of the entire manuscript. David Brion Davis was kind enough to read what he aptly called a pilot essay in which I toyed with some of the ideas I would develop in more detail later. Many thanks to Nell Painter, whose invitation to participate in the "Works in Progress" seminar at Princeton pushed me to think seriously about the war's impact on Britain. Finally, my greatest thanks to Lorna Lutes Sylvester, an old friend and coworker for a number of years at the *Indiana Magazine of History*. Lorna has that rare gift of savaging your prose while at the same time making you feel that she had done you a favor.

My wife, Cheryl, and sons, Victor and Peter, suffered through my long absences from home without much protest. There were times when I got the distinct impression they were enjoying these separations. That was enough of an incentive to finish the research. My daughters Leila and Lavinia, who live in London, always thought that this study was a rather flimsy excuse for me to visit them. I can say with a straight face that my interests were driven by more exalted motives. On the other hand, they became my British bankers of record, willingly depleting their accounts to cover the cost of books and the reproduction of documents that had to be paid in sterling.

Divided Hearts

Introduction

On a crisp Indian summer afternoon in October 1875 nearly thirty thousand gathered at the Capitol Square, Richmond, Virginia, for the unveiling of a statue of Stonewall Jackson. The statue, a gift from friends of the Confederacy in Britain, was the work of John Foley, probably contemporary Britain's most gifted sculptor. Money for the statue had been raised in the weeks following Jackson's death in 1863 by a group of Confederate supporters who were active in the movement to win recognition for the secessionists. Work on the statue had been suspended as the tide of war turned against the South, and plans for finishing it had been shelved in the wake of Union victory. When a former Confederate general was elected governor of Virginia and it appeared the old order had reasserted its political hegemony in the state, leaders of the Association of the Army of Northern Virginia made contact with old friends in London and had the statue completed. The Reverend Moses Hoge, a Presbyterian minister and principal orator of the day who on a visit to Britain during the war had collected twenty thousand dollars worth of Bibles for Lee's army, appealed to cherished contacts between Britain and old Virginia. The gift, he declared, was "the visible symbol of the ancient friendship which existed in colonial times between Virginia and the mother country." Virginians, an "English-speaking and an English-descended people," a local editor agreed, who were "politically separated from the mother country for nearly a hundred years," were "yet bound to her by strong ties of kinship and affection." Governor James Kemper's opening remarks were also laced with classical and knightly imagery. Virginia's lineage, he asserted, led through classical Greece and Rome and more recently through aristocratic

England.[1] For Hoge and Kemper the statue symbolized the links between aristocratic Britain and Virginia, the first state of the Confederacy.

More that one hundred years later, an equally symbolic act was enacted in a small square in Manchester renamed for the occasion Lincoln Square. The occasion was the relocation of a statue of Abraham Lincoln that had stood in a public park for over fifty years. At the time of its completion, the controversial statue by George Grey Bernard had been dismissed by the London *Times* as the "Tramp with the Colic." The inscription on the new plinth challenged directly the Richmond interpretation of events by venerating competing links between the peoples of Britain and the United States. If Richmond claimed aristocratic connections, Manchester emphasized "the support the working people of Manchester gave in the fight for the abolition of slavery during the American Civil War."[2] Committed to the abolition of slavery and to the principles for which the American republic stood, the working people of the city, the inscription continued, had stayed the course, in spite of the economic devastation caused by the Cotton Famine. Whereas in 1875 the organizers of the Richmond event had emphasized their links to people such as Alexander Beresford-Hope and other aristocratic supporters of the Confederacy, in 1986 their Manchester counterparts spoke of working-class solidarity and in a profoundly symbolic act gave the honor of unveiling the Lincoln statue to an African American, Arthur Mitchell, director of the Dance Theater of Harlem. Such symbols of solidarity reached back to the Civil War and beyond. In late 1864, for example, the African American John Brooks, representing the U.S. Consul in Glasgow, presented two volumes of government documents and a flag of the United States to the Newmilns Anti Slavery Society. A small weaving town in Ayrshire, Scotland, with a long radical tradition, Newmilns came to cherish the gifts. For many years afterward, a local historian recalled, "the *Lincoln Flag* was brought forth and paraded in company with the *Blue Blanket* which had been

1. *Richmond Daily Dispatch*, 26, 27 October 1875; James M. Morgan Jr., *The Jackson-Hope and the Society of the Cincinnati Medals of the Virginia Military Institute* (Verona, Va., 1979), 2–5; Kate Mason Rowland, "English Friends of the Confederacy," *Confederate Veteran* 25 (May 1917): 198. For a recent discussion of these issues see James M. McPherson, *Is Blood Thicker than Water? Crises of Nationalism in the Modern World* (New York, 1998), especially chapter 2.

2. Words transcribed from the base of the statue. For a history of the statue see Merrill D. Peterson, *Lincoln in American Memory* (New York, 1994), 209–14.

carried at Drumclog," where in 1679 the Covenanters had defeated Claver-house.[3]

Through these symbolic displays, both sides attempted to keep alive their competing memories of the Civil War. Such rituals were expressions of collective action and solidarity. Almost forty years after the end of the war in a recollection of his schoolboy days in Burnley, James E. Holden recalled the arrival of the first bale of American cotton following the end of hostilities. People (working people it is implied) from all parts of Lancashire gathered on the docks at Liverpool, where the cotton was placed on a cart and "trimmed with flowers and bunting, . . . and the flag under which I was born, . . . and between them the picture that you love, that my father loved, that you suffered for, the plain picture that appeals to the plain people in all the world— ABRAHAM LINCOLN."[4] Both Newmilns and Liverpool drew political solace from transatlantic abolitionist and working-class solidarities, which sought to mute racial divisions and to glory in working-class progress. The tradition held that during the war the Union found its greatest support among the working class and those committed to an expansion of the franchise, while the opposition took comfort from the aristocracy and all those determined to limit the right to vote. Not surprisingly, friends of the Confederacy saw things differently. The loci of economic progress, social stability, and political advancement, they insisted, were to be found in the historical links between aristocratic Britain and the descendants of the cavaliers who had settled in Virginia.[5]

These opposing traditions were appealed to during the political conflict

3. *Evening Standard* (Manchester), 13 November 1986; *Advertiser* (Ayr), 22 December 1864; John Strewhorn, "Newmilns: The Story of an Ayrshire Burgh," *Publications of the Ayrshire Archeological and Natural History Society*, 2d ser., 1 (1947–1949): 89; *Historical Aspects of Newmilns* (Darvel, Ayrshire, 1990), 16. There were frequent expressions of these symbolic political links between Britain and the United States during the war. In Skelmanthorpe, Yorkshire, for example, the "flag of freedom," which was produced in 1819 to commemorate the Peterloo massacre and used frequently during reform meetings, was flown to celebrate the end of the war. See James Vernon, *Politics and the People: A Study in English Political Culture, c.1815–1867* (New York, 1993), 109.

4. *The Outlook* (22 March 1902): 719.

5. See, for example, Percy Greg, *History of the United States from the Foundation of Virginia to the Reconstruction of the Union,* 2 vols. (London, 1887), an open attack on American democratic traditions backed by a nostalgic yearning for the days when the country took its lead from its natural leaders.

that raged in Britain as a result of the war in America. Writing five years after the end of the war, John Morley recalled that in "the American Civil war partisanship with the sides there was the veil of a kind of civil war here."[6] This study seeks to explore the nature of that strife, to determine to what extent class and other factors influenced reactions to the war. Historians have generally acknowledged that the war had a profound effect on the political culture of Britain. No other event, not those in Poland, Hungary, or Italy, or for that matter sporadic wars in the colonies, had as decided an effect on British life as did the Civil War. This is not to suggest that the country's gaze was averted from all other international events during those four years, only that the war was the one event whose impact reached deep into the political life of the country. The editors of the *Times* said it best: "The Civil War in the United States affects our people more generally even than the Indian Mutiny."[7]

Generally two schools of thought have developed around the issue of British attitudes toward the antagonists in the Civil War. On the one hand there are those, mainly early historians of Anglo-American relations during the war, who, drawing on the abolitionist tradition, argued that reactions were largely determined by class. The aristocracy and upper middle class, fundamentally opposed to democratic institutions and the extension of the franchise and fearful of competition from the United States, gave their support to the Confederacy. Those beneath them, particularly professionals and Dissenting ministers, long the backbone of British abolitionism and political reform, generally supported the Union. At the bottom, the working class, aware that slavery was the antithesis of everything it stood for, supported the Union and its class interests in the war. This neatly discrete class-based analysis has come under sustained attack since the 1950s. Examinations of the national press, the attitudes of Conservative, Liberal, and Radical politicians, as well as regional studies have all suggested that support for the Confederacy was more widespread than earlier studies suggest. By far the most compelling is Mary Ellison's study of Lancashire cotton workers, which raised questions concerning the nature and extent of working-class support for the Union. Ellison argues that, confronted by the shortage of cotton and a loss of jobs, Lancashire workers acted out of self-interest and supported the Confederacy. Those areas hit hardest by the shortage of cotton, she argues, were most vociferous in their support of the secessionists. Workers at meetings there voted for intervention,

6. John Morley, "England and the War," *Fortnightly Review,* 1 October 1870.
7. *Times* (London), 21 August 1862.

demanded that the government intervene to break the blockade of Southern ports that had cut off the flow of cotton to Lancashire mills, and called for the recognition of the Confederacy as an independent nation. This is not to suggest, she maintains, that Lancashire workers were proslavery, only that they were both antislavery and pro-South.[8]

But the question lingers: Do these findings hold up under closer scrutiny, and can one infer from Ellison's conclusions, as some historians have done, that the Confederacy won support beyond Lancashire? That is one of the aims of this study. But interest in the war reached well beyond the British working class. Determining who supported one side or the other and why they did requires a sociological examination of the membership of pro-Union and Confederate societies as well as an intellectual and political exploration of the arguments employed to justify positions taken. The study takes as its point of departure the assumption that these issues are best understood if they are placed in a wider transatlantic context. An examination of the impact of the war has to take into consideration the nature and changing contours of transatlantic abolitionist connections, of the ways in which nationalism framed the debate, and how race, among other issues, affected the public's perception of conditions in America. Although this is not a study of the Palmerston government's policies, it is, nonetheless, interested in fundamentally political issues, for it explores the ways in which friends of the protagonists attempted to influence how the public viewed the war. Operating on the assumption that in a democracy pressure from without can and frequently does influence how a government acts, both sides in the war made every effort to win public support for their position. Finally, in examining these and other issues, the study broaches the question of the extent to which the involvement in the public agitation over the war helped to consolidate alliances that, in the midst of the war, would begin to redirect their gaze toward political reform at home. John Morley put it boldly: "The triumph of the North . . . was the force that made English liberalism powerful enough to enfranchise the workmen, depose official Christianity in Ireland, and deal the first blow at the landlords."[9]

8. Mary Ellison, *Support for Secession: Lancashire and the American Civil War* (Chicago, 1972).
9. Morley, "England and the War," 479.

1

America: Its Politics, Its Society, and Its War

By the domestic fireside, on the exchange, and in the counting-house intelligence as to the war and its progress has been looked forward to, and
the details eagerly perused, and every tide of events have been anxiously
watched, and that not on account of the great commercial interests involved but a feeling that those taking part in the contest are bone of our
bone and flesh of our flesh.

—Leicester *Guardian*, 9 September 1861

The American Civil War had been a mere five months old in
September 1861, yet if the editor of the Leicester *Guardian* is to be believed, it
had touched the lives of a broad cross section of the British public. In the
counting houses there was concern about investment; on the exchange—particularly in Manchester—worry about the availability and price of cotton, the
source of Lancashire's prosperity; and in the homes fear for the fate of sons
who had emigrated to America in search of greater opportunity but who now
found themselves involved in a war that seemed to defy logic. How could a
nation, many wondered, that had been cut from the same historical, cultural,
and political cloth find itself in such a terrible impasse at the very moment
when it seemed poised to join the league of great nations? It was, to use

Goldwin Smith's analogy, as if John Hampden and George Washington, the founding fathers of the two branches of the transatlantic family, had suddenly gone their separate ways. But there was still hope. America had "been able to do great things," Smith lectured a Boston audience near the close of the war, "because your forefathers did great things for you."[1] Others less inclined to see any political hope in the future of the American system of government viewed the war as the death knell of the experiment in democracy. Like the French before them, the Americans were now hoisted on their own democratic petard. Yet for many, America continued to hold promise. It was, in the words of John Bright, the "ark of refuge" for all those in Europe who were denied political rights and an opportunity to advance economically.[2]

No other international event, not Italian unification nor the struggles in Poland and Hungary, had such a profound effect on the economic and political life of Britain as did the war in America. The shortage of cotton, the result of the Union blockade of Confederate ports, had led by the end of 1862 to severe economic dislocations in the textile towns in Lancashire, Cheshire, Derbyshire, Scotland, and Ulster. Those most affected by the Cotton Famine demanded the creation of alternative supplies of cotton, greater and more equitable distribution of relief for the unemployed, and aid to emigrate. The war also brought into stark relief the debate over the course of political reform at home. Radicals such as John Bright had long looked to the experiment in American democracy for pointers on the future of reform. Similarly, those opposed to the extension of the franchise warned of dire consequences should the country follow in the footsteps of the United States. By and large, those in favor of reform supported the Union; those opposed, the Confederacy. As "Antislave" of Blackburn saw it, democratic America held out the greatest opportunities for workingmen. There he was "acknowledged as a man and invested with the full rights of citizenship. At home his way [was] walled in on every side. A Whig and Tory aristocracy [had] monopolised power and seized the soil; and a mimic millocracy and mercantile class the capital of the country. Working men in their daily avocation [were] treated as serfs. When they ask[ed] for political rights, they were snubbed as rabble. The preachers say be quiet, and the employers turn the screw a little tighter."[3]

Such views must have been influenced in part by the generosity of New

1. Goldwin Smith, *England and America: A Lecture Read before the Boston Fraternity* (Boston, 1865), 10–12.
2. *Observer* (Rochdale), 7 February 1863.
3. *Times* (Blackburn), 17 January, 1863.

York and Philadelphia merchants who had recently sent thousands of barrels of flour, bacon, corn, and pork to those hit hardest by the Cotton Famine. Not long after the shipment's arrival, Blackburn workers met to discuss their plight and to thank the Americans for the gift. William Crossley, active in the weavers association, while critical of workingmen for not having saved more, laid the blame for the economic crisis at the door of uncaring employers and parsimonious relief officials. The unemployed, Crossley concluded, were left with few alternatives but to emigrate. Supporting the call for emigration, James Heaton promoted America as the refuge for the economically and politically oppressed. A fellow mechanic, Benjamin Hornbury, observed that the entire institutional apparatus of the country had operated against the interests of working people. "This war will come to an end," he argued, "slavery will be abolished; then there will be a grand opening for the intelligent artizans, operatives, and agricultural labourers of England. . . . You have never been looked upon as men in your own country; you have been deprived of the rights of citizenship. In every sense of the word you have been treated as an inferior order of men. When you get into the United States, you are invested with the full rights of man in every respect." The meeting adopted a memorial to the American merchants, thanking them for the gift, expressing the hope that the war would soon end in liberty for all regardless of color, and suggesting that the money invested in supplying the goods would have been better spent in helping the unemployed get to America.[4]

These men were not provincials, concerned only with the protection of their livelihood; they possessed an acute sense of the ways events abroad influenced politics at home. Eugenio Biagini and others have argued convincingly that the constant turmoil of international events between the Crimean War in 1853 and the assassination of Lincoln in 1865 helped to "revive working class interest in politics."[5] But if the Civil War helped to regenerate interest in reform among the working class, it also created deep political fissures.

4. *Times* (Blackburn), 31 January 1863, 8 April 1865. The memorial is enclosed in Dudley to Seward, Liverpool, 3 February 1863, Despatches from United States Consuls in Liverpool, 1790–1906 (microfilm), General Records of the Department of State, RG 59, National Archives. Unless otherwise noted, all following consulate dispatches are from RG 59, National Archives.

5. Eugenio F. Biagini, *Liberty, Retrenchment, and Reform: Popular Radicalism in the Age of Gladstone, 1860–1880* (New York, 1992), 372–75; Frances E. Gillespie, *Labor and Politics in England, 1850–1867* (Durham, N.C., 1927), 75, 213; Owen Ashton, *W. E. Adams: Chartist, Radical, and Journalist (1832–1906), "An Honour of the Fourth Estate"* (Tyne and Wear, 1991), 51; F. M. Leventhal, *Respectable Radical: George Howell and Victorian Working-Class Politics* (New York, 1971), 45–46; Nigel Todd, "Black-on-Tyne: The Black Presence on Tyneside in the 1860s," *North East Labour History* 21 (1987): 79.

Working-class and trade-union leaders did not speak with one voice. T. J. Dunning, a bookbinder and one of the founding members of the London Trades Council, was scathing in his denunciation of the Union, while fellow council members George Howell, G. Odger, R. Applegarth, and W. R. Cremer opposed an independent Confederacy. Like the leaders, the rank and file were divided over the war. A working-class group meeting in Leicester, for example, struggling to make sense of the war and its impact on the economy of neighboring communities, could find no common ground. Some thought that the war resulted from disputes over tariffs, others that slavery had driven the two sides apart.

The war also raised a more intractable question: when was rebellion justified? "A Dock Labourer" in Liverpool believed that a just war was one that was "grounded in justice and a public sense of right"; a Mr. Lewis of Edinburgh believed rebellion justified when "oppression becomes intolerable—when the moral and spiritual convictions of a people are concussed by armed hosts." Such was the case in Poland, Hungary, and Italy, but not in the Confederacy, not among that "hoard of perjured traitors and man-stealers," who were attempting "to consolidate an empire whose foundations [were] laid in human gore, and whose corner-stones [were] cemented with the blood and knit together by the heart-strings of the millions they [had] enslaved."[6]

Such lofty rhetoric when thousands were being thrown out of work as a result of the shortage of cotton struck some as misplaced. Self-interest would seem to dictate the immediate recognition of the Confederacy. J. Wilkins, a Bristol workingman, argued that in the American Civil War the issue of slavery was subordinate to the right of a separate nationality to establish its independence. A "Power-Loom Weaver" in Ashton agreed, in addition insisting that no country that had fought for the establishment of free trade could turn its back on a nation committed to the same principles. The South was also a nation of "little *white* men," "A Working Man" of Birmingham wrote, full of "perseverance and pluck ... doing desperate battle for liberty's sake."[7] For these workingmen, their support of the Confederacy turned on the issue of the right to economic and political independence, tinged, as it not infrequently was, by a sense of racial solidarity.

Conversely, John Plummer, a Kettering operative, believed that slavery

6. *Leicestershire Mercury*, 20 December 1862; *Mercury* (Liverpool), 28 July 1864; *Caledonian Mercury*, 20 February 1863.

7. *Post* (Bristol), 28 March 1863; *Reporter* (Ashton and Stalybridge), 30 November 1861; *Daily Gazette* (Birmingham), 22 January 1863.

was the central issue and must be considered: "So strong, so bitter, and so un-changeable is the popular hatred of negro slavery, that the industrial classes of this country would endure almost any degree of suffering and privation, if by so doing they could procure freedom for the slave; and by the same rule, they would refuse to be identified with a system which they hold as unscriptural and accursed." For a Liverpool "Working Man," solidarity with the slave turned on the fact that implicit in all forms of slavery was the control of labor. It struck him as illogical that a class fighting to extend its freedoms at home would support an oligarchy in America that insisted it had fashioned the ulti-mate form of labor control. The working class had other important obliga-tions, "Another Working Man" from Birmingham insisted they had to be the guardians of Britain's antislavery honor now that it was under assault from supporters of the Confederacy.[8]

All of these concerns were captured in a series of letters between R. Bell, a Union supporter, and "A Factory Operative," a defender of the Confederacy, in Todmorden, West Yorkshire, England. The latter, who admired the Confederacy for its courage, pointed to the shortcomings of democracy, par-ticularly its inability to differentiate between what he thought was "manly and unmanly." With an eye on the debate over political reform at home, he pointed to the tendency of republican forms of government to become tyran-nical and even monarchical once they abandoned consent for force. Evidence of this was to be found in President Abraham Lincoln's suspension of habeas corpus, his restrictions on newspapers' ability to freely report on the war, and his imprisonment of political rivals. But "A Factory Operative" leveled his most impassioned criticism at abolitionist demagogues, who, taking a page from the book of their predecessors in the West Indian movement, were at-tempting to force emancipation before its time. There was much about the civilizing influence of slavery to extenuate its evils. What, he asked rhetori-cally, was "the state of the negro in his native wilds? We already know that the efforts of the missionary have been unavailing to civilize him, and so, I believe will continue to be. Facts prove that so long as the negro remains at home, no influence can be brought to bear upon him which will sufficiently counteract the attractions of his barbarous customs."[9]

Obviously, the working class did not speak with a united voice. While

<hr />

8. *Bradford Review*, 16 November 1861; *Reporter* (Ashton and Stalybridge), 1 August 1863; *Daily Gazette* (Birmingham), 23 January 1863; *Caledonian Mercury*, 25 February 1863.

9. *Times* (Todmorden), 17, 24 October 1863; 14, 21, 28 November 1863; 5, 12, 19 December 1863; 2, 9, 23, 30 January 1864; 6, 13, 27 February 1864; 5, 12, March 1864.

some workingmen identified their hopes for political reform with the resolution of the war, among Liberals there was concern that the fallout from the strife in America could seriously undermine the very fabric of British political life. After a particularly acrimonious and indecisive set of meetings in Leicester in 1863 dealing with the merits of forming a local antislavery society, "Peacemaker" worried that the public debate could cripple local Liberals: "Does any one, who knows the town—believe that the North has made an additional friend, or that the South has reduced the number of its enemies by the late meetings? I for one do not—but this I do believe, that the question at issue—from being a mere *sentiment*, possessing no power whatever to influence the civil war in America—has become a bitter cause of animosity amongst very many who a short time since were on every other subject—religious, political, and social—cordially agreed." The Tories were with the Confederacy, so too were the Whigs, but among Liberals there were deep divisions, enough to undermine the unity and strength of the party. A fellow Liberal in Bradford had similar concerns. While he acknowledged that Liberal "sentiment still ran very strongly in favour of freedom," he thought it "most confusedly bewildered when it comes to deal with American affairs; hence we have men really wishing for the universal abolition of slavery expressing earnest wishes for the success of the section of a nation who are the most deeply tainted with the crime of slavery." [10]

Both correspondents were struck by these stark contradictions if for no other reason than the fact that America with its liberal constitution, lack of an established religion, abundance of cheap land, thriving economy, and universal suffrage had long appealed to the political sensibilities of Liberals and Radicals. Experience of America over the previous thirty years, however, had chipped away at this image. Some political exiles, particularly those who had fled in the wake of the Chartist uprisings in the 1840s, returned disillusioned with what they considered America's unconstrained political culture. Among these was William Aitken, an Ashton schoolteacher. Others who had gone in search of economic opportunity returned convinced that, in spite of all its hardships, life in Britain was decidedly preferable. Both John B. Horsfall and Mortimer Grimshaw, leaders of the movement for improved working conditions in Lancashire in the early 1850s, were disillusioned by their experiences in America. Early in the war Horsfall said of America, "[H]er citizens have all got votes, but that does not prevent her roughs and her rowdies from exercis-

10. *Leicestershire Mercury*, 19 December 1863; *Observer* (Bradford), 19 June 1863.

ing the right to carry and use bowie knives and revolvers." The convulsions in the country's commercial and political institutions were but "the natural result of a long course of commercial and political rottenness" filled with bribery and corruption. The image of the revolutionary, agrarian, and democratic America of Tom Paine had for many been replaced by a grasping, uncaring, corrupt, if not anarchic, republic.[11]

Even many supporters of the Union expressed concerns about the country's tendency to excess. To Goldwin Smith, the Oxford don who believed that many of Britain's political problems stemmed from the existence of a state church, American democracy tended to address the "shallower interests of man." These problems were compounded by the absence of limits on universal suffrage, which resulted in "the ignorant and penniless emigrant, Irish and German," being permitted to vote. The separation of church and state, however, compensated for most of these shortcomings. In this land where no state religion existed, there was no stark long-term poverty, little class conflict, and considerable pride in labor. As a result, "[t]here seems to be an approach on the whole to an adjustment of mutual rights between the two classes less by the angry clash of adverse interests and more by intelligence and the common sense of justice."[12] Henry Vincent, the old Chartist, saw little to criticize. Even if slavery had not been an issue in the war, he would have supported the Union on the grounds that it was "a government resting on universal suffrage, without an hereditary monarch or aristocracy, without a state church, or laws of primogeniture, or game laws or poor laws."[13] Lincoln's reelection in 1864,

11. Henry Pelling, *America and the British Left from Bright to Bevan* (New York, 1957), 2; G. D. Lillibridge, *Beacon of Freedom: The Impact of American Democracy upon Great Britain, 1830–1870* (Philadelphia, 1955), 35; Ray Boston, *British Chartists in America, 1839–1900* (Manchester, England, 1971), 19–20, 37; Jamie L. Bronstein, "From the Land of Liberty to Land Monopoly: The United States in a Chartist Context," in Owen Ashton, Robert Fyson, and Stephen Roberts, eds., *The Chartist Legacy* (Rendlesham, 1999), 147–70; Gregory Claeys, "The Example of America a Warning to England? The Transformation of America in British Radicalism and Socialism, 1790–1850," in Malcolm Chase and Ian Dyck, eds., *Living and Learning: Essays in Honour of J. E. C. Harrison* (Aldershot, 1996), 66–80; *Guardian* (Manchester), 18 May 1861.

12. Goldwin Smith, *The Civil War in America: An Address Read at the Last Meeting of the Manchester Union and Emancipation Society* (London, 1866) 4–5, 19.

13. *Journal* (Stroud), 3 June 1865. Like so many of his contemporaries, Vincent wrapped his republicanism in monarchist cloth. The longevity and success of Queen Victoria's reign had become a metaphor for the nation's potential. In the wake of Lincoln's assassination Vincent told a West Hartlepool audience that while he was an admirer of America and republican principles

in the midst of a civil war, testified to the resiliency of democratic institutions. To those in Britain who were denied the vote, the message was clear, argued Ernest Jones, the old Chartist and lawyer. Opponents of the extension of the franchise had warned that it would lead to violence. The election in America shattered that argument. In the midst of a war, two parties contested an election, and men who "when in England, were denied the possession of the franchise" voted without violence, proof of "the educational influence of the franchise in causing men to know and to maintain their rights."[14] In the weeks after the election, groups throughout Britain adopted memorials congratulating Lincoln and the nation for demonstrating that democracy worked even under the most trying of circumstances. No one, a meeting in the small Scottish town of Newmilns declared, but "an aristocracy who have viewed the American Republic with the same eye as Milton's devil viewed the garden of Eden when he scanned the world in its infancy" would deny the power and resiliency of democratic institutions.[15]

If there was debate among Radicals and working-class supporters of the Union concerning America's society and polity, Conservatives, who overwhelmingly endorsed the Confederacy, had no such scruples. As demonstrated in America, democracy, where it was not a failure, was a threat to ordered governance. America, the editors of the *Times* insisted, was brought to this sorry pass because it was governed by a majority, "the less wise, less practiced, less considerate, less circumspect, less adroit, and less informed part of her population." The war provided an opportunity to reaffirm British political traditions. In America the "preponderance of popular will without check or limit is at least as likely to hurry a nation into war and debt as the caprice of the most absolute despot or the intrigues of the most selfish of aristocracies." Those who over the preceding ten years had been calling for political

---

he was, nonetheless, a monarchist because he believed "it was just as possible to have a just and peaceable government under the reign of Queen Victoria as under any other form of rule." *Mercury* (Darlington), 3 May 1865; *Free Press* (Hartlepool), 6 May 1865.

14. *Guardian* (Preston), 22 February 1865. Hyperbole got the better of Jones when he told a Bury Parliamentary Reform meeting that the strength of democracy was fully demonstrated when in an election in the midst of a war not a "window was smashed or head was broken." But for his audience the point was well taken. *Times* (Bury), 29 April 1865. For discussion on how the election was viewed see also *Western Daily Press*, 4 January 1865; *Post* (Bristol), 4, 6, 11 January 1865; and J. R. Pole, *Abraham Lincoln and the Working Classes of Britain* (London, 1959), 32.

15. *Advertiser* (Ayr), 22 December 1864; memorials included in Adams to Seward, London, 1, 16, 23 December 1864, Despatches from United States Ministers to Great Britain, 1791–1906.

reform and the adoption of the American system now found themselves "utterly destitute." A quick glance at developments in America, they argued, should overwhelm those who would have the British constitution remodeled. While the editors admitted that American democracy had given "men all the blessings of freedom and all the benefits of equality," it had, after a very short trial, proven that "equality creates discontent as fatal as those of inequality; that freedom may degenerate, for want of regulation, into mere lawlessness, and that men who have been accustomed to bully all other people end up fighting among themselves." The result of this misconceived experiment in democracy was a government "at once tyrannical and stupid," led by a "rural attorney for Sovereign and a city attorney for Prime Minister."[16]

Conservative supporters of the Confederacy such as James Spence, Liverpool merchant, contributor to the *Times*, and author of the most expansive treatise on the war, were generally of one mind. When men were reduced to the same level, as they were in democracies, Spence declared, they acted like herded animals: "Any great impulse affects all alike, and originates a movement simultaneous, vast, and imposing." Such was the bane of the French Revolution. "Shoeless, shirtless, paid in assignats, they, too, went onward in eager hosts. But that movement, which began with songs of liberty, ended in erecting despotism, and in piling up, as an altar to brotherly love, a hecatomb of human bones." Whenever democracy was practiced on so vast a scale as it was in America, Spence argued, "the minority becomes abject, the majority despotic. The essence of freedom, its completeness in the individual man, becomes extinguished, and men move no longer by the guidance of reason and choice, but as fish move in a shoal, by the volition of the mass." Other Southern supporters, like "Homo" of Bristol, took Spence's argument one step further, insisting that, over time, democracy practiced on so vast a scale led to "national decadence, and of the increasing inferiority of the race—the pale, sickly, whiskerless countenance—the long, lank hair—the spindling legs— the effeminate foot—the cunning, over-reaching eye—the habitual stoop— the contracted chest—the eternal quid—the constant expectoration—the vile corruption of the noblest of living languages."[17] One can only marvel at the ability of such a physical and moral degenerate to fight a war. Borrowing

16. *Times* (London), 12 December 1864, 12 August 1861, 11, 12 August, 4 November 1862.

17. *Times* (London), 22 March, 21 November 1862; *Post* (Bristol), 15 August 1861. The editors of *Blackwood's* described the Union as "an imbecile executive above, a restless, purposeless multitude below, linked together like a kite tied to a balloon. . . ." Quoted in Robert Botsford, "Scotland and the American Civil War" (Ph.D. diss., Edinburgh University, 1955), 605.

extensively from Charles-Louis de Secondat Montesquieu, Spence, like the American Antifederalists before him, was convinced that so vast a territory, with its varied climate, production, and interests, and "great differences of manners, habits, and customs," could never be successfully melded into a single united republic.[18]

Back of this position was a conviction that America was populated by two different peoples with two distinct cultures. Writing in the late 1880s, Percy Greg, journalist, historian, and a major propagandist for the Confederacy, insisted that from its early years America had been settled by people with varied traditions, so much so that Virginia and Maryland "preserved visible traces of the loyalty, moderation, and English patriotism which were the proudest traditions of their cavalier ancestry." An unbridled democracy "aggravated by the absence of a class possessed of hereditary wealth, culture and leisure" ruled elsewhere, especially in New England. Not surprisingly, the American Revolution, which he considered a rebellious and disloyal movement, would have its origin in New England. Now that the South was fighting for independence, patriotic Englishmen had few alternatives but to support those who had stood with them during the American Revolution against the great-grandchildren of New England, who had inherited the Puritan leaven, "the feeling of rebels and regicides, the temper of the Winthrops and Endicotts, the spirit that had mutilated the national ensign, and had once at least threatened a transfer of allegiance to England's most powerful maritime rival."[19] After a brief visit to the Confederacy, Lord Wolseley saw the American Civil War pitting the descendants of the noble cavaliers against the pharisaic Puritans; the inheritors of "our banished cavaliers" against those who were the product of the "offscourings of every European nation."[20]

18. For a discussion of these points see Gordon S. Wood, *The Creation of the American Republic, 1776–1787* (Chapel Hill, N.C., 1969), 499.

19. Percy Greg, *History of the United States*, 1: 133–37. There is no way of identifying Greg's editorials and articles during the war. All of the evidence suggests, however, that his *History* was largely a rearticulation of the positions he took while working with Herny Hotze and other Confederate representatives. Anthony Trollope believed that the country was not homogenous and was made up of two sections with "different instincts, different appetites, different morals, and a different culture." Anthony Trollope, *North America* (1862; reprint, London, 1968), 1: 10.

20. *Blackwood's Magazine*, January 1863; Emory Thomas has argued that cultural life in the antebellum South celebrated southern life and linked it "to romantic visions of courtly love, chivalry, Greek temples, feudal knights, cheerful peasants (slaves)." *The Confederate Nation, 1861–1865* (New York, 1979), 28; Henry Hotze, the Confederacy's principal propagandist in London, consistently appealed to these purported links. "Southern America, in manners, forms

The Civil War provided Greg and other Conservatives with an opportunity to revive and exploit the deep sense of betrayal that many still felt at the loss of the American colonies. Virginia, which had been settled by the British, Spence maintained, had remained loyal to the crown during the revolution. The rowdy Celts and Germans in Massachusetts, on the other hand, were "turbulent, arrogant, and seditious. An intense and selfish fanaticism marked that people from the first, as it does this day. In the South, with the exception of Louisiana, in which there is a population of French origin, the people are almost of purely British descent." The Reverend William W. Malet, vicar of the small Hertfordshire village of Ardeley, following a visit to his sister on a South Carolina plantation, declared that the inhabitants of the Palmetto State were true Englishmen. "I could not resist a feeling of national pride, thinking of this people, claiming to be of the genuine stock, exemplifying in a wonderful manner some of the finest features of the character of man in self-government."[21] In this call for Anglo-Saxon solidarity can be found the stirring of a more fervent racism.

This idyllic picture of a people hewing closely to English traditions, a people, Conservatives argued, who should be warmly supported, was challenged, as Biagini has pointed out, by those who saw the slaveholding Confederacy as the aristocratic ancien régime and the Union as the embodiment of liberty and equality.[22] Although the North had attracted some rapscallions and outcasts, Vincent argued, "the brightest and best portion of the American people—he meant the early American people—represented . . . the industry, the energy, the faith, the perseverance, and the progressive instincts of the Old World." Ernest Jones agreed. America was "the noblest republic" the world had ever known, a place where democracy reigned. Comparing Massachusetts and South Carolina, an anonymous author found the former bustling, free, and educated; the latter backward and hamstrung by little education.[23] John Bright, manufacturer, M.P. for Birmingham, and by far the most prominent

---

of speech, and habits of thought and business, resembled Old England, while Young England resembled more Northern America." For generations the South had been "proud of its closer affinity of blood to the British parent stock, than the North, with its mongrel compound of surplus population of all the world could boast of." *Index*, 15 May 1862.

21. *Herald* (Glasgow), 27 November 1863; William Wyndham Malet, *An Errand to the South in the Summer of 1862* (London, 1863), 211.

22. Biagini, *Liberty, Retrenchment, and Reform*, 69.

23. *Express* (Huddersfield), 1 November 1862; Ernest Jones, *The Slaveholders' War: A Lecture Delivered in the Town Hall, Ashton-under-Lyne . . . On November 16th, 1863* (Ashton, 1863), 40; Anonymous, *The American Question: Secession, Tariff, Slavery* (Brighton, 1862), 40–41. George

British supporter of the Union, saw America as "prosperous, without emperor, without king, without the surroundings of a court, without nobles, except such as are made by eminence in intellect and virtue, without state bishops and state priests," a country where "labour has met with the highest honour." If Spence and other Conservatives attributed the crisis in part to the rapid geographical expansion of the country and the attendant collapse of democratic institutions, Radicals such as Bright held out hope for the survival of a vast, stable republic, a symbol of hope for all those fighting for political reform. "I see one vast confederacy stretching from the frozen North in unbroken line to the glowing South, and from the wild billows of the Atlantic westward to the calmer waters of the Pacific," he told a meeting of constituents in 1862, "and I see one people, and one law, and one language, and one faith, and over all that wide continent, the home of freedom, and a refuge for the oppressed of every race and clime."[24]

Where one stood on the nature of the American union was to a significant degree a reflection of one's political creed. Conservatives generally spoke with one voice: the country's size, diversity, and political institutions militated against unity. Radicals and Liberals were not always of one view, nor was the working class. To some, America was a beacon of hope, a place where the experiment in democracy had been a success; to others, it was a hope betrayed. Into this equation must be added those who, regardless of their political beliefs, were part of the organizational fabric of the transatlantic benevolent community: abolitionists and advocates of peace, temperance, and women's rights, among others. Abolitionists, uncertain about the causes and significance of the war, mirrored the ambivalence of this community. The problems were particularly acute for those who were members of the Garrisonian alliance. For more than twenty years they had insisted that emancipation was best assured by the secession of the nonslaveholding states from the Union. British members of the alliance were caught off guard by the ease with which their American colleagues shelved their commitment to separation in favor of support for the Union once war began. American Garrisonians in turn were stung by the dismissive tone of much of the criticism emanating from Britain. James Haughton, an Irish abolitionist, insisted in the first month of the war that the South should be allowed to leave and the North should remove all

---

Howell called America the "glorious Republic . . . the offspring of that great Anglo-Saxon race." *Bee Hive*, 28 March 1863.

24. John Bright, *Speeches of John Bright, M.P., on the American Question* (1865; reprint, New York, 1970), 129, 177–78; *Bee Hive*, 28 March 1863; *Observer* (Rochdale), 7 February 1863.

protective tariffs. Given the inflamed passions of both sides, war meant "extermination, or a fierce and horrible encounter of long duration." Should the South be allowed to "quietly secede," the North would be freed of complicity with slavery. Haughton reminded his American coworkers of the movement's creed: "No Union with Slaveholders." American Garrisonians such as Wendell Phillips defended themselves against this criticism. They had not abandoned principle, for they had never rejected the concept of union, only of one that was built on slavery, "a Union whose cement was the blood of the slave." Now that the North was determined to break the shackles, to make "the pledge of '76 . . . a reality," to insist that the "corner-stone of the Union should be justice," it should be supported. If this were the case, British friends countered, why had the Lincoln government not committed itself to emancipation and why were some federal officials still returning fugitive slaves to their masters?[25] Those were questions for which American Garrisonians had no ready answer until Lincoln's preliminary emancipation order in the fall of 1862.

These differences unleashed nationalist passions that surprised abolitionists on both sides of the Atlantic. An alliance that had prided itself on its internationalism confronted its differences by taking refuge behind nationalist lines. Harriet Martineau, an English author, journalist, and abolitionist who knew America well, for a while parted company with her American friends over what she saw as their abandonment of internationalist principles. Richard Webb, a Dublin abolitionist, stayed involved, but he too was deeply concerned about the signs of increasing nationalism among colleagues such as Phillips. Some in America considered such criticism the equivalent of the abandonment of a friend at the time of greatest need. When Britain faced mutiny in India, "M" of Philadelphia recalled, it found support among Americans. Now that America faced similar dangers, British friends were nowhere to be found. What galled "M" most, however, was European sanctimoniousness. Who among them, "M" demanded to know, had not experienced sanguinary wars? Not France, nor "you, O' England, whose red sword is still wet with the blood of 100,000 Sepoy victims. Great as is the sin of this country, culpable as is its government, and unworthy as are its leaders, America is the peer of all other nations; and, in her recent sacrifices for liberty, without a peer among the nations of the earth. It is in comparison with

25. *Liberator*, 21 June, 16 August 1861, 17 January 1862; *National Anti Slavery Standard*, 14 September 1861; S. May Jr. to Webb, Leicester, 10 February 1863, Webb to Anne Weston, Dublin, 31 December 1861, American Anti Slavery Society Papers (hereafter cited as AASS Papers), Boston Public Library, Boston.

our own ideal that we condemn our country as the 'chief of sinners'; but in comparison with other nations, we have no reason to be ashamed." [26]

The war reignited nationalist passions that had lain dormant for more than a decade. During the 1850s there had developed improved Anglo-American relations coupled with a growing sense of community across the Atlantic; a sense that, differences aside, Britain and the United States were "distinguished from the rest of the world by their commitment to human progress, representative government, and individual liberty." The growth of free-trade ideas in Britain had led, in the view of H. C. Allen, to a "profound . . . rethinking of the lessons of the American Revolution and of the nature of the Second British Empire" and to reconciliation based in part on the recognition that colonies invariably fell off "the imperial tree like ripe plums." [27] The Atlantic might stand between them, Goldwin Smith told a Boston audience, but "you are still nearer to us than all the world beside." A Coventry meeting put it differently: "[S]prung from the same Anglo-Saxon stock, you and we must ever be one in the bonds of brotherhood." [28] If by midcentury many in Britain had generally discarded as too arrogant, and even pejorative, the image of America as the wayward child, they still saw Americans as their cousins, a term Marcus Cunliffe has argued, that implied fondness, "but also the intrinsic complications of a familial relationship, with the right—one might almost say duty—to criticize which is recognized with families." [29]

At times of crisis, the fulfillment of such perceived duty tends to grate on nationalist sensibilities. In Britain, friend and foe alike were quick to advise the federal government in the United States on the best course of action. Whatever form such advice took, whether it called for a recognition of the inevitability of secession or insisted on immediate emancipation, it was delivered ex cathedra, something not guaranteed to palliate America's injured na-

26. Liberator, 7 February, 4 April 1862; National Anti Slavery Standard, 25 January 1862.

27. Martin Crawford, "British Travelers and the Anglo-American Relationship in the 1850s," Journal of American Studies 12 (August 1978): 210; H. C. Allen, "The American Revolution and the Anglo-American Relationship in Historical Perspective," in H. C. Allen and Roger Thompson, eds., Contact and Connection: Bicentennial Essays in Anglo-American History (London, 1976), 169.

28. Smith, England and America, 18; Weekly Times (Coventry), 8 April 1863.

29. Marcus Cunliffe, "America at the Great Exhibition of 1851," American Quarterly 3 (summer 1951): 116. See also William Brock, "The Image of England and American Nationalism," Journal of American Studies 5 (December 1971): 244, who argues that as America became an established power the defensive rhetoric of Anglophobia, which he associates with a young nation, was no longer a "necessary ingredient of nationalism."

tional pride. Charles Fairbanks, an American who had paid a short visit to Britain early in the war, was struck by the country's sincere opposition to slavery, but was critical of the tone of its remonstrances, which, he lamented, were always "dictatorial and almost always patronizing." Because the English thought they were superior to all, he wrote, they tended to "assume a lofty tone" when addressing others. Toward America, because it was a "young nation," they conducted "themselves with the bearing of a very high superiority."[30] This attitude went far beyond the accepted propriety of one cousin scolding or advising another. Aware of this, William Leng, a Dundee editor and friend of the Union, called for restraint: "It is not for us, whose Empire is scattered all over the globe, to endorse the principle of secession. It is not for us, who lately bound our own rebels to the muzzles of cannon and blew them into quivering atoms, to lecture the North about *habeas corpus* acts and constitutional forms."[31] Leng's advice was generally ignored, especially among conservative editors, who seemed to take a perverse joy in crafting inventive ways to condemn the Americans. One editorial, which spoke of national differences, was not uncharacteristic. Among the national traits of America, the editor declared, was "no repose, no moderation, none of that *otium cum digitate*, which is itself (what the Americans profess to despise) aristocratic. Their vices, habits, and faults are exaggerations of English faults, habits, and vices. Where we trade; they speculate. When we, in bad times, curtail; they smash. We walk, planting one foot firmly before we take another step; they 'go ahead' on the slipperiest ground, until they fall."[32] Louis Blanc, a French Radical living in exile in England, placed the blame for such nationalist angst on the Americans for whom humiliating England was "a luxurious and exquisite enjoyment." As a result, many in Britain, he surmised, took a "malicious satisfaction" in America's troubles.[33]

---

30. Charles Fairbanks, *The American Conflict as Seen from a European Point of View* (Boston, 1863), 12.

31. William C. Leng, *The American War: The Aims, Antecedents, and Principles of the Belligerents. A Lecture Delivered on the 10th of December 1862 in Castle Street Church* (Dundee, 1863), 33. At the end of the war Thomas Dudley made the same point in response to British editors who criticized the policy of offering a reward for the capture of Jefferson Davis. Such criticism, he wrote, came from a people who "blew the Insurgents in India from the cannon's mouth, and tried to Court martial the Insurgents in Ireland in 1798 and after death cut off their heads and displayed them on the ends of pikes." Dudley to Seward, Liverpool, 19 May 1865, Despatches from United States Consuls in Liverpool, 1790–1906.

32. *Guardian* (Halifax), 12 October 1861.

33. Louis Blanc, *Letters on England* (London, 1866), 1: 213–14. Wilbur Shepperson argues

Whatever the source of the antagonism, two major events in the first year of the war—Congress's adoption of the Morrill tariff and the *Trent* affair—helped to raise nationalist hackles. Passed in February 1861 after the withdrawal of Southern members from Congress, the tariff reversed a trend of progressively lowering rates. Although moderate, the tariff was an affront to the widespread belief that cheap food necessitated free trade. Fifteen years earlier the repeal of the Corn Laws had vanquished protectionism; now, it appeared, it was being revived across the Atlantic. The Morrill tariff drove Harriet Martineau to denounce her American coworkers in the most uncompromising terms. Bright called it a "stupid and unpatriotic act," and Richard Cobden expressed dismay that a democratic government could enact such legislation. The existence of the tariff instantly became a public-relations disaster for the Union, and opponents moved quickly to exploit the Confederacy's commitment to free trade.[34] If the tariff caused Union supporters considerable anxiety, the controversy created by the *Trent* affair almost led to war. In November 1861 Charles Wilkes, a Union naval officer, removed Confederates James Mason and John Slidell from the *Trent*, a British mail packet. Many considered Wilkes's actions a gratuitous insult to Britain, as well as a violation of international law. The Lincoln administration, one editor recommended, had to be given "alternatives of instant apology or instant war." There were also calls for reparations, and when word arrived in Britain that Wilkes had been feted as a hero, there were calls for retribution. "We are pretty well accustomed to Yankee bluster and hot headedness," one editorial fumed, "but we cannot think that they [the United States] will be so utterly blind as to provoke a collision with a power which with little difficulty could blow to the four winds their dwarf fleet and shapeless mass of incoherent

---

that many British emigrants to America returned "irritated by the nationalism of Americans, by the confidence, which verged on arrogance, and particularly by the constant demand that all Englishmen offer unqualified praise of the new order." *Emigration and Disenchantment: Portraits of Englishmen Repatriated from the United States* (Norman, Okla., 1965), 29.

34. "Letters of John Bright, 1861–1862," *Proceedings of the Massachusetts Historical Society* 45 (November 1911) & 46 (October 1912): 100; Kenneth Fielden, "Richard Cobden and America" (Ph.D. diss., Cambridge University, 1965), 409; Sheldon Van Auken, "English Sympathy for the Southern Confederacy: The Glittering Illusion" (Bachelor's thesis, Oxford University, 1957), 14; Eugenio F. Biagini, "Popular Liberals, Gladstonian Finance, and the Debate on Taxation, 1860–1874," in Eugenio F. Biagini and Alastair Reid, eds., *Currents of Radicalism: Popular Radicalism, Organized Labour, and Party Politics in Britain, 1850–1914* (New York, 1991), 137. Interestingly, while the February 1861 Confederate tariff on cotton met with some criticism, it never generated anywhere near the same public disapproval as did the Morill tariff.

squads."[35] The Union's slow response to the demands for an apology and the British government's decision to send troops to Canada threatened open hostilities between the two countries. Richard Cobden and other peace advocates tried to defuse the situation by organizing a series of public meetings, memorials to the prime minister, and interdenominational prayer meetings that appealed to the government to submit the dispute to arbitration.[36] Although the Federal government's apology in late December finally eased tensions between the two countries, the affair left a residue of bitterness and suspicion, even among allies. American Garrisonians were stunned by the hauteur of British friends. One editor labeled such arrogance "John Bullism," the assumption of the "impeccable nature of the British government and of the invincible power of the British empire." In turn, Webb and others wondered how American abolitionists could ever have supported so blatant an attack on the rights of asylum and suggested that they were blinded by a misguided nationalism.[37]

All of these factors, and more, determined how the British viewed the struggle and what they considered to be the true causes of the war. Much of the debate about secession centered on two major issues: Did the South have a right to leave the Union, and to what extent was slavery at the heart of that decision? Ernest Jones declared the South's actions groundless, insisting that two conditions were necessary to justify any rebellion: grievances had to be intolerable, and all means of redress had to have been unavailing. In the absence of these two conditions, insurrection "without warranty of law, insurrection without legal attempt at redress, insurrection without grievance, is rebellion." A war that does not seek to eliminate oppression and promote justice could never be a just war.[38] The Reverend W. Croke Squire, a Unitarian

35. *Times* (Leeds), 30 November 1861; *Mercury* (Cardiff), 30 November 1861. For a history of the crisis see Norman B. Ferris, *The* Trent *Affair: A Diplomatic Crisis* (Knoxville, Tenn., 1977), and Howard Jones, *Union in Peril: The Crisis over British Intervention in the Civil War* (Chapel Hill, N.C., 1992), especially chapter 4.

36. *Caledonian Mercury,* 13 December 1861; *Guardian* (Brighton), 1 January 1862; *Guardian* (Halifax), 28 December 1861; *Morning Star,* 25 December 1861, 1, 6, 8, 9 January 1862; *Daily Post* (Birmingham), 3 January 1862; *Mercury* (Bristol), 14 December 1861; *Post* (Bristol), 12, 13 December 1861.

37. *National Anti Slavery Standard,* 4 January 1862.

38. Jones, *The Slaveholders' War,* 36. Newman Hall agreed. Secession, he argued, is only justified and legitimate when a people have experienced "glaring abuse," something, given the political strength of the South in the federal government, that could not be claimed for the Confederacy. Newman Hall, *The American War: A Lecture to Working Men, Delivered in London, October 20, 1862* (London, 1862), 11–12.

minister and former Garrisonian abolitionist who had broken with the Preston Anti Slavery Society over its support for the Union, saw things differently. Squire believed that, as a rule, people had a right to the government of their choice. There was a higher law that governed the actions of men, one that permitted people to change governments as they saw fit. The British, for example, had turned the Stuarts out only to recall them before dismissing them once again. Furthermore, how could "the children of revolution," as were the Americans, deny the same right to others? William Scholefield, a merchant, manufacturer, banker, and Liberal M.P. for Birmingham, argued that the South had a moral right to secede for the simple reason that a country created out of rebellion had no grounds on which it could oppose political separation.[39] Knitting all these positions together was the conviction that the Washington government was much too weak and had neither the strength nor the resolve to force the seceding states back into the union.

While agreeing with Squire that forms of government, especially those born in rebellion, could never be permanent, Anthony Trollope, novelist, insisted that the Union had every right to prevent separation in an effort to protect its political integrity. No supporter of the Union would have disagreed with Trollope's contention about a government's obligation. Eccles Shorrock, a Darwen manufacturer, challenged those who argued the contrary to find parallels in the way Britain responded to rebellions in Ireland and India. No British government had ever conceded the legitimacy of calls for independence in either place.[40] The Reverend J. Page Hopps, a Unitarian minister who, like Squire, had broken with his abolitionist past to support the Confederacy, differentiated between the political nature of empires and federations. The former, the result of conquest, could brook no separation; the latter, the creation of free and consenting states, must concede what he called the "abstract right" of secession. The Reverend James W. Massie, a Congregationalist minister and Union supporter, thought history disproved Page's contention. Using Ireland as an example, Massie insisted that, on the contrary, conquest did spur demands for separation.[41]

39. *Chronicle* (Preston), 28 November 1863; *Daily Post* (Birmingham), 19 December 1862.

40. Trollope, *North America* 1: 9–10, 15, 217; *Times* (Blackburn), 21 March 1863.

41. *Reporter* (Ashton and Stalybridge), 24 September, 1 October 1864; *Inquirer*, 6 May 1865. Newman Hall called this argument for an inherent and a constitutional right to secede destructive of the original political intent of unity. Implicit in this right of states to leave is the recognition that other entities—counties, and cities—have similar rights. Clearly, Hall was accusing opponents of advocating a form of anarchy. Hall, *The American War*, 11–12.

No one in Britain, with the possible exception of representatives of the Confederacy, would have disagreed with the assertion that slavery was deeply implicated in the war. Some Southern supporters such as T. B. Kershaw, a Manchester overlooker, skirted the issue by insisting that it was Northern imposition of burdensome tariffs that finally pushed the South to secede. The role of tariffs in the war continued to be featured prominently in the Confederate propaganda arsenal. Even at the end of the war there were those who insisted that unfair tariffs, "an injustice persevered in for many years," by a "band of monopolists" against "free-trading communities," had led directly to the conflict. Had such policies not been abandoned in Britain by the "landed aristocracy," it is very likely that those in counties such as Yorkshire and Lancashire who had suffered most under the continued imposition of such taxes on bread and food would have demanded separation. But such arguments had little appeal. Even someone as unsympathetic to the Union as Trollope rejected such explanations as "trifling." T. Perronet Thompson, the old abolitionist warhorse, dismissed these and other explanations as subsidiary grievances, the equivalent of "mosquito bites added to a broken leg." William E. Baxter, a leading Dundee merchant, M.P. for Montrose, and author of an authoritative account of a visit to the United States, frequently recalled that never once while he was in the South did he hear anyone complain about tariffs.[42] The Confederacy, most argued, was nothing more than a design by slaveholders to ensure the survival of slavery. Ernest Jones was fond of quoting at length from southern politicians to show that, even before the outbreak of hostilities, the protection of slavery was what concerned the South most. "It is slavery from the top to the bottom, and slavery in the middle, and slavery all the way through. For slavery we will go to war; for slavery we will make a compromise; slavery is the ultimatum which we present to you." As the Leicester M.P. Peter Taylor graphically put it, the North, having adopted free-soil principles, was attempting to "surround the scorpion slavery with a ring of fire, so that it must either die or sting itself to death."[43]

A number of those who were willing to concede that slavery had been the

42. T. Bentley Kershaw, *The Truth of the American Question: Being a Reply to the Prize Essay of Mr. Rowan* (Manchester, 1864), 4; *Chronicle and Mercury* (Leicester), 6 May 1865; Trollope, *North America*, 2: 53; *Advertiser* (Bradford), 8 March 1862; W. E. Baxter, *America and the Americans* (London, 1855); *Northern Warder*, 7 November 1862.

43. *Courier* (Halifax), 14 November 1863; *Leicestershire Mercury*, 31 January 1863; *Chronicle* (Leicester), 31 January 1863. For similar arguments see the views expressed by workingmen in *Newcastle Chronicle and Northern Counties Advertiser*, 25 July 1863, and *Caledonian Mercury*, 20 February 1863.

cause of the war had considerable doubt about how this should affect British reactions to the protagonists. There were some who thought it pointless to discuss what triggered the war, for once put in motion, secession had become an accomplished fact. Resisting such facts was as fruitless, one editor believed, as Mrs. Partington trying "to sweep the ocean at springtide from her doorstep. . . . It is vain to defy the Atlantic with a mop." A fellow editor took a different tack but arrived at the same conclusions. Saying that slavery was the cause of the war was the equivalent of saying that two highwaymen were fighting over plunder acquired in a robbery.[44] The inventive imagery aside, one's view of the origins of the war determined to a measurable degree the position one took in the public debate. Here was a gallant band of men, scions of British traditions, fighting against overwhelming odds to establish a country that reflected their values. Tradition also dictated, as it did in the case of Poland, Hungary, and Italy, that Britain support those who were fighting for their independence. Even before the end of the first year of fighting there were those who went further and insisted that, to all intents and purposes, the Confederacy, by its victories on the battlefield and its creation of a government and armed forces, had already become an independent nation. Given this fact, Britain had no alternative but to recognize the South. Even if opponents were willing to concede that all the trappings of independence could be found in the Confederacy, they demanded that Britain first examine the basis on which the new nation was to be founded. A country "which declares in its pride that it stands first among the free," said W. E. Adams, the Radical journalist writing under the nom de plume "Caractacus," could not extend "the best aid to the most revolting despotism the world has ever seen." How can a people who have "welcomed Kossuth," he asked, "who have sheltered Worcell, who have applauded Garibaldi—we who have sympathised with every effort however desperate, and rejoiced over every victory however small, on behalf of human freedom—shall we of all the peoples in the world be the means of re-uniting the already broken chain of the slave?" Reason, compassion, and tradition dictated that sympathy go not to the South, John Stockdale of Bury insisted, but to those who "although black in colour, . . . were still men entitled to the rights of citizenship."[45]

A country that still took considerable pride in the fact that it had freed its slaves found it publicly difficult to sustain appeals that, if they did not endorse,

44. *Guardian* (Nottingham), 20 July 1861; *Gazette* (Yorkshire), 21 March 1863.
45. *National Reformer*, 13 December 1862; *Times* (Bury), 21 February 1863.

did at least concede the fact that slavery would continue for the foreseeable future in the Confederacy. As a result, supporters of the South, unable to refute the assertions of opponents such as Adams and Stockdale, countered that the surest way to emancipation was through an independent Confederacy, a proposal opponents derisively dismissed as "emancipation by escapement." There were few Confederate supporters who did not argue for the proposition that, in time, emancipation would be best guaranteed by separation. It was not a position unique to pro-Southerners. Early in the war a number of abolitionists, particularly those identified with the Garrisonian wing of the movement, continued to insist that the South be allowed to leave. They would soon abandon this position, persuaded by their American colleagues and later by the actions of the Lincoln administration that this was indeed a war for emancipation. By and large, supporters of the South considered emancipation a peripheral issue, something that would be best left to time and the considered judgment of those who ran the plantations. The "defence of slaveholders," Radical M.P. W. E. Foster told his constituents, had "gone forward into a defence and apology of slavery." H. D. Rickards of Bristol insisted, to the contrary, that the Union had been the principal guarantor of slavery. It was a system maintained by the North out of self-interest, for it enabled them "to bully and domineer over the world in general, and England in particular." Without such domination there would be increased contacts with Europeans whose moral influence would immediately be brought to bear on the slaveholders, producing a "moral conviction of the iniquity of slavery," which was the only true means to emancipation. Only when public opinion in the South turned against slavery, Rickards concluded, would the system be abolished. Bad as slavery is, he wrote, it is not an "arbitrary or casual incident of human society" that can be easily removed, but a "natural and necessary result of certain developments of human character and certain conditions of human life, and until these are corrected or altered it is useless to rail against slavery as it is to kick against fate."[46]

Rickards and other proponents of independence and emancipation were caught on the horns of an intractable dilemma. The proposal struck many observers as a mere subterfuge and a violation of the country's long-standing abolitionist tradition. Even James Mason, the Confederate commissioner, was

<hr />

46. *Free Press* (Leicester), 12 December 1863; *Press* (Bristol), 5 February 1863; *Observer* (Bradford), 5 February 1863. Arguments such as Rickards's were developed more fully by James Spence. See his *The American Union: Its Effect on National Character and Policy, with an Inquiry into Secession as a Constitutional Right and the Causes of the Disruption* (London, 1862), 159–63.

impressed by this tradition—he called it a "sentiment"—which he observed was "akin to patriotism." Writing many years after the war, another Confederate agent, Edwin DeLeon, laid the blame for the Confederacy's failure to win British recognition on the Union blockade of Southern ports and "the pernicious adherence to the institution of slavery which the moral sense of the civilized world condemned."[47] Proposals for Southern emancipation ran up against a stark reality: the Confederacy and its agents in Britain held fast against any plans to free the slaves. As a result, British supporters of the South found themselves publicly promoting a form of gradual emancipation, while in the company of Southerners eschewing all such plans. Prodded by the opposition, and, as Conservatives, genuinely committed to the notion of incremental change over time, proponents of Southern emancipation, such as the Reverend Edward A. Verity, the incumbent of Habergham Eaves, insisted that abolition was inevitable because slave labor was clearly more expensive than free labor and, more significantly, because the South would always be reproached if it did not free its slaves. Many would have agreed with Spence when he declared that he was opposed to slavery, not because of any idea that all men were created equal, but because a man should not be a chattel.[48] Spence tried as best he could to rein in those in the Southern Independence Association who insisted on a public declaration of support for emancipation. His efforts failed to appease Confederate agents such as Henry Hotze, however, who wrote his superiors of his suspicion that both Spence and the association were conceding too much to British antislavery traditions. The problem for Spence (and by extension for all other pro-Southerners), Hotze declared, is that "he assumed to occupy at one and the same time two opposite and irreconcilable positions, that of a high official of our Government owing it allegiance, and that of a disinterested alien friend." As far as Hotze was concerned, if the South was forced to choose "between independence and the maintenance of our domestic institution," it would not be prepared to abandon slavery.[49]

Hotze was astute enough to recognize, however, that public support for the

47. Mason to Benjamin, Paris, 25 January 1864, James Mason Papers, Library of Congress, Washington, D.C.; Edwin De Leon, *Thirty Years of My Life on Three Continents* (London, 1890), 2: 68–70.

48. *Reporter* (Ashton and Stalybridge), 30 January 1864; Spence, *The American Union*, 132.

49. Spence to Mason, Liverpool, 22 January 1864, Mason Papers; Hotze to Benjamin, London, 31 October, 26 September 1863, Henry Hotze Papers, Library of Congress, Washington, D.C.

Confederacy would have quickly evaporated without some timetable for free-ing the slaves. He therefore did not publicly oppose Manchester supporters' call for a plan of gradual abolition that was to be achieved "not abruptly or without due consideration, but by a system such as prevailed in the West Indies; not, however, to degenerate into 'squatting' and idleness, such as has cursed emancipation in the British colonies." Immediate emancipation, Beresford-Hope argued, would cause the freedmen the "greatest misery," for they would be thrown onto their own resources unprepared. It would also re-sult in "bloodshed, outrage, destruction of property, and perpetual starvation over the South, by the letting loose of a race half-savage, half-childish," attendant with all "kinds of horrors—murder, arson, rapine and outrage."[50] Few went as far as Beresford-Hope, but even among Union proponents there was some support for gradual, rather than immediate, emancipation. John Stockdale, for example, supported a plan proposed some years earlier by Thomas Chalmers, the Scottish divine, in which slaves would start by gain-ing control of one-sixth of their time, the fraction to be progressively in-creased over time. Edward Irving, a fugitive slave who had been living in England since 1856, called for gradual abolition because he feared that sudden freedom would create unspecified problems for both the freedmen and society. Irving was a lone voice among African Americans living in Britain, and Stockdale was generally out of step with fellow Union supporters. More typi-cal was David Thomas, a Bury journalist, who challenged proponents of grad-ual abolition to show an instance where "speedy emancipation" was not a success.[51]

Advocates of gradual emancipation were driven by two major considera-tions. On the one hand, their vision was limited by national pride. Britain had effected emancipation in its West Indian colonies in this way; thus logically it was the only tried and tested road to freedom. West Indian emancipation was a noble act, "a great self-sacrifice at the shrine of duty," Spence insisted. In fol-lowing this course, Britain had not forgotten justice or the rights of property owners. On the other hand, compensated emancipation, reinforced by a pe-

50. *Anti Slavery Reporter*, 2 November 1863; Beresford-Hope, *The American Disruption*, 10, 67, 92–93. See *Times* (London), 17 January 1862 and *Independent* (Sheffield and Rotherham), 27 May 1863, for similar arguments.

51. *Times* (Bury), 21 February 1863; *Examiner* (Huddersfield), 1 October 1863; *Courier* (Hali-fax), 1 October 1863. For a discussion of the rejection of gradual compensated emancipation by abolitionists on both sides of the Atlantic see Betty Fladeland, "Compensated Emancipation: A Rejected Alternative," *Journal of Southern History* 42 (May 1976): 169–186.

riod of transition in which the planter would be assured a supply of labor and the creation of institutions to look after the interests of the freedmen, would guarantee a peaceful move from slavery to freedom.[52] This approach seemed the only way to avoid the bloodshed that many predicted would follow in the wake of President Lincoln's Emancipation Proclamation. The fear of servile insurrection, which conjured images of mutilation, pillage, torture, and rape, dominated reaction to the proclamation among Union opponents. They drew on ancient history and the experiences of the French and Saint-Domingue revolutions to warn against the consequences of Lincoln's policy. Spence dismissed the proclamation as the last desperate act of an impotent government and military, the "poisoned arrow" of fanaticism that encouraged the slaves to revolt. Beresford-Hope saw it as the "unparalleled last card" played by a "reckless gambler." Drawing on the same theme, the editors of *Punch* called it "Abe Lincoln's Last Card; or Rouge-et-Noir."[53] The proclamation, the editors of the *Times* predicted, would result in a bloodbath reminiscent of Haiti. "A general revolt of the slaves would end only in their destruction where they are weak, and their return to a state of savagery wherever they won the country for themselves." It was a scheme for subjecting "an Anglo-Saxon people to horrors equalled only by those which fell upon the English in India five years ago." William S. Lindsay, a Liberal M.P., warned that it was a call to the slaves to massacre "your masters, massacre your mistresses, and massacre their children, so that you may obtain your freedom." "GRT" of Lichfield declared it a "scheme of sanguinary revenge" that would have results equaled only by "the frightful scenes of the Indian mutiny or amongst the cruel reckless Chinese." To one editor it brought back memories of "Paris of 1790."[54]

The fear of servile insurrection was not limited to defenders of the Con-

52. *Guardian* (Halifax), 13 February 1864.

53. *Times* (London), 16 January 1863; *Telegraph* (Maidstone), 24 January 1863. *Punch* quoted in Oscar Maurer, "'Punch' on Slavery and the Civil War in America, 1861–1865," *Victorian Studies* 1 (September 1957): 24. Similar reactions greeted word of John Brown's attack on Harpers Ferry in 1859. See Seymour Drescher, "Servile Insurrection and John Brown's Body in Europe," *Journal of American History* 80 (September 1993): 506–07.

54. *Times* (London), 19 September 1862; *Times* (Sunderland), 6 October 1863; *Mercury* (Liverpool), 22 July 1862; *Northern Warder*, 10 October 1862; *Chronicle* (Bath), 26 February 1863. Bernard Semmel has argued that the wars fought to maintain British colonial possessions, especially the Indian mutiny and the Maori wars, affected the public's attitude toward colonial subjects. These formerly "peaceful children of nature" had become "bloodthirsty savages." Bernard Semmel, *Democracy versus Empire: The Jamaica Riots of 1865 and the Governor Eyre Controversy* (Garden City, N.Y., 1969), 19.

federacy. In the wake of the Union defeat at First Bull Run, Cobden worried that the torch and the dagger would be put "into the negroes' hands" and would result in "the working of a servile insurrection on a tenfold scale of horrors to that of St. Domingo." In a letter to British friends, Harriet Beecher Stowe played on the same image in her defense of the Union's decision not to permit African Americans into the armed forces. To do so, she said, would unleash an "awful whirlwind of conflicting races." It was the match that could "ignite that powder magazine" and result in "barbarities hitherto unknown in civilization." Such an insurrection, she concluded, "would be the most unfortunate thing possible for that injured race, whose freedom is coming on the wings of every hour. Untaught, and furious, they would perpetrate deeds which would check the rising sympathies of the world, and needlessly complicate the majestic movement, we trust, is destined at last to humble and destroy the power of their oppressors." [55]

Ironically, this image of the bloodthirsty slave clashed with the cherished belief of Confederate supporters that the slaves were loyal and deeply attached to their master. As Winthrop Jordan has argued, it was a portrait of "the loyal darky as barbarous fiend." Following a hurried visit to the South in late 1862, W. C. Corsan, a Sheffield manufacturer, reported that he did not expect the slaves to rise up against their masters. They were too isolated and lacked leadership, and most importantly, it was not in their character to do so. "Isolated on plantations chiefly, in small numbers, remote from each other, mostly unable to read, naturally docile and attached to their homes and masters, more than any other existing race devoid of the power of combination, absolutely without leaders or self reliance, what could such a people do?" [56] William Andrew Jackson, a Virginia fugitive slave and Jefferson Davis's former coachman, found an explanation for the slaves apparent docility in the fact that they were a "praying people." This is not to suggest that they were not interested in ways to end the system, he maintained, for they talked about the subject constantly. They were, for instance, aware of John Brown's raid on the arsenal at Harpers Ferry, seeing it as moving the system one step closer to

55. Cobden to Bright, London, 8 August 1861, Richard Cobden Papers, British Library, London; Stowe quotation in *Anti Slavery Reporter*, 1 November 1861.

56. Winthrop D. Jordan, *Tumult and Silence at Second Creek: An Inquiry into a Civil War Slave Conspiracy* (Baton Rouge, 1993), 160; W. C. Corsan, *Two Months in the Confederate States: An Englishman's Travels through the South* (1863: reprint edition, Benjamin H. Trask, ed., Baton Rouge, 1996), 138. See also *Index*, 8 August 1862 for similar arguments.

collapse. "They worked slowly, and when the time came," he predicted, "they would be found ready."[57]

Some Union supporters welcomed the prospects of widespread slave uprisings. "Servile war, the wretches!" James Sinclair, secretary of the Glasgow Emancipation Society, boldly exclaimed. "Why sir, if it had resulted in the oppressed of these people rising and putting out of existence every man of their oppressors—not so much as the shadow of a tear would have wet the corner of one of my eyes." Henry Vincent insisted that a servile war would be the fault of those who were morally responsible for slavery, for slavery, J. Sella Martin, the fugitive slave agreed, was only war by another name. If there was a repeat of Saint-Domingue, Radical editor George Reynolds laid the blame at the door of those were responsible for the system. Generally, Union supporters dismissed the fear of servile uprisings as nothing more than a red herring designed to distract the public's attention from the real issues of the war. More significantly, they argued, the Union's policy of enlisting free blacks and freedmen negated the possibility that such an event would occur. Early in the war T. Peronnet Thompson had reasoned that the recruitment of Negroes in the army was the only way to save slaveholders from unnecessary loss of life and property. The experience of the British in the War of 1812, one editor observed, demonstrated that this approach had the added advantage of placing "disaffected persons" among the rebels.[58]

Much of the defense of Lincoln's proclamation, however, skirted the issue of violence. While many were critical of its limited reach, it was greeted as a major step in the right direction. Most observers were more restrained than the editor who trumpeted that the "Rubicon [had been] crossed at last." To W. E. Adams the proclamation meant that America, like Britain thirty years earlier, was moving toward abolition. It might have been the result of political necessity, as so many critics insisted, but governments, Adams responded, rarely acted on principle and are more generally moved by expediency. Of one thing Adams was certain, the Proclamation "cuts the ground from under the feet of those who profess to sympathise with the South on the ground that

---

57. *Advertiser* (Heywood), 13 June 1863; *Observer* (Wigan), 17 July 1863.

58. *Examiner* (Glasgow), 18 April 1863; Robert LeBaron Bingham, "The Glasgow Emancipation Society, 1833–76" (M.Litt. thesis, University of Glasgow, 1973) 223; *Examiner* (Huddersfield), 1 November 1862; *Reynolds's Newspaper*, 19 October 1862; *Advertiser* (Bradford), 22 June, 27 July, 3, 31 August 1861; *Staffordshire Sentinel*, 17 January 1863. For Martin's view see *National Anti Slavery Standard*, 7 December 1861.

slavery was likely to be sooner abolished by it, than by the North. It is now more than ever evident that pro-Southern sentiments are pro-slavery sentiments also." Ernest Jones agreed that Lincoln had acted out of political necessity, but his move was a sound approach based on the calculation that the Border States should not be alienated. Jones made something of a virtue out of necessity: the "sword for those who have drawn the sword; but our moral example for those who, though erring brethren, have maintained the peace. . . . [P]hysical force in the one hand and moral force in the other."[59]

The proclamation was for supporters of the Union confirmation of their conviction, held ever since the firing on Fort Sumter, that the war would lead to emancipation. While the Confederacy sought to reconfirm its commitment to the perpetuation of slavery, the arguments of its supporters notwithstanding, the Union had been making significant incremental steps toward the total elimination of slavery. Slavery had been abolished in the District of Columbia and in the territories; two Confiscation acts, which helped to free some slaves, had been adopted; the Union had at last conceded to the wishes of the British that suspected slave ships flying the American flag could be boarded and searched; and the governments of Haiti and Liberia had been recognized, cutting the ground away from those who insisted that the refusal to exchange diplomats with either country was symptomatic of the North's deep and abiding racism. Compared with the South, which maintained that the Negro was best suited for slavery, the Reverend R. Bell of Leicester pointed out that the North was doing all that it could to end slavery.[60]

Working-class supporters of the Union saw the proclamation as the final refutation of the Southern apologist's argument that slavery was the most efficient organization of labor. The document, a Mr. Somerville observed, gave workingmen an opportunity to declare their sympathy with four million "working men and women who are defrauded of the fruits of their labour, and the ownership of their own bodies, because they are guilty of having 'a skin not coloured like our own.'" John Turner, secretary of the Ashton branch of the Union and Emancipation Society, all of whose officers were workers, had no doubt that the issue of emancipation was a "working man's question, for if it was right for slavery in one part it was right in another; and it behooved the

59. *Advertiser* (Dundee), 6 October 1862; W. E. Adams, *The Slaveholders' War: An Argument for the North and the Negro* (London, 1863), 15, 17; *National Reformer*, 18 October 1862; *Morning Star*, 16 October 1862; Jones, *The Slaveholders' War*, 25.

60. *Leicestershire Mercury*, 27 June 1863; *Examiner and Times* (Manchester), 6 February 1863; *Independent* (Sheffield and Rotherham), 1 January 1863.

working classes to give no help to scoundrels who wanted their work done for nothing." Mr. Johnson of Leicester equated the Negro's lack of political rights in America with the condition of workingmen in Britain who were considered "the scum, and were machines, or were ignorant and requiring to be better educated." The time was not far distant, he predicted, "when not only the slave in America but their [Britain's] own political slavery would be done away." Aware that the cornerstone of the Confederacy was the "enslavement of the working man white as well as black," "A Factory Operative" of Bamber Bridge regarded the "future peace and prosperity of a great people, the emancipation or consignment to hopeless bondage of four million human beings as questions of greater moment than those that relate to the removal of any temporary suffering amongst ourselves."[61]

Laudable as such expressions of solidarity were, working-class supporters of the Confederacy saw the proclamation, and emancipation, differently. While few were willing to accept the calculation of Mr. Heyworth of Newchurch that for every Negro freed, three white men lost their lives, many had serious reservations about the merits of emancipation. Joseph L. Quarmby, an Oldham bookseller and for a time secretary of the local branch of the Southern Independence Association, rejected the proclamation as an effort to make "the nigger a stepping stone to empire" and a blatant attempt to ravish Southern white society. His reactions to the war, and more specifically Lincoln's policies, were driven by a combination of national pride, an abiding racism, and a visceral rejection of any position espoused by John Bright, the leading representative of the Manchester school, which, Quarmby insisted, had opposed all efforts to improve working conditions for British workers. The English constitution was the finest in the world, and consequently Englishmen the freest citizens. Had the Americans still been living under its mandate, they would have avoided the carnage of a civil war. The American government, the "greatest despotism in the world . . . the creature of the mob, an emanation of the rabble," was callously attempting, through the proclamation, "to free 'sambo' the better to enslave the white man in America and England."[62]

There were many in Britain, however, who chose not to support either side and who instead declared a pox on both houses. They were in large part opposed to slavery and therefore unable to support the Confederacy, yet found the Union's lack of an emancipation policy totally unacceptable. Abel Swann,

61. *Caledonian Mercury*, 20 February 1863; *Leicestershire Mercury*, 9 May 1863; *Reporter* (Ashton and Stalybridge), 3 January 1864; *Guardian* (Preston), 18 April 1863.
62. *Times* (Bury), 20 June 1863; *Standard* (Oldham), 25 April 1863.

a Stalybridge tailor, auctioneer, and associate of the Reverend J. Stephens, could not bring himself to support either side, the South because of slavery, the North because it had "shown a gross amount of ignorance and stupidity." Both sides treated the Negro "as an animal and not as men." The issue for Swann was not whether to recognize the Confederacy, but how to feed the unemployed. To some such as Mary Carpenter and her brothers, members of a prominent Unitarian family who had been active in the abolitionist movement, America had become so corrupt since the passage of the Fugitive Slave Law in 1850 that to associate with it was to risk corruption. The only way to avoid such an eventuality, James Martineau, the Unitarian divine, believed, was to adopt a "negative policy of abstinence and forbearance." [63]

The outbreak of hostilities prodded the Carpenter brothers to shelve their criticism of the Union in the interest of emancipation, but for many others, especially peace advocates, war for any cause was simply unacceptable. Following the attack on Fort Sumter, Henry Richards and Joseph Pease, leaders of the Peace Society, called on the two sides not to go to war, warning that military establishments suffocated countries wherever they existed. From the founding of the peace movement in 1846, Richards, Cobden, and others had called for the submission of disputes to arbitration. As in the Crimean War, they saw no reason why both sides in the Civil War could not have their differences arbitrated. "Our proper business is always to withstand the erroneous notion so widely prevalent, that wrong should be met with violence," wrote James Haughton, "that rebellion should be met with force of arms, even to bloodshed." Richards agreed, rejecting the notion that it was possible to promote "a purpose of pure Christian philanthropy by rapine, and slaughter, and extermination." [64]

Because of their universal opposition to war, peace advocates did not speak with one voice on the issue of emancipation. Richards remained firmly committed to abolition by moral suasion and absolutely rejected all forms of violence. Though holding in "the utmost abhorrence the blasphemous avowal of the Southerners that they mean to found their commonwealth upon slavery, as its chief cornerstone," Richards had "no faith whatever in the efficacy of the brutal butcheries of war either to protect civilization or to promote philanthropy." Conversely, though he generally agreed with Richards, Cobden remained open to the proposition that, in this case at least, war was acceptable

63. *Reporter* (Ashton and Stalybridge), 27 September 1862; Douglas Charles Stange, *British Unitarians against American Slavery; 1833–1865* (Rutherford, N.J. 1984), 116, quotation on 155.

64. *Morning Star*, 3, 4 June 1861; *Liberator*, 4 October 1861, 7 November 1862.

if the result was emancipation. "Though I would not have begun the war for the emancipation of the negroes," he wrote Charles Sumner, "and though I cannot urge its continuance for that object, yet I have always felt that the only result which could justify the war was the manumission of every slave on the Northern Continent of America." To "Pax et Libertas" of Bristol, war was a greater evil than slavery and had to be opposed at all costs. Some of his colleagues in the local Peace Society disagreed. Handel Cossham, a prominent businessman and Union supporter, insisted that he would have opposed the war if he had thought it had been started as a means to abolish slavery. As far as Cossham was concerned, however, the war had been forced upon the North by a South fighting to maintain slavery and as such was justified. While Richards stood above the fray, Cobden and Cossham supported the Union.[65] Even among Quakers, some of whom were the most active proponents of peace, there were differences of opinion over whether a war for emancipation was justified. The leadership of the British and Foreign Anti Slavery Society, the majority of whom were Quakers, withdrew the society from active participation in the public debate because of their opposition to war. Yet many Quakers who had been partial to the society's objectives agreed with W. Brook of Halifax, who insisted that "if ever there was an occasion when war could be justified in favor of any question, surely the existence of a nation like America would justify it, especially when they saw becoming more and more apparent the fact that the great question of slavery was involved in the contest." [66]

The complexity and subtlety of reactions to the war are almost staggering, yet there was considerable agreement on one point: the war had reaffirmed the superiority of the British system of government. National pride in the mixed monarchy acted as a lens through which views on the war were refracted. Even among those who were promoting political reform or who took heart from America's electoral system, there remained an abiding commit-

65. *Independent* (Sheffield and Rotherham), 25 June 1863; *Herald* (Brighton), 19 April 1862; *Post* (Bristol), 21 November 1862, 29 January, 29 June 1863, 13 September 1864; Beverly Wilson Palmer, ed., *The Selected Letters of Charles Sumner* (Boston, 1990), 2: 190; Nicolas C. Edsall, *Richard Cobden: Independent Radical* (Cambridge, Mass., 1986), 377–79. For tensions among peace advocates in America see Valerie H. Ziegler, *The Advocates of Peace in Antebellum America* (Bloomington, Ind., 1992), 149–52; Merle Curti, *The Learned Blacksmith: The Letters and Journals of Elihu Burritt* (New York, 1937), 139.

66. *Guardian* (Halifax), 3 December 1864. Brook and others would have agreed with W. E. Adams: "If justice can be won by war, war with all its horrors, is better than injustice conserved by peace." *National Reformer*, 2 August 1862.

ment to a constitutionalism centered on Parliament and the monarchy.[67] There is little doubt that in some instances a few, such as Thomas Wrigley, a Bury paper manufacturer, still smarted over the American Revolution. What right had they to leave "the great British empire," he asked. One did not have to agree with Quarmby that the American government was "the greatest despotism in the world," a creation of the mob, an emanation of the rabble, to believe that the English constitution was the finest in the world and Englishmen the freest. John Rowlinson, who had been active in the Bury movement for West Indian emancipation and who was a stalwart in the local pro-Union organization, rejected all calls for recognition of the Confederacy on the grounds that it would involve receiving the ambassadors of slavehold-ers. The "loyalty of Great Britain loathes the very idea of such an indignity being offered the royal lady we delight to venerate, as that her pure matronly and widowed hand which wields only the scepter of love over the free and brave should ever be contaminated by the kiss of any representative of so foul a conspiracy against civilization, humanity, and God."[68] The Reverend Thomas Guthrie of the Free Church of Scotland, who never quite forgave abolitionists for their condemnation of his church's decision to accept dona-tions from southern states in the early 1840s, was equally as dismissive of the American system of government as was Quarmby, although he would give lukewarm support to the Union. "Britons are envious of no nation," he told a Dundee audience. "We have a Sovereign who is entrenched in the hearts of her people. With her tears we have mingled our own. . . ." Should anyone in America or France "touch a hair of Queen Victoria's head 10,000 arms would rise in Britain to defend her."[69]

Many thought that such unalloyed patriotism pulled Britain away from those grand traditions of internationalism on which the abolitionist and other philanthropic movements had been founded and into a limiting nationalism that muted the British voice for justice abroad. Frederick Douglass thought he saw disturbing signs of this trend during his visit in 1859. Compared to his first visit in 1845 when all he met seemed committed to the eradication of slavery

67. For a discussion of these issues see James A. Epstein, *Radical Expression: Political Language, Ritual, and Symbol in England, 1790–1850* (Oxford, 1994); Margot C. Finn, *After Chartism: Class and Nation in English Radical Politics, 1848–1874* (New York, 1993), especially chapter 1; Linda Colley, *Britons Forging the Nation, 1707–1837* (New Haven, Conn., 1992), 18, 50.

68. *Guardian* (Bury), 13 June 1863; *Standard* (Oldham), 25 April 1863; *Times* (Bury), 7 February 1863.

69. *Northern Warder*, 6 March 1862.

in the United States, this time he saw signs of retreat. Where once there was interest in the ways Britons could aid the movement in the United States, now Douglass faced questions about the legitimacy of foreigners interfering in the internal affairs of another country. He would have been even more surprised had he remained in England during the war, for what Douglass worried was a growing sense of "non-intervention" in 1859 had by the middle of the war been transmuted in some quarters into a call for support for the Confederacy. Much of the change can be attributed to a growing disillusionment with the success of emancipation in the West Indies and to what Douglass rightly identified as the troubling rise of racism. As far as Douglass was concerned, the two were related and the product of a growing American influence in Britain. In contrast to the absence of any manifestations of racial discrimination during his first visit, in 1859 he found "American prejudice" on the "streets of Liverpool and in nearly all . . . commercial towns." This development, he surmised, was the work of the many "pro-slavery ministers" who were now welcomed in Britain—something he had fought against in 1846—and that "pestiferous nuisance, Ethiopian minstrels" who had imported into the country "the slang phrases, the contemptuous sneers all originating in the spirit of slavery." Now the Negro was being portrayed as a happy slave and as "thoughtless of any life higher than a merely physical one."[70]

Douglass may have chosen to locate the source of British racism in the United States, but in reality much of it was locally grown and closely allied to the retreat from emancipation's promise of equality. West Indian emancipation, Thomas Carlyle boldly asserted in his essay "Occasional Discourse on the Nigger Question," published in 1849, had been an abject failure, for it freed a people incapable of appreciating the boon of freedom and failed to put in place a new order that regulated labor. In a situation where labor was no longer controlled by either necessity or the regimen of the plantation system, the freedman had refused to work, and as a result, the economies of the West Indian colonies had collapsed.[71] Southern supporters saw little to dispute in Carlyle's analysis and warned against the danger of repeating the failures of the West Indian experiment. Lord Wolseley was convinced that West Indian

70. John Blassingame, ed., The Frederick Douglass Papers (New Haven, Conn., 1979–), 3: 335–36.
71. Thomas Carlyle, "Occasional Discourse on the Nigger Question," in Carlyle, Latter-Day Pamphlets (London, 1858). On the retreat from the principles of equality that informed British colonial policy in the aftermath of emancipation see Thomas C. Holt, The Problem of Freedom: Race, Labor, and Politics in Jamaica and Britain, 1832–1938 (Kingston, Jamaica, 1992), 179–82.

emancipation had been "a failure in every respect." Echoing Carlyle, "TM" of Kirkdale opposed immediate emancipation: "Frantic nigger worshippers howl for immediate emancipation; but wise men pause and search for a slow but effectual remedy. . . . To abolish slavery at once would be to take away the only available labour in the South, for it is a demonstrative fact that the negroes will not work as free men where they have once been slaves; they find it very inconvenient to be thrown on their own resources." As Trollope put it, "the freedman has always thrown away his hoe, has eaten any man's hog but his own,—has too often sold his daughter for a dollar when any such market has been open to him."[72] The picture painted by Carlyle of the freedman idly lying around up to his ears in pumpkins had by the outbreak of the war imprinted itself on the minds of those who were partial to the South, drawing as it did on a store of ideas developed by defenders of West Indian slavery.[73] It was an impression reinforced by some who had experienced emancipation firsthand and who were willing to testify to the accuracy of Carlyle's description. Hugh Fraser Leslie, who went out to Jamaica in 1823 to manage his mother's property, which included a coffee plantation and an animal pen, is a case in point. Leslie at first seemed to support emancipation, but within a few years was writing home of the freedman's refusal to work. By 1838 he was forced to sell the pen at a loss. The other properties were also sold at a loss in 1853, six years after Leslie's return to Aberdeen. When war broke out, Leslie, convinced that emancipation was not in the interest of either property owners or slaves, threw his support to the Confederacy.[74] This notion that the freedmen would not work and that, as a result, the colonies had reverted to barbarism was widespread enough to worry Thomas B. Butcher, a former missionary in the West Indies. "These alleged calamities," he wrote Lord Brougham, "are I find in the minds of many attributed to emancipation which though acknowledged to have been a splendid instance of philanthropy, was politically an error, and commercially a misfortune."[75]

Even if one were not willing to go as far as the editors of the *Times*—as

72. For Wolseley's view see *Proceedings of the Massachusetts Historical Society*, 14 October 1913; *Mercury* (Liverpool), 17 November 1862; Trollope, *North America*, 2: 69–70.

73. For analysis of these ideas see Alvin O. Thompson, "'Happy—Happy Slaves!': Slavery as a Superior State of Freedom," *Journal of Caribbean History* 29 (1995): 93–119.

74. John George Burnett, ed., *Powis Papers, 1507–1894* (Aberdeen, 1951), 112. For Leslie's support of the South see the membership list of the Southern Independence Association, John Rylands Library, Manchester.

75. Butcher to Brougham, Doncaster, 7 October, 1861, Lord Brougham Papers, University College, London.

many were not—and to argue that nowhere in the Bible was slavery condemned, there were those who believed that slavery was a civilizing institution and that emancipation ran the risk of disrupting its work. "There is much to be said for the continuance of slavery," A. Gwillym wrote his local newspaper. "You cannot change the fetish living African into a hopeful religious negro in the lapse of one generation or two. Slavery is an evil: it is a permitted evil for a certain time;—permitted by the same Diety who, for his own good purposes and wise ends, *permits* other evils to exist—evils that chafed the Greeks and alike fret the Welshman now. Were we not enslaved by the Saxons?" While Beresford-Hope was willing to concede that slavery was a curse and "a misfortune to the country in which it exists," he thought that the "best of slaveowners" made the chains "as light as possible—they educate their blacks, they make them Christians, while in Africa they would have remained untaught and uncivilized."[76]

The Reverend Malet's idyllic plantations were the training grounds for the backward Africans who were, in the words of Heywood schoolteacher W. Salisbury, being schooled for "a high state of civilization." Echoing the arguments of George Fitzhugh, a Virginia apologist for slavery, an editor in Brighton insisted that not only had the slave population increased dramatically since 1790, but also slaves were, compared to "their African progenitors, in a considerably advanced condition of civilization." Nowhere in Europe, not even in Britain, he concluded, had "the peasantry made an equal improvement in civilization and so increased in numbers as the Africans imported into the Southern States of America." The former Chartist Joseph Barker, who had emigrated to the United States in 1851 and who would return to Britain as one of the Confederacy's most active proponents, recalled at the end of the war that he was never very uneasy about the impact of slavery on the slaves. They were as "happy a people, previous to the war as any class of working people I know. I have been in some of the southern states and never saw a slave that was ill clad, and that seemed to be ill fed. . . . And slavery has not degraded the Negroes as is often said but raised and blessed them."[77]

76. *Times* (London), 6 January 1863; *Telegraph* (Merthyr), 7 December 1863; Beresford-Hope, *The American Disruption*, 11; *Telegraph* (Maidstone), 24 January 1863.

77. *Advertiser* (Heywood), 10 January 1863; *Guardian* (Brighton), 28 October 1863; Joseph Barker Diaries: 1865–1875, Vol.1, 12 May 1865 through 29 October 1869, Joseph Barker Collection, Nebraska State Historical Society, Lincoln, Neb. See also editorial in *Guardian* (Bury), 21 November 1863, and the letter of Tubal Cain in *Express* (Nottingham), 12 February 1863, for similar views.

Such views were not unimportant in the midst of the uncertainty (and, for some, economic dislocation) caused by the war. They fed directly into the growing skepticism about the results of West Indian emancipation and the utility of continued efforts to work for the elevation of backward peoples. They were also a decided influence on public perceptions of the war. One measurement of their impact is to be found in the way African Americans were received in Britain during the war. While there was continued support for efforts to aid destitute fugitive slaves then living in London to settle in Africa and while fugitive slaves such as Jacob Green of Kentucky found work in Britain, the passions unleashed by the debate over the war led to rising instances of racial discrimination, which, with a few minor exceptions, had not occurred during the antebellum period. William Andrew Jackson lamented the fact that he could go nowhere without "meeting with some prejudice, and ... thought that there was quite as much prejudice in England as in America." The treatment of Thomas Arthur created a minor furor that resulted in a petition to Parliament. Arthur, who was married to a white woman, was refused admission to his pew at a church in London. To complicate matters, the pew-door opener had allowed Arthur's wife to take her seat. None of these incidents could compare, however, to the reception William Watson received in Blackburn. Watson, a Kentuckian and former student at King's College, London, was scheduled to give a lecture on "The Bible, Trades, the Education of Blacks, and the American War and Its Future Events,"— a relatively uncontroversial topic—in early December 1864 at the local Rechabites Hall. Much to his and the local organizers' surprise, Watson was attacked outside the hall. There is no doubt that supporters of the Confederacy had set out to disrupt the lecture rather than to attack Watson, but the situation got out of control. Watson was kicked, his coat torn, and, as more than one observer reported, he was racially insulted. The attack convinced one local editor that "the hatred of the negro is not confined to either the North or South. . . ."[78]

78. *Times* (Bury), 9 May 1863; *Reporter* (Ashton and Stalybridge), 23 February 1863; *Journal* (Newcastle), 4 May 1863; *Leicestershire Mercury*, 28 February 1863; *Guardian* (Manchester), 2 May 1863; *Times* (Blackburn), 3, 10, 17 December 1864; *Guardian* (Preston), 10, 17, 24 December 1864. Watson's treatment challenges Pole's declaration that the "absence of racial feeling, of any conception of colour as a factor dividing worker from worker or man from man, was distinctive throughout the whole period." Pole, *Abraham Lincoln and the Working Classes of Britain*, 16. For an analysis of changing racial attitudes in the decade before the war see Douglas A. Lorimer, *Colour, Class, and the Victorians: English Attitudes to the Negro in the Mid–Nineteenth Century* (New York, 1978).

Writing in the wake of the Jamaican Morant Bay Rebellion in late 1865, Sarah Parker Remond, an African American who had been living in London since 1859, lamented this change in British views of the Negro. "Since the civil war in the United States the Confederates and their natural allies, these former West Indian planters," she wrote, "have united together to endeavor to neutralize the interest felt for the oppressed negroes, and to hold them up to scorn and contempt of the civilized world."[79] In intellectual circles, that alliance centered on the London Anthropological Society, which was founded in January 1863. An offshoot of the Ethnological Society, which had concentrated on the study of scientific issues and whose work was heavily influenced by humanitarian considerations, the Anthropological Society mixed science with politics. Among its founders were Dr. James Hunt; Sir Richard Burton, the British explorer; and Henry Hotze, the Confederate commissioner, all of whom thought little of the African's capacity for civilization. The Society's objectives, Hotze wrote his superiors, was to question the "heresies that have gained currency in science and politics, of the equality of the races of men." Inviting Hotze to join the society, Hunt wrote: "You should and must take a strong interest in our objects, for in us is your only hope that the negro's place in nature will ever be scientifically ascertained, and fearlessly explained."[80]

Hunt did exactly that in a paper, "On the Physical and Mental Character of the Negro," that he delivered at the annual meeting of the British Association for the Advancement of Science in Newcastle in mid-1863. Hunt insisted that scientific evidence pointed to the inferiority of the Negro. All those who were held up as examples of Negro capability were, he observed, of mixed race. Hunt was preceded at the meeting by John Crawfund, president of the Ethnological Society, whose paper "The Comixture of the Races of Man as Affecting the Progress of Civilization" argued that, over time, the mixing of superior and inferior races led inevitably to the decline of civilization. It would appear that Hunt and Crawfund were arguing at cross-purposes,

---

79. *Inquirer*, 22 November 1865.

80. Ronald Rainger, "Race, Politics, and Science: The Anthropological Society of London in the 1860s," *Victorian Studies* 22 (Autumn 1978): 51; Seymour Drescher, "The Ending of the Slave Trade and the Evolution of European Scientific Racism," *Social Science History* 14 (1990): 440–41; Edward Rice, *Captain Richard Francis Burton: The Secret Agent Who Made the Pilgrimage to Mecca, Discovered the Kama Sutra, and Brought the Arabian Knights to the West* (New York, 1990), 369–70; Hotze to Benjamin, London, 27 August 1863, Hotze Papers. Hotze, who was born in Switzerland in 1833 and settled in the United States as a minor, translated Arthur de Gobineau's treatise on the inequality of the races. Charles P. Cullop, *Confederate Propaganda in Europe, 1861–1865* (Coral Gables, Fla., 1969), 18–19.

for inherent in Hunt's position was the possibility that more race mixing would lead to permanent advances for the Negro. The apparent contradiction, however, was obviated by the belief that, while mixing could lead to some short-term progress for the Negro, in the long run civilization would be irreparably damaged.

The leaders of the Anthropological Society, and proponents of the Confederacy, were well aware that, widely reported, such views could work to their mutual advantage. The opposition, also aware of possible damage to their cause, made every effort to rebut Hunt and Crawfund. Joseph Cowen Jr., a prominent local manufacturer; W. E. Adams, who at the time was working for one of Cowen's newspapers; and the secularist and Radical George Holyoake led in these endeavors. It seems that they arranged an invitation for William Craft, an American fugitive slave who had been living in England since 1851 and who had just returned from a trip to Dahomey, to deliver a report on his visit to West Africa. A symbol of self-sacrifice and resistance to oppression, Craft must have caused Hunt some discomfort. When Craft rose to denounce Hunt and Crawfund for using "scientific fact" to justify the oppression of blacks, Union supporters could hardly contain their joy. A sympathetic correspondent for the Newcastle *Chronicle*, one of Cowen's newspapers, observed that comments about the Negro's anatomy were "an outrage to every kindly feeling, and an insult to humanity. . . . Mr. Craft's clear, open, generous and manly countenance contrasted most successfully with that of his bitter opponents." Hunt thought otherwise: Craft's criticism of scientific evidence was nothing more than "poetical clap-trap."[81]

Britain's new wave of colonial expansion in Africa gave greater urgency to the debate in Newcastle over the Negro's place in nature. As Philip Curtin has shown, the African, sometimes pitied, other times despised, now became in the eyes of Hunt and others someone to be feared, a threat to European civilization and colonial interests. Hunt was also well aware, as he told Hotze, that their views lent scientific legitimacy to the Confederacy's refusal to commit itself to emancipation. So, too, were their opponents. Moncure Conway, who moved to England in 1862 to promote the cause of the Union though he was the son of a Virginia slaveholder, published a pamphlet refuting Hunt's claims. The editor of the *Inquirer*, a Unitarian weekly, deplored the "altered tone of moral sentiment with which Englishmen, especially of the more edu-

81. Nigel Todd, *"The Militant Democracy": Joseph Cowen and Victorian Radicalism* (Tyne and Wear, 1991), 72; *Chronicle* (Newcastle), 19 September 1863; *Anthropological Review* 1 (1863): 390–91.

cated classes, are beginning to regard the great question of slavery." This "moral corruption" had now spread to science, where discussions about the Negro commenced from "a point of view derived from outside political and social sympathies."[82]

If Frederick Douglass is to be believed, what he witnessed on the streets of Liverpool and other major cities suggested that views about Negro inferiority were pretty widespread. What Hunt and Crawfund did for the educated classes, Douglass might have argued had he been in Britain during the war, the Ethiopian minstrels did for the masses. Douglass was not alone in his scathing criticism of what had become, by 1860, one of the most popular forms of entertainment. Writing some years later, Sarah Parker Remond condemned those who derived their view of the Negro partly from that "class of vulgar men called 'Ethiopian Minstrels.'"[83] Initially, Douglass had been ambivalent about minstrelsy, aware that, in many instances, the songs performed were sympathetic to the slave. His change of heart may have come as a result of the minstrels' widespread popularity in Britain. By the time of his second visit, there were buskers who performed on street corners, at fairs, and at the seaside; professional companies who played in theaters and concert halls; and amateur productions that were performed in workingmen's clubs and at village fetes. The group of "Amateur Ethiopians" that was formed in Newcastle to raise money for the building fund of the local Mechanic Institute and the local Colored Minstrels who raised money for the Coal Club and for the building of a library in the villages of Market Harborough and Husbands Bosworth attest to minstrelsy's popularity. Even before Douglass's first visit in 1845, minstrelsy had established itself as a component of working-class entertainment. In 1842 a gathering of Chartists in Calverton, near Nottingham, welcomed their leader, Fergus O'Conner, with tea, cakes, dances, games, and other amusements including "a Nigger, a real Nigger, accompanied by two fiddlers, dancing Jim along Josey in real Nigger style." Minstrel dialect speeches were published "for reading at home and for amateur delivery," Caroline Clayton points out, and costumes were offered for hire by "amateur minstrel troupes that proliferated in works and institutes." "Nigger dancing," along

82. Philip D. Curtin, *The Image of Africa: British Ideas and Action, 1780–1850* (Madison, Wis., 1964), 379–80; Moncure D. Conway, *Testimonies Concerning Slavery* (London, 1864), 61; *Inquirer*, 5 September 1863. The *Anthropological Review*, organ of the society, was a strong supporter of the Confederacy and the continuation of slavery. Lorimer, *Colour, Class, and the Victorians*, 149.

83. *The Freed-Man*, 1 February 1866.

with prizefighting, dogfighting, and drinking, had by midcentury become an integral part of working-class pastimes.[84]

These minstrel groups, as J. S. Bratton has shown, drew on local traditions and the needs of their audiences, adapting American materials to British tastes and addressing British issues and concerns. By 1860, Bratton concludes, minstrel troupes were a common feature of public entertainment. Newcastle, where at least nine troupes performed, sometimes more than once, between 1860 and 1864, was not atypical. Lorimer has estimated that there were fifteen "permanent minstrel companies" in English theaters in 1860.[85] Minstrelsy also had wide "cross-class appeal" because, when divested of its more risqué material, it was viewed as wholesome family entertainment. Harry Reynolds, one of the most prominent figures in British minstrelsy in the second half of the nineteenth century, remembered the time when a "minstrel show was the only approach to a variety entertainment that many respectable citizens permitted themselves to indulge in," especially those who preferred their "amusement to be free from items that leave a nasty taste in the mouth." Praising the performance of the Christy Minstrels, one reviewer wrote of "a charm in the performances and the excellence of the performers; there is a freedom from even a suggestion of indecency in even the most extravagant of the 'nigger absurdities,' while the harmonised melodies are so ex-

---

84. George Rehin, "Blackface Street Minstrels in Victorian London and its Resorts: Popular Culture and its Racial Connotations as Revealed in Polite Opinion," *Journal of Popular Culture* 15 (Summer 1981): 20; *Newcastle Chronicle and Northern Counties Advertiser*, 18 April 1863; *Journal* (Hinckley), 8 March 1862; *Midland Workman*, 7 December 1861; James Epstein, "Some Organizational and Cultural Aspects of the Chartist Movement in Nottingham," in James Epstein and Dorothy Thompson, eds., *The Chartist Experience: Studies in Working-Class Radicalism and Culture, 1830–1860* (London, 1982), 248; Caroline Clayton, "Black Face Power: The Construction of Black Face Performance in England and Their Contribution to Attitudes to Race, 1832–1867" (master's thesis, University of Warwick, 1991), 30; Robert D. Storch, "The Problem of Working-Class Leisure: Some Roots of Middle-Class Moral Reform in the Industrial North: 1825–50," in A. P. Donajgrodzki, ed., *Social Control in Nineteenth-Century Britain* (London, 1977), 153. For a discussion of the rise and impact of minstrelsy on British attitudes during Douglass's first visit see Sarah Meer, "Competing Representations: Douglass, the Ethiopian Serenaders, and Ethnic Exhibition in London," in Alan J. Rice and Martin Crawford, eds., *Liberating Sojourn: Frederick Douglass and Transatlantic Reform* (Athens, Ga., 1999).

85. J. S. Bratton, "English Ethiopians: British Attitudes and Black-Face Acts, 1835–1865," *The Yearbook of English Studies* 11 (1981): 128, 136–37, 140; *Newcastle Chronicle and Northern Counties Advertiser*, 30 August, 2 December 1862, 7 March 1863; *Journal* (Newcastle), 22, 23 April 1862; Nigel Todd, "Black-on-Tyne," 17–18; Lorimer, *Colour, Class, and the Victorians*, 86. See Douglas C. Riach, "Blacks and Blackface on the Irish Stage, 1830–1860," *Journal of American Studies* 7 (December 1973): 231–41 for a discussion of minstrelsy's popularity in Ireland.

quisite as to render them readily acceptable favourites in every dining-room of the land." [86]

Such popularity, as George Rehin has argued, had little to do with the effects of economic dislocation on the lives of the British working class.[87] In fact, the years prior to the Civil War were ones of relative economic prosperity and political stability. Nor did African Americans pose a threat to the livelihood of the working class. Hence the popularity of minstrelsy with its caricature of blacks could not be explained by a psychological need to belittle in order to dismiss a potential competitor. In spite of its adaptations to British tastes, however, minstrelsy's central concern was the Negro, an American obsession. Ultimately then, it was the American image of the Negro and life on the plantation that pervaded all aspects of a troupe's performance. There is no doubt that much of this image was filtered through national sensibilities, which in the years of greatest concern about the slave and freedman pitied the plight of the Negro and praised Britain for having the wisdom to free her slaves. As antislavery sentiment waned, however, pity for the Negro gave way to ridicule, and caricature became reality. Concerned about a critical review of his play, The Octoroon, Dion Boucicault, the Irish-American playwright, may have best explained changes in the popular view of the Negro that had occurred since the publication of Uncle Tom's Cabin ten years earlier. Boucicault was taken aback by the audience's reaction to a theme he thought Harriet Beecher Stowe had exploited to great effect: "The audience hailed with every mark of enthusiasm the sunny views of negro life; they were pleased with the happy relations existing between the slaves and the family of which they were dependents; they enjoyed the heartiness with which these slaves were sold, and cheered the planters who bought them. But, when the Octoroon girl was purchased by the ruffianly overseer to become his paramour, her suicide to preserve her purity provoked no sympathy whatever." [88]

86. Michael Pickering, "White Skin, Black Masks: 'Nigger' Minstrelsy in Victorian England," in J. S. Bratton, ed., Music Hall Performers and Style (Milton Kaynes, 1986), 83; Harry Reynolds, Minstrel Memories: The Story of Burnt Cork Minstrelsy in Great Britain from 1836 to 1927 (London, 1928), 47, 71; Guardian (Nottingham), 14, 18 October 1861; Journal (Aberdeen), 21 January 1863, 1 February 1865.

87. George F. Rehin, "Harlequin Jim Crow: Continuity and Convergence in Blackface Clowning," Journal of Popular Culture 9 (Winter 1975): 689. See Eric Lott, Love and Theft: Blackface Minstrelsy and the American Working Class (New York, 1993), for a discussion of the causes and consequences of minstrelsy's popularity among the working class in New York City.

88. Pickering, "White Skin, Black Masks," 83; Bratton, "English Ethiopians," 132; Lorimer, Colour, Class, and the Victorians, 82; Times (London), 20 November 1861; Richard Fawkes, Dion Boucicault: A Biography (London, 1979), 107.

In the heat of the public debate over the Civil War, minstrelsy's caricatures came increasingly to be interpreted as fair representations of the Negro's char- acter and as such to reinforce the views of southern apologists such as James Hunt. Hotze thought he could discern a growing appreciation of the South's opposition to emancipation. "Even among the masses," he observed, "these juster ideas gain ground, and Mrs Beecher Stowe and negro fanaticism are sat- irized and ridiculed on the popular stage." Even among pro-Union sympathiz- ers there was a tendency to conflate minstrel depictions and antislavery. For example, in a lecture to workingmen at Rothwell, Yorkshire, the Reverend E. Lewis made humorous references to "the general habits and feelings of the Negro, his dread of punishment, dislike of hard work, excitability, tendency to sing, and change solemn tunes into jigs." Less surprising was an unsympa- thetic report of a lecture by William Andrew Jackson in southern Wales. Jackson had allegedly addressed the meeting "in a pompous, inflated manner characteristic of the American negro, and created the impression upon the audience that the caricature of negro life displayed by the Ethiopian troupes travelling in this country are not exaggerations." Speaking of a lecture by the African American, Thomas Morris Chester, a correspondent for the *Index*, the Confederate organ in London, observed that the lecture was "a rich joke from beginning to end, and teemed with those self-evident absurdities which, in the mouth of the negro, amounts almost to a new and unnamed variety of wit." Jackson's lecture led another correspondent to conclude that slavery had and would always have a beneficial role to play, for the "fetish living African" could not be brought to Christianity in one or two generations. While slavery was an evil, it was a "permitted evil for a certain time," permitted by the same God who "in his infinite wisdom allows other evils to exist."[89]

With its use of heavy dialect and caricature, minstrelsy managed (inten- tionally or otherwise) to portray the Negro as silly and quick to break into song. Visiting African Americans might have played an unwitting role in per- petuating this depiction of the Negro as compulsively musical. It was not un- usual for lecturers to end their meetings with a short musical rendition. Jacob Green sang "Negro sacred songs"; William Watson, slave labor songs; Henry Box Brown, freedom songs. Jackson even promised to sing an "Ethiopian melody" if a meeting in Banbury would adopt pro-Union resolutions. Even the famed Shakespearian actor Ira Aldridge added "Opossum Up a Gum Tree,"

89. Hotze to Benjamin, London, 14 February 1863, Hotze Papers; *Journal* (Hinckley), 11 November 1861; *Telegraph* (Merthyr), 7 February 1863; *Index*, 28 January 1864.

a song made popular by minstrel troupes, to his "Classical Entertainment," which was a mixture of dramatic readings, lectures, and singing.[90] In the passions unleashed by the public debate over the Civil War, the popular image of the Negro came to influence peoples' perceptions of slavery, emancipation, and the future of the freedman. That a large cross section of the public attended these performances, and thoroughly enjoyed the entertainment, meant that these distortions of the Negro's character reached a wide audience.

While the Ethiopian minstrels did have an effect on the way the country viewed the Negro, Douglass was wrong to think that the changes in British attitudes toward the Negro were the result solely of American influences. The trajectory of a more strident racism was rooted, as Douglas Lorimer has argued, in the decade before the Civil War. That Britain did not speak with one voice concerning this and other aspects of the war should come as no surprise. As David Thomas, a Bury journalist, constantly reminded his listeners, he was old enough to know that the West Indian slaves were not freed "without a struggle. A great amount of agitation was required, for although there had been so much said about the twenty millions paid for their liberation, there was at the time great opposition; and not before the act was passed there could not be found more than five bishops in the House of Lords who were favourable to emancipation." In times of strife—and this was such a time—no nation thinks singularly. "It is not true that England with her whole heart hates slavery and desires its extinction," T. Perronet Thompson wrote early in the war. "She has not got a whole heart, any more than America."[91] The question for Thompson, Thomas, and other Union supporters was: to what extent did this divided heart reflect a loss of British abolitionist traditions; to what extent would a country that had freed its own slaves lend its support to the perpetuation of the institution elsewhere?

90. *Courier* (Halifax), 2 April 1864; *Times* (Blackburn), 10 December 1864; *Leigh Chronicle*, 11 January 1862; *Guardian* (Banbury), 24 December 1862; Herbert Marshall and Mildred Stock, *Ira Aldridge: The Negro Tragedian* (New York, 1958), 150–51.

91. *Times* (Bury), 13 February 1864; *Advertiser* (Bradford), 26 October 1861.

2

Have We Departed from the Faith of Our Fathers?

Another name to noble Nelson's link,
Another victor doomed of death to drink,
Even as the cries of victory resound,
Life's tide is ebbing from the fatal wound!
Mourn, Southern States, your ablest leader's end,
The gallant general, and generous friend . . .

—Sheffield *Telegraph*, 18 June 1863

One could dispute this Derbyshire poet's contention that Stonewall Jackson was the Confederate States' foremost general, but no one could doubt the genuine sense of loss felt by British supporters of the South following the general's death at Chancellorsville in May 1863. The cause had its first martyr. Like Admiral Horatio Nelson at the battle of Trafalgar, Jackson died at the moment of his greatest victory. The comparison reaches for Arthur William Devis's ethereal depiction of Nelson's death on the deck of his ship, the *Victory*, surrounded by what Linda Colley calls "his disciples of the sea." Others saw in Jackson some of the same heroic qualities found in leaders such as Arthur Wellesley Wellington and Giuseppe Garibaldi. Mills in Stockport flew flags at half staff, and a Sheffield meeting passed motions of sympathy for

Jackson's wife.[1] In early June a committee of prominent Confederate supporters led by A. J. B. Beresford-Hope began raising funds for a monument in
honor of Jackson. The commission went to John Henry Foley, one of Britain's
foremost sculptors. Designed and executed in London and placed in a prominent location in Richmond, Virginia, the statue would symbolically cement
the ties between Britain and the Confederacy. Although much of the money
for the statue was raised within a few months, the plans met with some opposition. Questions surfaced about the unseemly haste to honor someone so recently dead and, more significantly, a person so intimately involved in the
effort to establish a country based on slavery: "Cannot the children of the
zealous admirers of this modern hero be trusted to do this commendable work
when the crucible of time has tried the merits of this controversy for the establishment of slavery, and tried the character of the men engaged in it by the
unerring test of truth and justice."[2]

The speed with which the money was raised for the erection of a statue in
memory of a general fighting to defend a slave society appeared to support the
growing suspicion that something had gone awry in British abolitionist traditions. Indeed, historians have confirmed a general pattern of retreat beginning
in the late 1840s. Membership was on the wane, societies were hard pressed to
finance their operations, and the public seemed less inclined to get involved
in the issues that interested abolitionists. Part of the problem for those who
continued to advocate the cause of the slave stemmed from the fact that, long
before the outbreak of the war, the immorality of slavery had come to be
widely accepted. While success bred apathy, time also took its toll. The majority of the generation that had fought against West Indian slavery were now

1. *Telegraph* (Maidstone), 24 January 1863; *Advertiser* (Stockport), 29 May 1863; *Independent*
(Sheffield and Rotherham), 11 June 1863. Two biographies of Jackson appeared within a few
months of his death, the first by Sarah L. Jones in August, the other by Catherine C. Hopley later
in the year. See Charles P. Cullop, "English Reaction to Stonewall Jackson's Death," *West
Virginia History* 29 (October 1967–July 1968): 4; Colley, *Britons*, 180.

2. Committee broadside in Mason to Benjamin, London, 2 July 1863; Mason to William
Smith, London, 17 March 1864, both in Records of the Confederate States of America. Spence
to Mason, Liverpool, 1 June 1863, Mason Papers; *Chronicle* (Preston), 29 August 1863; *Post*
(Bristol), 8 October 1863; *Times* (London), 2 July 1863. The statue was not completed until
1874, months before Foley's death. Work on it had been suspended following the defeat of the
Confederacy, and it was not until the election of a Democratic governor in Virginia that the
statue was unveiled, with much fanfare, in Richmond. *Richmond Daily Dispatch*, 26 October
1875; Morgan Jr., *The Jackson-Hope and the Society of the Cincinnati*, 2–5. It is difficult to prove
Cullop's claim that Jackson's death gave a boost to the cause of the Confederacy. See Cullop,
"English Reaction to Stonewall Jackson's Death," 2, 5.

dead or largely retired, and the almost thirteen hundred societies that they created had been reduced to fewer than two dozen, most of them moribund.[3] The Bristol and Clifton Ladies Anti Slavery Society, for example, held its last meeting in November 1861; the Glasgow Emancipation Society had been inactive for some time; and little was heard from organized societies in Ireland. In December 1863 Isabelle Waring Maxwell complained about her inability to resuscitate the Colgher Anti Slavery Association. A few months earlier during a tour of the country to rally support against the continued slave trade to Cuba, Louis Chamerovzow, secretary of the British and Foreign Anti Slavery Society (BFASS), observed, "Disease, and other causes, have removed from the scene the Society's chief co-adjutors of the past times." Many of those who remain, he said, "were incapacitated by age and infirmities, from taking part in a public movement."[4]

When Frederick Douglass returned to Britain in 1859, thirteen years after his very successful first tour, he was surprised by the extent to which British antislavery views had changed. Wherever he went he was faced with two surprisingly contradictory realities. There were those who continued to explore ways to help the slaves and freedmen, donating to aid fugitive slaves in Canada, settle freedmen in Africa, and abolish the slave trade in Cuba while continuing to work for the emancipation of American slaves. There were others who had grown weary of such agitation and philanthropy and demanded to know "What have we to do with American slavery?" Douglass was taken aback by what he called this new doctrine of nonintervention, for the foundation of a successful antislavery movement had been the willingness of men and women of good will to work for the elimination of slavery wherever it existed. As he would repeatedly assert, the reform of the dram shop had to come "from the regions of sobriety," that of the "house of ill-fame . . . from the regions of probity"; so, too, must slavery be exposed by countries "uncontaminated by slavery."[5]

Everywhere Douglass went he saw disturbing signs of a loss of interest in

3. For a discussion of changes in the movement see Howard Temperley, *British Antislavery, 1833–1870* (Columbia, S.C., 1972), 251; Seymour Drescher, "Public Opinion and the Destruction of British Colonial Slavery," in James Walvin, ed., *Slavery and British Society, 1776–1846* (London, 1982), 24; Brian Jenkins, *Britain and the War of the Union* (Montreal, 1980), 1: 174.

4. Isabelle Waring Maxwell to Chamerovzow, County Tyrone, 4 December 1863, BFASS Papers, Rhodes House Library, Oxford University; Chamerovzow quoted in Lorimer, *Colour, Class, and the Victorians*, 117.

5. Blassingame, ed., *The Frederick Douglass Papers*, 3: 334, 281, 336.

American slavery. Gone were the days when the London *Times* would repub-
lish, as it did in 1850, an item from an American newspaper reporting the attack on Douglass by a "mob" enraged by the spectacle of a black man walking
arm in arm with two white women. Douglass had written to thank the *Times*,
and by extension all of Britain, for its sympathy: the "influence exerted upon
the more intelligent class of American people by the judicious expression of
British sense of justice and humanity is immense, and, I believe, highly beneficial." [6] By 1859, however, the British voice of justice seemed muted, if not si-
lenced. Samuel Joseph May, an American who had visited Britain a few
months before Douglass, was also struck by the growing indifference to slavery
in Britain. Most of the country, May reported emphatically, thought slavery
"none of their business." [7] Douglass's and May's frustrations were understandable. The ravages of time had taken their toll on the British antislavery movement. And, as Douglass and May intimated, perceptions of the country's
moral responsibility to the slave had undergone important changes. Douglass
thought the source of the change lay in the growing influence of American
racial prejudice on British public opinion. Early in the war, his English
coworker Julia Griffiths Croft attributed the problem to the British accep-
tance of American arguments that there were unstated "peculiar difficulties"
associated with emancipation, that the slaveholders would free their slaves if
it were at all possible, and finally that Negroes were incapable of taking care of
themselves. [8]

Although May's and Douglass's criticisms were justified, they may have
been a bit too harsh. British public opinion had undergone significant changes
since Douglass's first visit in 1845, but so too had the abolitionist movement,
which by the outbreak of the war was devoting most of its limited energies to
promoting the abolition of the slave trade to Cuba and encouraging the cultivation of free-grown produce. The movement's free-labor principles were dis-
armingly simple: it was cheaper to produce goods by wage rather than slave
labor. Thus, one of the ways to undermine slavery was to find alternative
sources of free-labor goods. Once confronted by this economic logic, slaveholders in the Americas, and those who supplied them with slaves in Africa,
would have no recourse but to free their slaves. The success of the movement's
goals in the West Indies justified the efficacy of such an approach. The lessons

6. *Times* (London), 10, 11 June 1850, 18 July 1850.
7. Donald Yacovone, *Samuel Joseph May and the Dilemmas of the Liberal Persuasion,
1797–1871* (Philadelphia, 1991), 166.
8. *Douglass Monthly*, July 1861.

learned there had now to be applied wherever slavery continued to exist. The ill-fated abolitionist effort to establish a string of free-labor settlements along the Niger River in 1841 raised serious questions about the wisdom of venturing into Africa, but did little to undermine the persuasiveness of free-labor principles.[9]

The free-labor movement gained a new lease on life in the late 1840s largely because of black American Henry Highland Garnet, who conducted a series of lecture tours throughout Britain between 1848 and 1851. Garnet's success can be measured by the number of free-labor associations that were formed as a result of his tour. The British movement could be sustained, however, only if it could be shown that freedmen in the West Indies could produce goods more cheaply than slaves. For many the jury was still out. For this reason Garnet accepted an appointment as a missionary to Jamaica from the Scottish United Presbyterian Church. He was expected to minister to the religious needs of the freedmen as well as to encourage the revival of cultivation in the area around his station at Sterling. Other African Americans, such as Samuel Ringgold Ward in Jamaica and Alexander Crummell in Liberia, also took up the challenge of implementing free-labor principles.[10]

The growing concern among Lancashire cotton manufacturers about their industry's almost total reliance on American cotton buttressed the efforts of Britain's free-labor movement. Possible disruption in the supply of cotton led in 1857 to the formation of the Cotton Supply Association, which aimed to encourage the cultivation of cotton in different parts of the world. The concern was well placed. Thomas Bazley, M.P. for Manchester, estimated that in 1861 the loss of supplies from America had cost Lancashire manufacturers nearly £10 million.[11] While the association did not become directly involved in the effort to find alternative sources of cotton, one of its members, Thomas Clegg, had worked for years with the Church Missionary Society to encourage the cultivation of cotton in Abeokuta in West Africa. Others tried to replicate Clegg's efforts in the West Indies, spurred on by the failure of West

9. For an engaging account of the Niger River expedition see Howard Temperley, *White Dreams, Black Africa: The Antislavery Expedition to the Niger River, 1841–1842* (New Haven, 1991). Clare Midgley, "Slave Sugar Boycotts, Female Activism, and the Domestic Base of British Anti-Slavery Cultures," *Slavery and Abolition* 17 (December 1996): 137–62.

10. For a broader discussion of these efforts see R. J. M. Blackett, *Building an Antislavery Wall: Black Americans in the Atlantic Abolitionist Movement, 1830–1860* (Baton Rouge, 1983), 162–94.

11. *Guardian* (Manchester), 9 November 1861.

Indian sugar production to maintain levels attained before emancipation. The driving force behind this effort was Stephen Bourne, who had spent thirteen years as a stipendiary magistrate in Jamaica and British Guiana. On his return to England in 1850, Bourne contacted a number of prominent abolitionists and cotton manufacturers in an effort to persuade them to back his experiment in Jamaica. His British West Indian Cotton and Fibre Company and its successor, the Jamaica Cotton Company, aimed to prove that cotton could be raised more cheaply by free labor. As Bourne never tired of telling audiences, the logic and reality of free-labor economics was on his side: while it cost slaveholders in the United States fifty pounds per year to buy and maintain slaves, he could grow more cotton paying Jamaican laborers twenty pounds. In a resolution of support for Bourne's company, the Newcastle and Gateshead Anti Slavery Society called for the encouragement of cotton cultivation in Jamaica and its importation into Britain as being good for commerce, as a protest "against the sin and crime of slavery, and as a lawful means of hastening the overthrow of the system."[12]

Try as he might, however, Bourne could not persuade Lancashire cotton men to invest in his enterprise. They could not envisage a future without American cotton. Even among philanthropists who were interested in such experiments less for their potential to generate profits than for what they did to undermine the slave trade and slavery, Bourne met with competition from the African Aid Society, which had been formed in London in July 1860 to facilitate the efforts of African Americans to establish a settlement in Abeokuta. Six months earlier Dr. Martin R. Delany, a proponent of African American settlement in Africa, and Jamaican schoolteacher Robert Campbell had reached an agreement with the local authorities in Abeokuta to establish a settlement there. As was true of the efforts of the Niger River expedition and the Jamaica Cotton Company, the appeal of Delany and Campbell's planned settlement turned on its ability to produce cotton for the British market on free-labor principles. The American Civil War put paid to these plans. African Americans who might have been willing to try their luck elsewhere took heart from the war's potential to undermine slavery and decided to stay at home. By the end of the decade the society had

12. Bourne to Brougham, London, 10 November 1858, Brougham Papers; Douglas Hall, *Free Jamaica 1838–1865: An Economic History* (New Haven, 1959), 126–27; *Nonconformist*, 22 May, 7 August 1861; *Daily Post* (Bristol), 12 July 1861; *Times* (Sunderland), 5 October, 9 November, 7 December 1861; *Daily Chronicle and Northern Counties Advertiser*, 7 September 1861.

evolved into little more than a supporter of British colonial interests in West Africa.[13]

Schemes such as Bourne's and Delany's caused traditional abolitionists considerable anxiety, in part because they attracted support from people with little or no abolitionist credentials. More worrying still was the fact that by the late 1850s these plans had won the tentative endorsement of abolitionists such as George Thompson, who not too many years before would have rejected them outright for deviating from the path of true abolition. Time had reduced the numbers still involved in the abolitionist movement, but the free-labor approach, following in the wake of the failure of the Niger River expedition, was also responsible for weakening British abolitionist traditions. To an unmeasured degree, the vibrancy of the movement had also been sapped by a pride, bordering on the xenophobic, in Britain's antislavery legacy. Most in the country were proud of this tradition. The movement not only had its origins in Britain but had been sustained without interruptions since the 1780s. It was a sentiment, Confederate emissary James Mason rightly observed, "akin to patriotism." But such feeling could and did breed inactivity and a profound feeling of resentment and hubris whenever British commitment to the cause was questioned. Angered by such accusations, an unknown correspondent wrote his local newspaper that the English were by nature antislavery, for they had drunk in "the love of freedom, and hatred of slavery and oppression, with [their] mother's milk."[14]

Although such flights of metaphorical fancy may have overestimated the strength of British antislavery feeling at the beginning of the war, they contained, nevertheless, an element of truth. There is little doubt that the movement was not as strong as it had been, but there is also ample evidence that a strong undercurrent of abolitionist sentiment continued to exist. The overwhelmingly positive popular reaction to efforts to free fugitive slave John Anderson is a case in point. Anderson, who had settled in Canada, was taken into custody in 1859 for the murder of a slave catcher during his escape from slavery in Missouri six years earlier. His former owner insisted that he be extradited to the United States under the terms of the Webster-Ashburton Treaty. When the Canadian courts decided in favor of Anderson's former

13. For a general discussion of Delany, Campbell, and the African Aid Society see R. J. M. Blackett, *Beating against the Barriers: Biographical Essays in Nineteenth-Century Afro-American History* (Baton Rouge, 1986), 160–70.

14. Mason to Benjamin, Paris, 25 January 1864, Records of the Confederate States of America; *Guardian* (Bolton), 28 February 1863.

owner, local and British abolitionists had little difficulty organizing public opposition to the decision. Affiliates of the BFASS petitioned the colonial secretary to release Anderson, and in London, Chamerovzow organized the John
Anderson Defence Fund. The pressure worked, and Anderson was released on
a legal technicality. Others, led by the London Emancipation Committee, invited Anderson to London, where he arrived in June 1861 to a warm welcome
at a meeting at Exeter Hall attended by more than six thousand. Anderson's
British supporters raised sufficient funds to pay for his education and arranged
for his settlement in Liberia.[15]

If Samuel May was distressed by the loss of British support for the cause in
the United States, other America visitors, taking their cue from reactions to
the Anderson case and the welcome they received, were more upbeat. Sarah
Parker Remond, a black American who traveled to Britain with May and
stayed throughout the war, saw things differently. "I feel quite at home in
Great Britain," she wrote home. "I feel so much more freedom here than at
home." William Powell, who had moved his family from New York to Liverpool in the early 1850s to escape growing racial restrictions, continued to
prosper at the end of the decade, as did William G. Allen, who left America
for Britain in 1853 because of violent resistance to his plans to marry a white
woman, one of his former students.[16] Thousands turned out to hear Douglass,
Remond, William Howard Day, George B. Cheever, and Delany lecture, a
clear indication of continued public interest in the struggle to free the slaves
in America. So, too, was the public's response to the debates between
Douglass and George Thompson over whether the American Constitution
was a proslavery document, an arcane and often mind-numbing topic at the
best of times. Scattered throughout the country were pockets of locally active
societies that continued to organize lectures. In December 1859 Remond conducted a tour of Yorkshire at the invitation of the Leeds Young Men's Anti
Slavery Society. During her visit to Wakefield, the local antislavery society
was reorganized. At the same time, Thompson delivered twenty-nine lectures

15. R. C. Reinders, "Anglo-Canadian Abolitionism: The John Anderson Case, 1860–1861,"
Renaissance and Modern Studies 19 (1975): 82–94; Patrick Brode, *The Odyssey of John Anderson*
(Toronto, 1989), 9, 65–70, 75–76, 102–20; *Nonconformist*, 26 June, 31 July 1861. Petitions to
the colonial secretary can be found in the Duke of Newcastle Collection, University of
Nottingham.

16. Remond to S. J. May, London, 18 October 1860, AASS Papers. For a biography of
Powell, see Philip S. Foner, *Essays in Afro-American History* (Philadelphia, 1978), 88–111; for
Allen see R. J. M. Blackett, "William G. Allen: The Forgotten Professor," *Civil War History* 26
(March 1980): 39–54.

in four months in northeast England, Scotland, and Ireland. As in the past, antislavery bazaars supplemented the lectures. Goods were sold to support, among other activities, the work of Douglass in Rochester, the exile fugitive slave communities in Canada, and the New York Vigilance Committee.[17] Finally, Britain continued to be a refuge for African American exiles, more than forty of whom would participate in the effort to win public support for the Union.

It is clear that by the end of the 1850s, British antislavery activity did wax and wane as circumstances dictated. In spite of Isabella Waring Maxwell's lament that she could do nothing to resuscitate the local society in Colgher, the experience elsewhere was different. The Bristol Anti Slavery Society had no trouble organizing a bazaar that ran for two months and included public lectures by African Americans William Howard Day and William Craft. Many of the ladies' societies organized by Julia Griffiths Croft, Douglass's English coworker in Rochester, during her tour of Britain in 1856 were still active in 1861.[18]

These pockets of antislavery activity, however, did little to alleviate the disappointment of many on both sides of the Atlantic who felt that, on the whole, Britain seemed to have lost sight of its abolitionist traditions at the outbreak of the war. Some in America were despondent. In Bristol, it was reported, Mary Estlin, the leader of a once-vibrant society, now found herself alone. Many had simply drifted away over the years; but the decision of the United States to use force to keep the seceding states within the Union troubled a number of abolitionists, especially those, such as Bristol Quaker Robert Charleton, who refused to endorse war as an antislavery instrument. Charleton spoke for others in the British and Foreign Anti Slavery Society whose peace principles trumped their opposition to slavery. Their inactivity frustrated J. Sella Martin. He dismissed the society as an "antiquated affair, the members of which met but once a year for the purpose of instituting deputations, that did nothing but sprinkle rose water on the feet of a few conservative lords."[19]

The decision about what course to pursue was made even more difficult by

17. *Anti Slavery Advocate*, 2 February, 1 March, 2 April, 1 May 1860; *Douglass Monthly*, July, September 1861; *Post* (Bristol), 4 February 1863.

18. *Post* (Bristol), 13, 14 February, 10, 11, 14, 17 April 1862; *Mercury* (Bristol), 15 February 1862. For Griffiths's activities see Clare Midgley, *Women against Slavery: The British Campaigns, 1780–1870* (London, 1992), 141–42.

19. May's letter in Clare Taylor, ed., *British and American Abolitionists: An Episode in Transatlantic Understanding* (Edinburgh, 1974), 516; *Post* (Bristol), 29 January 1863; *Liberator*, 28 February 1862.

the position long held by British supporters of Garrison that the solution to the problem in America lay with the separation of the free states from the Union. If, as they argued, the Constitution was fundamentally a proslavery document, then no government that adhered to its principles could ever hope to be free. It therefore came as a surprise, and created some resentment, when Garrison abandoned a position held for more than twenty years and gave his support to the Union. American visitors such as Martin had to contend with both the inactivity of the BFASS and the skepticism of old Garrisonian allies. Martin's initial discussions with Thompson and others did little to alleviate the concerns of British Garrisonians; but Martin, aware of the potential disaster of doing nothing, persevered.[20] He held forty-seven public meetings between August 1861 and February 1862, even though frequent bouts of illness curtailed his activities.[21] Martin's success confirmed one editor's observation that while "the tide of antislavery feeling in England seemed to have ebbed, the ocean which supplied it is full as ever, and . . . the great waters are again rising in their ancient channels."[22]

Martin's concern was not so much with the extent of popular support for antislavery as it was with the inactivity, and in some cases the hostility, of some prominent British abolitionists. While the leaders of the BFASS, with the noted exception of its secretary Louis Chamerovzow, stood on the sidelines and refused to take part, others were openly hostile to the Union. Prominent figures such as Wilson Amistead of Leeds and Lord Brougham, whom Chamerovzow called the Nestor of British antislavery, condemned the Union for going to war. Amistead would later condemn Lincoln's preliminary proclamation of emancipation as motivated by "statecraft not human brotherhood." The slaveholders' strength would have been sapped, bloodshed avoided, and the slaves made free had emancipation been proclaimed at the beginning of the war, he argued. Charles Buxton, son of Thomas Fowell Buxton, a contemporary of William Wilberforce and one of the moving forces in the effort to get the West Indian emancipation bill through Parliament, rejected the proclamation as nothing more than a sop to a small band of radical abolitionists.[23] Observing the situation from the American legation, Charles

20. F. W. Chesson diary, 22 September 1861 to 31 December 1862, Raymond English Deposit, John Rylands Library, Manchester.

21. *Weekly Anglo African*, 1 March 1862.

22. *Inquirer*, 28 February 1863.

23. *Mercury* (Leeds), 18 October, 12 December 1862; Chamerovzow to Brougham, London, 5 July 1863, Brougham Papers; *Times* (London), 26 December 1862.

Francis Adams lamented that the successors of those who had fought against West Indian slavery had not "inherited their impressions." The evidence suggests, however, that he may have been too pessimistic. Others saw things differently. The editor of the *Morning Star*, partial though he was to the Union, insisted that the tradition remained intact. Careful to differentiate between those who in the past had been active in the movement and those who had simply paid lip service to its objectives, he insisted that the descendants of "the working leaders of the old abolitionist movement are standing in their fathers' places." Each generation had to attract new fighters to the cause: "Time affords to each rank of . . . children in succession a share of honour by assigning to each a share of duty." The activities of the younger generation of Croppers and Braithwaites in Kendal, Sturgeses in Birmingham, and Wedgewoods in the Potteries, for example, proved unequivocally that the baton had been passed safely. Following a meeting in Kendal organized by the younger Cropper and Braithwaite, the local newspaper observed that "the spirit of their fathers will live again in every utterance that aims to raise the downtrodden abject slave into the life of manhood."[24] Some such as Congregationalist minister John Nelson Goulty of Brighton, William Lang of Stockton, Radical T. Peronnet Thompson, and the little-known John Rowlinson of Bury, all of whom had long antislavery pedigrees dating back to the struggle for West Indian emancipation, were still involved. Others such as Radical solicitor William Shaen and Joseph Lupton of Leeds, both Unitarians, and Arthur O'Neill, a Christian Chartist minister, came to the movement in the mid-1840s as founding members of the Garrisonian Anti Slavery League. Thomas H. Barker, a Manchester teetotaler, joined the movement after meeting Garrison, Douglass, and Thompson in 1846; as did John Mill, the economist, banker, and poet who was active in the effort to raise a subscription to buy Douglass's freedom. William Rathbone of Liverpool, William Dillworth Crewdson and John Somerville of Kendal, and Robert Ferguson of Carlisle followed in their fathers' footsteps. So, too, did Henry Joseph Wilson of Mansfield, whose father, William, was chairman of the Nottingham Anti Slavery Committee and whose mother was the author of the antislavery poem "The Hope of the Slave." Many born after West Indian emancipation joined the movement in the 1850s. T. Burt and George Howell, Radical labor leaders, were influenced by *Uncle Tom's Cabin*. Edward Owen Greening, a Manchester

24. Adams to George Thompson, London, 16 November 1862, Charles Francis Adams Letterbook, Adams Family Papers, Massachusetts Historical Society, Boston; *Morning Star*, 4 February 1863; *Mercury* (Kendal), 7 February 1863.

iron and wire fence manufacturer and leader of the cooperative movement, at sixteen was appointed secretary of the Manchester Anti Slavery Society.[25]

The spirit of the fathers seemed to be alive. But all was not well. Unable to condone war, yet unwilling to criticize publicly the Union, many quietly folded their tents and left the field not to appear at public meetings again until the end of the war, when the cause of the freedmen brought them back to what they considered the true cause of benevolence. True Christian benevolence, many insisted, had to be divorced from political association. It was on these grounds that a small group of old-line abolitionists in Leicester opposed the formation of a local chapter of the London Emancipation Society. To support the Union, as the society did, was to taint "abstract" emancipation with politics. Printer and former editor Joseph Foulkes Winks, active in the movement in the 1830s as a member of the original Anti Slavery Society, pleaded with his colleagues not to repeat the errors of their predecessors. Politics divided the movement then; it would do so now. True abolitionists should do no more than work for emancipation through moral suasion. Winks was supported by the Reverend James Phillippo Mursell, a radical Baptist minister and old-line abolitionist, who, ironically, was named for the Reverend James Phillippo, the Baptist missionary to Jamaica who was at the center of what became known, on the eve of emancipation, as the "Baptist Wars." The political and philanthropic, Mursell insisted, ought not to be mixed. Let the war end, and "slavery would end; but let North or South come together again, and slavery would last till their children's children."[26]

25. Newspaper clippings, Brighton (England) Public Library; for Thompson see Betty Fladeland, *Abolitionists and Working-Class Problems in the Age of Industrialization* (Baton Rouge, 1984), 93–110; Joseph O. Baylen and Norbert J. Gossman, eds., *Biographical Dictionary of Modern British Radicals* (Brighton, 1984), 2: 450–54, 391–94; Stange, *British Unitarians against American Slavery*, 61, 84; biographical card index, Leeds Public Library; R. C. Gammage, *History of the Chartist Movement, 1837–1854* (1894; reprint, London, 1969), 140, 144, 159; J. Bellamy and J. Saville, eds., *Dictionary of Labour Biography* (London, 1972–1993), 6: 193–98, 1: 136–39; Barker to Garrison, Manchester, 27 August 1864, AASS Papers; Isabel Mills, *From Tinder-Box to the Larger Light: Threads from the Life of John Mills, Banker (Author of "Vox Humana"), Interwoven with Some Early Century Recollections by His Wife* (Manchester, 1899); Eleanor F. Rathbone, *William Rathbone: A Memoir* (London, 1905), 191–92; Sheila Marriner, *Rathbones of Liverpool, 1845–1873* (Liverpool, 1961), 5; Robert Ferguson, *America during and after the War* (London, 1866); *Carlisle Examiner and Northern Advertiser*, 21 February 1863; Mosa Anderson, *Henry Joseph Wilson: Fighter for Freedom, 1833–1914* (London, 1953), 9; Biagini, *Liberty, Retrenchment, and Reform*, 71; Tom Crimes, *Edward Owen Greening: A Maker of Modern Co-operation* (Manchester, 1923), 10, 18–19, 29.

26. *Leicestershire Mercury*, 14 February 1863; *Midland Free Press*, 14 February, 4 April 1863; Alan Betteridge, "The *Baptist Reporter*," *Leicestershire Historian* 2 (Winter 1972): 12–15; Arthur

If Barker and Greening were at one end of the antislavery spectrum in 1863 and Murcell and Winks were at the other, then Dundee Congregational minister George Gilfillan represented the middle ground. Active with Douglass in 1845 in the effort to get the Free Church of Scotland to return money it had collected in the slave states, Gilfillan refused, as he put it, to be "a partizan of the North." He dismissed the North as insolent, full of swagger, and much too sensitive to criticism, the "uncommon combination of the bully and the coward." Continued unification of the country was impossible without the consent of all its parts. Only a miracle or, failing that, military despotism could hold together so vast an empire. "Overgrown Empires, like overgrown Churches," he declared, "have been the curse of the earth." Gilfillan admitted that the Confederacy was fighting to maintain slavery. The British, therefore, were duty bound to "watch both parties—to give more sympathy to the North than the South—to give our full sympathy to neither; but especially to watch over the cause of negro emancipation—to be jealous over it with a godly jealousy, lest, by some miserable mischance, it should be lost or crippled amidst the tremendous agitations and confusions which have environed the American continent."[27]

No one could doubt Gilfillan's sincerity or Winks's antislavery views. Both were genuine, and the two men were not to be confused with those who argued simultaneously for emancipation and the Confederacy. Very rarely did advocates of positions similar to those of Winks or Gilfillan espouse the cause of Southern independence. The two positions were simply incompatible. As Gilfillan saw it, while the protagonists in the war were "the brothers Cain,"

Mursell, *James Phillippo Mursell: His Life and Work* (London, 1886); D. B. Ellis, *Catalogue of Local Portraits* (Leicester, 1956), 39; A. Temple Patterson, *Radical Leicester: A History of Leicester, 1780–1850* (Leicester, 1954), 188.

27. *Advertiser* (Dundee), 25 April 1863, 3, 24 June 1861; *Northern Warder*, 20 January 1863; David C. Carrie, "Dundee and the American Civil War, 1861–65," *Abertay Historical Society Publication* 1 (1953): 6; C. Duncan Rice, *The Scots Abolitionists, 1833–1861* (Baton Rouge, 1981), 137. When Chesson invited Gilfillan to join a delegation of London Emancipation Society members who were planning a meeting with Adams to congratulate Lincoln on his reelection, Gilfillan declined, insisting that the president's reelection was "a heavy blow and great discouragement to the real interests of America—as a pledge for the continuance, with increased ferocity, of a wretched and hitherto useless contest, which has already appalled the civilized world, and sown curses and calamities broadcast in the fairest countries of the earth—as a renewed proclamation of war to the knife with a people who, though deeply guilty in the matter of slavery, and in other respects besides, have covered their multitude of sins by a courage, a constancy, a self denial, a unity, and a generosity of conduct which have seldom been paralleled in the history of nations." *Advertiser* (Dundee), 14 December 1864.

the South was fighting to maintain slavery and so was unworthy of the support of any committed abolitionist. Nevertheless, the range of positions taken by supporters of emancipation seemed to confirm Winks's worst fears. Not since the strife over West Indian emancipation had the country been so politically wracked by public dissension over the issue of freedom for the slaves. Then, as in the present crisis, people lined up on each side of the issue, and every effort was made to win converts to the cause. Whether one was for union and emancipation or simply emancipation, antislavery advocates found themselves at a political disadvantage as early as the summer of 1862. By then the *Trent* affair had done incalculable damage to the British public's views of the United States. Fears that the country's major industry and its people would be devastated by the shortage of cotton were being confirmed. And from where Adams sat at the American legation, it appeared that most major newspapers, both in the capital and the provinces, supported Southern independence.

Southern supporters made the first move to rally public opinion to their side with the organization in London in August 1862 of the Confederate States Aid Association. Little is known of this small and ephemeral society. Southerners living in London, with the support of James Mason and Matthew Maury, emissaries of the Confederacy, formed the backbone of the organization. Its secretary was Dr. Rector Smith, formerly of Kentucky and at that time practicing in London. Most of the financial support for the association came from Alexander J. B. Beresford-Hope, who continued to contribute significantly to all other pro-Confederate organizations. The son of a rich Dutch banker and diamond merchant, Hope attended Harrow and Trinity College, Cambridge. He served two terms as a Conservative member of Parliament for Maidstone from 1841 to 1852 and again from 1857 to 1858. Hope spent a great deal of his time and the fortune he inherited from his father and stepfather on the restoration of Anglican churches. To this Tory Anglican, American democracy raised the specter of a return to the Jacobin terror of the French Revolution. He believed that "levelling democracy and universal suffrage" was forcing the Northern states into "a perfectly Assyrian despotism," one far worse than that of France, Russia, or Austria, a despotism not of a "single sovereign, who may be, and often is, enlightened and benevolent,—but the despotism of irresponsible committees, of dark agents working in secret, and pulling the invisible strings with ubiquitous hands." Not surprisingly, Hope's support for the Confederacy was based on his calculation that it stood in the way of the spread of democracy, but it was also influenced by his views on slavery. Although Hope found slavery a "bad thing which ought manifestly to be improved off the face of the earth," he did not see how anyone who be-lieved in "the authenticity of the Epistle to Philemon, not to quote other New Testament texts," could say that it was not permitted.[28]

Even with Hope's deep pockets, the association accomplished little. If it hoped to reach the public, then it was an abject failure. Many of its activities were limited to small weekly meetings held at a private home in London. Fearful of possible disruptions, members kept these meetings closed to the general public. Admission was by card only, and a policeman was always pre-sent to ensure order. There is no evidence that the association made any con-certed effort to lobby the government. It did print and circulate one pamphlet in late 1862, a small return on Hope's substantial investment. One observer suggested that behind the front to influence public opinion lay the true inten-tions of the association: raising funds to supply the Confederacy with arms and ammunition.[29]

Equally secretive about its membership and objectives was the Liverpool Southern Club (LSC). Its inspiration was the ubiquitous James Spence. At the beginning of the war an acquaintance described Spence as a dealer in "plate and iron repair commissions in a rather small way." It appears that the depression of 1857 had severely affected Spence's once extensive trading con-tacts with the United States; in 1852 he had supplied the Illinois Central Railroad with more than 81,000 tons of railroad iron. It is safe to say that without Spence there would have been no pro-Confederate movement in Britain. Wherever and whenever there was a need to organize national and regional societies, Spence was on the spot. Whenever discussions were held about the best way to influence public opinion and government policy, Spence played a critical role. And it was Spence who was responsible for rais-ing funds for and offering advice to those who attempted to win working-class support for the Confederacy. His pro-Confederate treatise *The American Union,*

28. Morgan, *The Jackson-Hope and the Society of the Cincinnati Medals,* 18–23; A. J. B. Beresford-Hope, *The American Disruption: In Three Lectures Delivered by Request before the Maidstone Literary and Mechanical Institution* (London, 1862), 9–10, 82; Henry and Irene Law, *Book of the Beresford-Hopes* (London, 1925), 207; *Staffordshire Advertiser,* 30 August 1862.

29. Adams to Seward, London, 18 December 18, 1862, Despatches from U.S. Ministers to Great Britain, 1791–1906 (microfilm), General Records of the Department of State, RG 59, National Archives. Unless otherwise noted, all following ministerial dispatches are from RG 59, National Archives. Thompson to Garrison, London, 5, 12 December 1862, AASS Papers; *Anti Slavery Reporter,* 1 January 1863; *Daily Gazette* (Birmingham), 24 September 1863; *Bee Hive,* 26 September 1863; *Reporter* (Ashton and Stalybridge), 10 December 1864; Donaldson Jordon and Edwin J. Pratt, *Europe and the American Civil War* (Boston, New York, 1931), 171.

published in September 1861, quickly went through many editions and remained the most devastating and reasoned argument for the disruption of the Union. The book's arguments were supplemented by a couple of pamphlets and more than forty articles published in the *Times* between February 1862 and January 1865. His friend James Mason described Spence as "a man of large research, liberal and expanded views and great labor, full of enterprise and an able and experienced merchant." To opponents such as Benjamin Moran at the American legation, however, he was nothing more than that "scamp Spence."[30]

Spence reported that the Liverpool Southern Club, formed in fall 1862, drew its membership from among "leading Southerners" living in Liverpool, "several English merchants [and] friends of the cause." He could have added those who had a vested interest in the success of blockade-running activities, which were centered in Liverpool. Although the exact size of the membership is in doubt, Thomas Dudley, the American consul in Liverpool, put it close to two hundred and insisted that the club was dominated by those involved in the Southern trade. Among its members were Charlestonian Charles L. Prioleau, who moved to Liverpool in 1854 as the principal resident partner of Fraser Trenholm and Company, a major South Carolinian merchant company. The company operated five ships between Liverpool and Charleston in 1860. Throughout the war Prioleau would provide credit for the purchase of arms and ships for the Confederacy. Other members included the shipowner and Tory leader Arthur B. Forwood. Early in the war Forwood's son was arrested in New York on "suspicion of Southern tendencies." When a member of the royal family visited Liverpool in September 1861, Forwood chose to express his feelings, and perhaps protest the treatment of his son, by flying the Confederate flag from a window of his office. Tory Edward Lawrence, whose Anglo-Confederate Trading Company was one of the more prominent British firms involved in blockade running, joined Prioleau and Forwood.[31]

30. Frank Hughes, "Liverpool and the Confederate States" (M.Phil. thesis, Keele University, 1998), 112–13. For Spence's commission to write for the *Times* see Mowbray Morris to Spence, 9, 22 January 1862, *Times* (London) Archives; Spence to Mason, Liverpool, 28 April 1862, and Mason to Benjamin, London, 6 May 1862, both in Records of the Confederate States of America; Moran to Dudley, London, 18 May 1862, Thomas H. Dudley Collection, Huntington Library, Pasadena.

31. Hughes, "Liverpool and the Confederate States," 120, 315, 320; James D. Bulloch, *The Secret Service of the Confederate States in Europe or How the Confederate Cruisers Were Equipped* (1883; reprint, London, 1959), 1: 51–53; Stephen R. Wise, *Lifeline of the Confederacy: Blockade Running during the Civil War* (Columbia, S.C., 1988), 46, 203; Patrick Joyce, *Work, Society, and*

Trading and political interests seemed to be the principal criteria for English membership in the Liverpool Southern Club. Headquartered at the office of J. H. Ashbridge, an American from New Orleans, the LSC was both a political organization and a private club. It not only represented the interests of the Confederacy—and those who traded with it—it raised money from Southerners to support the war. Within weeks of its establishment, members had raised in excess of £3,000 from "patriotic Southerners in Europe." The club also acted as something of a benevolent society, providing aid to Southerners in distress in Europe. With membership fees of £10.10, annual dues of £5.5, and a committee to regulate the price of wine, the membership, not surprisingly, was very selective.³² But in spite of Liverpool's extensive trading connections with the South and the impressive list of names claiming membership in the club, Spence had little success generating public support in what many considered the most pro-Confederate city in the nation. Unsure about whether the government would intervene to stop their blockade-running activities and their involvement in building and purchasing ships for the Confederacy, LSC members might have thought it prudent to stay out of the spotlight. Not long after the club's formation, Spence persuaded the local Chamber of Commerce to adopt a memorial that called on the British government to join with other European nations in recognizing the Confederacy. But fearing opposition from those opposed to taking such a "political position" and a public influenced, as Spence put it, against any form of intervention by those "holding cotton and interests in India," he decided not to transmit the memorial to the government. Faced with no serious organizational opposition in a city known for its Confederate sympathies, Spence and the LSC still had difficulty imposing their will. It was not for want of trying. In October 1862, for instance, members arranged a meeting to hear Charles S. Morehead, the former governor of Kentucky who had been imprisoned by Federal authorities in September 1861. Released the following January, Morehead fled to Canada and then England where he spent a good part of the war.

Politics: The Culture of the Factory in Late Victorian England (New Brunswick, N.J., 1980), 256; P. J. Waller, *Democracy and Sectarianism: A Political and Social History of Liverpool, 1868–1939* (Liverpool, 1981), 489; *Times* (London), 29 October 1861, 21 April 1863; *Mercury* (Liverpool), 17 January 1862.

32. Dudley to Seward, Liverpool, 9 June 1862, Despatches from U.S. Consuls in Liverpool, 1790–1906; "Rules and Bye-Laws of the Southern Club of Liverpool Established 1862," Dudley Collection; Spence to Wharncliffe, Liverpool, 23 January 1865, Lord Wharncliffe Muniments, Sheffield Archives, Sheffield, England; Mason to Benjamin, Paris, 29 September 1864, Records of the Confederate States of America; *Daily Post* (Liverpool), 27 September 1862.

As a victim of Lincoln's suspension of constitutional rights, Morehead, it was hoped, would help to increase public support for the Confederacy. Nothing of the kind occurred.[33]

If Spence had surprisingly little public presence in Liverpool, he was involved in the formation of more politically active Southern clubs in other cities. Although not the driving force behind the formation of these clubs—the impetus usually came from local supporters of the Confederacy—whenever needed, Spence was there to lend a hand and offer advice. The first club was formed in Oldham in March 1863 at a meeting of "influential gentlemen," several of whom were members of the town council. Within three months the club had enrolled nearly one hundred members. All the men in Oldham, a correspondent partial to the cause observed, were "desperately South and the women were even worse than the men." Nothing, unfortunately, is known about the general membership of the club, but it was led by the Harrop brothers, Eli and Robert, cotton spinners; Abraham Leach, a doctor; and Joseph Lockwood Quarmby, a bookseller and former Owenite socialist who was active in the anti–poor law and short-time movements. Quarmby's position on the war was driven by a concern to protect what he considered to be Britain's imperial interests, which, he insisted, required a dismantling of the American empire.[34]

Where Oldham led, Manchester soon followed. But while Oldham's was a local club, the Manchester Southern Club (MSC) drew its membership, at least those who were vice-presidents, from across the nation in an effort to counter the national reach of the recently formed Union and Emancipation Society. Thirteen of the MSC's vice-presidents were from London, including Beresford-Hope; his brother-in-law Lord Robert Cecil; and the M.P.s John Arthur Roebuck, William Schaw Lindsay, and William H. Gregory. There were 3 from Scotland and 1 each from Wales and Ireland. Of the remaining 106 vice-presidents, all but 8 were from Lancashire and Cheshire. Surprisingly, given the name of the club, there were only 21 from Manchester. It could just as well have been called the Preston Southern Club, as that city provided 54 vice-presidents, almost one-half the

33. Spence to Mason, 3, 15 October 1862, Mason Papers; *Mercury* (Liverpool), 13 October 1862, 7 April 1865.

34. *Standard* (Oldham), 7 March, 13, 20, 27 June, 29 September 1863; *Index*, 22 October 1863; Miscellaneous Newspaper Cuttings, vol. 1, Oldham (England) Public Library; John Foster, *Class Struggle and the Industrial Revolution: Early Industrial Capitalism in Three English Towns* (New York, 1974), 136, 158.

total.[35] The formation of local affiliates followed in quick succession during the summer of 1863. By September there were thirty-four.[36]

One would have surmised that the MSC and its local affiliates were numerous enough to accommodate all those who were partial to the Confederacy. Even while the MSC was being organized, however, another association, the Central Association for Recognition of the Confederate States, was being formed in Manchester. Early in 1863 an opponent spoke of the existence of a "little club in Manchester somewhere, where gentlemen met to read the Southern newspapers; but they keep it excessively quiet." From this group would evolve the Central Association, which was led by Conservative Lord Wharncliffe, a mine owner and a former M.P. who had held minor posts in the last months of Peel's administration and under Palmerston in 1856. The association's executive committee included Spence; Robert Munn of Stackstead, one of the largest millowners in the Rossendale Valley; W. Romaine Callender and Thomas Hornby Birley, prominent textile manufacturers from Manchester; Asa and J. W. Lees from Oldham and Mossley, heads of one of the largest engineering firms in Oldham, which had considerable interests in cotton and coal; and R. Rayford Jackson of Blackburn, an honorary colonel in the Volunteers.[37] With the exception of the Leeses, who were Whigs, all were Tories and men of property and standing. The Central Association spawned one regional affiliate, the Yorkshire Association for Recognition of the Confederacy, formed sometime in June 1863. It is impossible to determine the size of its membership, but among its known associates were Charles Broadbent, a solicitor; J. Page Hopps, a young Unitarian minister; R. King, a printer; Edward Siddall, an auctioneer; Henry Wostenholm, a manufacturer and commercial agent; John Lister, a physician; Samuel Jackson, a nailmaker; George Lemon Saunders, a dance teacher and former harlequin actor; and William Harvey, an auctioneer and valuer.[38]

In June, Spence visited Manchester in the hope of bringing the Central

---

35. *Anti Slavery Reporter*, 1 September 1863.

36. *Chronicle* (Preston), 26 September 1863.

37. *Examiner and Times* (Manchester), 13 August, 23 September 1863; *Times* (Bury), 7 February 1863; *Dictionary of National Biography* 19: 113; Chris Aspen, *Mr. Pilling's Short Cut to China and Other Stories of Rossendale Enterprise* (Helmshore, England, 1983), 13–14; cumulative index, Blackburn Public Library; newspaper cuttings, Manchester Public Library; Foster, *Class Struggle and the Industrial Revolution*, 229.

38. *Independent* (Sheffield and Rotherham), 1 January, 4, 27 June, 2 October 1863, 18 June 1866, 1 August 1870; *Telegraph* (Sheffield), 13 December 1863; William White, *General Directory and Topography of the Borough of Sheffield* (Sheffield, 1864).

Association and the MSC together. He had won a promise from Alexander Collie, the originator of the scheme to run the Federal government's blockade of Southern ports, to support the merger and help finance the new society. A provisional committee was established in July to promote the merger and enlist new members.[39] Discussions were protracted and, one suspects, difficult. The new society—the Southern Independence Association (SIA)—was finally announced with much fanfare at a public meeting in Manchester in October. The association, Wharncliffe, its president, stated, aimed to dispel the notion held by some in government that large sections of the public were in favor of the Union. Once they were disabused of these notions, they could be persuaded to recognize the South as an independent nation. None of the SIA's members, he insisted, favored the continuation of slavery, but that problem was best left to those who knew best how to deal with it. Slaves were treated much better by their masters than were free blacks (whom he referred to as "slaves") in the North. Assured of class amity in Britain, Wharncliffe painted a rosy picture of race relations in the South where "the two colours were joined together side by side. They knew the affection which was entertained by the negro population towards their young masters and mistresses, a sentiment much akin to that which prevailed largely in England between the owners of an estate and those resident among them who were treated kindly, justly, and generously."[40]

Two months later a group headed by Beresford-Hope and a number of pro-Confederate M.P.s formed a London branch of the SIA with the expressed purpose of lobbying the government to recognize the Confederacy. As the leaders of the association saw it, Manchester would concentrate most of its efforts on organizing public opinion, while London lobbied Parliament.[41] Such practical considerations may have affected the nature of the leadership of

39. *Examiner and Times* (Manchester), 6 October 1863; *Guardian* (Manchester), 6 October 1863; *Times* (London), 7 October 1863; *News* (Bacup and Rossendale), 10 October 1863; *Advertiser* (Stockport), 2 October 1863; *Index*, 31 December 1863; Hotze to Benjamin, London, 31 October 1863, Hotze Papers; Spence to Mason, Liverpool, 19 June 1863, Mason Papers; Jenkins, *Britain and the War of the Union*, 2: 319–20.

40. *Examiner and Times* (Manchester), 6 October 1863; *Guardian* (Manchester), 6 October 1863.

41. *Daily News* (London),10, 12 December 1863; *Saturday Review*, 16 January 1864; Hotze to Benjamin, London, 17 January 1864, Hotze Papers. Dudley described the leaders of the London society as "active, unscrupulous with characters that won't tarnish." Dudley to Seward, Liverpool, 12 December 1863, 19 January 1864, Despatches from U.S. Consuls in Liverpool, 1790–1906.

each organization. Beresford-Hope had insisted that to be successful in its lobbying efforts, the London association would have to be "composed of men of
good political and social standing." Its leadership was composed of nine M.P.s,
including Roebuck, Lindsay, Birkenhead shipbuilder John Laird, and William
Scholefield of Birmingham; a number of members of the House of Lords;
Edward Akroyd of Halifax, head of the "largest worsted spinning and manufacturing complex in the country"; Spence; and Beresford-Hope. On the other
hand, the leadership of the society was of a mixed social hue. Joining
Wharncliffe, Thomas Hornby Birley, Thomas Briggs, and Mortimer Collins
were James Nield Sr. of Mossley, who once described himself as "an old man
. . . connected with the cotton trade nearly all his life" and who, evidence
suggests, had been a local working-class leader in the 1830s and 1840s;
Joseph Parker (not to be confused with the Manchester Congregational
minister of the same name) of whom nothing is known; and Thomas B.
Kershaw, an overlooker at a mill in Ancoats, an industrial suburb of
Manchester. Little is known of either Briggs or Collins, although Briggs was
a member of the Manchester Royal Exchange, which suggests he was a person of some economic substance. If the leadership of the SIA was drawn
from different classes, politically they were Tories or Whigs or, as in the case
of Kershaw, working-class men who had been allies of the Conservatives for
some time.[42]

The leadership of the SIA and other pro-Confederate societies made a
concerted effort to attract members from all classes but was not always successful. The evidence suggests that both the Manchester Southern Club and
the Central Association had difficulty meeting this objective. Following a trip
to Manchester in early summer 1863, Spence wrote Mason of the existence of
two pro-Confederate associations in the city and of his efforts to bring them
together. The MSC, he observed approvingly, was made up not of "the rich
spinners but young men of energy with a taste for agitation but little money."
Its members were to be differentiated from the group described by Hotze as
"respectable local merchants and manufacturers."[43] Little is known of the
leaders of the MSC, all of whom were drawn from Manchester, although, as

42. John Bigelow, *Lest We Forget: Gladstone, Morley, and the Confederate Loan of 1863, a
Rectification* (New York, 1905), 13; Eric Webster, "Edward Akroyd (1810–1887): Also a Brief
History of James Akroyd and Son," *Transactions of the Halifax Antiquarian Society* (1987): 35;
Daily News (London), 10 December 1863; *Saturday Review*, 16 January 1864; Hotze to Benjamin,
21 November 1863, Hotze Papers.

43. Spence to Mason, Liverpool, 16 June 1863, Mason Papers; Hotze to Benjamin, London, 6
June 1863, Hotze Papers.

has been shown, a significant number of vice-presidents came from other towns such as Preston. Its president was Daniel Lee, a calico printer and the only known Catholic to be involved publicly on either side of the dispute. A Liberal, Lee frequently allied himself with Tories, especially in the struggle to remove Catholic disabilities. Nothing is known of the vice-chairman M. N. Elliott or the treasurer James Armstrong. Both secretaries, M. Chadwick and T. Malan Walker, worked at the same mill in Ancoats. Walker was described by an opponent as a "cashier at Ancoats Mill, the proprietor of which holds a heavy mortgage on an extensive cotton plantation in the South." Spence, never one to pull his punches, later dismissed Chadwick as "not a man of any standing at all or of much judgement."[44]

If one's social standing and class position can be measured by listings in city directories and obituary notices—admittedly a less than reliable yardstick— then class played some indeterminate role in the choices made about which organization to join. For some unexplained reason, four of the original members of the MSC chose not to join the SIA. Of the nineteen who did join, twelve were neither listed in available directories nor appeared in obituary indexes. Of the remaining seven, four were commission agents, one a cotton manufacturer, one a calico printer, and one a merchant. In comparison, all eighteen listed members of the Central Association joined the SIA, only two of whom are unidentifiable. Of sixteen, five were cotton manufacturers, three Church of England ministers, two calico printers, and the remaining six a merchant, land agent, bleacher, spindle and fly maker, barrister, and lecturer. The profile of those who came to the SIA from the Central Association seem to fit Hotze's description.

The case of Preston may help to bring the picture into sharper focus. Forty of the fifty-four MSC vice-presidents from Preston chose not to join the SIA. There is evidence that politics had played no role in the decision of some men who had signed on with the MSC in the first place; they may have joined simply because an associate had. William Fisher, a bank manager, for example, "never took any prominent part in public matters. . . ." He may have been influenced to join by J. B. Gilbertson, a friend, the family's doctor, and a prominent figure in local pro-Confederate circles.[45] Among the eleven who did not

44. *Times* (London), 30 September 1863; Chamerovzow to Brougham, London, 9 December 1863, Brougham Papers; Spence to Wharncliffe, Liverpool, 20 June 1865, Wharncliffe Muniments. Catholics and the church would play a more active role in the effort by Confederate supporters to collect signatures for the 1864 "Peace Address," which called for an armistice and peaceful separation. *Index*, 15 September 1864.

45. *Guardian* (Preston), 14 March 1877.

join the SIA were Fisher, three physicians, two agents, one cotton spinner, one clothier, one factory manager, one printer and stationer, and one druggist. In comparison, among those who joined the SIA were six cotton spinners, including William and Edmund Birley, who were among the largest manufacturers in the city, and John Cooper, the owner of several mills; four solicitors and lawyers, including William Gilbertson, the brother of J. B. Gilbertson; two ministers, D. F. Chapman, the vicar of Saint Peter's, and W. Croke Squire, a Unitarian; one officer of Volunteers, Colonel Birchall; and finally, Robert Townley Parker, an attorney and the "bigoted Protestant squire of Cuerden Hall," who, according to one historian, exploited anti-Irish sentiment for political ends.[46] Although as a whole those who joined the MSC and not the SIA were slightly younger than local members of the SIA and so only marginally conformed to Spence's description of the initiators of the MSC, it seems that Spence's and Hotze's assessment of SIA supporters as men of means was close to the mark. One local report described members of the Preston chapter of the SIA as "gentlemen of influence and position." According to the report, they were manufacturers, merchants, tradesmen, and artisans. From the list of those whose names appear on the SIA membership roster, however, there is no evidence that tradesmen and artisans joined the local branch in any appreciable numbers. Reflecting the policy of the national organization, the local society was led by a group that included Joseph Dawson, a bank cashier, as secretary and John Worthington, a printer and stationer, as treasurer. Whatever the officers' class affiliation, the general membership was overwhelmingly Anglican, Tory, and Whig, reflecting the town's dominant political culture.[47]

With some variations the membership profile of the Preston SIA chapter was replicated in branches across the country. For instance, of the twenty-six members in Bolton and surrounding towns, fourteen were major figures in the cotton industry, including four members of the Cannon family, prominent

46. *Guardian* (Preston), 12 October 1870, 19 July 1873, 13 August 1879, 25 August 1886, 11 February 1888, 23 November 1893, 24 March 1894, 18 January 1908; *Lancashire Evening Post*, 14 September 1889; Paul T. Phillips, *The Sectarian Spirit: Sectarianism, Society, and Politics in Victorian Cotton Towns* (Toronto, 1982), 62–63; H. I. Dutton and J. E. King, *"Ten Percent and No Surrender": The Preston Strike, 1853–1854* (New York, 1981), 79, 90, 119, 122, 124; Henry N. B. Morgan, "Social and Political Leadership in Preston, 1820–60" (M.Litt. thesis, University of Lancaster, 1980), 190, 262, 312.

47. *Guardian* (Preston), 27 June 1863, 19 September 1885, 10 June 1893; *Chronicle* (Preston), 10 October 1863; *Herald* (Preston), 13, 20 June 1863; Dutton and King, *"Ten Percent and No Surrender,"* 80.

cotton spinners, and Peter Rothwell Arrowsmith; one was a papermaker; one a railway and bridge contractor; one a cashier; one a doctor; and two were ministers, one an Anglican, the other, Woodville Woodman, the only known Swedenborgian involved on either side of the issue. In addition, there were two pro-Confederate supporters active in the local movement who were not members of either the national or local society. One was the innkeeper Robert Handley, the other, the former Chartist and newsagent Thomas "Radical" Grimshaw. Of the fourteen men associated with the cotton industry, eight were Conservative and three were Liberal; the political affiliation of the remaining three is unknown. Of the three Liberals, two, Joseph Crook and Arrowsmith, both Unitarians, had Radical backgrounds. Crook was a leading figure in the Bolton Reform Union formed in 1837. Arrowsmith backed Fergus O'Conner, the Chartist leader in the late 1830s, and supported the idea that the mass platform was the best way of extracting political concessions from the aristocracy. Apparently Arrowsmith speculated heavily in Egyptian cotton at the beginning of the war and lost. His company failed in early 1865 with more than £200,000 in liabilities. The religious affiliation of only five of the twenty-six members of the chapter have been determined; all were Dissenters.[48]

In late 1864 J. W. Burns, a "working man," insisted that Confederate support in Sheffield consisted of only "three gentlemen." Burns may have been alluding to the number who were publicly involved, for the SIA's membership list shows there were seventeen. Of these, nine were involved in steel and knife manufacturing, the city's main industry; five were doctors; one was a mining engineer; and one was an Anglican minister. Confederate supporters who did not join the SIA included a manufacturer, a solicitor, an auctioneer and valuer, a nailmaker and shopkeeper, an engraver and printer, and a music seller and dance teacher. These occupations suggest that, if Sheffield was not atypical (and the case of Bolton suggests that it was not), then supporters of the Confederacy were much more occupationally and po-

48. Newspaper clippings, Bolton Public Library; *Chronicle* (Bolton), 17 February 1877; *Journal* (Bolton), 1 September 1877, 30 August 1890, 1 April 1893; *Journal and Guardian* (Bolton), 23 October 1897; Michael Brook, "Confederate Sympathies in North East Lancashire, 1862–1864," *Transactions of the Lancashire and Cheshire Antiquarian Society* 75 and 76 (1965–66): 215; Edward Royle, *Victorian Infidels: The Origins of the British Secularist Movement, 1791–1866* (Manchester, 1974), 206; John Kelly, "The End of the Famine: The Manchester Cotton Trade, 1864–1867—A Merchant's Eye View," in H. B. Harte and K. G. Ponting, eds., *Textile History and Economic History* (Manchester, 1973), 363; Peter Taylor, *Popular Politics in Early Industrial Britain: Bolton, 1825–1850* (Keele, 1995), 65, 67, 69, 73–74, 108–09, 188–89, 199.

litically diverse when nonmembers of the SIA are added to the equation. Both William Harvey, the auctioneer and valuer, and George Lemon Saunders, the dance teacher and seller of music scores, were nonmembers and described by Burns as "democrats." Saunders called for manhood suffrage and voting by ballot, for which he was accused of trying to Americanize British institutions. In both cases their position on the war may have been the result of local political developments, particularly their break with Isaac Ironside, a former Chartist and the most dominant pro-Union voice in the town.[49]

When the Rochdale chapter of the SIA was formed in April 1864, one local report observed that it was made up of "merchants, manufacturers, and general tradesmen." Based on an analysis of a number of SIA chapters, it appears that this observation about the extent of participation by tradesmen is valid only when nonmembers are added to the mix, and then only marginally. The evidence also suggests that, by and large, the overwhelming majority of those who took the side of the Confederacy were Conservatives and of those who could be classified as Liberal, most saw themselves as Whigs. There were some notable exceptions. There is also some evidence for the existence of a couple of pro-Confederate groups in which working men took an active role. The first, the Committee of Employers and Employees, was formed in Ashton in August 1862 by a group of cotton masters eager to encourage the breaking of the blockade and to promote recognition of the Confederacy. The organizers were fully aware that the success of their objectives required the kind of public pressure only the working class could stimulate. William Aitken, schoolteacher and former Chartist, was the committee's most visible agent, while William Boon, a young cotton twister from Dukinfield, acted as secretary. Over the next few months the group organized a number of public meetings. By the end of 1863, however, it appears that, with the exception of Aitken, all the leading working-class figures were no longer active. By mid-1864 most of the pro-Confederate meetings were attended by "respectable gentlemen." In mid-1863 a working-class association formed in Blackburn, but nothing is known about its origins or officers. There is no evidence that it organized any public meetings. Most of its activ-

49. *Independent* (Sheffield and Rotherham), 1 January, 4, 27 June, 2 October, 12 December 1863, 18 June 1866, 1 August 1870; Sidney Pollard, *A History of Labour in Sheffield* (Liverpool, 1959), 162; John Salt, "Local Manifestations of the Urquhartite Movement," *International Review of Social History* 13 (1968): 358.

ities were limited to weekly meetings for members at its committee rooms in a local pub.[50]

Membership in pro-Confederate organizations is not, of course, an adequate measure of artisanal and working-class support of the South. The frequency with which these groups debated the issues of the war in their debating and fraternal societies and the number of times resolutions backing the Confederacy were adopted suggests the existence of strong approval of the cause of secession. Not surprisingly, the attitudes expressed at these meetings found their way into public forums. In mid-1864 "Bill the Blacksmith" of Birmingham wrote a local newspaper about the existence of a pro-Confederate club: "I happen to be one of a few who hold a sort of club amongst ourselves, and on each occasion that we meet to express our joy or grief for the brave Southerners, we collect a trifle, and give it to be disposed of in a way we think proper." In the closing month of the war "A True Southerner and A Working Man" predicted that six hundred workingmen planned to observe Jefferson Davis's call for a day of fasting, humiliation, and prayer by staying at home.[51]

Whatever the source of support, two months after the formation of the SIA, propagandists claimed an estimated membership of twenty thousand, the majority of them "operatives and men employed in other forms of labour." These figures seem somewhat exaggerated given what is known of the extent of working-class support for the Confederacy and the tendency of both sides to inflate the number of their supporters. The SIA was on firmer ground in its claim for the existence of thirty-three affiliates by the end of 1863. Two additional chapters, one in Leicester and the other in Rochdale, were added in the first few months of 1864. All but seven of the branches were in Lancashire and Cheshire; there were two in Suffolk and one each in Glasgow, Northampton, Newcastle, and Glossop. Some of these local societies may have been

50. Janet Toole, "Workers and Slaves: Class Relations in a South Lancashire Town in the Time of the Cotton Famine," *Labour History Review* 63 (1998): 160–81; *Reporter* (Ashton and Stalybridge), 27 September, 4 October 1862, 14 November 1863, 25 June 1864; *Standard* (Blackburn), 16 September 1863; Philip John Auger, "The Cotton Famine, 1861–1865: A Study of the Principal Cotton Towns during the American Civil War" (Ph.D. diss., Cambridge University, 1979), 254.

51. For the frequency of debates on the war and the votes taken see the Minutes of the Birmingham Sunday Evening Debating Society, Birmingham (England) Public Library; Margaret Wendy Corke, "Birmingham and the American Civil War" (master's thesis, University of Liverpool, 1963), 46; *Daily Gazette* (Birmingham), 27 June 1864, 6 March 1865.

stillborn. Newcastle probably did not have a society, for there are no recorded members from that city on the SIA membership list.[52]

To some extent, the Society for Promoting the Cessation of Hostilities in America, which was formed in fall 1863, duplicated the work of the SIA, at least in London. Unlike the SIA, which sought to win recognition for the Confederacy, this society, as its name implied, was more interested in pressuring the British and European governments to use their influence to force each side to end the war. In practice there was little to separate the organizations; cessation of the war and negotiations would have achieved recognition by different means. Freeman Morse, the United States consul in London, described the society as "a powerful, foreign organization" working with "disloyalists and tories in the Northern States of the Union" to destroy the country. The impetus for the formation of the society and much of its financial support came from Matthew Maury, the noted nautical scientist who arrived in England in November 1862 on a mission to purchase and build ships for the Confederacy. Its president was Talavera V. Anson, a retired navy commander, but its driving force was its secretary the Reverend Francis William Tremlett, rector of Saint Peter's Church, Belsize Park. Verifying the size of the society's membership is impossible. Very likely, many of the five thousand claimed as members in 1864 were also enrolled in the SIA. Many of the leaders, for example, including Lord Wharncliffe, Henry de Hoghton, and William Scholefield, were also prominent in the SIA. Although there were plans for a chapter in Burslem, Staffordshire, in late 1864, there is no evidence that the society made any concerted attempts to form auxiliaries outside London.[53]

Much of the steam had gone out of Confederate organizations by the summer of 1864. Tremlett and the Society for the Cessation of Hostilities continued to lobby the government, but after a meeting with Palmerston in July failed to win approval for its proposals, the society folded its tent. There were rumors of plans to form another organization, the National Coalition, with

52. *Index*, 19 November, 31 December 1863. The difficulty in determining the true size of membership is complicated by the fact the SIA membership list contains fewer than one thousand names. *Chronicle* (Leicester), 4 June 1864; *Midland Free Press*, 28 May 1864; *Pilot* (Rochdale), 9 April 1864.

53. Tremlett to Mason, London, 2 June 1864, Mason Papers; Morse to Seward, London, 29 July 1864, Despatches from U.S. Consuls in London, England, 1790–1906; Frederic Boase, ed., *Modern English Biography* (1892; reprint, London, 1965), 4: 140–41; Jenkins, *Britain and the War of the Union*, 2: 334–35; Frances Leigh Williams, *Matthew Fontain Maury: Scientist of the Sea* (New Brunswick, N.J., 1963), 412; *Staffordshire Advertiser*, 17 September 1864.

objectives very similar to those of the SIA, but nothing came of them.[54] The failure of pro-Confederate groups to achieve their objectives was attributable in no small measure to the vigorous opposition they encountered from societies that supported both the Union and emancipation. Organizationally, this support did not come as easily or as expeditiously as Americans had hoped. Separation, British abolitionists of all persuasions had long insisted, was the best solution to the crisis and the one best guaranteed to destroy slavery. Lincoln's initial refusal to declare the slaves free deepened abolitionists' skepticism about the wisdom of maintaining the Union. If this was not a war about slavery, then why should British abolitionists become involved? Even among some who believed that slavery was the cause of the conflict, there existed a passionate opposition to all forms of war. As a result, supporters of the Confederacy had a relatively free run of things during the first year of the war. Cheever, Thompson, Remond, Day, and others tried as best they could to keep the public aware of the issues involved in the war in the months after the firing on Fort Sumter, but the forces of public opinion seemed to be pulling against them. With a few major exceptions, the press, with the London *Times* in the lead, supported the independence of the South. By the summer of 1862 it was rumored that the government was seriously considering recognition of the Confederacy. That, Lincoln's preliminary proclamation of emancipation in September, and growing concern about the continued shortage of cotton, were the impetuses for the emergence of sustained pro-Union activity.

The first of the new pro-Union groups was the Committee on Correspondence with America on Slavery, formed in late 1862. Not a society in the organizational sense of the word, it was the brainchild of a several Congregationalist ministers who were frustrated by the Congregational Union's refusal to take a position on the war at its October meeting. The committee, a direct descendent of the free-produce movement, hoped to influence public opinion to continue the country's antislavery tradition, to counter any efforts to recognize the Confederacy, to work to aid those at home thrown out of work because of the shortage of cotton, and to promote the cultivation of free-grown cotton. The Congregationalists were joined by ministers from other denominations and a number of laymen who would later play prominent roles in the London Emancipation Society and the Union and Emancipation Society,

54. John Ravens to n.n., London, n.d., Mason Papers.

including P. A. Taylor, John Stuart Mill, James Stansfield, Edward Dicey, Edmond Beales and Professor E. S. Beesly of London, Joseph Cowen of Newcastle, and Abel Heywood and George Wilson of Manchester. Little is known of the committee's officers except that its secretary was the barrister Frederick Tomkins, who would later play a prominent role in the British freedmen's aid movement.[55]

The Committee of Correspondence with America on Slavery was short-lived. It issued just two pamphlets before going out of business in early 1863, its place taken, at least in London, by the London Emancipation Society. Although the society attracted members from across the abolitionist spectrum, Garrisonians were its driving force. Since 1859 Garrisonians on both sides of the Atlantic had been exploring ways to resuscitate the movement. Samuel May Jr. had spoken to Richard Webb of Dublin, editor of the *Anti Slavery Advocate*, about the need to reactivate the Anti Slavery League, which had been formed during Garrison's visit in 1846, but which had long been inactive. Never one to pull his punches, Webb dismissed the idea as impractical. There were simply not the means or the men of talent needed for such an effort. For example, William Powell, an African American living in Liverpool, was a "poor man in the employment of others" and was insensitive to social conventions. His wife was a "born lady," but one of his sons, a doctor, was "very intemperate, and one of the stupidest men I ever met with." Webb was only slightly less intolerant of the talents and social graces of many who May thought could play a role in the proposed society. But other antislavery advocates persevered in their efforts to revitalize the movement. In May 1859 Thompson, F. W. Chesson, William and Ellen Craft, Remond, William Farmer, a member of the original league, and others met to form the London Emancipation Committee. The name was changed fifteen months later to the Anti Slavery League. One year later a group of about thirty members of the league met at the Whittington Club in London and adopted the name of the London Emancipation Society (LES).[56]

The society aimed to rally public opinion in an effort to counteract the "alleged sympathy" of Britain for the South and to encourage the Federal gov-

---

55. *Nonconformist*, 17 December 1862; Gillespie, *Labor and Politics in England*, 214–15; Jordon and Pratt, *Europe and the American Civil War*, 142–43; C. F. Adams to Tomkins, London, 5 January 1863, Adams Papers.

56. Taylor, *British and American Abolitionists*, 437–39; Chesson diary, 1 June 1858 to 22 July 1859, Raymond English Deposit; *Morning Star*, 14 October 1861, 14 November 1862; *Liberator*, 28 February 1862; *The Inquirer*, 2 September 1865.

ernment in the "prosecution of its anti-slavery policy."[57] The exact size of the society's membership is unknown, although there are indications that it drew support from a wide area of the country, with auxiliaries in a few of the towns around London, as well as in Sheffield, Liverpool, Leicester, Bristol, and Bury, and "committees" in Newark and Merthyr Tydfil. There may have been some duplication in membership, particularly in Liverpool, where a number of the leading figures in the society were also vice-presidents of the Union and Emancipation Society. Similarly, the Bristol branch, formed in March 1863, was led by Handel Cossham, a prominent figure in the Union and Emancipation Society. At the end of 1864 the branch claimed an "honorary" and executive committee of forty, many of them leading Liberals. It was reported that all students at the Bristol Baptist College were members. The branch in Bury seemed to have done very little. Much of the organization of meetings in that town was not the work of the society's leading figure, John Rowlinson, but of David Thomas, a reporter on the local newspaper.[58]

The LES was led by William Evans, about whom nothing is known except that he had extensive investments in the United States. Peter Alfred Taylor, Radical M.P. for Leicester and heir to the silk manufacturer Courtauld, was one of two treasurers; the other was W. T. Malleson, about whom there is no information. The secretary was F. W. Chesson, the son-in-law of George Thompson, a journalist and secretary of the Aborigines Protection Society. Forty-seven of the 204 members of the "General Committee" were ministers. All but one, Joseph H. Rylance, curate at Saint Paul's, Southwark, were from Dissenting churches, and many of them were former members of the Committee of Correspondence with America on Slavery. Thirty-three could be classified as professionals. Surprisingly—given the view that the press was generally hostile to the Union—thirteen were involved with newspapers and/or publishing, including Samuel Lucas, managing proprietor of the London *Morning Star*, and William Tweedie, printer of antislavery tracts and slave narratives. Eight were members of the legal profession, among them the Scottish Radical John Gorrie, a regular contributor to the *Morning Star* who

57. C. F. Adams to Seward, London, 29 November 1862, Despatches of U.S. Ministers to Great Britain, 1791–1906; Morse to Seward, London, 21 November 1862, Despatches from U.S. Consuls in London, England, 1790–1906.

58. *Morning Star*, 28 March 1863; *Post* (Liverpool), 16 January, 31 October 1863; *Post* (Bristol), 13 March 1863; *Mercury* (Bristol), 10 December 1864; *Times* (Bury), 7 February 1863; Dudley to Seward, Liverpool, 17, 20 January 1863, Despatches from U.S. Consuls in Liverpool, 1790–1906.

later became a prominent figure in the colonial judiciary in Mauritius, Fiji, the Leeward Islands, and Trinidad. Seven were doctors, including homeo-pathic physician John Epps. There were four professors, with Positivist Edward Spencer Beesly of University College, London, being the most promi-nent. Fourteen, with safety matches manufacturer William Bryant among them, could be classified as manufacturers, businessmen, or merchants. Radi-cals and long-time Chartists such as Charles Henry Elt and Henry Vincent were a strong presence. At least eight on the committee, including William Shaen, can be classified as old abolitionists. Others had either joined the movement in the last decade or were recent recruits. These included Bromley starch, baking powder, and ink manufacturer Harper Twelvetrees and Dr. John Epps, both of whom were involved in the effort to win John Anderson's re-lease; and Plaistow Independent minister John Curwen, who seemed to have joined the movement during J. Sella Martin's first visit to England in 1861. Politically, there were no known Conservatives on the "General Commit-tee."[59]

The membership of the Ladies London Emancipation Society (LLES), formed in March 1863, has a similar profile. With the exception of its presi-dent, journalist Frances Cobb, all were avowed Liberals or, like Mentia Taylor, founder of the society and wife of Peter Alfred Taylor, from families with strong Radical traditions. Although dominated by Londoners, the LLES was a national society, which recruited many of its estimated two hundred members from throughout England. Many of its subscribers were from families, or were themselves, long active in the abolitionist cause, including Mary Estlin of Bristol, Harriet Martineau, Eliza Wigham of Edinburgh, Elizabeth Pease Nichols of Glasgow, George Thompson's daughter Amelia Chesson, Harriet Lupton of Leeds, and African Americans Sarah Parker Remond and Ellen Craft. The majority of the executive committee, however, were new to the cause.[60]

Unlike the Union and Emancipation Society, the LES had difficulty estab-lishing branches outside of London and the Home Counties. Where they were

59. Baylen and Gossman, *Biographical Dictionary of Modern British Radicals*, 2: 55, 203–04, 497–99, 519–22; Boase, *Modern English Biography*, 1: 795, 990; ibid., 2: 525, 3: 1055–56, 4: 528; Royden Harrison, "Professor Beesly and the Working-Class Movement," in Asa Briggs and John Saville, eds., *Essays in Labour History* (London, 1960), 219; Bridget Brereton, *Law, Justice, and Empire: The Colonial Career of John Gorrie, 1829–1892* (Kingston, Jamaica, 1997), 19–21, 55; John Epps, *Diary of the Late John Epps, M.D.*, ed. Mrs. Epps (London, n.d.), 585.

60. Midgley, *Women Against Slavery*, 180–81; *Anti Slavery Reporter*, 1 January 1864; *Boston Commonwealth*, 29 May 1863.

successful, the societies, like the one in Bury, remained relatively inactive. Leicester, where there was a heated debate over the need and wisdom of founding societies, is a case in point. The inspiration for the society came from Thomas Cook, the organizer of inexpensive tourist travel who had attended the founding meeting of the LES in November 1862. He must have been surprised by the divisions that came to light at the founding meeting. Thomas Burgess, Joseph F. Winks, and the Reverend James P. Mursell, all declared abolitionists, expressed strong opposition to a society they thought had allowed politics to intrude into the debate over slavery. The reactions of others were more ambivalent. R. Bell, a Wesleyan minister, condemned the extent of proslavery sentiment in the North, although he believed there were "genuine Christians . . . and anti-slavery advocates of the strongest order" there. More importantly, he was convinced that "the slavery question was at the bottom of the war." As a result, Bell could support a motion that condemned the Confederate's proslavery policy and at the same time withhold support for the Union. Three months later Bell abandoned his neutrality on the war. He came to support the North, he reasoned, because the war was unconstitutional, because the South was adamant that the Negro belonged in slavery, and finally, because the Federal government was doing all it could to end slavery.[61]

While Burgess attended the founding meeting and continued to engage members of the society on the wisdom of its approach, nearly all the ministers who were invited to join declined and boycotted the society's public meetings. Leicester was atypical in this regard; in no other city were Dissenting ministers so unanimous in their opposition to the formation of an antislavery society. Bell seemed to have been the lone exception, and he would leave the city in September 1863 after a short three-year residence. Such tepid support from traditional antislavery sources undermined the effectiveness of the branch, particularly when it came under attack from opponents. Taking his cue from the London *Times*, a local editor insisted that the society was led by "smaller local luminaries" and "talkative nobodies who, like the Tooley-street tailors, have come to consider themselves 'the people of England.'"[62] Among those who raised the editor's ire was Thomas Emery, a bookseller and former Owenite who supported practical incremental changes in the suffrage laws as the best means of ensuring continued middle-class support for electoral reform. He was joined by Samuel Baines, a tea dealer and grocer, and Thomas Viccars,

61. *Leicestershire Mercury*, 14 February, 27 June 1863; *Midland Free Press*, 14 February 1863.
62. *Journal* (Leicester), 20 March, 18 December 1863.

a woolstapler. Francis Drake, an architect and surveyor, became a member of the LES because he considered the leaders of the Confederacy revolutionists and because of his opposition to the perpetuation and extension of slavery. Although the sample is small, what is known of the members suggests that the society attracted shopkeepers, artisans, and those who were politically Radical, not a group much in favor with Conservatives such as the editor of the *Leicester Journal*.[63]

While the branch remained small—only thirty attended its founding meeting, and there is no evidence that many more flocked to join later—support for the Union in Leicester was substantial. Supporters included Charles C. Coe, author and Unitarian minister, and William Biggs, who with his brother John ran one of the largest hosiery businesses in the city and had extensive trading contacts in the United States. The brothers had made frequent trips across the Atlantic, and much of their devotion to the tenets of political economy, one historian has observed, was due to their admiration of America's "democratic openness." Both actively supported the Italian and Hungarian independence movements. Coe, William Biggs, and J. Buckley, a shopkeeper, were the Union and Emancipation Society's only members from Leicester. Support for the Union also came from William Charlesworth, a shoe manufacturer, and William Forester Bramley, an ironmonger and brazier, neither of whom were members of either society.[64]

A mix of manufacturers, small shopkeepers, artisans, Dissenting ministers, and Radical politicians among Union supporters in Leicester—to which needs to be added substantial working-class support from elsewhere—best describes the membership of the Union and Emancipation Society (UES). If Burgess and Winks in Leicester were concerned about the implied political affiliation of the LES, there could be no mistaking where the Union and Emancipation Society stood. In fact, the organizational meeting of the society had voted by only the narrowest of margins to include the word "Union" in its name. Thomas Baily Potter, its president, later recalled that the name was insisted on by those who believed that in America the Union was the symbol of "the success of popular government," while emancipation broke the fetters of

---

63. *Midland Free Press*, 14 February, 4 April 1863, 30 April 1864, 22 August 1868; *Leicestershire Mercury*, 14 February 1863; *Drake's Directory of Leicester* (Leicester, 1861), 20, 64.

64. *Chronicle* (Leicester), 25 April 1874; *Chronicle and Mercury* (Leicester), 6 May 1865; *Leicestershire Mercury*, 14 February 1863; R. H. Evans, "The Biggs Family of Leicester," *Transactions, Leicester Archeological and Historical Society* 48 (1972–73): 30–47; *Drake's Directory*, 24–27.

the slaves and promised the rights of citizenship. But the choice of name was also freighted with domestic political implications. "We also need union, to give every man equal rights and justice, and emancipation from those remnants of feudalism, the privileges of which still trammel labour in this country."[65] Many of those who opposed the inclusion refused to join the society. Hugh Mason, an Ashton cotton manufacturer and member of the LES, rejected an invitation to join the UES because he did not "feel it to be his duty, and he had not felt it to be sound policy to identify himself with the society termed the Union and Emancipation Society, though that society included in its ranks a considerable number of men with whom he had the pleasure to work on many important subjects." Union was secondary to emancipation, and while Mason thought it would be a calamity if the Union was destroyed, he felt strongly that the future political map of the country should be left entirely to the Americans to decide.[66] In spite of his concerns, Mason continued to support the activities of the society.

The UES was launched following a massive meeting at the Free Trade Hall in Manchester on the last day of 1862. Arranged to coincide with the implementation of Lincoln's Emancipation Proclamation, the meeting was meant to demonstrate the depth of working-class support for the maintenance of the Union and for the president's antislavery policies. Resolutions were adopted that condemned slavery as a violation of all principles of liberty and praised Lincoln for his efforts to keep the Union together. In an address to Lincoln, the meeting assured the president, "[I]f you have any ill-wishers here . . . they are chiefly those who oppose liberty at home."[67] Up to this time, the Manchester gathering was the largest and most impressive to address British popular reactions to the war, and the fact that it was organized, financed, and dominated by the working class was not lost on many political opponents. The *Index*, British mouthpiece of the Confederacy, dismissed those seated on the platform as "men of no character or influence whatever." Across the Pennines range, an editor found the meeting all of a piece with other working-class demonstrations at which the speakers are "usually a few ambitious, and fluent, and (may we not add), self-conceited, members of the operative class,

---

65. *Bee Hive*, 6 May 1865; *Morning Star*, 5 May 1865; *Reynolds's Newspaper*, 7 May 1865.

66. Jones, *The Slaveholders' War*, 4–5. Jones later recalled that the suggestion that the claims of union and emancipation be kept separate was rejected as being unprincipled. *Times* (Bury), 29 April 1865.

67. *Examiner and Times* (Manchester), 1 January 1863; *Guardian* (Manchester), 1 January 1863.

and certain Popularity-loving politicians of a higher grade, who seek to ingratiate themselves with the audience by an amount of adulation absolutely sickening." Henry Lord, U.S. consul at Manchester, not surprisingly, saw things differently. The audience, he wrote his superiors, was so "respectable in dress and general appearance as to be hardly distinguishable from that gathered in the same place a year ago to hear Mr. Gladstone." Most of the speakers, he reported, were working men "but all were eloquent and logical."[68]

Who were these men dismissed by the *Manchester Guardian* as "practiced hands at agitation"? The UES had its origins in discussions among members of the largely working-class Socratic Debating Society. Nothing is known of the society, but in similar organizations in other cities, such as the Birmingham Sunday Evening Debating Society whose members were mainly artisans, there were frequent debates on aspects of the war.[69] Out of these debates came the decision to organize a society that would be the working class's voice on the war and one that would help to mold public opinion in favor of the Union. Much of the impetus came from John C. Edwards and Edward Hooson, Radical working-class figures active in political reform causes. Hooson, a Chartist and ally of Ernest Jones, was a leader in the trade-union movement, while Edwards, who was largely self-taught, was a proponent of the cooperative movement. They were joined by, among others, Thomas Evans, a former weaver who had been active in the trade-union strikes of the 1850s. Evans seemed to have divided his time between England and the United States, crossing the Atlantic twenty times. He was living in the United States when war broke out, but returned to England in late summer 1861. The Cropper brothers, James R. and Robert, former Owenites and Secularists active in reform politics, were leading figures, as was former Owenite Dr. John Watts. Finally, there was Thomas H. Barker, secretary of the United Kingdom Alliance for the Suppression of the Liquor Traffic, who authored the "Address to Lincoln." Arrangements for the Free Trade Hall meeting were made at the home of Max Kyllman, a German merchant who had invested in a cooperative cotton mill. Although subscriptions raised by working-class members of the organizing committee covered the expenses of the meeting, most of the society's operating funds were provided by Thomas

68. *Index*, 8 January 1863; *Intelligencer* (Leeds), 3 January 1863; Lord to Seward, Manchester, 1 January 1863, Despatches from U.S. Consuls in Manchester, 1847–1906.

69. *Guardian* (Manchester), 2 January 1863; Minutes of the Birmingham Sunday Evening Debating Society.

Bayley Potter, its president. A Unitarian with a pronounced Radical pedigree, Potter was independently wealthy.[70]

One suspects that it was the combination of working-class initiative and Radical politics that caused opponents of the UES so much concern. And what was true politically and socially for those who took a leading part in organizing the society was equally applicable to the general membership. A comparison of the UES and the Southern Independent Association to that of the Manchester Royal Exchange at the end of the 1860s provides an indication of the social status of those who belonged to the UES. The exchange, as Simon Gunn has argued, was "the key institution of Manchester business," and its leadership "remained effectively a Tory preserve throughout the second half of the century."[71] If one excludes doctors, lawyers, ministers, and others not directly involved in the business world, then fully one-half of the Manchester members of the SIA were to be found on the exchange. While more than half the Manchester UES vice-presidents were on the exchange, as were five of the executive council's twenty-four members—an indication that the UES saw the need to place individuals of standing in leadership positions—only 13 of an estimated 135 general members could claim the same affiliation. The finding suggests that economic interests and, more problematically, politics determined to some substantial degree, at least in the case of Manchester, the side one supported in the war.

Generally, the same conclusions hold true for Preston, considered by many observers one of the strongest pro-Confederate bastions in the country. There was, however, a substantial pro-Union presence in the city. The local branch of the UES was formed in June 1863 and for the rest of the war worked closely with the older Preston Anti Slavery Society. Founded in late 1860 following a visit by George Thompson, the Anti Slavery Society was unique in many re-

70. Newspaper clippings, Manchester Public Library; *The Pioneer*, 16 February 1889; *Bee Hive*, 7 February 1863; *Examiner and Times* (Manchester), 15 August 1862; *Liberator*, 29 April 1864; *New York Times*, 21 April 1863; Paul A. Pickering, *Chartism and the Chartists in Manchester and Salford* (New York, 1995), 191; Royle, *Victorian Infidels*, 309; Brian Harrison, *Drink and the Victorians: The Temperance Question in England, 1815–1872* (Pittsburgh, 1971), 475; Barker to Garrison, Manchester, 27 August 1864, and Thompson to Garrison, London, 15 January 1864, both in AASS Papers; Baylen and Gossman, *Biographical Dictionary*, 2: 418–22; Stange, *British Unitarians against American Slavery*, 207; Temperley, *British Antislavery*, 255.

71. Simon Gunn, "The Manchester Middle Class, 1850–1880" (Ph.D. diss., University of Manchester, 1992), 340.

spects. Although not a ladies' society, many of its officers were women. Those included president Elizabeth Abbott, an active ally of American Garrisonians; secretary Jane Clemesha; assistant secretary Sarah A. Halliday; and treasurer Anne Simpson.[72] Among the other members of its executive committee was the Reverend J. Croke Squire, a Unitarian minister who broke with the society over Union policy early in the war and who became an active member of the SIA. The society appears to have maintained communication with both Garrisonians and the BFASS. Such neutrality was rare in 1860, and much of the work of maintaining it seems to have fallen to Jane Clemesha. The daughter of a Quaker grocer and tea dealer, Clemesha assumed her post at the relatively young age of twenty. Nothing is known of the family's background or of her life after the war. Unlike others who became active in the women's rights movement after the war, Clemesha seemed to have ceased all public involvement after 1865. For the duration of the war, however, she was the voice of the Preston Anti Slavery Society, writing frequently to newspapers, corresponding with other societies and, when needed, publicly chastising opponents. When Squire left the society and castigated it in the press for violating the principles of moral suasion, it was Clemesha who came to its defense. It was she who insisted that the society would continue to support the "old and original abolitionists—those who advocated the abolition of slavery by moral means, of which the great and noble man W. L. Garrison, is the head."[73]

The grocer's daughter was typical of Union supporters in Preston. While the president of the UES chapter, Joseph B. Haslam, was a cotton spinner, the majority of its leaders, at least those whose occupations are known, were, like Clemesha's father, shopkeepers. Of the three vice-presidents whose occupations have been identified, Thomas Phillips was an oil and general merchant, Robert Benson a grocer, and William Boyden a Methodist Free Church minister. One of the two secretaries, Richard Lambert, was a bookseller and stationer, the other, William Thompson, a victualer. The treasurer, William Toulmin, was a provision dealer. The occupations of two of the five executive committee members are known: William Blackburn was a grocer, and John Salter a printer and publisher.[74] When supporters of the Union who were

72. Many thanks to Clare Midgley of Staffordshire University for this information.

73. *Chronicle* (Preston), 28 August, 19 October 1861, 21 February, 16 May 1863; *Liberator*, 19 February 1864.

74. *Guardian* (Preston), 4 July 1863, 18 August 1869, 6 July 1887, 26 September 1914; *Chronicle* (Preston), 4 July, 1 August 1863; Dutton and King, *"Ten Percent and No Surrender,"* 125; Taylor, *Popular Politics in Early Industrial Britain*, 124; A. Hewitson, *Preston Town Council or*

members of neither society are added, the occupational profile changes only slightly. There were two millowners, seven grocers and general merchants, two dentists, two printers and publishers, one stonemason, one bookseller and stationer, and one homebuilder. Compared to supporters of the Confederacy, who were solidly Anglican and mainly Conservative, backers of the Union were members of Dissenting churches and generally Liberal.

Had Jane Clemesha visited Stockport, she would have found herself in familiar company. Of the twelve members of the committee of the local UES chapter, six were ministers. Of the four whose affiliations have been identified, three were Independent and one Baptist. Five of the remaining six members included a cotton-waste spinner, a timber merchant, a provision dealer and beer retailer, a bookseller and stationer, and a butcher.[75]

Although there were some differences between the towns, Clemesha would have recognized the profile of Union supporters in the Bolton area. Of the fifteen persons on the UES national membership list, there were five cotton spinners or bleachers; one was a grocer, one worked as a manager at a cotton mill, and two were Congregational ministers: G. D. Macgregor, a vice-president of the UES from Farnworth, and John Crossley. Thomas Thomasson, owner of five mills, was the most prominent of the cotton manufacturers to support the Union. A former Quaker, Thomasson had converted to Anglicanism in 1834, only to break with the church during the Crimean War and join Bolton's Free Christian Church. He was an early supporter of the Chartists and of women's suffrage. Another member of the UES was Samuel Gee of Farnworth, one of the largest employers in Kearsley. Gee had once supported the South, but after what he insisted was careful study of the causes of the war, he changed his allegiances. Gee's initial position may have been influenced by a family member, the Reverend Woodville Woodman, one of the most active local supporters of the Confederacy. There was also Robert Heywood, a "stern opponent of smoking and intemperance," a supporter of women's suffrage and an opponent of capital punishment who had visited the United States in the mid-1830s. Of those who supported the Union but were not members of the UES, one, Thomas Barlow, owned a number of mills; two

---

Portraits of Local Legislators (Preston, 1870); Census of Population (England), 1861, RG 9, Family Records Center, London; P. Manner, *Preston and District: Being the First Volume of the Directory and Topography of North Lancashire* (Preston, 1865).

75. *Morris and Company's Commercial Directory and Gazetteer of Cheshire* (Nottingham, 1884); *Stockport and Cheshire County News*, 2 November 1861; *Advertiser* (Stockport), 3 July 1863, 31 December 1897; Phillips, *The Sectarian Spirit*, 84.

were tea dealers, and there was a bank manager, a waste dealer, a ware dealer, a coal proprietor, and a tailor. Here, as in the other towns, Union supporters, as far as they can be identified, were members of Dissenting denominations and Liberals; many, like Heywood, were long involved in Radical causes.[76]

The evidence drawn from these samples shows that while there were a number of cotton lords who supported the Union, a substantial portion of the strength of the UES came from the ranks of small businessmen and shopkeepers. Support also came from skilled workers. The Middleton society, for example, was made up mainly of artisans and small shopkeepers, including a clog maker, beer retailers, and booksellers, with a grocer, Abraham Stansfield, as its treasurer.[77] The UES was also successful in recruiting working-class members. Although it is impossible to determine with any precision the number of members who were from the working class, indications are that it was not insubstantial. Four of the registered members from Lees, Lancashire, for example, were workers. Those included an iron laborer, a carter, and two cotton doublers. It is very likely that it cost nothing to have one's name added to the membership of the UES; one was simply signed up by an agent. Nine of the thirteen leading figures in the Ashton chapter, all of whom were skilled workers, were registered members of the national organization. But dues must have been required for members of local chapters, for much of the money raised by this means went to support the local chapter's activities. No evidence has been found that indicates the amount members were expected to pay. On the other hand, the rather hefty fees charged members of pro-Confederate organizations must have limited their ability to recruit workers. SIA subscriptions started at one guinea; the London SIA double that amount. Although considerably cheaper at 2s. 6d., the Preston branch's dues were still beyond the reach of most workers. The Rawtenstall Southern Club tried to get around the problem by waiving the one-shilling fee for workers who could not afford it.[78]

At a time when many cotton workers were unemployed, membership dues,

76. Phillips, *The Sectarian Spirit*, 28, 155; Taylor, *The Decline of British Radicalism*, 64, 74, 115, 201, 206; W. E. Brown, *Robert Heywood of Bolton* (Wakefield, 1970), 12, 18–19, 57, 60; *Guardian* (Bolton), 21 February 1863, 4 February 1865, 9 June 1877; *Chronicle* (Bolton), 21 February 1863, 28 July 1900; Newspaper clippings, Bolton Public Library; *The Bolton and District Directory for 1870–1871, comprising All the Townships in the Bolton Union* (Bolton, 1871).

77. *Standard* (Oldham), 27 June 1863; Isaac Slater, *Royal National Commercial Directory of Manchester and Liverpool and the Principal Manufacturing Towns in Lancashire* (Manchester, 1861).

78. Census of Population (England), 1861, RG 9; "SIA Circular," Anti-Slavery Pamphlets, John Rylands Library; *New York Times*, 18 April 1864; *Guardian* (Preston), 27 June 1863; *News* (Bacup and Rossendale), 27 February 1864.

even for the promotion of a cause about which one felt passionately must have had a very low priority. Members of the UES chapter in Ashton-under-Lyne, which was made up exclusively of workers and artisans, came up with an ingenious scheme to raise money to finance their activities: they knocked on doors and solicited contributions. These were supplemented by the proceeds from the sale of Ernest Jones's pamphlet, *The Slaveholders' War*, the text of a speech given under the auspices of the society in November 1863. In spite of hard times the society reported income of £9 7s. 5½d. and expenditures of £7. 18s. at the end of 1864.[79] The society had been formed at a meeting attended by a handful of workers at the home of John Hague, a gardener. Eight of the thirteen members of its executive committee have been identified, including James Brooke, a baker and grocer; James Broadbent, a molder; James Wilson, a weaver; John Johnson, a carder; William Patten, an engineer and mill mechanic; and Thomas Storer, a master shoemaker.[80] They worked closely with the charismatic Jonathan Biltcliffe, a local member of the national society, a Secularist and proponent of the cooperative movement, and a union organizer. He was a leader of the South Lancashire Weavers Union, which unsuccessfully struck against wage reductions in early 1861 and throughout the war. Until his migration to the United States in summer 1864, Biltcliffe worked to increase the support provided to the unemployed during the Cotton Famine.[81]

By all measurements, antislavery seemed to have maintained its currency well beyond the middle of the century. If there was understandable concern among abolitionists on either side of the Atlantic about that legacy, they must have been surprised by the speed with which the tradition was mobilized once Lincoln issued his Emancipation Proclamation. In spite of this, however, abolitionists were dismayed by the strength and resilience of pro-Confederate and (as they interpreted it) proslavery sentiment in the country. Historians have long grappled with this apparent dilemma, finding explanations in a combination of national jealousy and class antagonism, a loss of interest in abolition, a rising tide of racism, and more recently, the simple need for cotton to keep

79. *Reporter* (Ashton and Stalybridge), 2 April 1864, 14 January 1865.

80. *Reporter* (Ashton and Stalybridge), 7, 28 March 1863, 8 October 1864, 14, 21 January 1865; Census, 1861. Information of Storer kindly supplied by Robert Hall.

81. *National Reformer*, 7 September 1861; Neville Kirk, *The Growth of Working-Class Reformism in Mid–Victorian England* (Urbana, 1985), 257; Royle, *Victorian Infidels*, 186; Michael S. Edwards, *Purge This Realm: A Life of Joseph Rayner Stephens* (London, 1994), 119, 123; *Reporter* (Ashton and Stalybridge), 13 August 1864.

mills operating and workers employed. Evidence heretofore untapped suggests two more persuasive explanations: one, that class and religious and political affiliations were important predictors of the position folks took on the war; two, that while British abolitionist sentiment had lost some of its bite with the passage of time and the death of many of those who had promoted the cause of West Indian slaves, there existed a residue, a tradition, that could be called upon in times of need. Abolition still had currency.

3

Which Side Are You On?

The owl shrik'd at thy birth, an evil sign;
The night crow cried, aboding luckless time;
Dogs howl'd and hideous tempests shook down trees;
The raven rook'd her on the chimney's top,
The chattering pies in dismal discords sung.

                —Bury and Rossendale *News*, 6 February 1864

So wrote an opponent of the Southern Club in Rawtenstall, a mill town nestled in the Rossendale Valley of Lancashire. The club had been formed in September 1863, one week after the formation of a chapter of the Union and Emancipation Society. Within a couple months it had established a reading room to provide information on the war to its members, who, if they could afford it, paid dues of one shilling. Dues were waived for workers, especially the unemployed. Within four months, however, the club had closed its reading room "on account of the small interest taken in the American question in this locality." Opponents saw no general waning of interest in developments in the war; the club, they insisted, had always been the exclusive preserve of a few prominent local figures who had failed in their efforts to win widespread support for a cause that "substituted Slavery, Subordination, and

Government, for Liberty, Equality, and Fraternity." The club's officers included Robert Munn of Stackstead, one of the larger millowners and employers in the valley; textile manufacturer Henry Maden of Bacup; and Peter H. Whitehead, one of the local "Cotton Lords."[1]

The history of Rawtenstall's Southern Club provides interesting insights into the nature of organized British support for protagonists in the Civil War. Major employers in the area dominated the leadership of the club. While it was not always true in all parts of the country, by and large the leadership of organizations favoring the Confederate cause drew heavily from this group. It was also true that these leaders made every effort to attract their employees to their cause, in the Rawtenstall case by waiving the membership dues for workers. In this regard they had some success. In other respects, however, the Rawtenstall case was unique. The three principal figures in the club—Munn, Maden, and Whitehead—were all Liberals, and earlier in their careers the first two had been active supporters of the Anti–Corn Law League, a major springboard for many subsequent reform causes. Munn and Maden were unusual in this regard; very few former supporters of the league allied themselves with the Confederacy.[2] There were others, such as William Tagg, who were not members of the club but who leaned toward recognition of the South, convinced that all wars were indefensible and that, in this case, the North had neither the means nor the ability to subdue the South. Tagg, a haberdasher and a member of the Peace Society, was described by someone who knew him as a young man as "a Chartist of the Quaker stamp."[3] In Rawtenstall at least, the Confederacy seemed to have drawn support from the "Cotton Lords," advanced Liberals, and an undetermined number of workers, a coalition that was most unusual. Further, if it is true that as a rule families tended to act with some degree of unanimity on political issues, in Rawtenstall the Civil War proved to be the exception. Three members of the Whitehead family parted

1. *Guardian* (Manchester), 10 October 1863; *News* (Bury and Rossendale), 5 September 1863, 6, 13, 20, 27 February 1864; *Times* (Bury), 30 January, 6, 13 February 1864.

2. Chris Aspen, *Mr. Pilling's Short Cut to China and Other Stories of Rossendale Enterprise* (Helmshore, 1983), 13–15. Not many former supporters of the league promoted the Confederate cause. The most prominent may have been Edward Akroyd of Halifax, head of the largest worsted spinning and manufacturing complex in the country and one of the main local contributors to the league. Webster, "Edward Akroyd (1810–1887)," 28.

3. *News* (Bacup and Rossendale), 23 May 1863; *Times* (Bury), 12 July 1879. See series of articles, "Rossendale Celebrities Past and Present" *Times* (Bury) 28 March to 16 May, n.y., provided by the local library.

company with Peter H. to join the larger and more active Union and Emancipation Society.[4]

The picture that emerges from the Rossendale Valley, then, is much more complex than either supporters of the Union or some historians have indicated. Since the publication of Mary Ellison's study of Lancashire cotton workers, scholars have generally accepted that there was some support for the Confederacy among those most affected by the shortage of American cotton. To this group could be added a number of workingmen who, like Mortimer Grimshaw, had grown weary of the growth of American capitalism and its wage slavery. After having spent a period of political exile from England in the northern United States in the early 1850s, Grimshaw expressed dismay at the country's political and economic developments: American freedom and liberty, he insisted, was nothing but a "farce and humbug."[5] Yet in spite of Ellison's useful corrective, little is known about those who joined, or their reasons for joining, organizations supporting either the North or the South. Even less is known about those, like Grimshaw, who did not pen their names to the membership rosters of societies but who, nonetheless, were ardent public supporters of one side or the other.

J. Sella Martin, an American fugitive slave and minister who spent most of the war years in London, believed that the Confederacy drew its British supporters from among the ignorant, who were led astray by erroneous press reports and letters to the editor; those with financial interests in the South; those opposed to the extension of the franchise; those who thought that the South had a constitutional right to secede; and those who believed that the North had not committed itself unequivocally to the abolition of slavery.[6] Martin's was a pretty comprehensive list, but to it could be added Moncure D. Conway's "magnates of English literature"—among them, Charles Kingsley—men who, Conway insisted, were generally not original thinkers, were more proslavery than pro-Confederate, and who couched their views in the language of Thomas Carlyle. Other literary figures—John Stuart Mill, Thomas Hughes, and Newman Hall, for example—by implication more original in their thinking, supported the Union.[7] The Confederacy also

4. See the Manchester Union and Emancipation Society membership list published in the *Examiner and Times* (Manchester), 18 August 1863.

5. Ellison, *Support for Secession*; *Guardian* (Preston), 25 May 1861.

6. *Liberator*, 9 October 1863; *Morning Star*, 19 September 1861.

7. *Boston Commonwealth*, 17 July 1863; Moncure D. Conway, *Autobiography, Memories, and*

drew support from those who were angered by what they considered the Federal government's Machiavellian foreign policy and, especially, Seward's apparent insults and slights. The nationalistic vitriol associated with the *Trent* affair in December 1861 pushed many into the ranks of Confederate supporters. For some, the passage of the Morrill Act, with its increased levies on British goods, violated every principle of free trade, for which they had fought since the early 1840s, as well as being a direct assault on British commercial interests. Others simply had too much invested in the South to abandon it. W. C. Corsan, a Sheffield cutlery and edge-tools manufacturer, visited the South in October 1862 in a desperate attempt to make contacts with trading partners and customers cut off by the Union blockade of Southern ports. On his return he published a pro-Confederate account of conditions in America, but he could do little to restore the health of his company. Others saw the chance of a lifetime to profit from participation in running supplies to the South through the Federal blockade. Many, if not all, of the members of the Liverpool Southern Club were involved in some way with blockade running or had substantial investments in or commercial ties to the South. James Spence, the driving force behind the effort to win popular support for the Confederacy, had fallen victim to the economic panic of 1857 only to see the firms with which he renewed contacts in the North collapse as a result of the war. Spence profited substantially from his investments in blockade runners that operated out of Liverpool and other British ports.[8] So, too, did Alexander Collie, a Manchester merchant who made a fortune speculating in American cotton and was the driving force

---

Experiences of Moncure D. Conway (London, 1904), 1: 362–63. See Charles E. Shaine, "The English Novelists and the American Civil War," *American Quarterly* 14 (fall 1962): 399–421, for a general discussion of reactions to the war among this group.

8. Corsan, *Two Months in the Confederate States*. Other and less well known cities relied on the American trade. Northampton, for instance, was the major supplier of shoes to both sides. See David Weller, "Northampton and the American Civil War," *Northampton Past and Present* 8 (1990); "Rules and Bye-Laws of the Southern Club of Liverpool Established 1862," Dudley Collection. Alexander Collie wrote Lord Wharncliffe in the summer of 1864 to inform him that Spence had gotten a return of £6,000 on "his joint account with you in four steamers." Alex Collie to Wharncliffe, London, 27 June 1864, Wharncliffe Muniments. Henry Ward, a Blackburn cotton manufacturer, made an estimated £1 million running the blockade. See J. H. Fox, "The Victorian Entrepreneur in Lancashire," in S. P. Bell, ed., *Victorian Lancashire* (Newton Abbot, England, 1974), 108. Botsford claims that Clyde shipbuilders' profits increased due to their involvement in blockade running and the destruction of the American merchant fleet. Robert Botsford, "Scotland and the American Civil War" (Ph.D. diss., Edinburgh University, 1955), 529–30.

behind the building of British ships to evade the federal blockade of Southern ports.[9]

R. M. Thomas of Chester confirmed Martin's observation that many British aristocrats and Conservatives, both Whig and Tory, considered slaveholders kindred spirits under assault from democratic forces. The Confederacy drew support, Thomas observed, from "old Tories, stick-in-the-mud Whigs, or paid partizans of Jeff Davis and Co." Those like Peter Mackenzie of the Glasgow *Gazette*, who had a profound antipathy for America and its democracy, insisted in September 1862 that as a system of government, democracy "ever resulted in setting fools in high places." Americans, he had declared in an earlier editorial, were no more than "braggarts, upstarts, and lying scoundrels. . . . They are the scum of the earth, and have completely lost caste, not only among themselves, but in the eyes of all civilized Europe." In her fond reminiscences of British supporters of the Confederacy, Kate Rowland paid particular homage to members of the aristocracy, among whom Southerners in England found so much solace and comfort. Both James Mason and Matthew Maury, Confederate commissioners, frequently retreated to the comforts of Bedgebury Park and other manorial homes for rest and recuperation.[10]

The Confederacy also drew support from among those such as John M'Adam, a Glasgow potter and glass bottle manufacturer who had lived thirteen years in Jackson and Vicksburg, Mississippi, before returning home to Scotland in the 1850s. A Radical by all measures, M'Adam broke company with his colleagues in the Italian and Polish independence movements to support the Confederacy. M'Adams's Radical politics were no match for his fond memories of time spent in Mississippi. Not surprisingly, personal and family contacts in the South played a critical role in deciding which side to support. Early in the war the Reverend W. W. Malet, the eccentric vicar of Ardeley, a small village in Hertfordshire, traveled to South Carolina to fetch his sister, who was stranded on her family's plantation following the death of her husband in battle. Malet's brother-in-law had been a classmate of Malet's older brother at Harrow. Malet returned from his trip convinced that the South should be independent.[11]

9. Collie's obituary, newspaper cuttings, Manchester Public Library.

10. R. M. Thomas to Dudley, Chester, 2 February 1863, Dudley Collection; *Gazette* (Glasgow), 6 September 1862, 18 January 1862; Rowland, "English Friends of the Confederacy," 198; Williams, *Matthew Fontain Maury*, 412.

11. *Times* (London), 28 September, 1 October 1864; see Malet, *An Errand to the South in the Summer of 1862*.

If Martin's assessment of the sources of Confederate support was essentially correct, then it would follow logically that the Union drew sustenance from Radicals, advanced Liberals, Dissenters, and members of the working class, including those long-suffering textile workers who were victims of the Cotton Famine. That judgment remains the conventional view in spite of the findings of several studies that have raised questions about the extent and nature of British support for the Union. More importantly, that opinion was also the considered conclusion of many observers at the time, even among those who had a partisan ax to grind. The editors of the London *Times,* no lovers of the Union, were adamant that very few people of social or political standing had allied themselves with the Northern cause. The newspaper labeled members of the executive committee of the London Emancipation Society as a "few struggling obscurities," a "half a dozen nobodies," who believed that Robespierre was right. Among those who addressed the large Exeter Hall meeting in favor of union and emancipation in late January 1863 were a "minor novelist and two or three Dissenting ministers, who seem to be of the usual intellectual calibre." The "weakminded men" who congratulated Lincoln on issuing the Emancipation Proclamation were pale imitations of the great emancipators who destroyed West Indian slavery; they were at best "rootless, and bottomless, and fruitless . . . sticks." Demonstrations in favor of the Union were nothing more than "cuckoo eggs, fraudulently laid in the old [antislavery] nest but utterly repudiated by the old birds." Never one to shun the mixed metaphor, the editor concluded that the leaders of the emancipation movement were "very small dogs" who had "taken possession of the old lion's den."[12]

Such scorn was echoed in other conservative quarters. *Blackwood's Magazine* had nothing but contempt for the membership of pro-Union associations, made up as they were of "Bottom the weaver, Smug the joiner, and Flute the bellows-mender." Not surprisingly, the *Index,* the weekly published by Henry Hotze, the Confederate government's agent in London, found such assessments apt. Reporting on the large pro-Union meeting at the Manchester Free Trade Hall at the end of December 1862, the correspondent of the *Index* observed that scarcely a "person of respectable character was present," with the possible exception of Thomas Bazley, who as usual was "pompous, dull, and slow," and Abel Heywood, "a second rate, but an honest and respectable citizen." On the platform sat men of "no character or influence whatever; the

12. *Times* (London), 31 January, 19 February 1863.

most prominent being a minor Chartist spouter, an infidel newsvendor, and an ex-Socialist lecturer."[13]

If the editor of the *Index* could be dismissed as a paid partisan, those of the *Times* and *Blackwood's* could not; both were major players in Britain's political life. More importantly, their views found considerable currency among people who felt some anxiety about the chances of political upheavals in the country. A telltale sign of such concerns was the frequent dredging up of political bogeymen such as Robespierre, whose name continued to be a metaphor for political discord well into the late nineteenth century. Support for the Union, in this view, was nothing more than a subterfuge. Pro-Union forces in Bolton, a local editor observed, were made up of the rump of emancipationists who had "certain affinities with the equally attenuated remnants of Radicalism and Chartism." Across the Pennines in Sheffield, an opponent of the local emancipation society warned that supporters of the Union were not motivated by a desire to see slavery abolished but by a longing to see democracy and a republican form of government established at home: "These opponents of the crown and aristocracy view with undisguised bitterness the failure of that form of government they believe to be the most perfect, and ultimately to become universal."[14]

The views of the *Times* and other Conservative opinions about the sources of Union support do not hold up under scrutiny. While it is true that the Union drew considerable backing from among those interested in political reform at home, other issues, such as abolition and a belief in the freedom and rights of workers, were important. In Rawtenstall, for example, support came from a wide cross section of the community. Cotton manufacturers such as Joshua Lord and Joseph Redman joined the three members of the Whitehead family as members of the local pro-Union society. Redman had lived a number of years in Pennsylvania. Other Union proponents included cotton workers such as Daniel Greenwood (known locally as "Big Dan") and Henry Cunliffe, who by the outbreak of the war had both worked up the ranks to supervisory positions as overlookers. They were joined by Thomas Newbigging, an engineer and manager of the Rossendale Gas Company who would later gain a reputation as the valley's historian. The Union also won the endorsement of George Lomax, who was active in the temperance movement, and of Dissenting ministers such as James Baimbridge. One "Working Man" won-

13. *Blackwood's Magazine*, November 1863: 650; *Index*, 8 January 1863.
14. *Chronicle* (Bolton), 14 February 1863; *Telegraph* (Sheffield), 5 June 1863.

dered how anyone could rally to the cause of those "brave chivalrous women whippers and violators" of the Confederacy. Will these people, he asked rhetorically, be "our friends when we demand an extension of the suffrage and a more just and adequate representation?" Workingmen, he concluded, must make it abundantly clear that they see no advantage in becoming "the slave, the property of our employer—nor do we consider it right for the black man to be the white man's chattel."[15]

There is sufficient in the views of "A Working Man" to confirm the *Times's* worst fears, yet it is clear that supporters of the Union in the Rossendale valley were motivated by more than domestic political concerns. D. G. Wright comes to similar conclusions in his study of Bradford, where he found that support for the Union came from among those interested in abolition and domestic political reform, an alliance of labor aristocrats (including overlookers, warehousemen, and clerks), the "radical oligarchy," and Dissenting clergy. Agitation over the Civil War brought together "middle class Radicals, the labor aristocracy . . . Positivists and trade unionists . . . radical Dissenters and freethinkers."[16] Those involved in the public debate over the war proffered remarkably similar explanations about the economic, social, political, and religious composition of the contending groups. Many Southerners in Britain agreed with Matthew Maury's observation that "the great masses of the people i.e. the middling and lower classes are against us." Even Confederate sympathizers from the upper classes, he lamented, were "what we would call abolitionists." Goldwin Smith, the Oxford don, explained to an American friend that the Confederacy drew its support from the aristocracy, the "great capitalists" who had been influenced by the London press, the clergy of the Church of England, the rich—with a few notable exceptions—who had "disregarded class feelings," and many in the middle class who aped the aristocracy. On the other hand, "a good deal of the intellectual, the religious heart of the middle classes, the ministers of most of the Free Churches, and the great mass of the intelligent lower classes" were with the Union.[17]

15. Union and Emancipation Society membership list; *News* (Bacup and Rossendale), 25, 30 May 1863; for "A Working Man's" view see ibid., 13 February 1864; *Pilot* (Rochdale), 16 January 16, 1864; James Ogden, "Fifty Years of Bacup Life," *Times* (Bacup) 1902 and "Rossendale Anthology, 1967," both provided by the Rossendale Public Library.

16. D. G. Wright, "Politics and Opinion in Nineteenth-Century Bradford, 1832–1880" (Ph.D. diss., University of Leeds, 1966), 512–13.

17. Maury to "Dear Frank," London, 21 January 1863, Matthew Maury Papers, Library of Congress, Washington, D.C.; Smith to Charles E. Norton, Oxford, 7 November 1862, Goldwin Smith Papers, Cornell University, Ithaca, N.Y.

Others disagreed with such a social and political assessment. A member of the Leicester branch of the Southern Independence Association dismissed as unfounded the view that its membership was a "Tory dodge." Members, he insisted, reflected all shades of "political and religious opinion—Tory, Whig, Radical, High Church, Low Church [and] Dissent." Francis Drake, a Leicester architect and surveyor, in giving his reasons for joining the local chapter of the London Emancipation Society, said he was motivated by the "[c]onservative principle of opposition to revolutionists and more particularly on the grander principle of opposition against the perpetuation and extension of slavery."[18]

While a study of the membership lists of Union and Confederate associations may do little to disentangle the mystery of why someone chose to join a society, it can provide a valuable, if impressionistic, social and political profile of the membership. There are problems, of course, with using lists for such a purpose. Membership rosters are notoriously inadequate predictors of involvement in a cause. Of the ten members of Bury's chapter of the Southern Independence Association (SIA), only Thomas Wrigley, who inherited his father's papermaking factory and who dabbled in banking, insurance, and railway construction, was ever publicly active. The same is true of Sheffield and Glasgow. John H. Eastcourt, one of the leaders of the Union and Emancipation Society (UES), recalled at the end of the war that most of the work fell to him and four others. Like subscription lists, membership rosters are, in J. R. Oldfield's words, "a form of self-advertisement." They may reveal more about how and by whom the list was compiled than about the extent of the signatory's commitment to the cause. In addition, numbers and names disclose little about the energy of individual members. As Brian Harrison points out, Unitarian ministers, who represented only a minuscule percentage of abstainers in the 1830s and 1840s, were "more important than their numbers suggest."[19] The lists also cannot assess the influence of individuals such as Union supporters David Thomas in Bury, Handel Cossham in Bristol, Samuel Goddard in Birmingham, and J. W. Burns in Sheffield; or for that matter, advocates of the South such as the Reverend E. A. Verity in Habergham Eaves near Burnley. And they cannot measure the influence of men and women who

18. *Chronicle* (Leicester), 4 June 1864; *Leicestershire Mercury*, 19 December 1863.

19. Sarah Agnes Wallace and Frances Elma Gillespie, eds., *The Journal of Benjamin Moran, 1857–1865*, 2: 1382; J. R. Oldfield, *Popular Politics and British Antislavery: The Mobilisation of Public Opinion against the Slave Trade* (Manchester, England, 1995), 45; Harrison, *Drink and the Victorians*, 180.

were nonmembers, particularly those of the working class, for whom annual membership dues were usually too prohibitive.

Because organizations' membership rosters tend to underrepresent the extent and range of working-class and women's involvement, it is therefore necessary to include in any study the names of those supporters who did not subscribe to any society but who made their views publicly known. Biographical detail has been gathered on 337 such supporters of the Confederacy and 530 advocates of the Union. An analysis of the composite lists provides an opportunity to assess the national and regional reach of the societies.

Beginning in late 1862 both sides of the public debate moved quickly to form national and regional societies. Three of them came to dominate the public dialogue during the war years: the London Emancipation Society (LES) and the UES on the side of the Union, and the SIA for the Confederacy. Prior to the outbreak of war, support for emancipation had centered on the British and Foreign Anti Slavery Society (BFASS), founded in 1839, and the much smaller London Emancipation Committee, formed in 1859. Time had taken its toll, however, on both the membership and activities of the BFASS. By 1861 the society had narrowed its sights and major activities to the abolition of the slave trade to Cuba. Although a brief flurry of activity around the John Anderson trial in 1859 showed that the society could act decisively, especially some of its local auxiliaries, little was heard from its leaders following the outbreak of the American Civil War. Ever since the demise of the Anti Slavery League in the late 1840s, British supporters of the Garrisonian wing of the American antislavery movement had toyed with the idea of forming a new national society. In May 1859 a number of them, including George Thompson, William Farmer, and black Americans William and Ellen Craft and Sarah Parker Remond, got together at the home of F. W. Chesson, Thompson's son-in-law, to form the London Emancipation Committee. The name was changed to the London Emancipation Society in November 1862. Within a few months female supporters of the organization formed the Ladies' London Emancipation Society (LLES).

Six weeks after the formation of the LES, a massive meeting at the Manchester Free Trade Hall, attended by more than three thousand people, agreed to the formation of the UES.[20] Both societies aimed to counter orga-

---

20. Chesson's diary, 1 June 1858 to 22 July 1859, English Deposit; *Morning Star*, 14 November 1862; *Inquirer*, 2 September 1865; Brougham Villiers and W. H. Chesson, *Anglo-American Relations, 1861–1865* (1919; reprint, Port Washington, N.Y., 1972), 182–83; Midgley, *Women against Slavery*, 174, 180.

nized pro-Confederate activity in London. They focused much of their attention on the Confederate States Aid Association, formed in London in August
1862, as well as on the Liverpool Southern Club, the brainchild of James
Spence. By mid-1863 the Liverpool club had given rise to a number of similar
organizations in many parts of Lancashire. The activities of these clubs were
reinforced by the work of the Central Association for Recognition of the
Confederacy, formed sometime early in 1863 and centered in Manchester.
The Central Association and the clubs united in October 1863 to form the
SIA, with headquarters in Manchester.[21] The pro-Confederate cause spawned
a number of other organizations, the most important of which was the Society
for Promoting the Cessation of Hostilities in America, formed in the fall of
1863.

Unfortunately, only three societies' membership lists have survived, those
of the UES, the SIA, and, in a more truncated form, the LES.[22] While the lists
present glimpses of the memberships at different stages, they were all published within nine months of each another. In December 1862 the LES's
"General Committee" membership stood at 204; in August 1863, the UES reported a general membership of 1,403; and a few months later the SIA listed
661 members. The Ladies' London Emancipation Society claimed a membership of about 200. The lists of the UES and SIA include names from most
areas of the country, while with a few notable exceptions, the LES drew most
of its support from London and the Home Counties. But even if the UES
could rightly claim widespread support, excepting Ireland, its greatest strength
lay in Lancashire, Cheshire, and Derby. Forty-three of its fifty chapters were
located in these three counties. The SIA displayed a similar pattern, with a
few marked and still unexplained exceptions. Three hundred thirteen of its
members lived in Lancashire, with Greater Manchester, not surprisingly, dom-
inating the membership with 163; Cheshire recorded 39; and Yorkshire 70. At
the end of 1863 all but seven of its thirty-three chapters were in Lancashire
and Cheshire. There were 23, 20, and 15 members respectively from Suffolk,
Lincolnshire, and Essex, largely agricultural counties. Seventy-eight members,
nearly 12 percent of the total number, came from Ireland, a reflection of the
determined effort on the part of Southern supporters to stem the flow of Irish

21. *Examiner and Times* (Manchester), 6 October 1863; *Guardian* (Manchester), 6 October
1863; *Times* (London), 7 October 1863; *Index*, 31 December 1863.

22. For the UES list see *Examiner and Times* (Manchester), 18 August 1863; the LES, *Times*
(London), 29 December 1863; and the SIA, "Southern Independence Association," Anti
Slavery Pamphlets, John Rylands Library, Manchester.

emigrants to the North. Seventy-four members of the SIA came from Scotland, and not surprisingly, given the centrality of the city to the Southern trade and blockade running, nearly half of them gave Glasgow as their address. What is surprising are the pockets of support in areas with no traditional trading or other contacts with the United States. More that half of the Scottish membership was drawn from Aberdeen and Peterhead, port cities surely, but neither with any known connections to the South.

The *Morning Star's* claim in 1862 that the Confederacy drew most of its sympathizers from the southern counties of England may confirm the SIA's strength in these predominantly rural counties.[23] While it is impossible to determine with any precision the number of supporters from small farming towns and rural areas—strongholds of the gentry, Tories, and the Church of England—significant numbers were, like the Reverend John Sneyd of Ashford Park, Cheddleton, near Leek, Staffordshire, substantial landholders. The first 43 names on the SIA's list can be identified as either marquises, viscounts, lords, or knights. Seventeen others, like Sneyd, were living in a "Castle" or "Manor Park." Ireland excepted, about 210 members came from rural or small-town Britain, and even many of those who claimed to be residents of cities had their homes outside city limits. In all, about 300, almost one-half of the SIA's members, lived in small towns and rural areas, in stark contrast to the UES, which drew most of its members from urban areas. When the pressures of his commission became too burdensome, James Mason retreated to Bedgebury Park in Kent, the country home of Alexander James Beresford-Hope, a man of considerable fortune and the principal financial backer of Confederate activity in Britain. Beresford-Hope's and Alexander Collie's London homes were the political and social centers of Confederate activities in the city. There plans were laid for the establishment of the London branch of the SIA in late 1863, and it is there that lavish dinners and social events were held.[24]

The editors of the *Morning Star* may have been wide of the mark in their assessment of the sources of Confederate support, but place was obviously important: the Confederacy drew much of its support from small towns and rural

23. *Morning Star*, 4 February 1862.

24. Morgan Jr., *The Jackson-Hope and the Society of the Cincinnati*, 18–23. In June 1863 Spence sent his friend Charles Prioleau the menu, written in French, of a lavish dinner held at Beresford-Hope's London home that was attended by fifty-two people, including Maury and Lord Elcho. Spence to Prioleau, London, 26 June 1863, Fraser Trenholme Collection, Merseyside Maritime Museum, Liverpool.

areas, while the Union was strongest in larger towns and cities. Although the implication of the *Morning Star*'s observation was that class mattered, membership cannot be explained solely in those terms. Over half of the SIA's members came from cities and large towns, and it is impossible to determine with any precision their class affiliation. There are, however, some indicators. Membership, it could be said with little exaggeration, was a family affair. Washington Wilkes, a Radical, and his brother John, a Congregationalist minister, were leading lights in the LES. So, too, were William Shaen, a London lawyer, and his cousin Henry Solly, founder of the Working Men's Club and Institute Union. Cousins Beresford-Hope and Lord Robert Cecil and the brothers J. Fernandez and J. Howard Clarke, both doctors, were prominent in the SIA. Three of Abel Heywood's children joined him as members of the UES. Thomas W., George, and Thomas Mellor, leaders of Ashton's Tories, threw their support to the Confederacy. Of the UES's 91 members in Mossley, 42 came from fifteen different families. Robert Hyde Buckley, a major cotton manufacturer and president of the local chapter, was joined by five members of his family. This web of family connections remained significant across towns. The Birleys, major cotton manufacturers in Manchester and Preston, were prominent figures in the SIA. But the war also bred divisions among families, as it did in the case of the Whiteheads of Rawtenstall. James Nield Sr. and James Nield Jr. of Mossley parted company over the war. The older Nield, a spinner "connected with the trade almost all his life," was secretary of the SIA; his son threw his lot in with the Union. Jesse Collings, a hardware merchant, spent the first two years of the war in Exeter, where he took up the cause of the Union in frequent letters to the local press. He continued these activities when he moved to Birmingham in 1863. His brother Henry left his position as captain of an American schooner to join the Confederate navy at the outbreak of hostilities. He was a member of the crew of the Merrimac before leaving to join the army. Henry was later taken prisoner at the fall of Richmond.[25]

If, as these examples suggest, class and family were important, but not absolute, predictors of where one stood on the war, other measurements help to bring the picture into sharper focus. Given the impact of the war on some sec-

25. *Chronicle* (Oldham), 11 July 1863; Foster, *Class Struggle and the Industrial Revolution*, 157; Jesse Collings and John L. Green, *Life of the Right Hon. Jesse Collings* (London, 1920), 84; Corke, "Birmingham and the American Civil War," 50; H. F. Hooper, "Mid-Victorian Radicalism: Community and Class in Birmingham, 1850–1880" (Ph.D. diss., University of London, 1979), 527.

tors of the British economy, especially those dependent upon cotton, it is not surprising that textile manufacturers played an important role in the public debate and in financing the efforts of the societies. Most were to be found in the ranks of the Confederacy. Of the 83 Southern supporters who can be identified as substantial manufacturers and businessmen, 49 were involved in cotton manufacturing. In Preston, for example, five of the town's leading millowners, among them William Birley, supported the South. The same is generally true of Stockport, where the Confederacy drew additional support from two ironmongers. In the Potteries, where the impact of the cotton shortage was minimal, 4 of the 6 members of the SIA were silk manufacturers from Leek. But support for the Confederacy did not come exclusively from cotton manufacturers and businessmen. In some cities, as in the case of Sheffield, other important players in the local economy backed the South. The town's economy rested on the production of steel, cutlery, tools, and machinery, with some work in gold and silver. The cutlery trade, which relied heavily on exports to the United States, was severely affected by the outbreak of war and did not recover until sometime in 1863 with the expansion of alternative markets in Europe. It was in an attempt to address this problem that W. C. Corsan made his futile visit to the South in late 1862. One local newspaper was adamant about the source of the trouble: America, the cutlery manufacturers' biggest customer, had destroyed the trade by "legislation and war."[26]

Although the Union relied less heavily on support from cotton manufacturers, surprising numbers (twenty-seven of sixty-two substantial manufacturers and businessmen) of those who backed the North were major figures in cotton, among them Thomas Thomasson, a Quaker manufacturer who owned many mills in Bolton, and Eccles Shorrocks, a Darwen millowner. This division among millowners seems to turn almost exclusively on politics: those, like Thomasson, with a tradition of support for political reform, especially the extension of the franchise to working men, were more likely to support the Union. The same is true of Handel Cossham, a wealthy Bristol coal-mine owner and "ardent Radical" who in his youth supported the Chartists. One of Cossham's most treasured possessions was a staff made from a rafter of one of John Brown's cottages, given to him by a group of women from New York.[27] A slightly larger number of merchants of one kind or another supported the

26. *Independent* (Sheffield and Rotherham), 5 December 1861.

27. Z. Eastman to Seward, Bristol, 13 September 1862, U.S. Department of State, Great Britain, Despatches from U.S. Consuls in Bristol, 1792–1906; *Post* (Bristol), 30 May 1864; *Gazette* (Bristol), 23 April 1866.

Union rather than the Confederacy. There were next to none in the Confederate camp to compare to the Manchunian Max Kyllman, a German immigrant who financed a cotton mill run on cooperative lines and at whose home plans were laid for the formation of the UES. John Patterson, a corn merchant, played a similar role in Liverpool. Finally, the evidence suggests that the Union drew support from a wider cross section of businessmen and manufacturers than did the Confederacy.

A larger number of professionals, described by one contemporary as forming "the head of the great English middle class," supported the Confederacy rather than the Union.[28] Included in this category are lawyers, solicitors, doctors, engineers, professors and teachers, geologists, architects, dentists, and journalists. The clergy are considered separately later in this chapter. Of the SIA's 88 London members, 15 were doctors or surgeons, 8 lawyers or solicitors, and 8 were either geologists, geographers, engineers, or zoologists. If one added to this group the 10 who were current or retired military officers, then almost one-half the London membership was professional.[29] Of those who can be identified, there were an additional 41 professionals from other parts of the country, among them 19 lawyers and solicitors, 6 doctors, 5 journalists, 1 accountant, 1 architect, 1 dentist, 7 professors and teachers, and 2 engineers. Of Sheffield's 17 members, 5 were doctors, and 1 was a mining engineer. Twenty-four professionals have been identified as members of the UES and LES. Of the 111 London members of both societies, there was 1 doctor, 4 who were either lawyers or solicitors, and 3 university professors, including F. W. Newman of University College, London. In the rest of the country there were 2 dentists in Preston, 3 lawyers or solicitors, 1 doctor, and 2 university professors, to whom could be added J. A. Langford, the historian of Birmingham. In addition, there were 2 accountants, including Duncan M'Laren of Edinburgh,

28. Quoted in W. J. Reader, *Professional Men: The Rise of the Professional Classes in Nineteenth-Century England* (New York, 1966), 1. The occupational breakdown relies heavily on those employed by Gareth Stedman Jones in *Outcast London: A Study in the Relationship between Classes in Victorian Society* (London, 1971), 350–57.

29. It is not always possible to differentiate between those who were active or retired members of the regular military and those who were officers in the Volunteers. The Volunteers were created in 1859 to defend the country against possible invasion from France. Four Manchester members of the SIA were founding officers of Volunteer battalions. Thirty-seven "military" men were members of the SIA; none joined the UES or LES. Simon Gunn has argued that while the Volunteers attracted support from moderate Liberals and a few Nonconformists, it was a movement, especially in the cotton towns, "identifiable with Toryism. . . ." Gunn, "The Manchester Middle Class, 1850–1880," 325.

John Bright's brother-in-law; 1 schoolteacher; and 1 artist, William Ibbitt of Sheffield.

During his tour of America, Goldwin Smith was frequently asked why Bishop Wilberforce, son of William Wilberforce, the British emancipator, opposed the Union. "You express surprise that the son of Wilberforce is not with you," Smith responded, "but Wilberforce was not, like his son, a bishop of the State Church."[30] Smith's analysis may have come as something of a surprise to most in his audience, for historically Anglican ministers had played a significant role in the antislavery movement. Even in the late 1850s, Anglican clergymen had lent support to the effort to have the fugitive slave Anderson freed from a Canadian jail where he was being held for possible extradition back to the United States. As late as 1861 it was not unknown for Anglican ministers to attend and sometimes chair the meetings of visiting African Americans, such as William Howard Day.[31] By and large, however, the Anglican clergy abandoned this tradition during the war. Of forty-four clergymen identified as supporting the Confederacy, thirty-nine were ministers of the Church of England, two were Unitarians, one Congregationalist, one Methodist New Connexion, and one Swedenborgian. The most active Anglican supporter of the South was Francis William Tremlett, vicar of Saint Peter's, Belsize Park, London, and secretary and mainstay of the Society for Promoting Cessation of Hostilities in America. His vicarage, known fondly as the "Rebels' Roost," was home to many Southern visitors to London. Tremlett was born in Saint John's, Newfoundland, in 1821. An avid seaman, he lived briefly in the United States in 1851. Two years later he moved to England and in 1860 took up his appointment at Saint Peter's.[32] Tremlett has left no record of the reasons for his support of the Confederacy, nor is there anything in his background that would explain his hostility to the Union. He divided much of his time after the war ministering to his parishioners, raising money for the establishment of colleges in the South, and taking long excursions on his boats. William Heffill of Dukenfield, Lancashire, was a different kettle of fish. An eccentric who took to wearing clogs, Heffill throughout the 1850s had been

---

30. Smith, *England and America*, 26.

31. See Oldfield, *Popular Politics*, 129, for a discussion of the role of Anglican ministers in the movement against the slave trade. See the petitions to the duke of Newcastle, secretary of state for the colonies, calling for the release of Anderson in the Newcastle Collection. In November 1861, the Reverend S. H. Waddington, vicar of Saint Michael's, Coventry, chaired one of Day's lectures. *Herald and Observer* (Coventry), 22 November 1861.

32. "Francis William Tremlett (1821–1913) Doctor of Divinity," typescript, Archives, University of the South.

working with the Reverend J. R. Stephens and others to create the "church of the people" as a counterweight to the Liberal establishment.[33]

The Reverend Edward R. Verity had a similar pedigree to Tremlett's. The son of a doctor, Verity, born in Wales in 1822, was the only one of seven sons not to follow his father's profession. He chose instead the church and from 1845 had been incumbent at Habergham Eaves, just outside Burnley. Like Heffill, a staunch Tory, Verity had been involved in trade union activity, becoming spokesman for East Lancashire weavers during the 1859 strike.[34] If Heffill, and Verity are fairly representative of Anglican ministers, then it appears that support for the Confederacy was driven to a significant degree by domestic political considerations; i.e. by passionate dislike of Liberal politics and the free trade economic policies associated with the Manchester school, of which John Bright and Richard Cobden were the most active proponents. For example, whatever John Bright proposed, Verity opposed, and Bright was the Union's staunchest advocate. Verity never tired of vilifying the extortionist policies of those mill owners who operated on the assumption that a totally free market benefited workers. Such policies, he insisted, made wage slaves of white workers, who had no alternative but to form trade unions to protect their interests. In the midst of the Cotton Famine, Verity formed the Padiham Operative Relief Committee so that area workers would not have to rely on relief committees dominated by mill owners, whose policies he likened to those of the Inquisition. There was little to differentiate between the experiences of the factory worker and plantation slave. Both systems created the "same dependence . . . the same cruelties, sufferings, envies, jealousies and quarrels, the same amount of crime and dissipation, ignorance and superstition, the same appeal to the fears and failings of the human heart." But these common experiences did not lead Verity to propose similar prescriptions for change. The slaves were not in a position to benefit from forms of collective activity such as trade unions. True to his political views, he proposed a twelve-point plan that aimed to elevate the condition of the slave to that enjoyed by "the Saxon 'serf' in olden times—an appendage of the estate."[35]

33. Robert G. Hall, "Work, Class, and Politics in Ashton-under-Lyne, 1830–1860" (Ph.D. diss., Vanderbilt University, 1991), 80; Joyce, *Work, Society, and Politics*, 253–56.

34. T. E. A. Verity, "Edward Arundel Verity, Vicar of Habergham: An Anglican Parson of the Industrial Revolution," *Transactions of the Lancashire and Cheshire Antiquarian Society* 9 (1977): 73, 84–85; Mary Brigg, "Life in East Lancashire, 1856–1860: A Newly Discovered Diary of John O'Neil (John Ward), Weaver, of Clitheroe," *Transactions of the Historic Society of Lancashire and Cheshire* 120 (1968): 127.

35. *Guardian* (Bolton), 11 May 1861; *Bee Hive*, 4 October 1862; *Independent* (Sheffield and Rotherham), 15 May 1862; quotations in Verity, "Edward Arundel Verity," 86–87.

The Union found few supporters among ministers of the Church of England. Of the eighty-nine clergymen identified as supporters of the Union, only eight were Church of England ministers; one, the Reverend William Hey of York, declared his neutrality. One of the six, the Reverend George Pinhorn, curate of Brimfield, Hertfordshire, and Ashford Bowdler, Shropshire, supported the South for a time following the tensions created by the *Trent* affair, but later shifted his support to the North, convinced that the war was largely the result of the growth of the slave power. Philip Hains and J. Jones worked to promote the Union cause in Liverpool before Hains moved to Wigan in 1863.[36] Two others, the Reverends Walter Irvine and W. L. Kay, both members of the Newcastle and Gateshead Anti Slavery Society, supported the cultivation of cotton in Jamaica as the best means of promoting the welfare of the freedmen, but could not bring themselves to support the Union. The war, Irvine insisted, had nothing to do with emancipation; it was a "conflict for political purposes of another character."[37] Of this small group, the most active person was Joseph H. Rylance, curate of Saint Paul's, Southwark, London, and a member of the general committee of the LES. Little is know about Rylance. Henry Solly recalled that he was one of the earliest supporters of the Working Men's Club movement. He traveled to America in mid-1863 carrying an address from British Protestant ministers expressing solidarity with colleagues in America working for emancipation. Rylance chose to settle in America, where he became an Episcopalian minister to churches in Cleveland, Chicago, and New York.[38]

The evidence confirms Jordan and Pratt's observation that, with very few exceptions, Anglican clergymen were "far more sympathetic to the South than the North." Rylance put it best: "*Though* a clergyman of the church of England," he wrote Seward, he had worked to win support for the Union.[39] But if the Anglican clergy favored the Confederacy, the opposite was true of the Dissenting denominations. Fully 335 members of the UES and LES were ministers compared to 100 who endorsed the SIA. Not all of these have been identified, but the figures suggest some general patterns. Ministerial member-

---

36. *Times* (Hartford), 19 September 1863; *Examiner* (Wigan), 3 June, 29 July 1864.

37. *Newcastle Daily Chronicle and Northern Counties Advertiser*, 7 September 1861.

38. Henry Solly, *"These Eighty Years"; or, The Story of an Unfinished Life* (London, 1893), 2: 275–76; *Anti Slavery Reporter*, 1 March 1864; *Bee Hive*, 28 February 1863; *National Anti Slavery Standard*, 12 March 1864.

39. Jordon and Pratt, *Europe and the American Civil War*, 132; Rylance to Seward, Washington, D.C., 25 July 1863, William Seward Papers, University of Rochester, Rochester, N.Y.

ship of the pro-Union organizations was strongest outside of major urban areas. There were, for instance, very few members in urban Lancashire. No members were recorded for Ashton, Stalybridge, Mossley, or Oldham. Only Bury showed a strong presence, where 6 of 18 members were ministers. Of the 89 pro-Union ministers identified, 19 were Congregationalists, 17 Baptists, 11 Methodists of one kind or another, 17 Independents, 6 Presbyterians, 7 Unitarians, and 4 Scottish Free Church. Congregationalists were particularly active in London, where they were largely responsible for the establishment of the short-lived abolitionist Committee on Correspondence with America on Slavery. Dissenting ministers also played pivotal roles in provincial commit-tees. Nine of the 10 members of the UES from Shropshire were clergymen, and in Wales, where Dissenting denominations were strong, 39 of 48 members were ministers of these chapels. In fact, many of the most important members of the LES and UES were clergymen: Baptist Noel and Newman Hall in London, Robert William Dale in Birmingham, Hugh Stowell Brown in Liverpool, J. H. Rutherford in Newcastle, Thomas Guthrie in Edinburgh, Henry William Crosskey in Glasgow, and F. W. Macdonald in Burslem. Even in cities where prominent clergymen such as George Gilfillan of Dundee, a man of impeccable abolitionist credentials, refused to join the UES on the grounds that it sought a political rather that a humanitarian resolution to the crisis, the Union won considerable support from Dissenting ministers. Gifillan's evident dislike of what he considered America's craven love of ma-terialism was never strong enough for him to abandon his abolitionist past. He gave the Union critical support, as did his wife, Margaret, who was president of the Dundee Ladies Anti Slavery Society.[40]

Of all the Dissenting groups the Quakers remained largely aloof from the public debate, surprisingly so given their long traditions in the antislavery movement. For many, the issue of peace took precedence over abolition. It was not that they had abandoned the struggle for abolition, but war, they be-lieved, was no way to effect emancipation, especially in this case when war was being fought exclusively for reunification. It was over this issue that the leadership of the British and Foreign Anti Slavery Society (BFASS) kept its distance from public discussions about the war. Even after Lincoln issued the Emancipation Proclamation, considered by most to be a recognition of the antislavery nature of the war, the BFASS declined to become involved.

40. Carrie, "Dundee and the American Civil War, 1861–1865," 6; Rice, *The Scots Abo-litionists, 1833–1861*, 137; *Advertiser* (Dundee), 25 April 1863; *Tenth Annual Report of the Dundee Ladies' Anti-Slavery Association* (Dundee, 1862), 4–7.

The same was true of Wilson Armistead, a Quaker mustard manufacturer and the mainstay of antislavery activity in Leeds. He rejected the preliminary proclamation of emancipation as an expediency, a "hostile movement against the insurgents . . . [not a] thorough declaration against slavery."[41]

In comparison to those who supported the North, the number of Dissenting ministers who backed the Confederacy was minuscule. Of these, the two most significant (and to some extent the most surprising) were the Unitarian ministers W. Croke Squire of Preston and John Page Hopps, who was minister at Sheffield until 1863 and then at Dukenfield. A Garrisonian abolitionist, Squire's decision to sever ties with the Preston Anti Slavery Society took his colleagues by complete surprise, for there had been no warning. One of the more active local associations, the society had kept abreast of developments in America through regular lecture visits by George Thompson. Squire took an active part in all the society's activities. Then suddenly in February 1863 he announced that he could no longer continue his support. He had become increasingly disillusioned with Lincoln's preliminary emancipation order and the levels of unemployment among cotton workers caused by the disruption in the supply of cotton from America. War, he insisted, violated his peace principles. No minister worth his salt could countenance the Union's war aims. Personally, he could not support American abolitionists who had "suddenly, as a war measure, set free 3,000,000 blacks, to perish from hunger, or to engage in the cruelties of a servile war. With thousands of my fellow-countrymen starving around me, or supported by public charity, I cannot sanction sending money or showing sympathy for either party in America." It mattered little who started the war, he said, it should be ended. Within three months, however, Squire had thrown his lot in with the Confederacy, which he now believed was fighting for its independence against superior forces bent on domination. Within a year, Squire was acknowledged as the major figure among pro-Confederates in the city.[42]

Only twenty-nine when the war broke out, John Page Hopps, like Squire, had been active in a number of Radical causes including those of Italian and Polish independence. Hopps had trained for the Baptist ministry at Baptist College, Leicester, but within two years of his ordination he converted to Unitarianism. Again like Squire, his public declaration of support for the Confederacy came in the wake of a lecture in Sheffield by George Thompson

41. Irene Goodyear, "Wilson Armistead and the Leeds Antislavery Movement," *Thoresby Society Publications* 54 (1974): 113–14; *Mercury* (Leeds), 15 October 1862.

42. *Chronicle* (Preston), 21 February, 11 and 25 April, 9 May 1863; *Index*, 6 June 1864.

in late 1862. To continue a "hideous and unnatural war for the restoration of what cannot be restored is madness," Hopps said, "if it is not desperate wickedness." The war, he admitted, was being fought over slavery; but the North was not fighting for abolition, nor did it care very much for the slave. With the North caring little for the slave and the South wanting to maintain the system, "nature" had brought home to the United States "the knowledge of its sin and turned its arms against the very thing it had been a *sharer* in." It was clear to Hopps that the South had to leave the Union. In the absence of the Southern states, the North would be "purified and free"; and freed from this incubus, it would be able to develop all "those liberal tendencies which only need to be purified to make them the wonder and admiration of the world."[43] Hopps differed from many Confederate supporters in his acknowledgment that slavery was at the center of the war, but his notion that the war offered the North an opportunity to free itself and gain salvation through separation was standard fare for many who saw emancipation being effected through separation.

When ministers are added to the list of other middle-class professionals, the number of Union supporters from the latter group is significantly higher. By and large, the war confirmed that the traditions of abolitionism endured among Dissenting ministers. Even some supporters of the Confederacy, such as Squire and Hopps, believed that with independence would come emancipation. When disaggregated, however, the "old professions" of law and medicine were more inclined to throw their support to the Confederacy. The picture is complicated by the fact that Radicals and Liberals such as Hopps and Squire were also involved in a wide range of other social and political movements. Squire was a peace advocate and a supporter of Solly's Working Men's Club. Hopps supported Italian and Polish independence and the cooperative movement, and he would become an active member of the Jamaica Committee, formed in the wake of the Morant Bay rebellion in Jamaica in October 1865. Late in life someone who had known Hopps at the time of the war described him as a staunch if not a servile Radical.[44] Hopps may have been his own man, as this fond recollection suggests, but his activities during the war cut across the grain of his other political activities. In this he was not

43. See name index, Leicestershire Record Office; Stange, *British Unitarians against American Slavery*, 199; *Independent* (Sheffield and Rotherham), 31 December 1862; *Inquirer*, 3 January 1863. See John Page Hopps, *Southern Independence: A Lecture* (London, 1865), where his arguments are developed further.

44. *Wyvern*, 1 (January 8, 1892), Leicester Record Office.

alone. John M'Adam, a Glasgow Radical, broke from colleagues in the reform movement and those who supported independence for Poland, Italy, and Hungary over the issue of the Civil War. He recalled his time in Mississippi when he had proposed a gradual emancipation scheme and settlement of the freedmen in Mexico as the best means of ending slavery and ensuring the elimination of social inequalities. His fond memories of the South and knowledge of the mistreatment of blacks in the North convinced him that those committed to emancipation in Britain should support the Confederacy. Years later he would come to question his pessimism. "I had no idea that the Negroes would settle down as they have among the whites under such adverse circumstances, and in this to some extent I was wrong, and differed with many of my most esteemed compatriots in other movements in this country. I am not sorry now that I was mistaken, and that the Negro himself will solve the difficulty, though at such a cost of blood and suffering to both North and South."[45]

In spite of their differences over the war, however, M'Adam continued to work with colleagues such as the Reverend Henry William Crosskey, a Glasgow Unitarian, and James Moir, an old Chartist, for parliamentary reform and with Radicals Joseph Cowen and W. E. Adams of Newcastle and others on continental issues. But splits of this sort were the exception. For the most part, leaders of parliamentary reform and supporters of European revolutions held together on the Civil War. Similarly, few opposed to further extensions of the franchise were to be found in the Union camp. The "Muswell Hill Brigade" typified those Radicals who endorsed the Union. The group was named after the area of north London where brewery owner and M.P. James Stanfield lived. There a small group of family and friends met to discuss political developments on the continent and at home. Included were William Shaen; Peter Taylor, M.P. and wealthy heir to a silk manufacturer; and John Humffreys Perry, a barrister and former moral-force Chartist. Giuseppe Mazzini, the Italian republican revolutionary, was a frequent visitor and participant in the discussions. All were members of the LES, and many female members of the brigade, as well as those who were married to its male members, were active in the LLES. Although dominated by Londoners, the LLES was a national society that recruited many of its estimated 200 members from throughout England. Many of its subscribers were from families, or were themselves, long active in the abolitionist cause, including Mary Estlin of Bristol,

45. Janet Fyfe, ed., *Autobiography of John McAdam (1806–1883)* (Edinburgh, 1980), 81–82.

Amelia Chesson, Harriet Lupton of Leeds, and the black Americans Sarah Parker Remond and Ellen Craft. The majority of its executive committee, however, were new to the cause, and all, with the exception of Tory Frances Cobb, were Liberals and members of Dissenting churches.[46]

These men and women, as well as many others involved in radical political activity, became important Union supporters. There were Edward O. Greening and Edward Hooson, leaders of the UES and longtime political allies of Ernest Jones in Manchester; the Kell brothers, S. C. and Robert, of Bradford, who worked closely with George Tatham and John Jowitt of Leeds and Joseph Cowen in Newcastle; and a number of Birmingham reformers, including J. Arthur Partridge, John Oxford, and Allen Dalzell. Disentangling these multiple political and social interests is not always possible. The fame of the eccentric Philip P. Carpenter, brother of Russell Lant Carpenter, the Unitarian divine, rested on his study of mollusks. But he was proud of the fact that he was "antitobacco, antiwine, antifilth, antisectarian, antiwar, and antislavery, but pro mollusca." There were other well-known "antieverythingnarians," including F. W. Newman, who once informed a dinner party: "Oh! I am antislavery, anti-alcohol, anti-tobacco, anti-everything."[47] Those involved in temperance, "the movement *par excellence* of the self-made man," and the cooperative movement, the majority of whose members were of working-class background, were more likely to support the Union.[48] There was also considerable Union support from the ranks of those who worked for peace and women's rights. Of the 60 Union supporters who were active in these various movements, 32 were involved in temperance, 14 in cooperation, 7 in peace, and 3 in women's rights. Not surprisingly, there were a few, such as Robert Heywood, a Bolton cotton manufacturer, who straddled many movements. In comparison, only 12 advocates of the Confederacy can be identified as involved in any of these causes, among them 3 in temperance, 1 in peace, and 1 in cooperation. The others, such as Charles W. Chapman and the Reverend

46. Baylen and Grossman, eds., *Biographical Dictionary of Modern British Radicals*, 2: 402–405, 450–54, 478–82, 497–99. For a discussion of the LLES see Midgley, *Women against Slavery*, 180–81.

47. Carpenter quoted in Stange, *British Unitarians against American Slavery*, 129. For Newman see Harrison, *Drink and the Victorians*, 225. Alfred Ephraim Eccles, a Manchester temperance leader, was a founder of the Anti-Tobacco Society, a member of the Peace Society, and an opponent of dancing. Newspaper cuttings, Manchester Public Library. *The Life and Labours of Alfred Ephraim Eccles of White Coppice, Chorley* (Chorley, 1909).

48. Harrison, *Drink and the Victorians*, 150; Kirk, *The Growth of Working- Class Reformism in Mid–Victorian England*, 142–47.

W. Croke Squire of Preston, were active in the Working Men's Club; and the Reverend John Griffith divided his time in Merthyr Tydvil between temperance and the fight to end prostitution. Proponents of peace were more likely than others to call for neutrality. Few were like Bacup haberdasher William Tagg, who favored separation on the grounds that war simply was indefensible. More were like those leaders of the British and Foreign Anti Slavery Society whose peace principles would not allow them to support either side in the war, even after Lincoln issued the Emancipation Proclamation.

Years after the war, Greening recalled that the UES was "closely allied with the Co-operative Movement, almost all the leading co-operators being on the side of the North and freedom." Seven of the leading figures in the UES, including Abel Heywood, the "father of Manchester Co-operation," were prominent figures in the movement. Having come to political age through his involvement in the public debate over the war, Greening went on to devote much of his life to the cooperative movement.[49] Much the same can be said for advocates of temperance. It was Thomas H. Barker, secretary of the United Kingdom Alliance for the Suppression of the Liquor Traffic, an ally of Frederick Douglass and William Lloyd Garrison during their visit to Britain in 1845, and a member of the executive committee of the UES, who wrote the "Address to Lincoln" adopted by the meeting at the Free Trade Hall, Manchester, at the end of 1862.[50]

A. F. Chuikshank has argued that temperance advocates provided the nucleus of the pro-Union support in Sheffield. Verification of this statement is difficult. At a public meeting addressed by J. A. Roebuck, nailmaker S. Jackson condemned temperance advocates for their support of the Union. Only Ralph Skelton, a shovelmaker, can be identified with the movement. But six of eleven pro-Union meetings between January and July 1863 were held at the Temperance Hall, a fact that would seem to reinforce Cruikshank's claim.[51] Cruikshank's observation, however, does appear to apply to Leeds, where five of the city's proponents of temperance were members of the UES.

49. Crimes, *Edward Owen Greening*, 31; Pickering, *Chartism and the Chartists in Manchester and Salford*, 196–97; Kirk, *The Growth of Working-Class Reformism*, 69.

50. Barker to Garrison, Manchester, 27 August 1864, AASS Papers.

51. A. F. Cruikshank, "J. A. Roebuck, M.P.: A Re-Appraisal of Libertarianism in Sheffield, 1849–1879," *Northern History* 16 (1980): 204; *Independent* (Sheffield and Rotherham), 27 May 1863, 18 May 1877. In his study of Scottish reactions to the war Robert Botsford claims that temperance and pro-Federalism were "intimately linked." Botsford, "Scotland and the American Civil War," 623.

Included were Jabez Tunnicliffe, founder of the Band of Hope, and John Andrew, a local pioneer in teetotalism.[52]

What was true of Radicals in the provinces and Scotland applied equally to London. Many of the leaders of the two major political reform movements in the 1860s, the National Reform League and the National Reform Union, supported the Union. Of fifty-four vice-presidents of the National Reform League, seventeen can be identified as members of the UES and LES. Joseph Bedford Leno, a Chartist printer and poet, was the only member of the league's executive committee who actively supported the Confederacy. From an examination of the major cotton towns, Philip J. Auger has discerned a similar pattern. Of fifty-six vice-presidents of the UES from Lancashire, twenty-nine held similar positions in the Reform Union, and "a further eleven were known reformers."[53]

Toward the end of the century George Howell of the Reform League recalled that "[f]or years one test of a man's Liberalism was—What was he on the American question? If for the South, he was put down as a Tory; if for the North, Radical; if neutral, he was a Whig."[54] The evidence suggests that Howell's recollections were close to the mark. Roydon Harrison has argued that, with some notable exceptions, the veterans of the class struggle, "reared in the hard school of the anti-poor law agitation, the factory reform movement and Chartism," unreconciled as they were to capitalism, favored the Confederacy. On the other hand, the younger generation, generally reconciled to class cooperation in industry and willing to form alliances with middle-class Radicals, were pro-Union. Howell fits well into the latter group. Born in Somerset in 1833, he was converted to abolition after reading Harriet Beecher Stowe's *Uncle Tom's Cabin*. The same can be said of three of the

52. The Reverend H. Marles, *The Life and Labours of the Reverend Jabez Tunnicliffe, Minister of the Gospel at Call Lane Chapel, Leeds, and Founder of the Band of Hope in England* (London, 1865); Boase, ed., *Modern English Biography*, 6: 716; Harrison, *Drink and the Victorians*, 156; Alexander Wilson, *The Chartist Movement in Scotland* (Manchester, England, 1970), 256–58.

53. Kirk, *The Growth of Working-Class Reformism*, 69; Wright, "Politics and Opinion in Nineteenth-Century Bradford," 429, 570–71; D. G. Wright, "Leeds Politics and the American Civil War," *Northern History* 9 (1974): 120. On Tatham see biographical typescript, Leeds Public Library. Hooper, "Mid-Victorian Radicalism," 385–86; Membership list, Reform League MSS, minute book, April 1865 to November 1866, George Howell Collection, Bishopgate Institute, London; Roydon Harrison, "British Labour and the Confederacy," *International Review of Social History* 2 (1957): 82; Auger, "The Cotton Famine, 1861–1865," 333–34.

54. *Reynolds's Newspaper*, 29 November 1896; Leventhal, *Respectable Radical*, 47.

major figures in the UES, John C. Edwards, E. O. Greening, and William E. Adams, who were born within four years of one another—Adams in 1832, Edwards in 1833, and Greening in 1836. A Radical journalist, Adams had been a regular feature writer for Charles Bradlaugh's *National Reformer* before moving to Newcastle to work on Cowen's Newcastle *Chronicle*. At seventeen, Greening became active in the short-lived Manchester Anti-Slavery Union, which raised money to support the activities of the Underground Railroad that helped to spirit slaves to freedom. Both men were significant players in the political reform movement.[55]

But the picture is not always as tidy as Harrison suggests. Of thirty-eight Chartists identified as Union supporters, eighteen were born before 1817. Their birth dates would have made them young men in the initial years of the movement. William Bell (1816–1892), a Heywood Chartist who was imprisoned for six months for his alleged involvement in the Plug Riots, was one of those who was active in trade union activity and in the cooperative movement. The same was true of James Moir (1805–1880), a Glasgow Chartist and later president of the Scottish National Reform League.[56] The picture might alter slightly if one added to the list those trade union leaders and working-class activists not identifiable as Chartists. Those activists include a group of artisans in Birmingham, among whom were John Oxford (carpenter), George Bell (metal operator), Henry Bishop (tin plate operator), and Allen Dalzell (pin and rivet maker). W. R. Cremer (1828–1908) and George Odger (1820–1877), leading figures in the London Trades Council, were also of the younger generation. One of the more intriguing individuals from this group was William Owen (1844–1912), a Burslem pottery labor leader who later played a major role in the labor movement as editor of a number of trade union newspapers. Owen was converted to the cause of emancipation and the Union when, as a nineteen year old, he attended a pro-Confederate meeting in Burslem at which the Reverend John Armstrong, rector of Burslem, spoke in

55. Roydon Harrison, "British Labour and American Slavery," *Science and Society* 25 (December 1961): 307–11; Biagini, *Liberty, Retrenchment, and Reform*, 71; Bellamy and Saville, eds., *Dictionary of Labour Biography*, 1: 111, 136–37; Ashton, *W. E. Adams*, 105; Crimes, *Edward Owen Greening*, 10, 18–19; *Momus*, 24 March 1881; newspaper clippings, Manchester Public Library.

56. Newspaper clippings, Manchester Public Library; *Times* (Bury), 10 December 1892; Pickering, *Chartism and the Chartists in Manchester and Salford*, 189; Wilson, *The Chartist Movement in Scotland*, 103, 161; Irene Elizabeth Sweeney, "The Municipal Administration of Glasgow, 1833–1912: Public Service and the Scottish Civil Identity" (Ph.D. diss., University of Strathclyde, 1990), 939–40.

recognition of the South. Armstrong was opposed by the Wesleyan minister, the Reverend Frederick W. Macdonald, who had been working among the potters, colliers, and navvies in the area. Owen found himself in total agreement with Macdonald.[57]

Some notable Chartist and trade-union figures did support the Confederacy. One, Joseph Bedford Leno, provides no explanation for his opposition to the Union, but other Chartists were not so reticent. Twelve Chartists have been identified as proponents of the Southern cause; two others, Henry Hodgson of Bradford and John Haywood of Birmingham, may also have been Confederate supporters.[58] Of the twelve, at least six were born before 1817, a fact that would seem to confirm Roydon Harrison's observation in one regard: that those among the Chartists who supported the Confederacy were drawn from the generation born before 1817. The most prominent of these men from the older generation were T. J. Dunning of London, William Aitken of Ashton, and the indefatigable Joseph Barker, who seemed to have had no fixed address during the war. Dunning (b. 1799), secretary of the Bookbinders' Society and the "father of London Trade Unionism," did all he could to undermine working-class confidence in the Union. He considered the North vulgar, timid, and apathetic and insisted that the Emancipation Proclamation was aimed more at destroying the South than aiding the Negro. Such political deviousness he located in the character of American (particularly northern) society. The North, he argued, was inhabited by three races, the Anglo-Saxon, Celtic, and Teutonic, and a good bit of the scum of each. In such situations, he believed, republicanism could be politically problematic, producing results no one desired. When coupled with the northern peoples' egotism, conceit, selfishness, and vanity, trouble was inevitable, especially when it clashed with the arrogant pride characteristic of southerners. To this inflammable mix the spark of slavery was added. The South had its faults, but they were nothing when compared to those of the North. Dunning's views seemed to be the result of a deep dislike of American society.[59]

A similar dislike of American economic, social, and political institutions

57. *Staffordshire Advertiser*, 19 October 1912; *Staffordshire Sentinel*, 14 October 1912; Paul Anderton, "The Liberal Party of Stoke-on-Trent and Parliamentary Elections, 1862–1880: A Case Study in Liberal-Labour Relations" (master's thesis, University of Keele, 1974), 252; Denis Stuart, ed., *People of the Potteries: A Dictionary of Local Biography* (Keele, England, 1985), 144–45.

58. *Daily Post* (Birmingham), 28 January 1865.

59. Harrison, "British Labour and American Slavery," 293, 296; Roydon Harrison, *Before the Socialists: Studies in Labour and Politics, 1861–1881* (London, 1965), 44–45; *Bee Hive*, 28 February, 16 May, 13 June, 11 July 1863.

seemed to have informed Aitken's stand on the war. A Chartist who had been involved in the agitation for shorter hours, Aitken, like so many others in the movement, was arrested and imprisoned for nine months in 1839. Three years later he and two other companions fled to the United States following the failure of the strike in which he was actively involved. They landed in New Orleans in November. Aitken spent the next two years in the United States, where he saw the effects of slavery in the South and racial discrimination in the North. He developed a deep admiration for the abolitionists. "Chartists in England and the Repealers in Ireland . . . are far more secure," he wrote in his account of his time in the United States, "than an Abolitionist in the slave-holding states of America." Racial prejudice was so pervasive that he doubted emancipation would come soon. His stay coincided with a deep economic recession that may have affected his views of the country, for although he held out the hope that "the people of America will justify that high opinion which the democratic party in England form of their country," he was deeply pessimistic about the prospects of poor British emigrants. Aitken saw no reason why hard-working folks should leave Britain for wretchedness and misery in the United States: "The condition of the tillers of the soil in the far west is far from being enviable." All of this, as well as the fact that the interest of the country was being sacrificed to what he called the "demon of party spirit," left Aitken deeply ambivalent about the United States. On the one hand, it was a country of enormous potential on which rested the hopes of many. On the other, it seemed incapable of bridging its multiple divisions.[60]

Nothing in the account of his stay, however, would have predicted Aitken's hostility to the Union. The depth of racism in the North may have come as something of a surprise, but he had seen firsthand the workings of the slave system and was aware that, while related, the two were not the same. Part of his antipathy may be explained by the fact that, like so many of his countrymen who visited the United States, Aitken returned from exile in 1844 convinced that, in spite of its many shortcomings, Britain was a superior polity and held out greater hope for the working man. This was reflected in Aitken's growing conviction, following his return, that the best chance of reform in Britain rested in alliances with the middle class. But it proved an uneasy alliance at best. Aitken frequently crossed swords with the Radical

60. *News* (Ashton), 2 October 1869; Robert G. Hall and Stephen Roberts, eds., *William Aitken: The Writings of a Nineteenth-Century Working Man* (Tameside, England, 1996), 7–8; William Aitken, *Journey up the Mississippi River from its Mouth to Nauvoo, the City of the Latter Day Saints* (Ashton-under-Lyne, England, 1845), 6, 14, 16, 30–31.

mill owners who dominated Ashton politics in the years leading up to the war. Many of those owners, whom he sometimes dismissed as a "bastard aristocracy," were supporters of the Union. Aitken was also disturbed by the havoc and dislocation caused by the Cotton Famine. These factors and his conviction that the Federal government was becoming more centralized and tyrannical may have influenced Aitken's decision to work for the Confederacy. He and a small group of working-class figures, including Mortimer Grimshaw, Kinder Smith, and others who were involved in the Lancashire labor strikes of the early 1850s, would become active agents of the Confederacy.[61]

When Aitken committed suicide in 1869, there were those who suggested that the split with political allies over the war left a lasting impression that led to bouts of depression. None of his contemporaries, however, suggested that Aitken's decision to support the Confederacy was the result of instability. The same could not be said for Joseph Barker (1806–1875), who many, at their most generous, considered mercurial. He seemed to flit from one cause to the other with relative ease, but with the most profound conviction that, this time, his decision was justified by the facts. Abolitionists were stunned when he deserted them for the enemy, and the hurt caused by his abandonment produced some of the most vituperative exchanges during the war years. No one questioned Barker's considerable talents. The Reverend J. Guiness Rogers of Ashton remembered him as "a man of considerable intellectual force, great public gifts, and, judging by the effect he produced on large numbers of people, he must have had somewhat of a magnetic personality." W. E. Adams, Barker's colleague on the *National Reformer*, never doubted Barker's "great natural ability," but thought he would have been much more influential had he been "less given to change, less saturated with egotism and pomposity." Dogmatic, Barker was "as cocksure after every turnabout as if he had always crowed from the same dunghill." When criticized for his tendency to change course and causes, Barker was fond of saying he was simply following the rhythms of cellular change. As all biologists knew, the human body replenished its cells every seven years. This meant that the Barker who supported immediate abolition in 1856 was molecularly not the same Barker of 1863![62]

Barker was born into a sternly religious, but desperately poor, weaving fam-

61. Hall and Roberts, eds., *William Aitken*, 10; see also Robert G. Hall, "Chartism Remembered: William Aitken, Liberalism, and the Politics of Memory," *Journal of British Studies* 38 (October 1999): 445–70.

62. J. Guiness Rogers, *An Autobiography* (London, 1903), 90; W. E. Adams, *Memoirs of a Social Atom* (1903; reprint, New York, 1968), 400–01.

ily in Bramley, Yorkshire, in 1806. He became active in the antislavery movement in the 1820s and aligned himself with the radical abolitionists in
America following Garrison's and Douglass's tour of Britain in 1845. Barker
made his first visit to the United States in 1849 and returned there to settle
two years later. Following the passage of the Fugitive Slave Law in 1850,
which increased the ability of slaveholders to reclaim slaves who had escaped,
Barker wrote Garrison that American slavery was "the most revolting piece of
inhumanity" and a prop to European tyranny. After a brief visit to England in
1855, Barker settled in Nebraska. Four years later he was back in England. His
long commitment to abolition appeared to be one of the few stable and pre-
dictable features of a life that by 1861 had shown all the impermanence for
which Barker was famous. Especially after 1863, when Lincoln issued the
Emancipation Proclamation, his should have been the cause of the Union and
emancipation, not the Confederacy and slavery. But like Aitken and the others, Barker's experiences in the United States and the outbreak of war pushed
him to abandon his former allies in the abolitionist movement. Given their
nonviolent traditions, Barker wondered how abolitionists could support war
as a means to emancipation. Although he insisted that slavery should be abolished ultimately, he nonetheless argued that as an institution, it had helped to
raise the African out of savagery. Under these conditions, immediate emancipation would be a disaster. History and logic showed that the abolitionists
were wrong in their belief that "negroes and white people were exactly alike."
By denying the South access to western territories, the North had fired the
first salvo in the war and consequently should be held responsible for the dis-
solution of the union. Finally, Barker insisted that protectionism, exemplified
by the Morrill tariff, was monopolistic and a violation of free-trade principles,
as well as damaging to the interest of the working classes on both sides of the
Atlantic.[63]

Barker joined Aitken and a small group of other labor leaders—including
Mortimer Grimshaw, John Matthews, Thomas Rhodes, Kinder Smith, and
Luke Wood, who were involved in the Ten Percent strikes of the early 1850s—
to win working-class support for the Confederacy. For a while Barker acted as

---

63. I have drawn heavily on the excellent biographical essay on Barker in Fladeland,
Abolitionists and Working-Class Problems in the Age of Industrialization, 132–70. See also Stephen
Roberts, "Joseph Barker and the Radical Cause, 1848–1851," *Miscellany*, Thoresby Society
(1990): 59–73; and Brook, "Confederate Sympathies in North East Lancashire, 1862–1864,"
211–17. Barker makes little or no mention of his activities during the war. See Joseph Barker,
The Life of Joseph Barker (London, 1880).

agent of the Central Association for the Recognition of the Confederacy and kept in regular contact with James Spence, who financed the activities of a group including Aitken, Grimshaw, Matthews, Rhodes, and Smith. Aitken was also agent of the Committee of Employers and Employees, an ephemeral organization formed to win public support for recognition of the Confederacy and for breaking the Union blockade of Southern ports. The war, Barker was fond of saying, cured him of his Garrisonian abolitionism and his democratic republicanism, both of which were infused with the spirit of Robespierre. Some of his working-class allies, especially those like Kinder Smith, an advocate of a Tory–working-class alliance, endorsed Barker's view. Aitken, however, while he might have agreed with Barker about the dangers of Garrisonian abolitionism, even, perhaps, with his rejection of republicanism, continued to put his hope in a Liberal–working-class alliance as the best means for achieving political reform.

While it is impossible to determine with any precision the extent of working-class support for either side in the war, it appears that at the level of leadership there was considerably more backing for the Union. Among those who were identifiably Chartists, age seemed to have mattered little; and here, too, a majority supported the Union. More significantly, as Biagini has suggested, the war united rather than divided "the labour leadership in Britain."[64] A more complete picture emerges if one adds to the mix small traders and shopkeepers, including booksellers, grocers, butchers, and tailors. Although, for instance, none of the 15 Bolton members of the UES fit this category, substantial support for the Union came from a group that included two tea dealers, a tailor, a coal proprietor, and a waste dealer. In comparison, among the 26 members and supporters of the SIA in Bolton there were only a newsagent and an innkeeper. A similar pattern can be seen in Preston, where the Union won support from two grocers, a printer, and a bookseller; the Confederacy could claim support from one tobacconist and a corn dealer. Away from Lancashire the pattern held true. In the west country town of Hereford, for example, pro-Union activity centered around the printer and bookseller Joseph Jones, at whose shop petitions were held and meetings organized.[65]

If support is to be measured by those who declared their position through membership in an organization, by participation in public meetings, by signing petitions, or in letters to newspapers, then some conclusions about the na-

64. Biagini, *Liberty, Retrenchment, and Reform*, 74.
65. *Times* (Hereford), 26 September 1863; *Morning Star*, 10 October 1863.

ture of British reactions to the war can be suggested. Significant support for the Confederacy came from members of the aristocracy, played a major leadership and financial role in the SIA, the Southern Clubs, and other organizations. While a few prominent Dissenting ministers threw their lot to the Confederacy, the majority favored the Union; however, ministers of the Church of England, with a very few exceptions, advocated the cause of Southern independence. The number of other professionals, particularly those in law and medicine, who endorsed the South suggests that in this case they were willing to become more involved in political causes, but why they chose to support the Confederacy may have more to do with domestic political considerations than with the contending merits of the warring factions in America.[66] While it is true that the UES was formed to give voice to working-class views of the war, the overwhelming majority of its members came from other social classes and occupations. Those with working-class roots whose names appear on the UES and LES membership lists were generally artisans, members of other organizations, such as temperance and cooperation, small traders, and shopkeepers. A cursory look at the 1861 census suggests that the UES attracted some support from the working class. In the small Lancashire town of Lees, for instance, 4 of the 11 members of the UES were unskilled workers.[67] Few ex-Chartists' names appear on any of the lists, but their public expressions indicate that, with a few notable exceptions, they supported the North and that their activities during the war may have helped, if only temporarily, to bridge the gap between those who came of age in the heyday of the movement in the 1830s and the younger generation. The same seems to hold true when labor leaders with no known Chartist connections are added to the mix. Whether in London, Glasgow, or the cotton towns of Lancashire, those involved in trade-union activity generally supported the Union. Further attempts to measure the extent of working-class support for one side or the other will be made in a later chapter. Support for the Union rested on old political (especially Liberal) alliances, and these, in turn, were critical to the success of a resurgent movement for political reform in Britain. The same can be said, if to a lesser degree, for the old Tory–working-class alliance. Such al-

66. Davidoff and Hall argue that in the case of Birmingham, Essex, and Suffolk, medical men were found more in the leadership of scientific and cultural societies, while lawyers and solicitors took a greater interest in political and economic organizations. Leonore Davidoff and Catherine Hall, *Family Fortunes: Men and Women of the English Middle Class, 1780–1850* (Chicago, 1987), 261.

67. Census of Population (England), 1861, RG 9, Lees, Lancashire.

liances helped Tories to take control of some town councils at the end of the decade. There were, however, some notable exceptions that complicate the picture. Nothing in his political background should have led the Reverend John Page Hopps into the Confederate camp. Nor, if one were to look exclusively at his support for the South during the war, would one anticipate his later involvement in Radical causes.

William Aitken, a schoolteacher and former Chartist who had spent two years in the United States, became an agent for the Confederacy.

Manchester Public Library

A. J. B. Beresford-Hope, leader of the pro-Confederate forces.

Courtesy of Gordon Batchelor

James Spence, the Confederacy's most prominent supporter.

from Edward F. Spence's *Bar and Buskin: Being Memories of Life, Law, and the Theatre*

John C. Edwards, one of the founders of the Union and Emancipation Society.

Momus, 21 March 1881

The Reverend Edward A. Verity was a pro-
Confederate advocate and Anglican parson.
Lancashire and Chesire Antiquarian Society, 1977

Joseph Barker, pro-Confederate advocate
From Ray Boston, *British Chartists in America,
1839–1900*.

William Andrew Jackson, Jefferson Davis's former coachman.

Harper's Weekly, 7 June 1862

J. Sella Martin, a fugitive slave and minister who spent most of the war years in London, actively campaigned against British support for the Confederacy.

Moorland-Spingarn Research Center, Howard University

Richard Ansdell's 1861 painting *The Hunted Slave* evoked great sympathy for the fate of fugitives. The painting remains on display at the Walker Art Gallery in Liverpool.

Courtesy of the Board of Trustees of the National Museums and Galleries on Merseyside.

This poster of an 1863 pro-Union meeting in Manchester skillfully incorporates a depiction of the lacerated back of escaped slave Gordon.

John Rylands Libarary, Manchester

Bazaars such as this held in Liverpool in October 1864 were important fund-raising tools, especially for supporters of the Confederacy.

Huntington Library

CAUTION to EMIGRANTS

PERSECUTION OF CATHOLICS IN AMERICA.

THE TABERNACLE OVERTHROWN !

The Blessed Host scattered on the ground !

Benediction Veil made a Horse Cover of ! All the Sacred Vessels carried off ! !

The Monuments of the Dead defaced !

The Priest imprisoned, and afterwards exposed on an Island to Aligators & Snakes ! His house robbed of everything !

Those and similar outrages, unparalleled in history, have been committed on Catholics by Massachusetts Soldiers, in the State of Louisiana, and published in the FREEMAN'S JOURNAL, New York. Irish Catholics should weigh well in their minds the position of the once United States of America, before they resolve on making them their future home—the country of their adoption. "Rather than endure the ills they know, they fly to those they know not of."

Let Irishmen remember the Know-Nothing Party that Orangeism gave birth to, the latter now prevailing all over the United States, some years ago, when they entered the Convents and insulted the Nuns at their devotion ! The same party openly and publicly avowing their intention to disfranchise all Foreigners, and wipe out Catholicism.

The right of Habeas Corpus is now suspended—the house of liberty is now the head quarters of military despotism—the great Republic of the West, now no longer exists—life and liberty is at stake.

It is well authenticated that many an Irish Emigrant on landing at the other side of the Atlantic, is set up, cajoled, and enticed away, to swell the ranks of the Federal Army. The moment that an Emigrant Ship reaches the port of America, the unpretending Emigrant, full of warm and friendly feelings to the Country, is persuaded by interested Agents to declare his intention to become a Citizen, (as they term it, a REAL AMERICAN); after his declaration being made, according to the late Act of Congress, he comes under the CONSCRIPTION LAW.

And no alternative is left. He becomes a SOLDIER. In 48 hours he is landed in the Swamps of the Carolinas, or on the Sand Bars of Charleston. Then to imbrue his hands in THE BLOOD OF HIS COUNTRYMEN, and fight for a People that has the greatest antipathy to his birth and creed.

Let Irishmen remember the fate of MEAGHER'S BRIGADE, on the bloody field of Fredericksburg, 5,000 strong ! now no more; and were refused permission to reorganise; some of the New York Papers stating that they could afford to lose a few thousand of the scum of the Irish.

Under these and many other circumstances, too numerous to mention, we would advise those of our Countrymen, who contemplate emigrating, to remain at home, until such times as this UNHOLY AND CRUEL WAR IS AT AN END ! !

Confederate agents distributed handbills such as this to dissuade Irish emigrants from settling in the Northern states. Enclosed in James Capson to Judah Benjamin, 11 November 1863.

Records of the Confederate States of America

Poster for an 1863 pro-Union meeting in Manchester.
Manchester Public Library

ABOLITION OF SLAVERY AND MAINTAINENCE OF
THE AMERICAN UNION.

MEETING IN THE FREE TRADE HALL,

MANCHESTER,

On Wednesday, December 31st, 1862,

TO ADOPT AN ADDRESS TO PRESIDENT LINCOLN.

Doors open at Six. Chair to be taken at Seven o'clock.

𝕻latform.

Ticket to the founding meeting of the Union and Emancipation Society.
Manchester Public Library

4

To Reach The People

English opinion is, after all, the opinion of the world, and we may hope
that, in spite of affected indignation and highflown eloquence, the good
sense which has uniformly marked our consuls in this affair may at length
prevail.

—London *Times*, 12 July 1862

So spoke the editors of the *Times* ex cathedra. Some thought the
feigned dispassion was the result of imperial hubris; others saw it as the product of an abiding arrogance born of the paper's sense of its own importance as
the voice of the country. But whatever contemporaries thought about the
newspaper's opinion, of one thing they were certain: the *Times* had its finger
on the pulse of a politically powerful sector of the society, reflecting and molding that group's views on all the important events of the age. To the editorial
writers at the newspaper, the country's reactions to important events such as
the Civil War were, as Beresford-Hope said in another context, to be molded
by those who mattered politically, and by any measurement the *Times* mattered. Commentaries by contemporaries on both sides of the Atlantic drew

from its editorials, and politicians in Washington and Richmond scanned its editorial pages in an effort to determine British reactions to the war.[1]

British public opinion might not have been the "opinion of the world," but what the country thought and what policies it adopted were of vital importance to the protagonists in the war. And in the political culture of mid-Victorian Britain, it was taken for granted that the way the public viewed a particular event influenced, in very concrete ways, the policies adopted by government. That was true of Catholic emancipation, of the abolition of the African slave trade and the emancipation of West Indian slaves, of the abolition of the Corn Laws, and of political reform. At the height of these movements, the government was pressured, nudged, appealed to, and pleaded with to adopt legislation that would bring about the desired changes. While experience taught that pressure from without did not always sway Parliament, there was ample evidence that, without it, important legislation was impossible. By the outbreak of the war, the mechanisms for molding public opinion had long been established. The movement against West Indian slavery, for instance, had employed a combination of meetings, lectures, pamphlets, newspapers, agents, and petitions in its effort to frame public opinion and pressure Parliament to free the slaves. The agitation around the Civil War drew on this tradition, but it was complicated by the fact that, in this instance, the issues involved matters over which the British government had no direct control. When, for instance, the Confederate government issued letters of marque in the early months of the war and the Federal government blockaded Southern ports, the British government could do nothing but try to protect its country's commercial interests. The British declaration of neutrality in May 1861 also influenced the way the public debate would be conducted. It frustrated Confederate supporters, who found themselves in the position of having to pressure the government to alter a policy that could result in direct involvement in the war, and it worried pro-Unionists, who saw neutrality as a possible first step toward recognition of Southern independence. Concerned though the pro-Unionists were, neutrality handed them the advantage. They simply had to persuade the country to stay the course. Supporters of the Confederacy, however, had to effect a reversal of policy. While governments need the support of pressure groups in the administration of established policy,

1. See Martin Crawford, *The Anglo-American Crisis of the Mid–Nineteenth Century: The* Times *and America, 1850–1862* (Athens, Ga., 1987) for a thorough analysis of the newspaper's views on America and its reactions to the outbreak of hostilities.

rarely do they require such backing to change policy. As a result, as Brian Harrison has argued, those desiring change must "attract attention by conspicuous displays of power."[2]

Before governments can be pressured to act, they have to be convinced that public opinion favors a particular policy. In the first year of the war neither pro-Confederate nor pro-Union groups were certain about where the public stood. In the midst of the *Trent* affair, Louis Blanc, a French exile, thought that while British opinion tended to be moderate, it was yet volatile and as unpredictable as the "scenery of an opera, where a horrible cavern is succeeded, all in a minute, by a smiling landscape." The aristocracy and politicians seemed to be moving toward recognition of the Confederacy, yet public meetings in many parts of the country were calling on the government to submit the conflict to arbitration.[3] Where Blanc discerned subtle class distinctions, another foreign observer, J. Sella Martin, found after four months in London only "mutual misunderstanding," which, he reported, dashed his hopes of winning "English sympathy with the North."[4] John Bright thought the public "languid and confused": the upper and ruling classes anxious to see the establishment of two republics; the middle class, he told Charles Sumner, supportive of emancipation, but angered by "your foolish Tariff." In August 1862 Bright wrote Richard Cobden that the government, the press, and "all our rich and ruling class" had done all within its power to sustain the Confederacy. "There is no other country in Europe in which the Statesmen, Public men and newspapers are so much for the South as in England." American government officials in Britain were equally pessimistic. Charles Francis Adams thought the prime minister was simply biding his time before acting against the Union. Thomas Dudley, consul in Liverpool, and his counterpart in Manchester, Henry Lord, thought opinion in both cities was running in favor of the Confederacy, as did W. L. Underwood, their colleague in Glasgow.[5] If representatives of the Union were generally gloomy, Confederate

2. For a discussion of the advantages of neutrality to pro-Unionists see Jordon and Pratt, *Europe and the American Civil War*, 165; Harrison, *Drink and the Victorians*, 227.

3. Blanc, *Letters on England*, 1: 64–65, 210–11, 252, 284.

4. Martin to J. A. Andrew, London, 13 December 1861, Executive Letters, Vol. 175, Box 42, Massachusetts State Archives, Boston.

5. "Letters of John Bright, 1861–1862," *Proceedings of the Massachusetts Historical Society* 45 (November 1911) and 46 (October 1912): 94–95; Bright to Cobden, Rochdale, 30 August 1862, John Bright Papers, British Library, London; Dudley to Seward, Liverpool, 10 May 1862, Despatches from U.S. Consuls in Liverpool, 1790–1909; Lord to Seward, Manchester, 13 September 1861, Despatches from U.S. Consuls in Manchester, 1790–1906; Underwood to

emissaries, at least in the first few months of the war, were optimistic about the prospects for recognition. William Yancey declared boldly: "Public opinion is for us." But he was merely indulging in wishful thinking. While some of Yancey's associates in and out of government might have led him to believe that recognition was imminent, there is no evidence that opinion outside Parliament favored a reversal of government policy. Public opinion was something that had to be tapped before it could be measured. When Confederate supporters did attempt to rally public support for their cause, they were surprised by the strength and breadth of the opposition they encountered.[6]

In July 1862, as the effects of the shortage of American cotton began to take its toll on textile workers in Lancashire, placards posted throughout Blackburn announced an open-air meeting in the marketplace to discuss ways to alleviate the problem. Scheduled speakers included Mortimer Grimshaw of Blackburn, William Aitken of Ashton, and John Matthews of Heywood. Days before the meeting, another set of placards appeared denouncing the organizers and speakers and raising questions about the meeting's true intent. Rather than proposing ways to alleviate the cotton shortage, organizers of the meeting, opponents insisted, were trying to win support for a parliamentary motion by John Turner Hopwood, M.P. for Clitheroe, calling on the government to recognize the Confederacy. These concerns were reinforced by fliers that were distributed throughout the crowd just as the meeting began. The opposition's suspicions were further confirmed when Grimshaw opened his speech with a resolution that called for recognition as the best way to tackle the problem of rising unemployment. William Crossley, a weaver, countered with an amendment that called on the government to use its influence with leaders of the Confederacy to persuade them that the interest of British commerce and peace would be best served if they rejoined the Union. The amendment was carried. Just before the meeting dispersed, the victors denounced Hopwood, wondering how anyone who opposed the extension of the franchise could ask workingmen to use their influence to pressure the government to intervene diplomatically in the war.

The defeat did not sit well with supporters of recognition. Over the next

to President, Glasgow, 4 December 1862, Despatches from U.S. Consuls in Glasgow, 1790–1906; Thomas Dudley, "Three Critical Periods in Our Diplomatic Relations with England during the Late War," *Pennsylvania Magazine of History and Biography* 17 (1893): 35.

6. James D. Richardson, ed., *A Compilation of the Messages and Papers of the Confederacy including the Diplomatic Correspondence, 1861–1865* (Nashville, 1905), 2: 136.

couple of weeks they laid plans for another meeting, this time determined that only "substantial" citizens, not the "tramping agitators," as one opponent described Grimshaw, Aitken, and Matthews, would speak from the platform. Rather than an open-air meeting conducted by workingmen, the organizers requisitioned the mayor for use of the town hall. Although the audience was made up mainly of workers, they took no active role in the proceedings. A week before the meeting, an opponent had predicted that operatives who worked at the mills owned by the organizers would be excused from work so they could pack the hall. None of those who sat on the platform, a position usually reserved for local nabobs, can be identified with any of the pro-Union organizations. A few, such as R. Rayford Jackson, would join the Southern Independence Association. Placards announcing the meeting stated that it would submit a memorial to the queen, asking her to work with other European powers to bring an end to hostilities. Control of the proceedings did not ensure the desired results. Jackson's call for recognition was opposed by J. C. Fielden, a prominent cotton manufacturer, who insisted that such action would only lead to war. Fielden proposed instead that the government make grants to the unemployed to see them through the difficulty. Fielden's amendment was countered in turn by another that called for arbitration. In the end, the meeting supported the call for arbitration, a far cry from the organizers' original intention.[7]

As the organizers of both meetings discovered, rallying public support was an unpredictable business. The meetings, however, provide useful insights into the mechanisms employed to influence public opinion. Although there were no national or local societies to provide organizational and financial support at this time, Grimshaw, Aitken, and Matthews were acting as agents of those who supported the Confederacy. One or more of them had met with James Spence in Liverpool a few months earlier when the decision was made to target the worst-hit cotton towns, on the assumption that support for Southern independence from the unemployed could not fail to influence the government. Such agents were a vital part of the propaganda machine utilized by both sides in the dispute. So, too, was the stream of petitions, addresses, and memorials sent to the government, the queen, and the Lincoln administration calling for the adoption or support of certain policies. Generally, meetings of this sort generated frequent editorial comments and letters to local and

7. *Chronicle* (Preston), 2 July, 6 August 1862; *Guardian* (Preston), 16 August 1862; *Herald* (Preston), 16 August 1862; *Standard* (Blackburn), 13 August 1862; *Guardian* (Manchester), 9 August 1862; *Times* (Blackburn), 31 January 1863, 8 April 1865.

regional newspapers. The Blackburn meetings, for example, were reported and commented on by newspapers in adjacent towns. John Hopwood, who would later become a member of the Southern Independence Association, might well have calculated that the Blackburn meeting would produce a ground swell of support for the Confederacy among Lancashire workers and pressure the government to act on recognition. If Hopwood did not, Spence surely did, and the pattern of activities that would unfold in subsequent months showed that petitions and memorials were organized to coincide in many instances with parliamentary motions in support of recognition or arbitration. Spence was convinced that the war could not be won without European (preferably British) intervention and that the only power that would move the government to act was public opinion.[8]

Organizing expressions of public support created ticklish problems at the best of times. Whether expressed through petitions or meetings, public reaction to an issue had to be large, extensive, and sustained over time to draw the attention of those in power. It also had to be called on at critical moments as reinforcement for proposed actions in Parliament. As Spence well knew, a large meeting in a major city or a memorial to Parliament that followed close on the heels of a Confederate victory on the battlefield improved the chances that the government would act in favor of the cause he espoused. Large meetings that generated substantial opposition did the cause no good; they had to be controlled and relatively trouble free. That, as will be shown in the next chapter, rarely happened. Petitions were more easily controlled; nevertheless, questions were always raised about the methods by which names were collected. Unfortunately, while the wording of petitions and memorials has survived, the names of those who signed them have not.[9] Thus it is impossible to determine with any exactness what Lee Benson has called the "quantitative *divisions* of opinion among the public . . . the *attributes* and *characteristics* of the individuals who held different positions on the issue."[10] An examination of the methods employed to influence the way the public viewed the causes of the war can, however, provide some insight into the nature and range of these divisions.

8. Spence to Mason, Liverpool, 3 October 1862, 12 December 1863, Mason Papers.

9. J. G. Randall, *Lincoln: The Liberal Statesman* (New York, 1947), mentions seeing the 1863 memorial sent to Lincoln by the inhabitants of Birmingham at the National Archives. The memorial has only recently come to light again.

10. Lee Benson, "An Approach to the Scientific Study of Past Public Opinion," *Public Opinion Quarterly* 31 (Winter 1967–1968): 533.

It is clear, as Spence and others realized, that place mattered, that it was important to tailor one's message to the particular needs and concerns of a community. This realization explains why Grimshaw, Aitken, and Matthews took their message to Blackburn, a town already feeling the impact of the shortage of American cotton in July 1862. If Blackburn did come out in support of recognition, then it was likely other cotton towns would follow. Charles Francis Adams saw the potential danger. He wrote Seward of troubling signs of a "disposition to get up agitation and to give to the discontent of the depressed operatives a political direction." The messengers—Adams called them "insurgent emissaries"—were as important as the message they carried. Grimshaw, Aitken, and Matthews were known to audiences for their long involvement in movements aimed at improving the economic, political, and social conditions of the working class. It is to agents such as these that both sides turned in their effort to fashion public opinion in their favor.[11]

Frank L. Owsley in his work on Confederate diplomacy identified three components to the Confederate propaganda apparatus: official diplomats, agents sent from the South, and a group he labeled "native propagandists." The latter included Spence, Beresford-Hope, and other prominent figures, but not the likes of Grimshaw, Aitken, or Matthews. Owsley, however, was only marginally interested in public reactions to the war. As a result, his categories are much too limiting. They pay too little attention to the leaders and agents of organizations such as the Union and Emancipation Society or the Southern Independence Association, to the influence of prominent local figures such as Aitken and Bright, or for that matter, to the ways newspapers (other than the *Times* and the *Economist*) through their editorials and extensive coverage of meetings framed the debate and provided a forum in which people tested their ideas and engaged opponents in sometimes heated exchanges.[12]

Aware of the need to win international endorsement of their fledgling nation, the Confederacy dispatched a number of official and unofficial agents to Britain soon after the outbreak of hostilities. The government in Washington, on the other hand, was too preoccupied with trying to stem the flow of states

---

11. Spence to Mason, Liverpool, 28 April 1862, Mason Papers; Adams to Seward, London, 3, 7 July 1862, Despatches from U.S. Ministers to Great Britain, 1791–1906; Benson, "An Approach to the Scientific Study of Past Public Opinion," 538–39.

12. Frank Lawrence Owsley, *King Cotton Diplomacy: Foreign Relations of the Confederate States of America* (1939; reprint, Chicago, 1969), 171–72. Cullop, *Confederate Propaganda in Europe*, considers a broader range of agents and activities than does Owsley, as does Jenkins in his wide-ranging study *Britain and the War of the Union*.

to the Confederacy to pay much attention to such matters. Such tardiness put the Union at a decided disadvantage. By fall 1861 many of its consuls were expressing anxiety about the successes of Confederate agents. John Young in Belfast reported that "Southern men have been actively at work here. The press, the mercantile class, and even the clergy have been subjected to their influence more or less." His colleague in Dublin, Henry B. Hammond, saw only evil consequences resulting from the presence of a number of secessionists. J. S. Prettyman wrote from Glasgow that he had been forced to spend a great deal of time and money to counter the activities of Confederate agents who were recruiting local engravers and engineers to go to Richmond.[13]

Who all these agents were or exactly when they arrived is unclear. What is certain is that the Confederacy invested a considerable amount of time and energy toward winning British recognition of its independence in the first few months of the war. Its chance of success increased considerably because both sides followed a course of action based on the premise that slavery had little or nothing to do with the conflict. As Howard Jones has shown in *Union in Peril*, both sides ducked the issue of slavery in this period: the Union was anxious to contain the departure of additional states, particularly those in the upper South; the Confederacy realized that recognition was more likely if the British could be convinced that secession was the result of factors other than the desire to protect the institution of slavery.[14] Try as they might, however, none of the Southern spokesmen could escape the fact that one of the major pillars of the new polity was an institution that most in Britain found abhorrent. Nor could they skirt the issue of slavery and at the same time palliate, if not openly endorse, the right of the new nation to continue the offensive and outdated institution.

The Confederacy's first group of commissioners to Europe left a great deal to be desired. Neither Pierre A. Rost, Dudley Mann, nor William Lowndes Yancey demonstrated much flair for diplomacy. Yancey, the most prominent of the trio, was recognized as one of the finest orators of his time, but he was a dyed-in-the-wool secessionist, a "fire-eater" who had urged the reopening of

13. John Young to Seward, Belfast, 30 October 1861, Despatches from U.S. Consuls in Belfast, 1796–1906; Henry B. Hammond to Seward, Dublin, 29 January 1862, Despatches from U.S. Consuls in Dublin, 1790–1906; J. S. Prettyman to Seward, Glasgow, 10 January 1862, Despatches from U.S. Consuls in Glasgow, 1801–1906. Peter Sinclair confirmed that during a two-month tour of Ireland in 1861, Confederate emissaries were "everywhere." Sinclair to Seward, Edinburgh, 25 July 1862, Seward Papers.

14. Jones, *Union in Peril*, 33.

the slave trade on the rather dubious grounds that the federal government had acted unconstitutionally when it abolished the trade. Owsley's assessment of the three is apt: they were "about the poorest choices possible." The same could be said about those who followed Yancey, Mann, and Rost a few months later. James Mason of Virginia had no experience in the art of diplomacy and, more damaging, was considered the author of the Fugitive Slave Law of 1850. John Slidell, who spent most of his mission in France, demonstrated more tact and finesse, but found his options limited by the need to defend slavery. Edwin DeLeon, a journalist, had some experience in foreign affairs, having served in the United States consulate in Egypt. By far the most effective agent, however, was Henry Hotze, a Swiss-born journalist who within one month of his arrival in London in early 1862 had a propaganda system in place that became the envy of his opponents. The Confederacy sent out a number of other agents, most of whom operated away from public scrutiny buying ships and ammunition for the military and raising loans for the country. The exception was Matthew Maury, a well-known nautical scientist who was sent on a mission to buy ships for the navy, but who also devoted considerable time and resources getting the Confederate message across to the public. Finally, there were numbers of unofficial emissaries who whenever possible used their talent, money, and connections in support of the cause. Among these were Charles S. Morehead, a former governor of Kentucky; Rose O'Neal Greenhow, who for a few months at the beginning of the war had been imprisoned as a Confederate spy; Moses D. Hoge, a prominent Richmond Presbyterian minister; and John Reuben Thompson, editor, literary figure, and associate of Thomas Carlyle, Charles Dickens, and Alfred Lord Tennyson.[15]

15. Owsley, *King Cotton Diplomacy*, 51–52, 162. The *Richmond Examiner* editorial writer Basil L. Gildersleeve dismissed Confederate emissaries as the "dregs and the froth of our society. . . ." See Ward W. Briggs Jr., ed., *Soldier and Scholar: Basil Lanneau Gildersleeve and the Civil War* (Charlottesville, Va., 1998), 172. William Davis describes Yancey as a proslavery loudmouth. Davis, *Jefferson Davis: The Man and His Hour* (New York, 1991), 386. For a biographical essay on Yancey see Eric Walther, *The Fire-Eaters* (Baton Rouge, 1992). Charles S. Davis, *Colin J. McRae: Confederate Financial Agent* (Tuscaloosa, Ala., 1961), 35–37, 49–50; Bulloch, *The Secret Service of the Confederate States in Europe*, 1: 48; *Mercury* (Liverpool), 13 October 1862; Lowell H. Harrison, ed., *Kentucky's Governors, 1792–1985* (Lexington, Ky., 1985), 63–65; James Morris Morgan, *Recollections of a Rebel Reefer* (Boston, 1917), 107–08; Jenkins, *Britain and the War of the Union*, 2: 317; Williams, *Matthew Fontain Maury*; De Leon, *Thirty Years of My Life on Three Continents*; Cullop, *Confederate Propaganda in Europe*, 18–19, 157; Ishbel Ross, *Rebel Rose: Life of Rose O'Neal Greenhow, Confederate Spy* (New York, 1954); Robert Bain, Joseph M. Flora, and Louis D. Rubin Jr., eds., *Southern Writers: A Biographical Dictionary* (Baton Rouge, 1979), 450–51. A more recent study of Confederate diplomacy is Charles M. Hubbard, *The Burden of Confederate Diplomacy* (Knoxville, Tenn., 1998).

None of the first group of Confederate representatives should have caused the American consuls much concern. Yancey met with some British government officials and tried to cultivate support among Conservative politicians, but had little to show for his efforts when he returned home in early 1862. His one public appearance, a meeting at Fishmongers' Hall in London in November, a semiofficial affair at which the mayor of London was present, produced such a torrent of opposition that Yancey decided to keep out of the limelight. J. Sella Martin condemned him as an advocate of slavery, and George Thompson reprinted one of Yancey's earlier letters to J. B. DeBow, the southern journalist, in which Yancey condemned the law abolishing the African slave trade as unconstitutional and the product of the "heat of radicalism spurred by the French revolution."[16] There is no evidence that other Confederate representatives were having any more success than Yancey. In the weeks after the attack on Fort Sumter, DeLeon had written the London *Times*, warning its readers that, by its actions, the Union was raising the watchword of the Jacobins, "*Fraternite, ou la mort.*" Should it not, asked DeLeon, "stir the pulses of free-born Englishmen when a new reign of terror is sought to be inaugurated once more under the desecrated name of liberty, over the smiling fields and happy homes of the sunny South[?]"[17] The comparison may have been too heavy-handed, and there is no evidence that DeLeon's warning had much effect at this stage.

If the American consuls in Dublin, Belfast, and Glasgow are to be believed, it appears that a number of unofficial agents were promoting the cause of secession through private meetings. There is no record of any lectures or meetings that can be identified as part of an effort to win public support for the Confederacy, but supporters of the Union on both sides of the Atlantic were so concerned about the activities of these unofficial agents that they pleaded with Seward to do something about them. The secretary of state thought the work of containing the Confederacy in Europe could be left to the country's consuls, although he did concede that periodic visits by prominent Americans could help to counter "the machinations of the agents of treason against the United States." Archbishop John Hughes, Bishop C. P. McIlvaine, and Thurlow Weed paid brief visits to Britain in late 1861, Weed taking with him funds to be used to promote the cause of the Union. Other missions soon followed. John Murray Forbes and W. H. Aspinwall arrived in Britain in March

16. *Morning Star*, 12 November 1861, 7, 9 January 1862; *Evening Star and Dial*, 27, 31 January 1862; *Liberator*, 28 February 1862.
17. *Times* (London), 25 May 1861.

1863 with enough funds to buy cruisers and ironclads being built for the Confederate navy, thus preventing them from reaching their destination. Other Americans with no official ties to the Federal government also played a part in the public debate over the war. They included George B. Cheever, a Congregationalist minister who was in Britain when the war broke out and who was for a time the lone voice warning against the dangers of recognition of the Confederacy; Moncure D. Conway, who left his prominent Virginia slaveholding family and in 1863 traveled to Britain, never to return; and Henry Ward Beecher, whose brief lecture tour in the fall of 1863 generated considerable interest. There were also lesser-known lights who worked for the cause, including W. D. Haley, a Unitarian minister from Washington, D.C.; Professor C. P. Grosvenor of Central College, New York; and, late in the war, Crammond Kennedy, a chaplain in the army and an agent of the National Freedmen's Aid Association. Finally, there were numbers of Americans permanently living in Britain, such as Samuel Aspinwall Goddard of Birmingham and A. F. Stoddard of Paisley, who were active in the cause of the Union.[18]

The Union could also count on the support of more than forty African Americans who, in one way or another, played an active role in the public debate about the war. It is impossible to determine with any precision exactly how many African Americans were in Britain between 1861 and 1865. The evidence suggests that the number increased during the war, as it had ten years earlier when many black Americans fled to Britain in the wake of the passage of the Fugitive Slave Law. J. Sella Martin was surprised by the large number: "Some are begging money to build churches, buy relations, establish newspapers and build schools. Indeed they are as much of a nuisance in this respect here as they are in Boston and what is painful the White People are tired of them."[19] Periodically, there were letters to London newspapers calling

18. Martin to Gerrit Smith, Boston, 2 July 1861, Smith Papers; Anna Loring to Mrs. Andrew, Beverly, 14 July 1861, John Andrew Papers, Massachusetts Historical Society, Boston; Seward to C. F. Adams, Washington, D.C., 7 November 1861, and Weed to Archbishop Hughes, London, 1 January 1862, both in Thurlow Weed Papers, University of Rochester, Rochester, N.Y.; Glyndon G. Van Deusen, *Thurlow Weed: Wizard of the Lobby* (Boston, 1947), 280; Jenkins, *Britain and the War of the Union*, 1: 188; Sarah Forbes Hughes, ed., *John Murray Forbes: Letters and Recollections* (Boston, 1899), 2: 4–5, 17; Conway, *Autobiography*, 1: 371; John d'Entremont, *Southern Emancipator: Moncure Conway, the American Years, 1832–1865* (New York, 1987), 183.

19. Martin to George Lewis Ruffin, London, 15 October 1861, Ruffin Family Papers, Moorland-Spingarn Research Center, Howard University, Washington, D.C.

for help to support destitute African Americans or to assist them in emigrating to Liberia. There is also evidence that some black Americans found jobs in the north of England and Scotland. Some, including Henry Box Brown, James Watkins, William G. Allen, William Howard Day, and William and Ellen Craft, were already in England when war broke out. Others, such as Martin, T. Morris Chester, and William Andrew Jackson, were in Britain specifically to campaign against the Confederacy. Still others, such as the Reverend W. Mitchell, were on missions to raise money for fugitive slaves in Canada and took the opportunity to work against the Confederacy. There were also a few attending British colleges or medical schools, including William Watson, R. M. Johnson, and C. J. Russell.

One of the most active of the African Americans was the Reverend J. Sella Martin, a Baptist minister from Boston who visited Britain twice during the war. Martin, a fugitive slave whose family was still in slavery, worked closely with the London Emancipation Society in and around London and with the Union and Emancipation Society in the north of England and Scotland. During his second visit he became pastor of a church in the East End of London, the congregation of which was composed mainly of working families.[20] Another was William Andrew Jackson, the twenty-nine-year-old former coachman of Jefferson Davis, who escaped from Richmond in April 1862. Jackson made his way through Union lines around the Confederate capital. By the time he arrived in New York he was already something of a celebrity, with a brief biography and sketch in *Harper's Weekly*. Aware of his public relations potential, abolitionists such as Garrison encouraged Jackson to visit Britain and provided him with letters of recommendation. Once in London, Jackson was taken under the wing of George Thompson and his family. If there was a pro-Union figure who dominated the public debate in 1863, it was Jackson. While Martin stayed in London, Jackson, acting as an agent of the Union and Emancipation Society, took the message to the north of England and to Scotland and Wales. "He is quite a sharp person," Zebrina Eastman wrote from Bristol, "and makes some telling hits; and as a colored man is here always an oracle, there is no gainsaying him."[21] The work of these African Americans put the Confederacy at a decided disadvantage, for although they did not speak with one voice about the causes of

20. For a biography of Martin see Blackett, *Beating against the Barriers*, 185–285.

21. *Liberator*, 23 May, 28 November 1862; *Harper's Weekly*, 7 June 1862; *Times* (Bury), 16 May 1863; Eastman to Seward, Bristol, 4 February 1863, Despatches from U.S. Consuls in Bristol, 1792–1906; Thompson to Garrison, London, 5 December 1862, AASS Papers.

the war, they were a constant reminder that slavery was at the center of the conflict.

In spite of these apparent advantages, Adams worried constantly that the presence of all these Americans did more harm than good to the cause. Hotze and his British supporters, however, saw an "indefatigable and unscrupulous agency" at work against them, an agency, one editor reported, "profusely supplied with gold from the Washington Treasury," the sole purpose of which was to purchase influence.[22] It is evident that a portion of the funds Weed took with him was earmarked for public agitation. Adams, however, was skittish about identifying himself too closely with such work. It seemed beneath the dignity of the office. He worried, as did Hotze, that such activity could be construed as foreign interference in the domestic affairs of the country. While Adams met with delegations from antislavery societies and with prominent politicians such as W. E. Foster and received memorials and petitions for transmission to Washington—activities that clearly fell within the purview of an ambassador's traditional duties—he stayed clear of any direct involvement in the effort to influence public opinion. Responsibility for these activities fell to Freeman Morse in the London legation and Thomas Dudley, the consul in Liverpool. Between them, they coordinated all intelligence gathering and political activity. Morse worked closely with antislavery societies and agents in and around London, providing support from both private and "secret service" funds for the publication of pamphlets and the organization of meetings. Dudley took responsibility for similar activities in the north of England and in Scotland.[23] There were times when consuls ignored diplomatic conventions and became directly involved in efforts to win public support for the Union. Zebrina Eastman in Bristol, for example, made contact with local antislavery folks in an effort to "undo

22. Adams to Seward, London, 25 June 1863, Despatches from U.S. Ministers to Great Britain, 1791–1906; Hotze to Hunter, London, 1 February 1862, Hotze Papers; *Weekly Times*, 19 January 1862; *Standard* (Oldham), 16 May 1863; *Times* (London), 10 April 1863.

23. Morse to Seward, London, 12 December 1862, 17 January, 6 February, 13, 20 March 1863, Despatches from U.S. Consuls in London, England, 1790–1906; Jenkins, *Britain and the War of the Union*, 2: 246–47. During the early months of the war, the Union effort to keep an eye on the activities of Confederate agents was run by Henry Shelton Sanford from his office in Belgium. This created logistical and other problems for Union representatives in England. As a result, Sanford's organization in England was disbanded in early 1862 and taken over by Morse. See Harriet Chappell Owsley, "Henry Shelton Sanford and Federal Surveillance Abroad, 1861–1865," *Mississippi Valley Historical Review* 48 (September 1961): 211–28.

the work of secessionists," and in Dundee, James Smith attended public meetings in early 1863.[24]

While Adams worried about the wisdom of American citizens and their
representatives becoming involved in the effort to influence public opinion,
Confederate and Union organizations sought the support of British citizens
who had spent some time in the United States. Joseph Barker was employed
as an agent of the Central Association for the Cessation of Hostilities in
America in 1863. When he ended his agency in late 1863, John Smith assumed the position as the British voice experienced in the ways of America.
Formerly of Worcester, Smith had lived in the South for over twenty years. A
small planter and slaveholder, Smith had his property confiscated, and he was
imprisoned at Camp Chase in Columbus, Ohio, early in the war.[25] As important as the agencies of Barker and Smith were, the support for the Confederacy of those returning Britons who had no official association with any
organization was equally as critical. Of these, the most influential was the
Baptist minister Joshua Balme, who was in England raising money to start a
newspaper. A prickly character who caused as much trouble for his friends as
for his enemies, Balme lectured throughout the country, wrote frequent letters
to the press, and published two pamphlets in which he excoriated the Union
as a pro-slavery arrangement and abolitionists (particularly Garrisonians) for
abandoning the struggle against racial discrimination. It appears that Balme
had run afoul of his congregation in Chicago when he insisted that the church
publicly declare its opposition to slavery and racial discrimination. Balme
soon left to form an antislavery church that ran a school and a newspaper.
Both were short lived, and Balme was forced to leave the city. Trouble seemed
to follow him wherever he went, and his visit to England in 1858 was meant
in part, as Frederick Douglass reported, to "indemnify himself" for losses in-
curred in supporting the cause. It also appears that Balme had been involved
in the founding of the Church Anti Slavery Society in New York and that he
had broken with the leadership over some unspecified slights. Even among his
friends Balme was described as a man "off whose roof there is a slate."[26] But

24. Eastman to Seward, Bristol, n.d., Despatches from U.S. Consuls in Bristol, 1792–1906;
Advertiser (Dundee), 22 April 1863.

25. *Boston Commonwealth*, 3 January 1864; *Review* (Nottingham), 17 July 1863. For a study of
prisons see William B. Hesseltine, *Civil War Prisons: A Study in War Psychology* (Columbus,
Ohio, 1930).

26. The Reverend J. R. Balme, *American States, Churches, and the War* (London, 1865),

because there was no slaveholding in his past, Balme could not be dismissed as easily as Smith. Like Barker, Balme brought to the public debate a peculiar personality, but solid antislavery credentials. While Smith could be embarrassed publicly for being a slaveholder, Barker and Balme had to be treated as old and trusted friends who had somehow lost their way.

Pro-Union organizations had to face no such complications. Their most important agent from the ranks of returning Britons was Peter Sinclair. A Scot who had long been involved in reform politics, Sinclair went to the United States on a temperance lecture tour in the mid-1850s and decided to settle there. He returned to Britain in the summer of 1861, concerned that the country appeared to be moving toward support for the Confederacy. Soon after his arrival he wrote the Manchester *Examiner and Times*, condemning John Bull for his inaction, for standing "with his hands in his pockets, feeling for his conscience." The double entendre was not missed by those who saw the need to prick the country's sense of revulsion against slavery and condemn it for its reliance on slave-grown cotton. Over the next few months Sinclair met with leaders of the Glasgow Emancipation and the British and Foreign Anti Slavery Societies and with prominent figures in Manchester, helped in the reorganization of the London Emancipation Society, participated at a number of public meetings, and published an influential pamphlet.[27] He worked closely with Morse. At some point after Sinclair's arrival in England, Morse placed him on retainer and would later pay for the publication of his pamphlet. By late 1862 Sinclair was reporting to the consul on his activities. In February 1863 Sinclair was hired as an agent of the Union and Emancipation Society, a position he would hold until the end of the year.[28] Other returning Britons with no official ties to pro-Union organizations or government officials also played an important role in influencing the way the public

---

479–500. His letters to the Liverpool *Mercury* in the first two years of the war were republished as *Letters on the American Republic; or, Common Fallacies and Monstrous Errors Refuted and Exposed* (London, 1865). For his activities in Scotland see Botsford, "Scotland and the American Civil War," 497–503.

27. *Liberator*, 26 July 1861; *Examiner* (Glasgow), 14 December 1861; *Morning Star*, 17 November 1862; Glasgow Emancipation Society, minute book 4, 1845–1876, Smeal Collection, Glasgow Public Library; British and Foreign Anti Slavery Society minute book, BFASS Papers; Sinclair to Seward, London, 14 November 1862, Seward Papers.

28. Morse to Seward, London, 12 December 1862, Despatches from U.S. Consuls in London, 1790–1906; J. Estcourt to Dudley, Manchester, 18 March 1864, Dudley Collection; Peter Sinclair, *Freedom and Slavery in the United States: Being Facts and Testimonies for the Consideration of the British People* (London, 1863).

viewed the war. One of the most interesting was J. W. Jones, editor of the American Welsh-language newspaper *Y Drych a'r Gwyliedydd* who on his return to south Wales in late 1864 gave a series of lectures about the war to large audiences.[29] Neither side had paid much attention to Wales, although as has been shown, the Union and Emancipation Society did draw considerable support from Dissenting ministers there, and the few pro-Union meetings that were held prior to Jones's arrival always drew enthusiastic audiences.

The nature of the agencies developed by both sides cannot be understood fully without looking at the group of Englishmen who worked to get the message across. None was more prominent than George Thompson, the workhorse of antislavery agitation whose record reached back to the struggle to abolish West Indian slavery. C. Duncan Rice calls him the "prizefighter of Victorian reform," a superlative orator "with somewhat vulgar good looks" and a gift for "inspiring intense personal devotion, especially among women." Some thought they could discern a loss of the Thompson charm and powers of oratory in the years before the war. Following one of Thompson's debates with Frederick Douglass in Scotland, an editor spoke sadly of the diminution of his oratorical powers: "Time and trouble and toil have all been dealing with him, and not very gently either as we should suppose from his personal appearance and vocal power. He is but a shade of what he was. He is comparatively shrunk and emaciated; his frame has lost much of its flexibility, and his voice has no longer that depth and fullness and resonate power which told with such an overpowering effect in his younger days."[30] Constant financial difficulties also helped to sap Thompson's energy. He believed that he could have done much more for the cause of peace and freedom, he wrote a friend, "[i]f my mind was at ease in regard to my worldly circumstances but they are so straitened, that I am constantly depressed, and cannot command the spirits and energy requisite for the work of agitation." Yet it was Thompson who led the public charge against the Confederacy in the first two and a half years of the war. In the end, his straitened circum-

29. *Telegraph* (Merthyr), 12, 17, 19, 31 November 1864. See Bob Owen, "Welsh American Newspapers and Periodicals," *National Library of Wales Journal* 6 (winter 1950), for a history of *Y Drych*.

30. Rice, *The Scots Abolitionists, 1833–1861*, 55–57; *Examiner* (Glasgow), 3 March 1860. Others, such as Lydia Child, were also struck by the fact that time had not been kind to Thompson. Child to Lucy Osgood, n.p., 26 February 1864, Lydia Maria Child Papers. Thanks to Ron Gifford for bringing the Child comments to my attention.

stances forced him to emigrate in early 1864 to the United States in search of better opportunities.[31]

The Confederacy could call on no one of Thompson's stature. Listeners might have disagreed with the position he took on the war, but none doubted the sincerity and commitment Thompson brought to the cause of antislavery. The South's most prominent British advocate was James Spence, a Liverpool businessman with no record of political activity who came to prominence with the publication of his book *The American Union* in the fall of 1861. Written in just fourteen weeks on what Spence offhandedly called "an impulse," the work was a tour de force. At its core it is a reasoned reiteration of conservative views on the shortcomings of republican democracies. Spence insisted that federal forms of government were successful only if undertaken on a small scale. In the case of the United States each unit was large enough to be a separate independent entity. That, as well as the sheer size of the country, bred arrogance and aggression, not moderation, the hallmark of a balanced democracy, and meant disruption was inevitable. Secession then was a welcome restraint on the effects of uncontrolled democracy. Size also complicated the ability to govern a country made up of two "distinct and rival communities." Like many supporters of the Confederacy, Spence insisted that the South was settled and was still dominated largely by an aristocracy that had its origins in Britain, while the North attracted settlers from among the residuum of Europe. In such a large country, democracy invariably led to the selection of those who were less skilled in the art of government. Spence compared the capabilities of the Founding Fathers, who governed at a time when the country was smaller, with the shortcomings of more recent presidents including Lincoln. Given these conditions, Spence insisted that slavery was not the proximate cause of secession, nor could it be abolished under the present political arrangement. Only separation and the moral influence of European powers could persuade the slaveholders to set the slaves free.[32]

The American Union, which was critically received by the Conservative press, went through four editions in six months and was translated into French, German, Spanish, and Italian. Opponents of secession were, not surprisingly, less enthusiastic, one insisting that it was filled with "*supressio veri,*" but even they had to admit that its publication could not have been more critical, coming as it did at a time when opinions on the war were still being

31. Thompson to George Wilson, London, 11 January 1862, George Wilson Papers, Manchester Public Library.

32. Spence to Mason, Liverpool, 28 April 1862, Records of the Confederate States of America; Spence, *The American Union,* 6–15, 28, 46–48, 87, 105–06, 163.

formed. Richard Webb called it "one of the ablest, craftiest and most dishonest books I have ever met with. It is studiously suited to the English taste, being moderate in tone, lucid in style, and free from personalities." *The American Union* became something of a sourcebook and was drawn on for information and arguments by supporters of the South throughout the country.[33] Nothing produced by pro-Union forces matched the range, reach, or influence of *The American Union*. Meant to be a rejoinder, John Cairnes's *The Slave Power* never attained the same prominence, partly because what it had to say about American political culture followed traditional abolitionist lines. Secession, Cairnes argued, had nothing to do with "commercial and fiscal differences" or with the desire for independence on the part of an oppressed minority. It was rather a recognition by the slave power, long accustomed to having its own way politically, that the election of Lincoln undermined its political authority and would lead, at best, to the confinement of slavery within its existing territory. Always aggressively seeking new territory as a means of augmenting its influence, the slave power was, by its very nature, aggressive. It was that need for new lands, rather than the desire to maintain political equilibrium between the two sectors, as Spence and others argued, that produced the crisis. Cairnes insisted that the subjugation of the South was justified, not because he wanted to maintain a union to which he personally felt no emotional attachment, but because the South sought to expand and consolidate a "barbarous tyranny," the defeat of which would be a "service to the civilized world." Where Spence saw the influence of that civilized world working on and over time encouraging an independent South to emancipate its slaves, Cairnes anticipated a continuously expanding and more aggressive slave economy. The solution, Cairnes thought, was to destroy slavery at its weakest point: the border states.[34]

33. Hotze to Hunter, London, 28 February 1862, Hotze to Secretary of State, London, 25 April 1862, Hotze to Benjamin, London, 9 May 1863, Hotze Papers. For favorable reviews see *Times* (London), 6 January 1862, and *Blackwood's Magazine,* April 1862. Smith, *England and America,* 44; *Anti Slavery Reporter,* 1 August 1862; *National Anti Slavery Standard,* 19 April 1862; Dudley to Seward, Liverpool, 6 January 1863, Despatches from U.S. Consuls in Liverpool, 1790–1906; *Advertiser* (Burnley) 14 February 1863; Donald Bellows, "A Study of British Conservative Reaction to the American Civil War," *Journal of Southern History* 51 (November 1985): 509–16. Four years later, in the heat of the debate over political reform, Professor Blackie would use Spence's bleak picture of political conditions in New York City to dismiss calls for an extension of the franchise. See Ernest Jones, *Democracy Vindicated: A Lecture Delivered to the Edinburgh Working Men's Institute on the 4th January 1867 in Reply to Professor Blackie's Lecture on Democracy, Delivered on the Previous Evening* (London, 1867).

34. John E. Cairnes, *The Slave Power: Its Character, Career, and Probable Designs* (1863; reprint, Newton Abbot, 1968), 2, 15, 18, 179, 204–05, 312–14.

Cairnes's work, which appeared in 1862 and was republished in an enlarged edition the following year, seemed to have had little influence on the way people viewed the war. Not so *The American Union*. The book's success made Spence the most important British figure in the public debate over the war. It would not be an exaggeration to say that Spence became almost ubiquitous in the months after its publication. He was involved in, if not at the center of, the formation of every national pro-Confederate organization and was regularly called on to assist in the formation of local societies. Although there were times when news from the battlefield distressed him, his spirits would soon be buoyed by developments at home or by some minor reversal of the Union's military fortunes. He took to the lecture and meeting circuits whenever he thought the cause needed a boost. One cannot imagine a Confederate movement in Britain without Spence. He was so invaluable, in fact, that Richmond thought it best to appoint him to a semiofficial post during the campaign to persuade Europeans to subscribe to the cotton bonds that were floated on the London, Paris, and Brussels markets in 1863. Such indispensability, however, bred suspicion among a few of Spence's coworkers. Charles Prioleau in Liverpool wondered whether Spence's past commercial and financial failures would undermine his ability to be an effective agent for the Cotton Loan. Hotze could not deny his usefulness but questioned Spence's pandering to British antislavery traditions. The problem for Spence, Hotze observed, is that "he assumed to occupy at one and the same time two opposite and irreconcilable positions, that of a high official of our Government owing it allegiance, and that of a disinterested alien friend." From Paris, Slidell expressed impatience with Spence's meddling in areas where he had no authority.[35] These concerns would lead to Spence's dismissal as commissioner of the Cotton Loan in late 1863. None of this, however, diminished Spence's standing as the most effective British propagandist for the cause.

Spence worked closely with the group of working-class agents that included Mortimer Grimshaw and John Matthews. Many in the cotton towns who remembered the role these two men had played in helping to break earlier strikes dismissed them as too willing to work for the highest bidder. John Ward, a Clitheroe weaver, recalled the day in March 1861 when a bellman announced a public meeting of striking weavers to hear from a delegation that

35. For Prioleau's views see Hughes, "Liverpool and the Confederate States," 112–13; for Slidell's views see L. M. Sears, "A Confederate Diplomat at the Court of Napoleon III," *American Historical Review* 27 (January 1921): 271; Hotze to Benjamin, London, 31 October 1863, Hotze Papers.

included Grimshaw and Matthews. The local strike committee, however, demanded to know why this "gang of notorious scoundrels" were in Clitheroe. The delegation, which insisted that the dispute with the masters be put to arbitration, were stoned, kicked, jeered, and forced to flee.[36] Even before the outbreak of the war, then, Grimshaw and the others had little credibility among the very people Spence hoped to bring into the Confederate fold. Other Confederate agents residing in Britain were more successful. Those included Edward Arundel Verity, the incumbent of Habergham Eaves, near Burnley, and T. B. Kershaw, an overlooker at a mill in Ancoats, Manchester. Kershaw was also one of the secretaries of the Southern Independence Association, the author of a pamphlet, and one of the driving forces behind both the massive pro-Confederate petition of 1864 and the Peace Address of the same year that called on the North to cease hostilities and recognize the South's independence. Relations between Kershaw and other leaders of the movement, however, were not all they should have been. Spence thought him a person of "much energy and some ability but little judgement—very little. The talent he really does possess he overstates enormously." Others questioned his use of funds.[37] With the departure of Joseph Barker in October 1863 and the ineffectiveness of John Smith, the Confederate agency had to rely almost exclusively on Verity and Kershaw. It did call on Spence occasionally, but it is clear from published reports of its meetings beginning in 1864 that without Barker, the agency lacked punch.

While the Confederate agency languished after 1863, that of its opponent flourished. Even after Jackson's departure in late 1863 and Thompson's move to the United States a few weeks later, the Union could call on a host of American and British agents to keep its message before the public. Old favorites with working-class audiences such as Ernest Jones, Henry Vincent, and Mason Jones, who visited the North in 1863, continued to draw large crowds to their meetings and lectures. Thousands turned out to hear Henry Ward Beecher in Liverpool, Glasgow, and Manchester in October 1863. Collectively, African Americans, both free blacks and fugitive slaves, reached

36. R. Sharpe France, "The Diary of John Ward of Clitheroe, Weaver, 1860–1864," *Transactions of the Historic Society of Lancashire and Cheshire* 105 (1953): 159–61.

37. *Times* (Oldham), 31 October 1863; *Chronicle* (Oldham), 14 November 1863; Hotze to Kershaw, London, 27 August 1864, Hotze to H. Chadwick, London, 20 March 1865, Hotze to Hasleham, London, 13 March 1865, Hotze Papers; Spence to Wharncliffe, Liverpool, 12 December 1864, Chadwick to Wharncliffe, Manchester, 20 March 1865, Wharncliffe Muniments; Kershaw, *The Truth of the American Question*.

audiences that Beecher would have envied. And if Adams worried about the potential harm American visitors could do to Anglo-American relations, the audiences who came to share their views with the visitors seemed to have no such concerns.

While the agency was the most critical feature of the propaganda apparatus employed by both sides in the dispute, it did not dwarf other devices used to reach and test public sentiment. Yancey and Mann might have failed in their efforts to influence British views on the war through public meetings, but by the fall of 1861 the friends of the Union thought they saw the hand of the commissioners in the rising tide of editorials and feature articles critical of the way the Lincoln government was conducting the war. While Bright was willing to concede that the London press, dominated as it was by "certain ruling West End classes," would speak to its class interests, he nevertheless was deeply concerned that there was "some tampering with a certain accessible portion of the Press" by Confederate agents. His friends at the *Morning Star* wrote of the existence of a "secret agency" that they acknowledged did have some success. Yancey and Mann, it appears, had also reached out beyond London, using money "without stint to secure the hireling services of the venal writers for our metropolitan and provincial journals." In Glasgow, John Moir denounced the Scottish press for its bias toward the Confederacy. From Ireland came word that only one newspaper in the entire island was partial to the Union. By the summer of 1862 it was reported that DeLeon was writing for and subsidizing the *Irish Times* and other Irish newspapers.[38] DeLeon had returned to Britain in April 1862 with a slush fund of $25,000 that he put to good use. Hotze preceded him by a few weeks and had set to work trying to win influence with major London newspapers. Within one month Hotze had won access to the London *Post* and was soon contributing articles to the London *Standard* and the London *Herald*.[39]

As journalists, both DeLeon and Hotze were familiar with the ways newspapers reflected and fashioned public opinion. In an era of rising literacy,

38. Bright, *Speeches of John Bright, M.P., on the American Question*, 123; "Letters of John Bright, 1861–1862," 99; *Morning Star*, 14 October 1861; *National Anti Slavery Standard*, 4 January 1862; *Gazette* (Glasgow), 18 January 1862; Webb to Chapman, Dublin, 15 October 1862, AASS Papers; Henry B. Hammond to Seward, Dublin, 28 August 1862, William B. West to Seward, Dublin, 28 August 1862, Despatches from U.S. Consuls in Dublin, 1790–1906.

39. Owsley, *King Cotton Diplomacy*, 157, 162; Virginia Mason, *The Public Life and Diplomatic Correspondence of James M. Mason* (Roanoke, Va., 1903), 293; Cullop, *Confederate Propaganda in Europe*, 21.

when the removal of taxes had led to a dramatic increase in the number of daily and weekly publications in Britain, newspapers were a formidable political force. They were by 1860 an important part of everyday life. Editors and editorial writers—few of whom were neutral—tried to influence their readers to support the cause they espoused. Banner headlines announced the results of battles, and articles, many reprinted from London newspapers, reported on political developments occurring both sides of the Mason-Dixon line. Following a well-established tradition, copies were posted outside municipal buildings so that townspeople could read or have read to them the latest news from across the country and abroad. Crowds gathered daily to get news of the war. In Stalybridge, for example, they met at the railway station and various newsagents to read about the latest developments. In such settings opinions were never simply the views expressed by the editor; they invariably were the result of spirited exchange. Years later, Samuel Fielden, one of the Haymarket martyrs, recalled that every night during the summer, crowds would gather in the small textile town of Todmorden, which straddled Lancashire and Yorkshire, "discussing the latest news and forecasting the next, and in these groups there was always to be heard the advocates and champions of both sides."[40]

Most studies of British views on the war ignore this exchange between readers and editors, so vital to an understanding of the nature of public opinion, and by concentrating almost exclusively on editorials, conclude erroneously that most newspapers favored the Confederacy. In a study of 250 newspapers, Thomas Keiser insists that, driven by a greater hatred of America than slavery, "no more than 10 were consistently pro-North." E. D. Adams argues for a shift in the summer of 1861 by the "majority of London newspapers" away from condemning the South for seceding to appealing to the North to accept the break up of the Union as an accomplished fact, to criticizing the Lincoln government for conducting a war of empire.[41] Such conclusions underestimate both the levels of support for the Union among editors and correspondents and, as Martin Crawford has argued, the degree to which newspapers "absorbed, reflected, and finally shaped" attitudes toward the war.[42]

40. Auger, "The Cotton Famine, 1861–1865," 294; Samuel Fielden, "Autobiography of Samuel Fielden," in Philip S. Foner, ed., The Autobiographies of the Haymarket Martyrs (New York, 1969), 142–43.
41. Thomas J. Keiser, "The English Press and the American Civil War" (Ph.D. diss., University of Reading, 1971), 25, 433; Ephraim Douglass Adams, Great Britain and the American Civil War (London, 1925), 1: 174.
42. Crawford, The Anglo-American Crisis, 13.

Hotze and DeLeon also knew from experience that the cause of the Confederacy stood little chance without the support of British newspapers, especially those in London. Surprisingly, representatives of the Union came to this realization much more slowly. Hotze's plan was simple: he would develop a cadre of skilled British writers who had access to major newspapers and supplement their efforts with his own editorials. His first appeared in the *Morning Post* just three weeks after his arrival. A few weeks later he sent his superiors extracts from major newspapers claiming responsibility for their tone, and by spring 1863 he reported that there were seven writers for London newspapers in his employ.[43] It is impossible to determine who all these journalists were. But certainly one was Percy Greg, a journalist, novelist, and historian who wrote frequently for the Manchester *Guardian*, London *Standard*, and *Saturday Review*. A "champion of feudalism and absolutism," Greg later wrote a history of the United States, which was filled with contempt for the country's democratic and republican traditions and with praise, if not for slavery as a whole, at least for its patriarchal traditions in Virginia.

> Supported by his master in infancy, in sickness, and old age, the slave was, as Carlyle said, a servant hired for life, and paid throughout life at a far higher rate than the Irish potato-grower or the Kentish hand. He received more than the European peasant, and did less than half the work. His old age especially presented to the English labourer a constant contrast of which English society might well be ashamed. No pauper's garb, no pauper's fare, no prison-like workhouse, no separation from wife and children, awaited the last years of the servant who could serve no longer. He occupied his cottage, he basked in the sun, his grandchildren playing round his knees, his gray hairs respected, his infirmities cared for, his temper and his vanities humoured.[44]

Such views of caring and benevolence had not yet become standard fare during the war years, but there were many among friends of the Confederacy who echoed Carlyle's nostalgia for those days of West Indian slavery when all was in its rightful place and all knew their place.

Hotze supplemented these efforts with the publication of the *Index*, which

43. Hotze to Hunter, London, 23 February, 11 March 1862, Hotze to Benjamin, London, 26 September 1862, Hotze Papers; Cullop, *Confederate Propaganda in Europe*, 49.

44. *Dictionary of National Biography*, 8: 529–30; Royle, *Victorian Infidels*, 311; J. F. Jameson, "The London Expenditure of the Confederate Secret Service," *American Historical Review* 25 (July 1930): 811–12; Greg, *History of the United States*, 2: 3.

spoke directly to the needs of the Confederacy. The newspaper first appeared in May 1862 and survived until the last weeks of the war. Much of the cost of publication in the first few months of its existence was covered by Hotze and friends back in Mobile, Alabama. It continued to operate on a shoestring until almost the final year of the war, when the government in Richmond allocated approximately £2,000, less than half of its needed operating expenses. Circulation never exceeded 2,250 copies, and Hotze was always hard-pressed to find adequate copy. In spite of these difficulties, the *Index* was a newspaper that the opposition could not ignore. It had the field to itself. Following the demise of the *Anti Slavery Advocate* in May 1863, only the *Anti Slavery Reporter* offered any resistance. The *Index* gave wide coverage of pro-Confederate meetings, especially those in Lancashire, and to the efforts to win support for secession. Hotze also utilized those journalists with whom he had worked earlier. Although their identities remain a secret, there were at least seven who regularly contributed to the newspaper, including Kershaw, who was its Lancashire correspondent.[45]

Although there is no evidence that Hotze attempted to influence, or even that he could have influenced, the editors of the London *Times* or any of its many correspondents, friends of the Confederacy were well aware of the advantage of having one of the most influential newspapers in their corner. Conservatives and advocates of free trade, the editors viewed developments in the United States with a mixture of praise and condemnation. On the brink of economic takeoff, and retreating from protective tariffs, the country was at the same time mired in the sort of political violence that saw an attack on a senator by one of his colleagues on the floor of the Senate and the ill-conceived attack by John Brown on Harpers Ferry. Martin Crawford has argued convincingly that as far as the editors were concerned, the United States posed no political threat to Britain. The British considered their system vastly superior to a form of government that relied on unchecked democracy, which always failed to elect its best men and was never strong enough to deal with renegade elements.[46] While most Americans could dismiss such criticism as patronizing, they could not ignore the fact that the *Times* was by far the most influential newspaper in Britain. It was assumed—and not illogically—that

45. Jameson, "The London Expenditure of the Confederate Secret Service," 822; Cullop, *Confederate Propaganda in Europe*, 40–44, 49, 50–51, 54. Moncure Conway points out that John Reuben Thompson worked with the *Index* during his stay in England in the last year of the war. Conway, *Autobiography*, 1: 365–66.

46. Crawford, *The Anglo-American Crisis*, 39–47.

the views from Printing House Square were the views of the country. Uncertainty about the future of the Union in the first few months of 1861 dominated the *Times*'s editorials. By the end of the year, however, the newspaper had thrown its lot in with the Confederacy. It put down its change of views to a pragmatism born of reality. Whereas in the weeks leading up to the attack on Fort Sumter it had opposed the breakup of the Union, once the attack occurred it was clear that the people of the South were determined to form their own government. All liberty-loving people were obliged to support this "natural" desire for independence, a desire that had made it possible for the weaker side to beat back all attempts at coercion. History had shown that at no time was so vast a country conquered. Secession, the editors insisted, was an accomplished fact.[47]

Americans could "lash themselves into a fury" over British neutrality, but the *Times* insisted that its support for Southern independence was driven solely by self-interest. Britain had an economic stake in what was happening across the Atlantic, for the shortage of cotton was ravaging the economies of many cities and the lives of their people. "Like monkeys grinning and chattering at mischief done in the mere instinct of wantonness, the American people have been triumphing in the distress they have been able to cause in our Cotton districts, and the press gains popularity by depicting starvation in Lancashire." Also the British needed to take an interest whenever republican forms of government came to grief. The expression of unchecked popular will on which such governments were based was "at least as likely to hurry a nation into war and debt as the caprice of the most absolute despot or the intrigues of the most selfish of aristocracies." Secession had also checked the expansion of a republic that could have threatened Britain's political interests in the future. It had saved Britain and Europe from a "Republic which should expand over the whole of North America, which should aggrandize itself by the spoil of England and degenerate Mexico, which should dictate to Europe with the authority of a united Continent." The editors longed for the promised day "which is to give us two friendly Unions of moderate power and temper."[48]

Frustratingly for friends of an independent Confederacy, however, the *Times* consistently eschewed any form of British intervention. The disappointment was felt even more keenly because the appointment of Spence as a

---

47. *Times* (London), 14 November 1861, 10 May 1862.
48. *Times* (London), 25 June 1861, 1 May, 15 July, 19 September, 15 March 1862.

special correspondent in January 1862 had raised expectations that the editors were about to call for some form of British involvement to end hostilities. No one could interpret the appointment as an effort by the editors to bring even a semblance of balance to their coverage of political and military developments in the war. By and large, except with one significant distinction, the positions of Spence and the editors converged: Spence never stopped calling for recognition. It is very possible that the Spence appointment was meant to give vent to, and so defuse, calls for direct British intervention. By the end of 1864 Spence was deeply frustrated by pro-Confederate newspapers such as the *Times* and the *Telegraph,* which were "dead against action of any kind."[49]

In January 1862 when nationalist hackles were raised over the *Trent* affair, all signs pointed to the possibility of British intervention in the war. In such a setting, regular articles by Spence aided immeasurably those promoting the cause of secession. Over the next three years, beginning in February, the *Times* published forty-five articles by Spence under the pseudonym "S." They were a sustained and unapologetic assault on the Union and an invaluable weapon in the Confederate's propaganda arsenal. Throughout his articles, as he had in his *American Union,* Spence took pains to demonstrate the political shortcomings of republican forms of government, which, he insisted, were unsuited for so large a political unit as the United States and which therefore tended naturally to disintegrate. Secession was a natural consequence of a country formed of disparate elements with differing economic interests, a society too large for proper management. Spence saw the war as a confrontation between two starkly opposing realities. On one side was the brave and undermanned South, on the other the better-equipped but incompetent North. Of the South he wrote: "Here is a people shut out from the world, deprived of all the comforts of life, starting without tools, money, credit, ships, or soldiers, disappointed in their political calculations, their commerce annihilated, the value of their property extinguished, overmatched in men and means of warfare, assailed by torrents of abuse, depressed by a long course of adverse events" yet holding their own.[50] The North in contrast was run by an incompetent president and a Congress bent on ruin with its tax bills and conscription, a country defended by an equally incompetent military that was defeated in most bat-

49. Mowbray Morris to Spence, London, 9, 22 January, 22 August, 22 September 1862, *Times* (London) Archives; Spence to Wharncliffe, Liverpool, 14 December 1864, Wharncliffe Muniments.

50. *Times* (London), 19 May 1862.

tles. A once proud land was now the home of "bastilles, passports, spies, informers, censors, [and] conscripts" from which many fled.[51]

Spence could not, however, ignore the fact that in spite of these apparent shortcomings, the Union seemed to be making slow but steady progress militarily. Good propagandist that he was, Spence did all he could to put the best face on Confederate military losses. In 1862 he was convinced that the South knew it was trying to defend too large a territory and so was retreating to more manageable positions. The capture of Island No. 10, for example, was not a real defeat, for it pushed the Confederacy to retreat to more defensible positions while forcing the Union to expend resources capturing militarily insignificant places. Spence did concede that the capture of New Orleans in April 1862 was a military setback, but he insisted that it in no way affected the most compact and important sector of the Confederacy, which remained intact.[52] These political and military realities, argued Spence, obligated European governments to recognize the Confederacy as an independent nation. Eight million people who were descended from the English and who spoke the same language had as much right to have their will respected as did one million Greeks. "We have respected the will of the Belgians, Tuscans, Neapolitans, Sicilians, Greeks—all manner and sorts of people. Is anyone of these," he asked, "a manlier race, more fit for self-government or better deserving of respect than our own kinsmen of the South have proved themselves?"[53]

The way in which Spence presented his information was as impressive as was the passion he brought to the cause. But knowledge and passion are no guarantees of influence, and it is impossible to gauge the impact of Spence's articles on the public. Leslie Stephens, a supporter of the Union, not surprisingly dismissed much of what Spence had to say in his articles. They were, Stephens declared, always erroneously predicting military defeat for the North, assuming incorrectly that the more territory the North captured the more it was forced to defend. Stephens was right, but he apparently did not understand that central to Spence's view of the war was the proposition that republics could only prosper and survive if they remained small: the war in many respects occurred because the United States had outgrown the natural and manageable limits of a republic. Other Union supporters were more concerned about the possible influence of Spence's articles on public opinion. A

51. *Times* (London), 29 August 1862.
52. *Times* (London), 28 April, 19 May 1862.
53. *Times* (London), 30 December 1862, 2 July 1863.

speaker at a meeting in Carlisle observed that the articles "astonished the people . . . by their daring effrontery and impudent assertions of what was not
true."[54]

Although not an official element in the Confederate propaganda machine,
newspapers such as the *Times* proved invaluable to Hotze. Many provincial
newspapers, even those with political views decidedly opposed to Printing
House Square, echoed in their editorial pages much of what the London *Times*
had to say about the war. Some of them, such as the Sheffield and Rotherham
Independent, an influential Yorkshire newspaper, remained steadfastly opposed
to the Union throughout the war. Its editor, Robert Leader, a Liberal and close
ally of John Roebuck, believed that the conflict was primarily political, an attempt by the North to subjugate the South. Like Roebuck, he also subscribed
to the notion that a people had a right to independence if they wanted it and
if they had the means to take it. Leader's editorials heaped scorn on the
United States, that "beau ideal of freedom, justice and good government."
The country was, he insisted, too prone to boast of its accomplishments, too
sensitive to accept criticism, too quick to pick fights with Britain at the least
provocation, and too big for its own britches. Leader was so committed to the
survival of the Confederacy that even after the fall of Richmond he insisted
that the war could still be won.[55]

Editorial views such as Leader's led many contemporaries to conclude that,
with a few notable exceptions, British newspapers, even those that catered to
a working-class readership, favored secession. Political affiliation seemed to
matter little. When John Moir complained about the Confederate bias of
Scottish newspapers, Peter Mackenzie of the Glasgow *Gazette* responded with
a rousing denunciation of Americans as "braggarts, upstarts, and lying
scoundrels. . . .They are the scum of the earth, and have completely lost caste,
not only amongst themselves, but in the eyes of all civilized Europe."[56] While
Mackenzie's position could be attributed to his monarchist tendencies, the
same could not be said of George Reynolds, a Secularist and staunch republican. Yet Reynolds promoted the cause of the South in the first year of the war.
Karl Marx and Frederick Engles believed that Yancey and Mann had purchased Reynolds's support. If this were true, it lasted only until Lincoln issued

54. Leslie Stephens, *The "Times" on the American War: A Historical Study* (London, 1865),
84; *Examiner and Northern Advertiser* (Carlisle), 21 February 1863.

55. For examples of Leader's views see *Independent* (Sheffield and Rotherham), 21 September
1861, 17 April 1865; Cruikshank, "J. A. Roebuck, M.P.," 202.

56. *Gazette* (Glasgow), 18 January 1862.

the Emancipation Proclamation, at which point Reynolds threw his support to the Union. Even then, however, he remained critical of Union policy, concerned that the North by its actions and the incompetency of its political and military leaders was giving democracy a bad name.[57] In his work on British labor and the Confederacy, Roydon Harrison has shown that other working-class newspapers, such as the Glasgow *Sentinel*, the *British Miner*, and the *Weekly Budget*, supported the South. The case of the *Bee Hive* was much more complicated. The newspaper, which first appeared in October 1861, originated in the nine-hour movement led by the building trades. Its early pro-Confederate position reflected the views of its first editor, George Troupe. Troupe's dislike of the United States and abolitionists had begun almost twenty years earlier during the abolitionist campaign to persuade the Scottish Free Church to return money it had raised in South Carolina and other slave-holding states. Although the campaign failed, Troupe never forgot the criticism leveled at the church and those who supported its decision to retain the money. The editor's position on the war, however, did not meet with the unanimous approval of the board of directors that supervised the newspaper. Troupe was ousted in October 1862 following a bitter dispute. The evidence suggests that the situation was complicated by the involvement of Confederate agents who had been helping the newspaper pay off its mortgage. When they threatened to withhold support if Troupe was fired, George Ogden, a member of the board, contacted friends of the Union, and money was found to assume the mortgage payments. Not surprisingly, with Troupe's departure the newspaper swung its support to the Union. Following a counter coup in 1864, however, Troupe returned, and the newspaper again became a promoter of Southern independence.[58]

As the case of the *Bee Hive* demonstrates, both sides devoted considerable money and energy to winning the endorsement of newspaper editors. Although friends of the Union lamented that British newspapers were almost universally opposed to their cause, the evidence does not bear out their contentions. Regardless of the national reach of the *Times*, numerous other London and provincial newspapers supported the Union. In addition, many

57. Karl Marx and Frederick Engles, *The Civil War in the United States* (3d ed., New York, 1961), 47–49, 144–45; *Reynolds's Newspaper*, 29 September 1861, 18 January, 21 June, 2 August 1863.

58. Stephen Coltham, "The 'Bee-Hive' Newspaper: Its Origin and Early Struggles," in Asa Briggs and John Saville, eds., *Essays in Labour History* (London, 1960), 174; *Banner of Ulster*, 30 December 1845, 12 January 1846; *Commercial Chronicle* (Belfast), 12 January 1846; *Reynolds's Newspaper*, 29 November 1896; Harrison, "British Labour and the Confederacy," 95–97.

more editors, publishers, journalists, and correspondents publicly supported the North through their membership in pro-Union organizations. Admittedly, many of them were connected to the *Morning Star*, the leading opposition to the *Times* in London, but they were also to be found in every geographical area, with the possible exception of Ireland. David Thomas, for example, was a reporter for the Bury *Times* who almost single-handedly kept the cause alive in his town. In 1868 Thomas would emigrate to South Carolina, where he became involved with a number of Republican newspapers, particularly the *Beaufort Times*, owned by W. J. Whipper, an African American from Michigan. William C. Leng was an editorial writer for the Dundee *Advertiser*, edited by his brother. James Smith, acting consul in Dundee, claimed responsibility for converting Leng from "being one of our worst enemies to being one of our ablest friends." Leng left Dundee in 1864 to edit the Sheffield *Telegraph*. Another Union advocate was William E. Adams, a Chartist, Radical journalist, and supporter of republican movements in Europe. For almost three years Adams was a regular correspondent for the Newcastle *Chronicle*. He was at the same time a regular contributor to the *National Reformer* under the pseudonym "Caractacus." Published by Charles Bradlaugh, the *National Reformer* encouraged the expression of opposing views on the war: Adams for the Union, Joseph Barker for the Confederacy. Barker would later sever ties with Bradlaugh to publish his own newspaper, *Barker's Review*; Adams became editor of the Newcastle *Weekly Chronicle*. R. M. Thomas, who worked closely with Dudley, was proprietor of the Chester *Record*. In Northampton, Albert Venn Dicey, publisher of the Northampton *Mercury* and brother of Edward J. S. Dicey of *Macmillan's* and the *Spectator*, was a friend of the Union.[59]

Of the metropolitan dailies, the *Morning Star* and the *Daily News* offered the most sustained support for the Union. The former was established in 1855 partly, as Martin Crawford observes, "to provide an alternative voice . . ." to the *Times* "on foreign affairs, particularly in regards to relations with the United States." The *Morning Star*, edited by Samuel Lucas (brother-in-law of John Bright), anticipating the logic of the Garrisonian argument on the pro-

59. Name index, Bury Public Library; *Columbia Daily Union*, 2 October 1872; Obituary notices, Dundee Public Library; James Smith to Dudley, Dundee, 4 May 1865, Thomas to Dudley, Chester, 2 February 1863, Dudley Collection; Leng, *The American War*; Carrie, "Dundee and the American Civil War, 1861–1865," 9; Ashton, W. E. *Adams*, 1–6, 104; Adams, *The Slaveholders' War*; Adams, *Memoirs of a Social Atom*, 402–403; David Weller, "Northampton and the American Civil War," *Northampton Past and Present* 8 (1990): 144.

slavery nature of the Union and repulsed by "an Invincible repugnance" to slavery, thought secession legitimate and in the best interest of the country. "Touch pitch, and you will be defiled; share a community of citizenship with the slaveholder, and you must expect to participate in his infamy." By the fall of 1861, however, Lucas had reversed course, insisting that the Union should be supported as the best guarantee of emancipation.[60] An independent Confederacy in which slavery would survive was unacceptable.

If the editors of the *Morning Star* initially doubted the wisdom of keeping the Union together, Harriet Martineau had no qualms about the need to oppose the Confederacy. Her triweekly editorials in the *Daily News* hammered away at the theme that slavery was the sole cause of the war. Given Martineau's knowledge of the United States and her long commitment to abolition, her opinions carried considerable weight. But Martineau was also a passionate advocate of free trade. The passage of the Morrill Tariff drove her to distraction and brought her to the brink of severing ties with American abolitionists with whom she had worked for thirty years. Her articles for the *National Anti Slavery Standard*, organ of the American Anti Slavery Society, condemned the tariff as an "insane protective policy" and suggested that there was no difference between those who enslaved labor and those who restricted trade. The *Trent* affair further strained relations, and Martineau accused her American friends of replacing their motto, "Our country is the world, our countrymen are all mankind," with a new slogan, "Our country, right or wrong."[61] Although the dispute led to a parting of the ways, it did not last long, nor did it diminish Martineau's value in the struggle to influence public opinion.

Newspapers also provided a forum in which issues surrounding the war were discussed, often extensively. Many an editor, in fact, had to intervene to end prolonged exchanges between adversaries. The letters between R. Bell and "A Factory Operative" in Todmorden is a case in point. The exchange, which lasted from October 1863 to March 1864, explored in great detail many of the issues involved in the war, ranging from whether slavery helped to civilize the African to the benefits of republican government.[62] Exchanges like these were reinforced by letters to the editors that attempted to engage

60. Crawford, *The Anglo-American Crisis*, 15; *Morning Star*, 3, 23, 24, 27 May, 30 October 1861.

61. Jenkins, *Britain and the War of the Union*, 2: 34–36; Midgley, *Women against Slavery*, 178–79; *National Anti Slavery Standard*, 13 April 1861; *Liberator*, 4 April 1862.

62. See issues of the Todmorden *Times* from 17 October 1863 to 12 March 1864.

issues on a broader front. Here the Union seemed to have had a decided advantage. There was no one among Confederate advocates to compare to Samuel Goddard of Birmingham. Born in Massachusetts in 1796, Goddard migrated to Birmingham around 1817 and joined a number of young Americans who had set up as merchants in the city. He became active in various Radical movements, including the Anti–Corn Law League. Whenever an article Goddard considered antithetical to the Union cause appeared in a local newspaper, he responded promptly. By the end of the war he had written and published 279 letters, which when published as a book at the end of the war ran to 583 pages.[63] What Goddard did in Birmingham, T. Perronet Thompson, a veteran of the West Indian abolitionist movement, did in Bradford. Many of his letters to the Bradford *Advertiser*, which called on the Union to create a black army to fight in the South and which insisted that the freedom of the slaves would work to the benefit of the British working class, were reprinted by newspapers in other parts of the country and in the United States.[64]

Both Union and Confederate organizations tried to influence editorial (and by extension public) opinion through the distribution of what the LES called fact sheets. By early 1863 they were sending these brief informative sheets to more than three hundred newspapers every week.[65] Widely circulated, these free tracts also disseminated information to the public. In late 1862 the BFASS produced two such pieces: "What Is the South Fighting For" and "The Address of the Committee on the American Crisis." A third, "British Aid to the Confederates," was published in March. Thousands of copies of each were in circulation by the summer of 1863. Going door to door, the Reverend John Curwen of Plaistow, London, alone distributed 5,000 copies of the second and third titles. The London Ladies Emancipation Society published a dozen tracts in 1864, over 12,000 of which had been distributed by the end of the year.[66] The SIA countered with its series Papers for

---

63. *Edgbastonia* 6 (August 1888): 113–18, Birmingham Public Library, Birmingham, England; John Thakray Bunce, "Newspaper Cuttings Relating to Birmingham Obituaries," Birmingham Public Library, England; Samuel A. Goddard, *The American Rebellion: Letters on the American Rebellion by Samuel A. Goddard, 1860–1865* (London, 1870).

64. For a biography of Thompson see Fladeland, *Abolitionists and Working-Class Problems in the Age of Industrialization*, 93–110. Thompson's letters can be found in the *Advertiser* (Bradford), 25 May 1861 to 18 April 1863.

65. *Morning Star*, 29 January 1863.

66. British and Foreign Anti Slavery Society minute book 4, BFASS Papers; Chamerovzow to Brougham, London, 15 May 1863, Brougham Papers; London Ladies Emancipation Society,

the People, some of which may have been the work of local chapters. It appears, for example, that the first in the series, "The Right of Southern Secession," was put out by the Bradford auxiliary. The SIA estimated that more than 85,000 of these tracts were issued by the beginning of 1864. It is not clear exactly how they were disseminated. In addition to being placed in the rooms of local societies for members to peruse, they were scattered through the audience at major SIA meetings.[67]

The tracts and fact sheets complemented the more substantial works—books, travelogues, and pamphlets—published independently or under the auspices of societies. While it is impossible to determine exactly how many were published or how many of each were put in circulation, it is clear from the advertisements in major newspapers such as the *Times* that dozens were printed. The frequency with which reprints appeared suggests that many of them attracted wide attention. They were a vital part of the propaganda apparatus. Freeman Morse called Sinclair's pamphlet "the armory" from which speakers and writers could marshal facts about the war. Hotze was convinced that the publication of two pro-Confederate pamphlets in late 1863 was symptomatic of the growing support for the cause in Britain: "The virus of anti-slavery prejudice was in the blood; no external application could cure it; but the antidote is now entered into the blood also, and follows it in its circulation through the body literary and politic." Matthew Maury printed and distributed to twenty thousand parishes one of the Reverend Tremlett's sermons calling for an end to the war. A few months later the Society for Promoting the Cessation of Hostilities in America began to print and distribute one thousand copies a week of an enlarged edition of Charles Morehead's "Essay." Seven hundred copies were sent to the Commons and four hundred to the Lords to coincide with a parliamentary motion calling for a joint British and European effort to end the war.[68]

The friends of the Union were equally active. The LES claimed to have

---

The Second Annual Report. . . . January 1865 (London, 1865); *Anti Slavery Reporter*, 5 March 1863; *Morning Star*, 14 February 1863.

67. *Index*, 31 December 1863; *Guardian* (Manchester), 30 January 1864. Copies were distributed at one of Spence's meetings in Glasgow. *North British Daily Mail*, 27 November 1863.

68. Morse to Seward, London, 6 February 1863, Despatches from U.S. Consuls in London, 1790–1906; Hotze to Benjamin, London, 26 December 1863, Hotze Papers; Williams, *Matthew Fontain Maury*, 412, 626; Tremlett to Mason, London, 2 June 1864, Mason Papers. For examples of pamphlets and books offered for sale see *Times* (London), 26 February, 2 May, 5 November 1863.

published two dozen pamphlets in 1863, many of them the speeches of prominent figures in the movement. Apparently only three slave narratives, long a staple of antislavery propaganda, were published during the war, those of J. H. Banks, Harriet Jacobs, and Jacob Green. Toward the end of the war George Thompson claimed that almost 600,000 copies of pamphlets supporting the Union had been circulated. It is not clear how many of these were the work of British friends of the Union, for the Loyal Publication Society, an organization formed in America to rally public opinion to the Union, estimated that it sent 7,000 of its pamphlets to Europe, most of them to Britain.[69] While Morse covered the cost of printing Sinclair's pamphlet from his "secret service" fund and distributed it free to the public, most pamphlets were published under the auspices of one of the national organizations or a local affiliate and sold cheaply to raise funds for local societies.

The dozens of pamphlets that circulated throughout Britain added to the corpus of information on the war and its effects on American society. William Howard Russell's detailed and influential accounts of his experiences in America during the early months of the war, which appeared in the *Times* and painted a grim picture of a country torn apart by irreconcilable differences, were read widely. Others published accounts of their travels to both North and South. Merton Coulter's tabulation shows that of ten British accounts of visits to America, eight were partial to the Confederacy. These included the details of W. C. Corsan's efforts to make contact with business partners in the South and the Reverend W. W. Malet's attempt to find his sister, who was stranded on the South Carolina plantation owned by her recently slain husband. Malet painted an idyllic picture of life on the plantation, where not one of the 350 slaves deserted and where he observed the coachman reading Bunyan's *Pilgrim's Progress*. "The negroes on the plantation have easy work," he reported. All had gardens and animals; no child worked before the age of

69. *Anti Slavery Reporter*, 1 March 1864; *Liberator*, 15 April 1864, 24 March 1865; J. H. Estcourt to Dudley, Manchester, 21 March 1864, Dudley Collection; Frank Freidel, "The Loyal Publication Society: A Pro-Union Propaganda Agency," *Mississippi Valley Historical Review* 26 (December 1939): 359–63; J. W. C. Pennington, ed., *A Narrative of Events in the Life of J. H. Banks, an Escaped Slave, from the Cotton State of Alabama, in America* (Liverpool, 1861); Harriet A. Jacobs, *The Deeper Wrong; Or, Incidents in the Life of a Slave Girl* (London, 1862); J. D. Green, "Narrative of the Life of J. D. Green, A Runaway Slave From Kentucky, Containing an Account of His Three Escapes, in 1839, 1846, and 1848" (1864; reprint in Yuval Taylor, ed., *I Was Born a Slave: An Anthology of Classic Slave Narratives* [Chicago, 1999, 1: 683–721]). Examples of pamphlets include Adams, *The Slaveholders' War*, which was translated in Gujratee; Jones, *The Slaveholders' War*; and Conway, *Testimonies concerning Slavery*.

fifteen; there were half tasks on Saturday; every evening some of the slaves came into the parlor of the Great House to read the New Testament to his sister; all owners to whom he spoke were opposed to the idea of splitting up families by sale; and superannuated slaves were "comfortably housed and cared for."[70] Anthony Trollope's travelogue spoke more to the political issues leading to secession than did Malet's, although as in his account of his visit to the West Indies in 1859, Trollope argued that the Negro had benefited little from emancipation. Convinced that slavery was the cause of the conflict and that no people were obliged to remain permanently attached to a form of government they despised, Trollope nevertheless argued that the Union had every right to fight to preserve its national integrity.[71]

Observers partial to the Union also had their say, although the volume of the work they produced was less impressive. Among the most popular was Edward Dicey's *Six Months in the Federal States,* which appeared in March 1863. A collection of articles that had first appeared in *The Spectator* and *Macmillan's Magazine,* the book was based on Dicey's six-month visit to the North and the border states early in 1862. Although no racial egalitarian, Dicey condemned slavery and was critical of the treatment of free blacks in the North. He also attempted to explain the constitutional and political limits that impinged on Lincoln's emancipation edict and provided a glimpse of ways in which the war affected life in the Union. Although not strictly a travelogue, Frances Kemble's account of the two years she spent on a Georgia plantation in 1838 and 1839 contrasted sharply with the picture of slavery provided by Malet and others. Published in 1863, Kemble's journal, with its stark descriptions of the conditions under which slaves were forced to live and the treatment they received from their masters, in many ways resembles the slave narrative. Throughout, Kemble is uneasy in her role as slave mistress and does all that she can to improve the conditions of her husband's slaves. In the end, the situation gets the best of her and she leaves, never to return. The planters who inhabit Kemble's journal are not the aristocrats of whom

70. Martin Crawford, ed., *William Howard Russell's Civil War Private Diary and Letters, 1861–1862* (Athens, Ga., 1992), xl; E. Merton Coulter, ed., *Travels in the Confederate States: A Bibliography* (Norman, Okla., 1948), xi; Corsan, *Two Months in the Confederate States;* Malet, *An Errand to the South in the Summer of 1862,* 45–68. For the impact of British travelers' accounts in the 1850s, see Crawford, "British Travelers and the Anglo-American Relationship in the 1850s." For an analysis of the views of British travelers to the United States before the war, see Max Berger, *The British Traveler in America, 1830–1860* (1943; reprint, Glouster, Mass., 1964).

71. Trollope, *North America,* 1: 15; 2: 48, 66; Eric Williams, *British Historians and the West Indies* (London, 1964), 89.

the friends of the Confederacy were so fond; rather they are impoverished landowners who live in dilapidated houses surrounded by large numbers of malnourished and exploited slaves.[72]

While the frequency of and numbers of people attending meetings are accepted as accurate measurements of public support for a cause, as are the scale and dissemination of printed materials, nothing seems a more potent reflection of the people's views than the petition. First established as part of the political landscape in the seventeenth century, petitions became important political tools to maintain and articulate the extent of "popular support on which extraparliamentary politics depends." They were, as Seymour Drescher has shown, the "symbol of the people mobilised," the result of "extensive expenditures of energy, ingenuity, material resources, organization, propaganda and public discussion."[73] Petitions to Parliament in the nineteenth century averaged ten thousand per year. Many on which the early abolitionist movement relied contained thousands of names. One historian has estimated that the 1792 petition against the slave trade contained the names of 13 percent of the adult male population of England, Scotland, and Wales.[74] By midcentury the tradition of "rolling in" to Parliament monster petitions signed by thousands had given way to more frequent appeals signed by a smaller number of people. No one petition to Parliament during the war could claim to represent as large a percentage of the population as did the earlier abolition documents, but petitions remained, nonetheless, the most immediate way of representing to those in power the people's views on a particular issue.

Not all these public appeals were aimed at affecting policy; they were also, along with addresses and memorials to the president and people of the United States, expressions of solidarity and provided a kind of people-to-people contact that spoke to traditions of independent political activity across national boundaries. Addresses of this kind, which aimed to support and encourage coworkers, were one of the features of the transatlantic abolitionist movement dating back to the 1830s. Over one-half million people added their names to the address from the "Women of England to Their Sisters, the Women of the

72. Dicey's book has been republished as *Spectator of America*, ed., Herbert Mitgang (Athens, Ga., 1989) 44, 52–53; Frances Anne Kemble, *Journal of a Residence on a Georgia Plantation in 1838–1839* (1863; reprint, Athens, Ga., 1971), 11, 150–51.

73. Colin Leys, "Petitioning in the Nineteenth and Twentieth Centuries," *Political Studies* 3 (February 1955): 59; Drescher, "Public Opinion and the Destruction of British Colonial Slavery," 25.

74. Oldfield, *Popular Politics and British Anti-Slavery*, 114.

United States of America" following the publication of *Uncle Tom's Cabin*. Local societies also initiated addresses that sought to make contact directly with organizations across the Atlantic without first winning the imprimatur of a national society. The "Address to the Inhabitants of the United States from the People of Warrington upon the Subject of Slaveholding," organized by William Robson in 1859 and signed by 3,522, is a case in point. When Peter Sinclair pleaded with the British and Foreign Anti Slavery Society to hold a series of meetings leading up to the anniversary of the Emancipation Proclamation and to use them as a means of preparing memorials to the people of the United States, he was, therefore, calling on a tradition that abolitionists on both sides of the Atlantic cherished. Such appeals, Sinclair pointed out, would bring British antislavery societies together to reaffirm the country's commitment to abolition; they would lend support to the movement in America; and they could persuade Lincoln to adopt a more comprehensive program of emancipation.[75]

Taken together, petitions, memorials, and addresses were possibly the most reliable indicators of the views of "the people." Not that they were spontaneous and independent expressions, rather they were the results of deliberate attempts by political factions to generate interest in a particular cause, but by the same token, they spoke to and reflected the concerns of the signatories. It might well have been easier to get people to sign a petition, either because other members of their family or coworkers did, than it was to encourage them to join a political cause, but the political significance of the act of adding one's name to an appeal to the government or the citizens of another country is not thereby diminished. The editors of the London *Times* could contemptuously dismiss such acts as "so common, so familiar, and generally so useless that we simply regard them as the ejaculations of weakness, or indifference, or contempt," but the vehemence with which opponents tried to discredit such efforts suggests that the act of signing an address or memorial was a supremely political act and as such had always to be contested.[76]

Both sides in the dispute employed a number of devices to gather names. Leading members of organizations often took on the task of collecting signatures. Kershaw, for example, was central in the effort to collect names for the 1864 Peace Address organized by the Southern Independence Association.

75. Betty Fladeland, *Men and Brothers: Anglo-American Antislavery Cooperation* (Urbana, Ill., 1972), 295–96. Information on the Warrington address kindly supplied by Janet Toole. Sinclair to Chamerovzow, Manchester, 26 September 1863, BFASS Papers.

76. *Times* (London), 12 October 1864.

The 1863 address to Lincoln from the people of Birmingham was the work of two men, J. Arthur Partridge and J. A. Langford. Using a network of priests, Kershaw and others were able to encourage parishioners to sign the Peace Address and the 1864 petition to Parliament. Priests in Ancoats, for example, opened their pulpits to Kershaw and encouraged their flock to add their names to the Peace Address, and the *Times* reported that in Ireland, signatures were being obtained through the "influence of the Roman Catholic priesthood." Over half of the 300,000 people who signed the Peace Address were Irish. Unemployed cotton workers were hired by the SIA, some at the rate of four shillings per day, to go door to door collecting names. John C. Edwards and Edward O. Greening reported from Manchester that names were being collected at homes and at mill gates for a pro-South petition that hid its true intent behind a plea for full-time employment. Tremlett even proposed that friends of the South emulate the abolitionists, who had employed foreigners such as Frederick Douglass, and engage Americans to agitate the issue. A "Factor's Clerk" in Birmingham volunteered to visit homes and shops after work to collect names for the address to Lincoln. Copies of petitions were left on "the drawing room or Hall Table of friends," and at bookstores, cotton exchanges, and Working Men's Institutes. National organizations also printed and sent to local societies copies of petitions with space provided for the chapters to add their names.[77]

As was true of all other political acts, the collection of names on petitions was vigorously contested. Questioning the drinking habits of those on whom the opposition depended was a tried and true method of denigrating one's foes. Conway, for example, insisted that the promoters of the Peace Address were "raking up the names from drunken groups in public-houses who didn't know the difference between America and Timbuctoo." Greening reported that memorials were "mostly promoted in mills, the owners of which are pro-South and pressure is put upon the mill hands to induce them to sign." Implicit in Greening's observation is the assumption that, left to their own devices, factory workers would not have signed such memorials. Opponents of the Peace Address also sought to undercut its success by assailing the influence wielded by the priesthood. Thomas Barker questioned Kershaw's re-

77. *Guardian* (Bury), 25 June 1864; *Times* (Bury), 2 July 1864; *Examiner and Times* (Manchester), 14 November 1863; *News* (Salford), 16, 23 July 1864; *Daily Post* (Birmingham), 20 January 1863; Tremlett to Maury, London, 1 January 1864, Maury Papers; *Times* (Hereford), 10 October 1863; *Free Press* (Burnley), 23 May 1863; Eastman to Seward, Bristol, 2 June 1864, Despatches from U.S. Consuls in Bristol, 1792–1906.

liance on the churches in Ancoats, where the Peace Address received "the signature of many women and children, and no doubt a good few men of the genuine Celtic stripe, who always do what the priest says must be done."[78] While such blatant anti-Irish views were rarely a part of the public debate over the war, their use in this case, one of the few occasions when the Irish made their position on the war known, shows the extent to which opponents would go to paint signers of pro-Confederate petitions as uninformed and politically dependent.

Heightened public agitation in 1863 produced a flurry of petitions to Parliament. Early in the war, there had been a couple of petitions condemning the South and pleading against recognition from small towns in Sussex and Hampshire. The following year, 1862, a group that included Aitken organized a petition from Lancashire and Cheshire pointing out the growing crisis brought on by the shortage of cotton and calling on the government to work for reconciliation between the warring factions as the best way of ensuring a resumption of the supply. But plans by John Roebuck to submit a motion to Parliament in mid-1863 calling for joint British and French intervention to stop the war generated a dramatic increase in the number of petitions. Supported by large public meetings in London, Liverpool, Manchester, York, and sixty other towns, an LES petition in May condemned the South, expressed concern about the construction of ships for the Confederate navy, and called on the government to continue its policy of neutrality. In late June another from the LES insisting that the public supported the Union's emancipation policy reinforced the plea of a UES petition that expressed concern about rumors of possible recognition. The LES and UES petitions stole a march on the opposition by raising serious question about the way the public would react to any move away from neutrality. Those in support of recognition organized a series of meetings in Lancashire, Cheshire, and Yorkshire beginning in late May in an effort to boost Roebuck's action in Parliament.[79]

78. *Times* (London), 9 September 1864; *Index,* 15 September 1864; Joseph M. Hernon Jr., *Celts, Catholics, and Copperheads: Ireland Views the American Civil War* (Columbus, Ohio, 1968), 105; *Liberator,* 4 November 1864; *Boston Commonwealth,* 5 November 1864; West to Seward, Dublin, 6 October 1864, Despatches from U.S. Consuls in Dublin, 1790–1906; Greening to Chamerovzow, Manchester, 31 December 1863, BFASS Papers.

79. *Reports of the Select Committee of the House of Commons on Public Petitions, Session 1861* (London, 1861); *Reports of the Select Committee of the House of Commons on Public Petitions,*

Although Roebuck's motion never reached the floor, supporters of recognition knew that without a change in government policy there was little chance secession would succeed. With the help of Tremlett and the Society for Promoting the Cessation of Hostilities in America, Maury and Mason initiated and financed a new campaign in late 1863 to coincide with plans by William S. Lindsay to reopen the debate on recognition when Parliament reconvened in 1864. An estimated thirty meetings were held throughout Lancashire in the weeks leading up to the submission of Lindsay's motion. The campaign organizers planned to direct their efforts toward both Parliament and Lord John Russell, the foreign secretary. The petition to the House of Commons contained sixty thousand names, including, according to the *Index*, "the whole list of mercantile and manufacturing firms that have done most towards making Manchester the commercial metropolis of these counties," as well as clergymen from all denominations and city councillors and aldermen. A second petition containing the names of an estimated ninety thousand operatives was submitted to Russell by a deputation of workingmen in July.

While there had only been fifteen petitions from both sides in 1863, the number increased dramatically in 1864. One or another of the pro-Confederate groups organized at least eighty-one in that year. Three of them called for peace and Southern independence, seventy-eight for termination of the war. About twenty-four of the latter came from Ireland, reflecting the recent attempts by Hotze and other Confederate agents to staunch the flow of Irish emigrants to the North. Of the seventy-eight petitions calling for cessation of hostilities, ten came from places so small that they do not appear on a modern road map; twenty-four were from small towns and villages; twelve were from London; and six from Lancashire and Cheshire. The limited number of petitions from the major textile towns suggests that the pro-Confederate lobby had changed the thrust of its appeal. No longer would recognition lead to a reopening of the supply lines to cotton fields in the South; thus the appeal now centered on the argument that the length of the war testified to the inability of the North to recapture the South. Given

---

Session 1862 (London, 1862); *Reports of the Select Committee of the House of Commons on Public Petitions, Session 1863* (London, 1863); *Independent* (Sheffield and Rotherham), 27 May 1863; *Morning Star*, 27, 29 June 1863; *Mercury* (Leeds), 2 July 1863; *Leicestershire Mercury*, 4 July 1863; *Times* (Blackburn), 4 July 1863; *Standard* (Oldham), 18 July 1863.

the impasse, the continuing loss of life could not be justified. These petitions reflected Tremlett's and the society's conviction that the best way to Southern independence lay through an armistice.[80]

Appeals, whether to Parliament or to the people of the United States, were invariably contested by the opposition. In Birmingham, opponents of the address to Lincoln tried unsuccessfully to mount a counterdemonstration expressing the town's abhorrence of Union policy. When a petition calling for the recognition of the Confederacy was sent to Parliament with the signatures of the "Mayor, magistrates, aldermen, town councillors, clergymen, solicitors, surgeons, cotton spinners, manufacturers, tradesmen and artizans" of Burnley, the local chapter of the Union and Emancipation Society organized a counterpetition pleading with the government to ignore such requests. The UES response came in the form of nine separate petitions containing two thousand signatures from Burnley. Similarly the SIA submitted an unknown number of petitions containing five thousand names. Although those signing the SIA petitions represented almost one-quarter of the town's population in 1861, the Burnley campaign containing multiple petitions signed by a relatively small number of people had by this time become the standard mode of operation.[81]

Petitioning, as Brian Harrison has shown, kept local organizations "in trim," gave focus to their campaign, educated the public, and at the same time tried to delegitimize the work of opponents. The abolitionist petition campaign, perfected in the early years of the agitation against the slave trade and used to great effect during the fight against West Indian slavery, remained a vital part of the antislavery propaganda apparatus down through the years. Held in reserve to be used whenever needed, the petition was periodically employed by abolitionists to influence policy. When it appeared that fugitive

80. *Reports of the Select Committee of the House of Commons on Public Petitions, Session 1864; Index*, 2, 9, 30 June, 7, 14, 21 July, 6 October 1864; *Weekly Observer* (Macclesfield), 16 July 1864; *Courier* (Macclesfield), 23 July 1864; *Times* (Bury), 2 July 1864; *Guardian* (Bury), 25 June 1864; *Stockport and Cheshire County News*, 2, 23 July 1864; *Examiner and Times* (Manchester), 19 July 1864; Tremlett to "Dear Sir," London, 13 July 1864, Spence to Mason, Liverpool, 18 July 1864, Mason Papers; Dudley to Seward, Liverpool, 5 January, 5 February 1864, Despatches from U.S. Consuls in Liverpool, 1790–1906; Jenkins, *Britain and the War of the Union*, 2: 317, 334–36; R. J. M. Blackett, "Pressure from Without: African Americans, British Public Opinion, and Civil War Diplomacy," in Robert E. May, ed., *The Union, the Confederacy, and the Atlantic Rim* (West Lafayette, Ind., 1995), 88–89.

81. *Daily Gazette* (Birmingham), 9, 10 January 1863; *Advertiser* (Burnley), 6, 13 June 1863; *Free Press* (Burnley), 23 May, 4, 11 July 1863; Brook, "Confederate Sympathies in North East Lancashire, 1862–1864," 213; *Advertiser* (Stockport), 26 June, 3 July 1863.

slave John Anderson might be extradited from Canada to face criminal charges in the United States, Chamerovzow and the BFASS organized a campaign that flooded the secretary of the colonies with petitions calling for Anderson's release. They came from local societies and churches from Cornwall to Newcastle, each containing a few dozen names.[82]

The tradition would be drawn on again a couple of years later when Britain appeared poised to declare war against the United States over the *Trent* affair. The seizure of Confederate commissioners Mason and Slidell from a British ship stirred deep nationalist resentment in Britain and led to calls for the payment of reparations by the United States and, failing that, war. "If the case be indeed true as reported," one editor insisted, "there are, we fear only two ways of settling the difficulty, an ample apology or an appeal to arms." Anxious to avoid a conflict, Richard Cobden and others, many of whom supported the Union, called for the organization of public meetings and the preparation of petitions calling on the government to submit the dispute to arbitration. John Epps, a homeopathic physician, denounced British hysteria: "It is indeed to me a regret to read the trash written respecting the honour of the British flag," he wrote the *Morning Star*, "while, at the same time, the justice of the British flag, a far higher attribute, is forgotten." Some thought the affair nothing more than a smoke screen for those eager to promote recognition of the Confederacy. A memorial from the mainly working-class congregation of Surrey Chapel, London, led by Newman Hall, called on the prime minister to submit the dispute to arbitration, insisting that with Britain, the United States was the friend of "Hungary and Italy and of popular freedom as opposed to despotism." War with America would result in Britain's fighting alongside slaveholders. Memorials from the BFASS and scores from ministerial alliances and working-class meetings throughout the country also called for arbitration.[83] These memorials met with opposition in some quarters. Following a meeting in Halifax that called on the government to adopt peaceful means to resolve the dispute—citing ancestral and commercial ties between the two countries and the fact that they had already

82. See petitions in the Newcastle Collection, University of Nottingham; Reinders, "Anglo-Canadian Abolitionism: The John Anderson Case, 1860–1861," 82.

83. Cobden to Bright, Midhurst, 12, 18 December 1861, Cobden Papers; Epps, ed., *Diary of the Late John Epps, M.D.*, 593; *Morning Star*, 25 December 1861, 1, 6, 8 January 1862; *Guardian* (Brighton), 1 January 1862; *Journal* (Newcastle), 10 December 1861; *Newcastle Daily Chronicle and Northern Counties Advertiser*, 28 November, 7 December 1861; *Times* (Cardiff), 10 January 1862; *Mercury* (Bristol), 30 November 1861; *Daily Post* (Bristol), 2, 3 January 1862.

fought two wars—a countermemorial, signed by three hundred, including "nearly every gentleman of standing and influence," called for prompt action, arguing that "the maintenance and defence of their insulted national rights and privileges must rest with the British people themselves, and is not the subject for arbitration by a foreign power."[84]

Organizers viewed petitions, addresses, and memorials, which were adopted at meetings and to which people could later add their names, as the most accurate measurements of the public's view of the war. This conviction explains why the Lincoln administration put such store in the memorial adopted by the thousands who met at the Free Trade Hall, Manchester, on December 31, 1862. It is why Charles F. Adams overcame his concerns about the diplomatic propriety of entertaining visits from representatives of public meetings and agreed to meet with delegations from antislavery societies and why he began to accept memorials and addresses from meetings expressing support for the Union. Every delegation that visited the legation was a public-relations victory for the Union. Members generally included some of the country's most prominent political figures. Among the five who brought the Birmingham address were Bright and Charles Sturge, the mayor of Birmingham. The prominent mayor of a major industrial city, Sturge was the son of the founder of the BFASS. Delegations that could not make the journey to London met with consuls in provincial cities. A deputation from the Parliamentary Reform Society of Paisley, for example, delivered an address to the consul in Glasgow in the summer of 1862 expressing support for Lincoln's conduct of the war.[85]

Nothing that the friends of the Confederacy did carried as much politically symbolic weight as British citizens meeting with representatives of the United States government to express public support for the Union. Agents of the Confederacy did have extensive contacts with members of the government and Parliament, but as in all matters of diplomacy, these usually took place away from the glare of public scrutiny. Not so the meetings with Adams and the American consuls, which were widely publicized. It was in an effort to counter this advantage that Tremlett arranged separate meetings with the prime minister and Russell in 1864 to submit the petitions calling for a stop to the war and why he made sure that meetings were well publicized. Concerned

84. *Guardian* (Halifax), 14, 21, 28 December 1861, 4 January 1862; *Courier* (Halifax), 28 December 1861, 4 January 1862.

85. C. F. Adams diary, Adams Papers; Prettyman to Seward, Glasgow, 29 July 1862, Despatches from U.S. Consuls in Glasgow, 1801–1906.

with more than the symbolic value of such meetings, however, Tremlett calculated that any call from the British government for an armistice would help the cause of the peace party in the United States in the upcoming presidential elections. Pressure on the government at home and an appeal to Washington signed by thousands and calling for cessation of hostilities, Tremlett hoped, would bring about Southern independence without involving Britain in the war. Kershaw and Joseph Parker, secretaries of the SIA, organized the effort to procure names for the Peace Address, with help from a group of agents and priests in Ireland. Within a matter of weeks the address had attracted 300,000 names, an impressive number by any account. The plan was to have Parker deliver the address to Horatio Seymour, governor of New York and one of the leaders of the peace party, in time to affect the outcome of the presidential campaign in November. Nothing, however, was heard from Parker for two months, during which time Lincoln was reelected. Unwilling to encourage so symbolic a statement of British interference in American affairs, Seymour had refused to accept the address. Following the elections, Parker made his way to Washington, D.C., where he failed to get an audience with Seward, who insisted that Parker first prove he was a bona fide emissary.[86]

Ignored by the Copperheads in New York and summarily dismissed by Seward in Washington, Parker cut a rather pathetic figure. Not only had the twin approaches failed to elicit a positive response from either Palmeston or Lincoln, but the Peace Address might even have violated all the constraints traditionally applied to appeals of this sort. The 1853 Appeal of the Women of Britain, following Stowe's visit in 1852, was made to the people, not the government of the United States, and so avoided political entanglements. So, too, did the Address to Ministers in the United States that was adopted by a meeting of British ministers at the Free Trade Hall, Manchester, in the summer of 1863. The address had its origins in a message from 750 French ministers to their British counterparts expressing opposition to slavery and

86. *Index*, 6 October 1864; *Times* (London), 12 October, 12 December 1864; *Boston Commonwealth*, 5 November 1864; Kershaw to Wharncliffe, Manchester, 23 August 1864, Wharncliffe Muniments; West to Seward, Dublin, 10 September 1864, Despatches from U.S. Consuls in Dublin, 1790–1906. Try as he might, Spence could not dissuade Parker and Kershaw from organizing the Peace Address, which he labeled "an absurdity." Parker must have borne most of the cost of his trip to Washington, for as late as August 1865 he was trying to persuade Wharncliffe to help him defray his debts. Spence to Wharncliffe, Liverpool, 28 August 1865, Wharncliffe Muniments; Joseph Parker, *For Peace in America: A Report from Mr. Joseph Parker of Manchester, to Sir Henry De Hogton, Bart., on His Mission as Bearer of the Peace Address from the People of Great Britain and Ireland to the People of the United States of America* (n.p., 1865).

the independence of the Confederacy on the grounds that it "would put back the progress of Christian civilization and of humanity a whole century." James Massie, a Congregationalist minister, and Joseph Rylance of the Church of England were commissioned by the Free Trade Hall meeting to take the address signed by 3,860 British ministers, to America. The address was received by churches throughout the Northeast, and only later did Massie request an official audience with Lincoln, Seward, and other government officials. Any other approach ran the risk of generating opposition. Hotze knew this from experience. When the Appeal to Christians throughout the World from nearly one hundred Southern clergymen arrived at his office in mid-1863, Hotze followed tradition: he had 200,000 copies of the appeal printed and paid to have it attached to "every respectable religious publication."[87] Experience showed that in such matters the most productive approach to government lay through the power of informed public opinion.

No examination of the devices used to influence public opinion would be complete without a look at the ways illustrations and other art helped to shape perceptions. In this venue pro-Confederate forces were at a distinct disadvantage. With the exception of portraits of Stonewall Jackson and other Confederate generals by B. F. Reinhardt, which were put on display at London galleries, the South lacked the sort of visuals that appealed to the values of the people. The movement on behalf of the Confederacy produced nothing to compare with the Wedgewood cameos of a kneeling male slave with the caption, "Am I Not a Man and A Brother," or the female equivalent, "Am I Not a Woman and a Sister," that were such a vital part of the movement to end West Indian slavery. Although the cameos were not replicated during the war, Staffordshire potters produced a number of portrait figures, including ones of Lincoln and John Brown. When at a Bury meeting William Andrew Jackson held up the illustration of the slave ship used so effectively at the end of the eighteenth century by those opposed to the slave trade, he was appealing to a tradition that resonated with his audience. Similarly, audiences were repulsed when fugitive slave Jacob Green donned a collar used to constrain slaves and J. Hughes showed a flapper used to punish female slaves. Richard Ansdell's

87. *Morning Star*, 4, 6 May 1863; *National Anti Slavery Standard*, 4 July, 1, 8 August 1863; *Guardian* (Manchester), 2 February 1864; *Anti Slavery Reporter*, 1 August, 1 September 1863; Jameson, "The London Expenditure of the Confederate Secret Service," 816; Hotze to Benjamin, London, 23 July 1863, Hotze to Chadwick, London, 20 March 1865, Hotze Papers.

famous painting *The Hunted Slave,* completed in 1861, drew on this tradition. An accomplished painter of animals, Ansdell first exhibited this work
at the Royal Academy, then at shows in the provinces and at the International Exhibition in 1862. It depicted a fugitive slave, broken shackles
still on his arms, defending his wife from an attack by a pack of furious dogs.
Prints were made and sold throughout the country. Reacting to the painting, a viewer declared it a "standing protest against slavery, speaking more
powerfully to the feelings than volumes of written descriptions."[88]

Nothing appealed more graphically to the feelings of revulsion against
slavery and the cause of the Confederacy than the *carte de viste* of the lacerated back of the slave Gordon. A fugitive slave from Mississippi, Gordon
entered Union lines near Baton Rouge, Louisiana, in early 1863. Not long
after, *Harper's Weekly* published three sketches of Gordon: one showed him
entering Union lines in tattered clothes; a second showed him dressed in a
soldier's uniform; and the third showed his back terribly scarred from a whip-
ping. A *carte de viste* of the third sketch, published in London in mid-1863 and
captioned "The Peculiar Institution Illustrated," was sold by the BFASS at
one shilling and six pence. With the Gordon *carte de viste,* pro-Union propagandists tapped into a popular art form. The card turned up everywhere. It
formed part of a placard announcing a Sinclair meeting in Halifax. A
Mr. Grant, described as an abolitionist and coffeehouse keeper, interrupted a
speech by Dr. Joseph M'Dowell, a surgeon in the Confederate army, by holding up the picture of Gordon's back. At a meeting in Padiham, E. O. Greening
held up a "large wood engraving, copied from a photograph of the back of one
of those well-used negroes three months after he had received his wages, and
pointed out where the hungry whip had dug into his flesh, leaving scars which
the negro would bear to his dying day." One opponent of the Union wrote of
a "republican newsvendor" in Blackburn who was in the habit of displaying a
"disgusting painting" of a slave with a lacerated back at the front of his shop.

88. P. D. Gordon Pugh, *Staffordshire Portrait Figures and Allied Subjects of the Victorian Era*
(London, 1970), 3; Oldfield, *Popular Politics and British Anti-Slavery,* 163; *Times* (Bury), 30 May
1863; *Courier* (Halifax), 3 October 1862, 2 April 1864; *News* (Hinkley), 16 January 1864. During the annual meeting at which Bright and Scholefield met their constituents, a slave whip was
brandished by someone in the audience as a protest against Scholefield's membership in the SIA.
Daily Post (Birmingham), 27 January 1864; Hugh Honour, *The Image of the Black in Western Art*
(Cambridge, Mass., 1989), 4: 212; *Chronicle* (Preston), 18 December 1861; *Weekly Scotsman,* 12
October 1861; *Times* (London), 23 May 1863; Norman Longmate, *The Hungry Mills* (London,
1978), 147.

The letter writer had no doubt that the newsagent was trying to turn the people against the South.[89]

Turning the people against the opposition was the aim of the apparatus employed by both sides in the public debate. By meetings and lectures, newspaper articles and editorials, petitions, addresses and memorials, pamphlets and fact sheets, and aided by such visual representations as the Gordon *carte de viste,* the public was appealed to and reasoned with to give its support to one side or the other. National societies initiated and paid for many of the activities, but much of the work of organizing local meetings and ensuring that petitions were available for signatures, fell to local chapters. The more vibrant the local auxiliary the more extensive was the agitation. In areas where local chapters were relatively inactive, individuals assumed the duties. It is very probable, for example, that without the commitment of David Thomas, the Union would have been swamped by the opposition in Bury. Thomas worked closely with the national office of the UES in Manchester to ensure frequent visits by agents of the society; to him fell the responsibility of arranging the meeting, preparing placards, renting halls, arranging that prominent townsmen would be seated on the platform, ensuring that the opposition did not gain control of the meeting, and always being present at pro-Confederate meetings to challenge speakers, if not disrupt the proceedings. On the eve of the most intense period of public agitation during the war years, F. W. Chesson insisted that the LES was acting not out of a desire to ferment a "fictitious agitation, or to put in motion an extensive centralized machinery; but to develop local public spirit—to make English citizens everywhere feel it was their duty to move and act for themselves."[90] No other agitation in the period, not the movements in support of Polish or Hungarian independence or Italian unification, engaged public interest so extensively as did the debate over the war in America.

89. William C. Darrah, *Cartes de Viste in Nineteenth-Century Photography* (Gettysburg, Pa., 1981), 148; Kathleen Collins, "The Scourged Back," *History of Photography* 9 (January–March 1985): 43–45; *Anti Slavery Reporter,* 1 August 1863; *Courier* (Halifax), 19 September 1863; *Herald* (Preston), 22 August, 12, 19 September 1863; Botsford, "Scotland and the American Civil War," 763–67.

90. *Morning Star,* 29 January 1863.

5

Reaching the People

Agitation helps us and injures the South. These men who have taken hold of this matter are good agitators. . . .

—Dudley to Seward, Liverpool, 20 February 1863. Despatches from U.S. Consuls in Liverpool, 1790–1906

One can assume that Thomas Dudley's observation was not a moral judgment, but rather a testament to the effectiveness of the propaganda machinery developed by partisans of the Union and to the influence of those who participated in the national and local movements to ensure that Britain not deviate from its position of neutrality. Real, not "fictitious agitation," to use F. W. Chesson's felicitous phrase, depended on the creation of a cadre of agitators, an agency, who could broadcast the message across the country. Abolitionists had perfected such a system in the years leading up to West Indian emancipation, and it was to this tradition that supporters of the Union turned in late 1862 after Lincoln's preliminary proclamation of emancipation. The system rested on a foundation of strong national and local societies that employed paid and volunteer agents, some, like George Thompson, with national reputations and others such as Washington Wilkes, who was well known in Radical and Dissenting circles in and around London. Agents were employed for varying lengths of time. Peter Sinclair and William A. Jackson, for example, worked for the Union and Emancipation Society for most of 1863. Volunteers such as John Patterson, a Liverpool corn merchant and temperance advocate, could afford to cover the cost of their activities, while others relied on local societies to meet the expenses of their tours. Pro-Union agents' efforts were reinforced by the presence of a group of African Americans, many of them fugitive slaves, who by their activities lent legitimacy to the cause of union and emancipation.[1]

Friends of the Confederacy employed a similar strategy. Among their national agents was Joseph Barker—a "capital lecturer," James Spence called him—who was employed by the Central Association for the Recognition of the Confederacy for about four months in 1863. T. B. Kershaw and the Reverend Edward Verity played similar roles for the Southern Independence Association following Barker's departure in late 1863. For a brief period in the spring and summer of 1862 Spence and Henry Hotze financed the activities of a group of working-class figures, including Mortimer Grimshaw, William Aitken, and John Matthews, who attempted to rally support for the Confederacy in Lancashire and Cheshire. Getting the Confederate message across also rested on the ability of chapters to sustain the activities of local agents such as Joseph L. Quarmby, a bookseller and former Owenite Socialist who was responsible for much of the SIA's success in and around Oldham. But the Confederate agency was hampered by its inability to sustain its activities over the course of the war. Replacing agents proved difficult. There was no one to fill the breach created by the departure of the ineffective John Smith. By early 1864 only Kershaw and Verity were active, and when Spence ventured out for infrequent meetings, he did so only reluctantly.[2]

The disadvantages under which the Confederate agency operated in no way diminished its determination to get its message across to the public. After all, the Confederacy's survival as an independent nation depended to a significant degree on its ability to win recognition from Britain. Recognition in turn rested on an almost universally accepted conviction that in democracies, governments were susceptible to public pressure. Consequently, agencies ar-

1. For Patterson see Dudley to Seward, Liverpool, 4 February 1863, Despatches from U.S. Consuls in Liverpool, 1790–1906; Patterson to Charles F. Adams, Manchester, 23 April 1863, Dudley Collection; *Daily Courier* (Liverpool), 28 April 1865.

2. Spence to Mason, Liverpool, 16 June 1863, Mason Papers. For Quarmby see Foster, *Class Struggle and the Industrial Revolution*, 158; *Standard* (Oldham), 25 April 1863.

ranged meetings and circulated petitions to coincide with policy debates in Parliament; friends of the Confederacy tried to exploit the dislocations caused by the Cotton Famine to win approval of their cause; and their opponents countered by arranging a series of meetings to coincide with the arrival of three ships carrying thousands of barrels of flour, pork, bread, bacon, and corn, a gift from major commercial figures in New York City and Philadelphia to the operatives hit hardest by the shortage of cotton.[3]

Little about this public agitation was spontaneous, as some historians have claimed; it was rather a well-conceived and organized effort that aimed first to win public approval and ultimately to influence government policy. While there were a few occasions when activities seemed to have been organized independently of national or local societies, much of what occurred was deliberate and calculated to have maximum effect on public opinion. "Let us by all means . . . avoid war" with Britain, one Boston editor declared in April 1863, "but let us turn our attention to the English people; not the Government, nor the literary men, nor the giants of the press, but the working men and working women. Let us avow ourselves the friends of these oppressed classes; let us, as we have done, relieve their starvation, offer them homes in the West, give them our sympathy in their political struggles, and in all ways identify our causes with theirs."[4] The editor was preaching to the converted. Both sides appreciated the political utility of this strategy and had already targeted the people of the working class, particularly those affected most severely by the shortage of cotton, the textile workers of Lancashire and Cheshire. While the famine also devastated, if not to the same degree, the lives of textile workers in other parts of the country, particularly around Glasgow, Belfast, Nottingham, and Hinckley, none of those areas became centers of dispute. Conditions in Duntocher, Lochwinnoch, and Barrhead were comparable to some towns in Lancashire and Cheshire. In late 1862 about one-quarter of the three thousand employed in the mills of Glasgow was idle; others were employed two to four days a week. In the Renfrewshire towns of Johnstone and Linwood, whose economies depended almost entirely on cotton, the lives of textile workers came to mirror those of their counterparts south of the border.[5]

3. For an account of the goods sent from the United States see Douglas Maynard, "Civil War 'Care': The Mission of the *George Griswold*," *New England Quarterly* 34 (September 1961): 301–02.

4. The idea of spontaneity is explored by Ellison, *Support for Secession*, 6; *Boston Commonwealth*, 17 April 1863.

5. Botsford, "Scotland and the American Civil War," 340; W. O. Henderson, "The Cotton Famine in Scotland and the Relief of Distress, 1862–1864," *Scottish Historical Review* 30 (October

Hosiery workers in Hinkley, where the distress showed no sign of easing until December 1864, fared little better. In Nottingham, as well as in the villages of Daybrook and Arnold north of the city, the crisis, which was largely the result of high frame rents, was exacerbated by the shortage of cotton. Thousands were thrown out of work. As in Lancashire and Cheshire, the unemployed did what they could to make ends meet, selling possessions, depleting savings, begging, busking, and tramping.[6] If Mary Ellison's contention that there existed a relationship between the most "searing distress and the strongest support for the Southern states" is to have applicability beyond Lancashire, one would expect to find a similar congruence in the cotton towns of Scotland and Ireland. Yet nothing of the sort occurred. If the number of meetings and lectures is a reliable indicator of the levels of interest in the war, as she posits, then the effects of the famine seemed to have generated comparatively little activity in the cotton towns of Scotland. There is also considerable doubt that the neat confluence of levels of distress and support for the Confederacy that Ellison proposes even existed in Lancashire.[7]

The devastation did, of course, influence the way textile workers saw the war. Their misery must have persuaded many that the solution to the crisis lay in recognition of the Confederacy and the reopening of the cotton trade. Others similarly affected, however, insisted that normalcy would only return when the United States was reunited. A Preston mother with two sons in the cotton mills captured the sense of dismay, uncertainty, and frustration felt by many who took the brunt of the economic dislocation caused by the war. The working class (the "backbone" of England and France, she called it) ran the risk of cracking under the strain caused by the high levels of unemployment. The governments of both countries, she thought, should take a leading role in the effort to stop the war, and if they did not, the working class should compel them to act.[8] But the question of exactly what the working class should pressure the government to do produced no easy an-

---

1951): 155; *Sentinel* (Glasgow), 6 December 1862. Hernon points out that the famine devastated the textile industry in Ulster, throwing almost 100,000 out of work. Hernon Jr., *Celts, Catholics, and Copperheads*, 5–7; *Banner of Ulster*, 25 October 1862.

6. *Leicestershire Mercury*, 20 December 1862; *Journal* (Hinckley), 29 November, 6 December 1862; *News* (Hinckley), 15 October, 5 November, 17 December 1864; *Express* (Nottingham), 6 July 1861, 13 February 1862, 4, 18, 23 April, 15, 16 May 1863, 12, 21 December 1864; *Review* (Nottingham), 5 December 1862, 1 May 1863.

7. Ellison, *Support for Secession*, 5.

8. *Herald* (Preston), 12 July 1862.

swers. Consequently, Lancashire became politically contested ground. The resolution of the county's problems became the country's concern, and as a result, the dispute over what, if any, role Britain should play in the war became universal.

Spence and working-class friends of the Confederacy stole a march on the opposition by organizing a series of meetings in Lancashire in the summer of 1862, aimed at exploiting the distress for political ends. The impetus seemed to have come from Mortimer Grimshaw, who ten years earlier had been a prominent figure in a series of strikes over wages in Lancashire. After the strikes he had emigrated to the United States. Grimshaw returned to England after four years, disillusioned with America—where, he wrote, he looked in vain for a "ten-hour bill, high wages, low rents, and cheap provisions"—and convinced that strikes were counterproductive. Even before leaving for the United States he had called for tactical alliances with Tories and Whigs and later formed the Lancashire, Yorkshire, and Cheshire Labour League, a "Tory-radical protectionist" group.[9] Grimshaw began trying to raise money to hold a series of public meetings in support of the Confederacy sometime in early 1862. He was joined by a number of former associates in the strike movement and in the Labour League, including John Matthews of Stalybridge, Thomas Rhodes and Luke Wood of Stockport, and Kinder Smith of Oldham. William Aitken of Ashton and James Williams of Stockport were also members of the group. Of these, only Williams had not abandoned his radical past, although even he, like so many other Chartists, was by 1858 calling for alliances between Radicals and middle-class reformers.[10] In April, Grimshaw and Aitken visited Spence, hoping to raise money to finance a series of proposed meetings. Spence and members of the Liverpool Shipowners' Association approved of the plan and lent their financial support. Spence also offered to help draw up a series of petitions to Parliament that Grimshaw and Aitken planned to submit to meetings all over Lancashire.[11]

Within two days of Grimshaw's and Aitken's return from Liverpool, a massive meeting in Ashton, attended by more than six thousand and organized by

9. Dutton and King, 'Ten Percent and No Surrender,' 46–47, 57; Guardian (Preston), 25 May 1861.

10. Dutton and King, 'Ten Percent and No Surrender,' 41, 57, 181–82; Carole Anne Naomi Reid, "The Chartist Movement in Stockport" (master's thesis, University of Hull, 1974), 490–94; Examiner and Times (Manchester), 4, 26 July 1862.

11. Spence to Mason, Liverpool, 28 April 1862, Mason Papers; Examiner and Times (Manchester), 29 July 1862.

the Committee of Employers and Employed, was asked to adopt a resolution calling for recognition of the Confederacy. Aitken called for a lifting of the blockade so that cotton could reach Britain; insisted that, unlike the Union, the Confederacy was committed to following a policy of free trade; suggested that the government be memorialized to recognize the South; and called for the formation of committees made up of all classes "to save the country from bankruptcy, want and disease." Matthews argued that recognition was inevitable and wondered, if this were so, why the government did not shorten the distress by doing what all knew it would ultimately have to do. The organizers ran into stiff opposition from a group who condemned them for exploiting the distress to win recognition for the slaveholding Confederacy. In placards posted throughout the town, opponents warned that a "number of evil-disposed agitators" had been hired by "the enemies of liberty, the advocates of slavery, and paid by the agents of the rebels of South America, in order to get the assent of the people of Lancashire in favour of breaking the blockade, and thus acknowledge the rebel government." The resolution supporting recognition was countered by an amendment that urged the governments of Britain and France to work with America to crush the abettors of slavery and oppression for, it declared, America was "the most liberal government in the world" and should be supported. To do otherwise would undermine "humanity, justice, liberty, civilization, and the future peace and prosperity of mankind." Partly because of the size of the crowd and the unrelenting clamor that greeted each speaker, it is not clear whether either the resolution or amendment was carried. In the end both sides claimed victory.[12]

Over the next few weeks opponents of recognition held a couple of meetings in Stalybridge and Ashton that declared in favor of finding alternative sources of cotton as the best way to deal with the crisis. Recognition, Jonathan Biltcliffe, leader of the South Lancashire Weavers Union, declared, was more likely to lead to war and to "dear bread, dear butter, dear cheese, and not cotton." James Nield Sr. of Mossley countered that only recognition would guarantee a regular supply of cotton, a call that was overwhelmingly rejected by the meetings.[13]

If Mary Ellison is right, then the impact of the famine should have led the textile workers of Ashton and Stalybridge to declare in favor of the Con-

12. *Reporter* (Ashton and Stalybridge), 3 May 1862.

13. *Reporter* (Ashton and Stalybridge), 10 May, 9 June 1862; Henry Lord to Seward, Manchester, 1 May 1862, Despatches from U.S. Consuls in Manchester, 1847–1906; Thomas Evans to George Wilson, Berwick, 4 July 1862, Wilson Papers.

federacy, but this clearly was not the case. By early 1862 there were already unmistakable signs that the Cotton Famine had taken hold in both towns. Only 40 of the 188 mills, employing 8,144 of 66,527 millworkers, were producing full time in April. Ashton's pauperism rate in June 1861 was 1.3 percent of a population of 134,761, the lowest rate in England; by June 1862 it had risen to 6.4 percent. Well over half of the Stalybridge workforce was idle in November 1862. One month later it was estimated that fully 25 percent of the town's population was on relief.[14] The result of the meetings suggests that the distress did not drive the towns' textile workers to declare in favor of an independent Confederacy. Nor did the situation change appreciably over the course of the war. If one combines the number of meetings and lectures held in both towns in the three years between April 1862 and April 1865, there were twenty-one in favor of the Union and thirteen in favor of the Confederacy.[15] What the slight differential suggests is that these towns were contested ground, a pattern common to all Lancashire, as well as to other parts of the country where the issues were debated. As a rule, contestation is not the result of spontaneous expressions of political differences, but is rather the outcome of deliberate and calculated attempts by partisans, both from within and outside the community, to exploit local conditions to generate support for the cause they espouse.

Rising unemployment, as Spence well knew, could provide political fodder for those supporting secession. The visit of Grimshaw and Aitken provided him with an opportunity to ride the coattails of a movement of Lancashire and Cheshire workers and mill owners who were actively seeking a solution to the economic crisis caused by the shortage of cotton. Condemning the "obnoxious labour tests" as demeaning, a Stalybridge meeting in early March had called for the formation of a committee, which included the Reverend J. R. Stephens and Biltcliffe, to discuss with local authorities the best way to allevi-

14. *Reporter* (Ashton and Stalybridge), 3 May 1862; Kirk, *The Growth of Working-Class Reformism*, 64, 116; P. M. Peers, "The Cotton Famine in Ashton-under-Lyne, 1861–1865" (Manchester College of Education, 1970), 20, 30, 36; Alice Lock, "The Role of Local Clergy and Ministers in the Stalybridge Riots of 1863," in Alice Lock, ed., *Looking Back at Stalybridge* (Tameside, England, 1989), 69; Michael Rose, "Rochdale Man and the Stalybridge Riot: The Relief and Control of the Unemployed during the Lancashire Cotton Famine," in A. P. Donajgrodzki, ed., *Social Control in Nineteenth-Century Britain* (London, 1977), 194–95.

15. Longmate, *The Hungry Mills*, 250, finds "at least 14 pro-Confederate meetings in Ashton and at least 5 petitions calling for support for the South were sent to Parliament." Longmate's numbers for meetings seem somewhat inflated, unless in his calculations he combined meetings and lectures.

ate conditions in the town. This was only the first in a series of similar meetings held throughout Lancashire and Cheshire over the next few months. At Stevenson Square, Manchester, three thousand workers praised those employers who were doing what they could to ease the situation and condemned the labor test for forcing skilled workers to break rocks and pick oakum before they were granted relief. Subsequent meetings pleaded with workers to be patient, called for the promotion of cotton cultivation in India, and suggested emigration as one way to relieve unemployment.[16] At one of the May meetings in Manchester, Grimshaw suggested that a deputation of workers be sent to meet with the prime minister and the secretary for India to discuss ways of increasing cotton production in India. A few weeks later a delegation met with Sir Charles Wood at India House in an effort to persuade the government to remove duties on Indian cotton goods. Two months later another delegation led by Aitken met with Lord Palmerston and the president of the Poor Law Board and called for the suspension of the labor test for at least nine months.[17]

The group associated with Spence aimed to exploit these economic and political conditions. Spence's spirits were buoyed when the delegation that visited him in April boasted that they could call out thirty thousand to an open-air meeting in Ashton and win endorsement for European intervention in the war. Over the next four months Aitken, Grimshaw, and the others held a series of meetings throughout Lancashire that proposed recognition as the best way to resolve the growing economic crisis.[18] The group of "insurgent emissaries," as Charles F. Adams called them, now included Aitken, Grimshaw, Matthews, and the Stockport contingent of Luke Wood; James Williams; Charles Cittie, a former Chartist; William Cleave, a textile worker; and Kinder Smith. Thomas Rhodes, a Stockport weaver and one of the heroes of the Ten Percent Strike of 1853, abandoned the group in the summer of 1862,

16. *Reporter* (Ashton and Stalybridge), 8 March 1862; *Guardian* (Manchester), 30 April, 5, 29 May, 13, 15 August 1862; *Examiner and Times* (Manchester), 9 May, 15 August 1862; *Times* (Blackburn), 19 April 1862.

17. *Guardian* (Manchester), 29 May, 13 August 1862; *Standard* (Blackburn), 25 May 1862; *Stockport and Cheshire County News*, 19 July 1862; "To the Associated Operative Cotton Spinners of Lancashire, Cheshire, Yorkshire, and Derbyshire," broadside, Tameside Central Library; Hall and Roberts, eds., *William Aitken*, 25–26.

18. *Guardian* (Manchester), 30 January 1864; *Stockport and Cheshire County News*, 28 June, 12 July 1862; *Examiner and Times* (Manchester), 4, 5 July 1862; *Chronicle* (Oldham), 9, 16 August 1862; *Courier and Herald* (Macclesfield), 5 July 1862.

only to return later in the war.[19] To try to give some organizational form to the group's effort and to add public support for Lindsay's proposed motion in Parliament calling for recognition, Aitken in mid-July called a meeting of delegates at Bolton from each of the affected towns. Unfortunately, among those in attendance were a few opponents of recognition, such as Thomas Evans, a Manchester weaver who had worked in the United States before the war, and James Handy of Stalybridge, who Grimshaw dismissed as an "old defunct Radical agitator of 1838–9 'pike and dagger' notoriety." More than half of the delegates were local, a fact that complicated Aitken's efforts to portray the meeting as representative of Lancashire workers. Opponents also challenged the organizers to prove that the meeting was not paid for with Confederate money. There was even the more prosaic accusation that some had been promised suits of clothes to attend. Whatever the merits of these accusations, they had the desired effect of raising questions about the legitimacy and independence of the meeting. The organizers did manage to carry a motion in favor of recognition, but by only a single vote.[20]

The opposition proved too much for Aitken, Grimshaw, and the others. The group disbanded permanently in early fall 1862, although many members would reappear as agents of the SIA in late 1864 in a brief flurry of activity that produced similar results.[21] But these working-class supporters of the Confederacy knew from long experience—from their involvement in the Chartist movement and the strikes of the 1850s—that success in public agitation rested on tailoring their message to the conditions of the people. Friends of the Union were also aware that rising unemployment could prompt textile workers to support the Confederacy. George Thompson almost pleaded with attendees at a Stockport meeting not to let their guard down. "I hope you will not allow any temporary suffering to lead you to give your sympathies to the enemies of human freedom on the other side of the Atlantic; I hope we shall

19. Adams to Seward, London, 11 July 1862, Despatches from U.S. Ministers to Great Britain, 1791–1906; Dutton and King, "Ten Percent and No Surrender," 52, 96; Reid, "The Chartist Movement in Stockport," 429–30, 475–76; Stockport and Cheshire County News, 28 June 1862; Reporter (Ashton and Stalybridge), 16 August 1862.

20. Guardian (Bolton), 19, 26 July 1862, 14 February 1863; Chronicle (Bolton), 26 July 1862; Examiner and Times (Manchester), 22, 26, 29 July 1862; Reporter (Ashton and Stalybridge), 2 August 1862; "To the Working Classes Dependent on Cotton," broadside calling the meeting, signed by Aitken and Joseph Wood, Tameside Central Library.

21. Observer (Rochdale), 19 November 1864; Spectator (Rochdale), 10, 19 November 1864; Examiner and Times (Manchester), 22 November 1864.

prove there is something we love better than cotton—that is, liberty of the human race."[22]

While the expressions of such lofty principles to an audience of the unemployed struck some as misplaced, if not callous, Thompson's experiences had also taught him the lessons of political agitation, namely, that the people had to be persuaded that their interests and those of the country were best served if they supported certain policies. But the issues raised by this war presented partisans with unique problems that did not lend themselves too easily to traditional solutions. While the debate over West Indian slavery, or even Polish and Italian independence, started with the assumption that by and large the people were uninformed and so had to be educated about the issues involved, in matters concerning the United States this was not the case. Since the beginning of the nineteenth century there had been a constant emigration and repatriation of British workers across the Atlantic. Wilbur Shepperson estimates that almost forty thousand English emmigrants returned to their home country from the United States between 1858 and 1860. Such movement bred familiarity with and sometimes contempt for American institutions and customs. But whatever the British thought of American ways, large sectors of the population were educated enough to make relatively informed judgments about the war. Many of those who had never been to the United States had relatives or friends who had gone there in search of work and who kept in touch. The Smith brothers of Crompton, north of Oldham, were not unique in this regard. Three of them had emigrated to Philadelphia in 1863, after the local mills closed. Letters home informed family and friends about conditions and chances for success. When young James Horrocks fled Farnworth and the angry father of a young woman he had made pregnant, he wrote home regularly, informing his family about life in the army and the state of the war. British newspapers frequently printed letters from British emigrants that provided firsthand accounts of the economic, political, and social consequences of the war.[23]

22. *Stockport and Cheshire County News*, 2 November 1861.

23. Shepperson, *Emigration and Disenchantment*, 24–25; W. H. Chaloner, "Letters from Lancashire Lads in America during the Civil War, 1863–1865," *Transactions of the Lancashire and Cheshire Antiquarian Society* 77 (1967): 137, 142; Alan Conway, ed., *The Welsh in America: Letters from the Immigrants* (Minneapolis, 1961), 291–92; T. P. Eckersley, "The Growth of the Cotton Industry in Mossley, with Special Reference to the Mayalls" (master's thesis, Manchester Polytechnic, 1991), 34; A. S. Lewis, ed., *My Dear Parents: An Englishman's Letters Home from the American Civil War* (London, 1982), n.p.; *Reporter* (Ashton and Stalybridge), 21 January 1865. See also the diary of John Sturrock, a Dundee millwright, "How I Spend My Leisure Time," in

Where such personal contacts did not exist, the British public made every effort to educate itself about the war. John Ward, an unemployed Low Moor weaver, frequently trekked the many miles to Clitheroe to read the newspapers. "There is a great excitement in the United States upon the account of electing Mr. Lincoln President," he recorded in his diary in January 1861. "All the slave states are talking of seceding from the states and forming a republic of their own, and the free states talk of using force to compel them to submit."[24] The war and its causes engaged the interests of debating societies throughout the country. The Birmingham Sunday Evening Debating Society, whose members were largely artisans, and the Birmingham and Edgbaston Debating Society, made up of masters, or factory owners, regularly debated issues surrounding the war. More than just a debating society, the former, "the center of artisan agitation in Birmingham," examined a range of questions, including, in 1861, whether Britain should recognize the Confederacy, the legitimacy of South Carolina's secession, and the legality of Jefferson Davis's decision to issue letters of marque. Later it discussed, among other topics, the merits of gradual emancipation and the wisdom of reelecting Lincoln.[25] Similar interest was evident in other parts of the country. The Discussion Club of Merthyr Tydfil, Wales, held a series of discussions in the fall of 1862, and the war and slavery were subjects of competition at Welsh *eisteddfods*. The Trinity College and Young Men's Christian Association explored the issue of secession at the Historical Society, Dublin, in the summer of 1864. The Working Men's Club of Cheltenham examined the benefits of Southern independence, while its counterpart in Nantwich explored whether abolitionists were the true friends of the slave. Every Wednesday evening for several weeks in late 1862, audiences of from three hundred to four hundred gathered at the Free Newsroom in Heywood, Lancashire, to listen to a debate on the war. In October members of the Stalybridge Mechanics' Institution met to respond to an essay by Walter Kenyon about the war. The

which he records receiving letters from family members in America and reading American newspapers that were sent to his father. My thanks to Joan Auld, archivist at the University of Dundee, for providing me with photocopies of pages from the diary.

24. France, "The Diary of John Ward," 153; O. Ashmore, "The Diary of James Garnett of Low Moor, Clitheroe, 1858–1865: Part 2, The American Civil War and the Cotton Famine, 1861–1865," *Transactions of the Historic Society of Lancashire and Cheshire* 123 (1971): 83.

25. Minutes of the Birmingham Sunday Evening Debating Society and minutes of the Birmingham and Edgbaston Debating Society, Birmingham (England) Public Library; Hooper, "Mid-Victorian Radicalism," 36; Corke, "Birmingham and the American Civil War," 43–46.

following month they engaged in another round of debates that lasted four weeks.[26]

Weather permitting, it was not unusual to find groups gathered at street corners or open spaces discussing the most recent developments in the war or expressing their views on the merits of the contenders. One editor referred to them as "warm street debates." Writing at the turn of the century, James Ogden of Bacup recalled that it was not uncommon for groups to "stand discussing matters in the streets" long after the conclusion of meetings. One observer reported that in the small town of Chadderton, north of Oldham, "groups of people are to be seen and heard daily in full and earnest debate upon the various movements of the two contending parties. Handloom weavers and others have been known to group together immediately after dinner and have continued to argue the question pro and con until late in the evening." Although the annual fair at Mossley was uncharacteristically drab in 1863, one observer reported that the "battle for the North was fiercely fought in the various bar parlours by the village politicians, and the 'eternal negro' found eloquent defenders amongst the white slaves of Lancashire—some even going so far [speaking of Jackson] as to kiss the ruby lips of the past-forging, God-fearing, temperance-promoting, runaway coachman of Jeff Davis."[27]

These debates and discussions were supplemented by frequent lectures to a wide array of audiences in all parts of the country. Some lectures were organized by national societies or their local chapters; others were the work of informed individuals with an interest in the public debate over the war. Regular lectures by Dissenting ministers, such as the Reverends J. Jones, John Davies, A. Matthews, and E. Jacobs; by Henry Vincent; and by fugitive slaves Francis Fredric and J. C. Thompson brought the pro-Union message to Wales.[28] Lec-

26. *Times* (Cardiff), 24 October 1862; Gwynne E. Owen, "Welsh Anti-Slavery Sentiments, 1790–1865: A Survey of Public Opinion" (master's thesis, University College of Aberystwyth, 1964), 113; William B. West to Seward, Dublin, 26 May 1864, Despatches from U.S. Consuls in Dublin, 1790–1906; *Free Press* (Cheltenham), 5 December 1863; *Record* (Chester), 7 February 1863; *Advertiser* (Heywood), 20, 27 December 1862; *Reporter* (Ashton and Stalybridge), 12, 19 October, 1, 8 November 1862.

27. *Advertiser* (Heywood), 22 August 1863. On Chadderton see Auger, "The Cotton Famine, 1861–1865," 294; *Times* (Bacup), 1902, kindly sent me by the local librarian; *Standard* (Oldham), 7 March, 11 July 1863. Friends of the Union frequently wrote Dudley about debates that occurred at railway stations and on board boats. See, for example, Charles D. Cleveland to Dudley, Cardiff, 21 March 1864, and James M. Meir to Dudley, Glasgow, 9 April 1864, Dudley Collection.

28. *Times* (Cardiff), 23 August, 6 December 1861, 5 September 1862, 2 January, 21 August, 18 December 1863, 19 February, 23 December 1864; *Telegraph* (Merthyr), 21 February, 12 September 1863, 26 November, 3 December 1864; *Daily Post* (Bristol), 2 December 1864.

tures were also delivered in out-of-the-way places, in towns and villages not immediately affected by the war, a reflection of wide-ranging interests in developments across the Atlantic. African Americans lectured throughout the country—William G. Allen in Ashford, Kent; R. M. Johnson in Kings Lynn, Norfolk; J. C. Thompson in Lemington Spa, Warwickshire; and J. W. C. Pennington and J. H. Banks in Rhyl, North Wales.[29] Many emigrants who had recently returned from the United States brought firsthand accounts of their experiences. Literally scores of lectures were delivered by returning Englishmen. In Bradford, for example, William Fenton lectured twice about his "Wanderings in America"; A. Sylvester gave a series of lectures about "America: Yankee Life; the War, its Causes, and Probable Results"; and the Reverend J. Bastow, who was educated in the United States, spoke on the relationship of slavery to the war. R. Redman Belshaw, who had lived in both the North and South, gave three lectures in Newcastle; and in Bristol the Reverend W. Adams, who had just returned from Kentucky, spoke of his experiences. A Dr. Poole, who claimed to have witnessed the Battle of First Bull Run, spoke on the war in Hanley, Staffordshire. Joshua Balme frequently condemned Union policies in many parts of the country, and Baptist minister the Reverend Charles Hill Coe, formerly of Birmingham, returned to his hometown after ten years in the United States to give a series of lectures in support of the Union.[30]

More popular than the lecture as sources of information and entertainment were the panoramas and dioramas that toured the country throughout the war. At least ten have been identified. Some were short-lived and targeted only certain sectors of the country; others were on display throughout the war and reached audiences in most of the major cities. Henry Box Brown, a fugitive slave who had settled in England in the early 1850s, had for some years been showing his panorama "Mirror of Africa and America." Sometime later in the decade he had added a supplement on the Indian mutiny. At the end of 1861 he announced a "Grand Moving Mirror of the American War." Mixing lectures with songs and instrumental music, panoramas and dioramas aimed to

29. *Telegraph* (Maidstone), 7 March 1863; *The People's Weekly Journal*, 13 May 1865; *Royal Lemington Spa Courier and Warwickshire Standard*, 13 February 1864; *North Wales Chronicle*, 18 January 1862.

30. *Review* (Bradford), 9 November, 12 December 1861, 23 January 1862, 5 March 1863, 7 January 1864; *Observer* (Bradford), 5 March 1863; *Chronicle* (Newcastle), 11, 25 March 1865; *Post* (Bristol), 6 May 1862; *Staffordshire Advertiser*, 22 February 1862; *Advertiser* (Burnley), 31 August 1861; *Chronicle* (Leicester), 11, 18 May 1861; *Chronicle* (Preston), 4 September 1861; *Weekly Scotsman*, 15 March 1862; *Daily Gazette* (Birmingham), 26 March, 13 August 1863.

both educate and entertain. A few, like Leslie's, came very close to aping the popular minstrel shows, with the inclusion of humorous and sentimental songs. Many ran for two or three nights, although a few were on display for longer periods. Henry Smith's played for an entire week in Cardiff, and W. H. Edwards's was in such demand in Nottingham that it continued to attract large audiences for twelve nights. Divided into three sections, Church's "Historical Panorama of the Civil War in America," depicted major battles on land and sea, slaves escaping, a cotton plantation on the Mississippi, and the inauguration of Lincoln. Brown lectured on the causes of the war and entertained his audiences with songs honoring the valor of fugitive slaves. Always inventive, he would later include a lecture on "electro-biology" and give away gifts at each entertainment. Tickets were not inexpensive, ranging from one shilling for front seats to three pence for the gallery.[31]

Few areas of Britain were untouched by these efforts. On matters relating to America and the war, the public was an informed one. While it showed little interest in the arcane constitutional issues involved in the dispute, family contacts, letters, discussions with returning emigrants, newspaper coverage, lectures, panoramas and dioramas, and meetings brought within its reach information on which informed judgments could be made. It was from this knowledgeable public that partisans hoped to win support. One of the mechanisms employed by national associations and their local chapters was the formal lecture. It is not always easy to differentiate between such lectures and public meetings, for both had many of the same characteristics. Traditionally, lectures ended simply with motions of thanks to the lecturer, but in a few instances, resolutions designed to measure levels of support were submitted. Support could also be measured in other ways. At the conclusion of Newman Hall's lecture in Birmingham, for example, there were three rousing cheers for Lincoln. In some instances it appears that the decision to give a lecture rather than hold a public meeting was driven largely by concerns about maintaining order. In towns where the opposition had become too disruptive, lectures pro-

31. *Chronicle* (Leigh), 11, 18 January 1861; *Guardian* (Bolton), 18 January 1862; *Spectator* (Rochdale), 8 February 1862; *Courier* (Halifax), 8 March 1862; *Daily Post* (Bristol), 1 January 1864; *Times* (Cardiff), 20 September 1861, 12 August 1864; *Review* (Nottingham), 9, 10, 11 September 1861; *Guardian* (Preston), 25 March 1865; *Times* (London), 10 November 1863. Norris's panorama on the war included a twenty-five-year-old comic singer depicting a man of seventy. See *Spirit of the Times* (Wolverhampton), 29 April 1865. During an engagement in Aberdeen, the Christy Minstrels mounted a panorama of "scenes in America." *Journal* (Aberdeen), 1 February 1865. For a biography of Box Brown and an analysis of his panoramas see Jeffrey Ruggles, *The Unboxing of Henry Brown* (forthcoming).

vided a means of controlling the setting. Delivered in churches, Mechanics Institutes, or small cooperative or temperance halls, to a select audience to whom tickets were sold or distributed free of charge, formal lectures lessened the chances of attracting organized opposition while at the same time providing the opportunity to get the message across. When, for instance, the Reverend Woodville Woodman of Farnworth spoke at the Oddfellow's Hall in Bacup in favor of Confederate independence, front seats cost two pence and back seats one pence. George Thompson was not likely to run into much opposition when he lectured to 250 pupils at a girls school in the northeast or when he spoke to Sabbath school pupils in the Potteries.[32]

It is in these controlled settings that women were more likely to become involved. Very few reports of public meetings mention the presence of women, although there were a few notable exceptions. In Preston, for example, where women such as Sarah Jane Clemesha were active in the leadership of local antislavery societies, they did sometimes attend public meetings. One Bacup newspaper suggested that it was the rowdiness and lateness of public meetings that kept women from becoming more involved. If women stayed within the bounds of Victorian conventions and did not attend what contemporaries liked to call promiscuous gatherings, however, many, especially supporters of the Union, were keenly aware of and involved in the public debate. Friends of the Confederacy were at a distinct disadvantage in this regard. Unlike their counterparts, they organized no societies, and with the possible exception of the Liverpool bazaar to aid Confederate prisoners in October 1864, had no public presence. There were still more than a dozen active local women's affiliates of the British and Foreign Anti Slavery Society at the outbreak of the war. Many of these, such as the Dundee society, continued to be involved in raising money for the cause. Others not affiliated with the BFASS, such as the Birmingham Ladies' Negro's Friend Society, although not publicly active in the early years of the war, reemerged as active players in the effort to raise support for freedmen in the South. Still others, such as the Manchester Ladies Anti Slavery Society, led by Rebecca Whitelegge, contin-

32. *Daily Post* (Birmingham), 21 February 1863; *News* (Bacup and Rossendale), 17 October 1863; Thompson to Amelia, Tynemouth, 19 June 1861, English Deposit. William Andrew Jackson gave three lectures in Rotherham at which resolutions were adopted. *Independent* (Sheffield and Rotherham), 9, 10, 20 January 1863. The same occurred at Verity's two lectures in Bradford. *Review* (Bradford), 25 February 1864. When Hall lectured at his church, Surrey Chapel, London, and the Reverend J. P. Chown at his Baptist church in Bradford, it was not unusual for more than three thousand to attend. *Review* (Bradford), 4 January 1862; *Observer* (Bradford), 2 January 1862.

ued to support the efforts of Garrisonian abolitionists.[33] But in many important respects, such traditional women's activities as the organization of fairs and bazaars were, as Deborah Van Broekhoven and others have argued, profoundly political acts. They enticed customers to buy goods that carried with them political messages. "In working for fairs," Van Broekhoven insists, "women were both educating themselves and organizing their communities." They brought together in public buildings men and women of all classes and, at least in abolitionist fairs, all races and in so doing reached and influenced a wider public. The April 1862 Bristol antislavery bazaar is a case in point. Gifts poured in from all across the country. Public meetings and lectures were held in the months leading up to the bazaar. Louis Chamerovzow spoke in January about the need to end the Cuban slave trade. He was followed by William Howard Day, who gave two lectures, the second at midday so that many of the women organizing the bazaar could attend. William Craft attended and lectured on the second and third days of the bazaar. While there, Craft took time to view R. Ansdell's already popular painting *The Fugitive Slave*, depicting a fugitive slave and his family defending themselves against bloodhounds. The bazaar raised nearly £500 to aid the work of antislavery societies in America.[34]

It is more difficult to measure women's contributions to the Confederate cause. There were no female national or local societies, and the cause produced no one comparable to Sarah Jane Clemesha. In fact, what evidence does exist suggests that female support for the Confederacy came almost exclusively from the ranks of the aristocracy. It is these ladies who managed and staffed a very successful three-day bazaar in October 1864, which raised in excess of £20,000 for the Southern Prisoners Relief Fund. In existence since late 1862, the fund was organized by the Liverpool Southern Club and had by 1864 already disbursed more than £3,000 to Confederate soldiers held in

---

33. *Guardian* (Preston), 1 August 1863; *Times* (Bury), 30 May 1863; *Anti Slavery Reporter*, 1 February 1861; *National Anti Slavery Standard*, 4 April 1863. See Midgley, *Women against Slavery*, for a discussion of women's involvement.

34. Deborah Van Broekhoven, "'Better than a Clay Club': The Organization of Anti-Slavery Fairs, 1835–1860," *Slavery and Abolition* 19 (April 1998): 28, 32, 37, 39. See also Lee Chambers-Schiller, "'A Good Work Among the People': The Political Culture of the Boston Antislavery Fair," in Jean Fagan Yellin and John C. Van Horne, eds., *The Abolitionist Sisterhood: Women's Political Culture in Antebellum America* (Ithaca, N.Y., 1994); Beverley Gordon, *Bazaars and Fair Ladies: The History of the American Fundraising Fair* (Knoxville, Tenn., 1998); F. K. Prochaska, *Women and Philanthropy in Nineteenth-Century England* (Oxford, 1980); *Anti Slavery Reporter*, 1 November 1861; *Daily Post* (Bristol), 20 January, 13, 14 February, 10, 11, 14, 17 April 1862, 4 February 1863; *Mercury* (Bristol), 12 April 1862.

Northern prisons. As in every other aspect of the cause, Spence was the inspiration behind the bazaar, which he began planning sometime that spring. A week before its opening Spence worried that he might not be able to find buyers "for the amazing quantity of contributions coming in. . . ." His concerns were misplaced. At least ten thousand attended the three-day affair and almost two thousand had to be turned away on the final day. Held in the ornate Saint George's Hall, the bazaar combined all the elements of the country fair with pony rides, music, stalls, games, a "piping bull finch," and even a "Southern mermaid." There were performances by an operetta company, piano recitals by a child prodigy, and a panorama depicting life in Liverpool. Fancy goods were sold at stalls, and ladies, each representing one of the Confederate states, moved through the crowd selling items. The raffling of a pony and Manx cat attracted a great deal of interest and patronage.[35] Although there were none of the public meetings traditionally associated with abolitionist bazaars, this was, nonetheless, a profoundly political event. A portrait of Stonewall Jackson was prominently displayed, visitors could examine a sword and Bible that were to be sent to Robert E. Lee, as well as a flag that was to be presented to Captain Semmes. "All the elite and Fashion of the town has been there," Dudley reported home, "indeed one may say it has been patronized generally by the whole people." It was, he insisted (and the evidence supports his claim), the most successful fair of its kind ever held in England.[36] Symbolically, there was also in the bazaar's Victorian splendor, its festooned bunting and military trappings, and its patronage by aristocratic women and their husbands, the reaffirmation of a natural alliance between British aristocracy and southern chivalry.

Even in these controlled settings, however, the organizers did not always have the field to themselves. Spence made sure there were enough policemen present in case of trouble. Such precautions were wise given the tradition of opposition and disruption. When John C. Harrington of South Carolina gave a series of lectures in Shepton Mallet and the little village of Butleigh, near Street, Somerset, local opponents organized a counterdemonstration in favor

35. *Mercury* (Liverpool), 19, 20, 22 October, 18 November 1864; *New York Times,* 9, 10 December 1864; Dudley to Seward, Liverpool, 22 October 1864, Despatches from U.S. Consuls in Liverpool, 1790–1906; Spence to Wharncliffe, Liverpool, 3 October 1864, Wharncliffe Muniments; K. F. Sirett and K. J. Williams, "Liverpool and the American Civil War: A Confederate Heritage in England," *Journal of Confederate History* 4 (1989): 114, 122.

36. Dudley to Seward, Liverpool, 22, 24 October 1864, Despatches from U.S. Consuls in Liverpool, 1790–1906. Prochaska estimates that the 1845 Anti–Corn Law League bazaar raised about £25,000 in seventeen days. Prochaska, *Women and Philanthropy,* 63.

of the Union. The opposition was led by William Stephens Clark and Thomas Bearen Clark, Quakers and heirs to the famous shoemakers. Family connections were crucial to the speed and thoroughness of the opposition to Harrington. William was married to Helen Bright, John Bright's oldest daughter. Soon after Harrington left Butleigh, the Clarks posted huge placards throughout the village denouncing the Confederacy and challenging its supporters to a public debate.[37]

These activities reinforced and made more far-reaching the work of the agents of organized societies. Especially in places like Butleigh where there were no local societies or where agents could not be expected to lecture or hold meetings, Harrington and the Clarks ensured that the message was heard. The group of official and unofficial agents was an impressive lot. The majority had gained their spurs in the rough and tumble of the hustings. Few of his contemporaries surpassed Joseph Barker in his command of the public stage. Mercurial, witty, brash, always well informed, and with a commanding voice that could reach every corner of a large audience, Barker was in turn feared, respected, and reviled by his opponents, as was the towering Edward A. Verity, who stood well over six feet tall and had a knack for vilifying those he thought wanting. Some thought Barker possessed a "magnetic personality," while others such as W. W. Broom, an opponent from Manchester who for a brief period in 1863 followed and pecked away at Barker's credibility, described him as a "Judas of freedom, who had received the bloodmoney, and sold himself to the enemies of mankind."[38] Verity's support of the right of workers to unionize, his support of strikes in the late 1850s, and his deep suspicion of the tenets of the Manchester school alienated many of those who agreed with him on the need to support an independent Confederacy to the point that they refused to attend his lectures. Barker and Verity were joined by T. B. Kershaw, an overlooker at an Ancoats mill and a man of considerable energy who became one of the secretaries of the SIA. Barker's agency lasted fewer than six months, ending in October 1863. Much of the work of taking the message to the public then fell to Verity and Kershaw, supported occasionally by Spence, who, with no stomach for public wrangling, chose very carefully where he spoke.

37. Information on the Clarks kindly provided by Richard Clark of Street; *Post* (Bristol), 11 November 1864. Poster enclosed in Zebrina Eastman to Seward, Bristol, 29 October 1864, Despatches from U.S. Consuls in Bristol, 1792–1906.

38. Rogers, *Autobiography*, 90; Spence to Mason, Liverpool, 16 June 1863, Mason Papers; *Albion* (Middleton), 10 October 1863.

The corps of pro-Union agents was much more impressive. It included, among others, George Thompson, Peter Sinclair, J. Sella Martin, William Craft, and William Andrew Jackson. They were joined by a supporting cast that included Moncure D. Conway, Charles Denison, and dozens of African Americans, who proved critical to the way the public debate was framed. Like the "big brawny negro mounted on a stone at the side of the Bayswater Road" in London who was speaking against intervention and to whom Benjamin Moran stopped to listen, many of these unnamed Negroes used the tradition of the soapbox to engage passersby in a discussion of the war. The streets, long "the fulcrum of the interlocking spheres of entertainment and retailing," as Hewitt asserts, provided ample space for those, such as this unknown Negro, who were unable to engage local notables to support their efforts. Wherever he went, Jacob Green, a Kentucky fugitive slave, employed a bellman to announce his street-corner meetings.[39] Green and other African Americans took the message of nonintervention to all parts of the country. William Howard Day, Craft, and Martin canvassed the west of England; the Reverend Isaac W. Davison, Green, Jackson, and Day, Yorkshire; the Reverend W. Mitchell, Benjamin Benson, and J. W. C. Pennington, Wales; Craft and Henry Highland Garnet, northeast England; and William Watson, Mitchell, and Jackson, the Midlands. Almost all the lectures and meetings held in Chester had as their principal speaker an African American.[40]

Relations between these African Americans and British organizations were not always harmonious. Louis Chamerovzow of the British and Foreign Anti Slavery Society, for instance, was concerned about allegations of fraud and insisted on the need to control these itinerant lecturers who in some instances were rumored to be milking the "anti-slavery community." Day, he wrote colleagues in the United States, had "obtained contributions which must in the aggregate have amounted to a considerable sum" and that he used for personal expenses. It is difficult to determine if Day had defrauded supporters, but there is evidence in one case that another did fall foul of the law. During a lecture tour in South Wales, Mitchell was brought before the Mayor of Cardiff for try-

39. Wallace and Gillespie, eds., *The Journal of Benjamin Moran*, 2: 1035–36; Martin Hewitt, *The Emergence of Stability in the Industrial City: Manchester, 1832–1867* (Aldershot, England, 1996), 185; *Reporter* (Ashton and Stalybridge), 16 August 1862. For another "coloured man" who used a bellman to announce his lecture see *Times* (Blackburn), 20 June 1863.

40. R. J. M. Blackett, "African Americans, the British Working Class, and the American Civil War," *Slavery and Abolition* 17 (August 1996): 56; *Record* (Chester), 21 September 1861, 21, 28 March, 11, 25 April, 12 September 1863.

African Americans Who Took Part in Public Debate

William G. Allen	schoolteacher
J. H. Banks	fugitive slave
Jacob Bell	fugitive slave (possibly Jacob Green misidentified)
J. Bennett	fugitive slave (there is also mention of a William Bennett)
B. Benson	unknown
John Brooks	unknown/working in Glasgow
Henry Box Brown	fugitive slave/owner of panorama
Robert Campbell	schoolteacher
T. Morris Chester	schoolteacher
Nelson Countee	fugitive slave/minister
Ellen Craft	fugitive slave/housewife
William Craft	fugitive slave/trader
Isaac W. Davison	minister
William Howard Day	schoolteacher/editor
Francis Fedric	fugitive slave
Henry Highland Garnet	fugitive slave/minister
Jacob Green	fugitive slave (see Jacob Bell)
Babba Gross	fugitive slave/minister
J. Hughes	fugitive slave/minister
Edward Irving	fugitive slave
John A. Jackson	fugitive slave (Some reports mention John A. Andrews; others an Andrew Jackson. These may all be the same person.)
William A. Jackson	fugitive slave
Madison Jefferson	fugitive slave
Robert M. Johnson	fugitive slave/minister/medical student
William Johnstone	fugitive slave
T. M. Kinnard	fugitive slave/minister
John Sella Martin	fugitive slave/minister
William Mitchell	fugitive slave/minister
William North	fugitive slave
James W. C. Pennington	fugitive slave/minister
William Powell	clerk
Sarah Parker Redmond	student
David Reed	unknown, living in Bury during the war
C. J. Russell	medical student
Lewis Smith	unknown
James C. Thompson	fugitive slave/barber
James Watkins	fugitive slave
William Watson	student

ing to slip away without paying his hotel bill. He had evidently done the same in Newport, Penmark, and Llancarfen.[41]

With the exception of the Mitchell case, these problems were never publicized. What the public saw was a close working relationship between supporters of the Union and these African Americans, the majority of whom were fugitive slaves seeking a safe haven and, in some cases, jobs in Britain. Not all of them, however, spoke with one voice on the causes and consequences of the war. Day told a large meeting of the African Aid Society in December 1861 that the war was a direct result of the arrogance of what he called the "Anglo-Saxon races," who refused to recognize the rights of black Americans. The Reverend N. Countee declared that both the Union and the Confederacy were cut from the same cloth, "twin brothers in the unholy transaction . . . an avaricious set of people [who] did not care who sank as long as they swam." As far as Mitchell was concerned, the Lincoln government was fighting to preserve the Union for free white labor and had no interest in granting black Americans their freedom. Those like William Craft who early in the war were still wedded to the Garrisonian view of the Constitution as a proslavery document nevertheless believed that the Confederacy could not long sustain itself with four million slaves in its midst. Green saw things differently. He insisted that the Constitution was "perfectly anti slavery" and that the Confederacy was attempting by war to transform slavery from a local into a national institution.[42]

In spite of these differences over Union policy, not one of these African Americans was sparing in his condemnation of the Confederacy. In the eyes of the public, their passionate promotion of freedom, especially after the preliminary proclamation of emancipation was issued, gave the Union a level of legitimacy that was the envy of the Confederate lobby. Southern supporters breathed a collective sigh of relief when Jackson returned to America at the end of 1863. The Union forces, one cheered, had lost their most potent weapon in the battle to win public opinion. They have "ceased to command an audience in Lancashire now that President Davis's mythical ex-coachman

---

41. Chamerovzow to "Dear Sir," London, 5 July 1865, American Missionary Association Papers, Amistad Research Center, Tulane University, New Orleans; *Anti Slavery Reporter*, 2 May 1864; *Times* (Cardiff), 14, 21 October 1864. On Mitchell's earlier visit see *Times* (Cardiff), 20 September 1861; *Mercury* (Cardiff), 7 September, 26 October 1861; *Nonconformist*, 9 April 1862.

42. *Midlands Counties Herald*, 12 December 1861; *Courier* (Halifax), 22 October 1864; *Pilot* (Rochdale), 15 October 1864; *Observer* (Rochdale), 22 October 1864; *Leicestershire Mercury*, 21, 28 June 1862; *Times* (Sunderland), 11, 19 May 1861; *Times* (Todmorden), 26 September 1863.

(who was really worth seeing and listening to) is no longer available for diversifying the humdrum of an anti-slavery speech with a racy natural joke worth all the money."[43] Coming as it did from an opponent, this statement was ample testimony to the potency of African American contributions to the Union cause. William and Ellen Craft, Sarah Parker Remond, William G. Allen, James Watkins, Henry Box Brown, and William Howard Day, among others, were in Britain working for American abolition when war broke out. Day had arrived in mid-1859 to promote a scheme for the settlement of a select group of African Americans on the west coast of Africa. When that fizzled after the outbreak of hostilities in America, he shifted his emphasis to the causes and consequences of the war. He was, one editor believed, the "most talented representative and advocate of the colored race that has ever addressed an assembly on the subject."[44] James Watkins, a fugitive slave from Maryland who had been in Britain since 1851, was in much demand as a lecturer. A sharp critic of Lincoln's plans to colonize freedmen outside of the United States, Watkins also won praise for his account of life in slavery. In Newcastle, Leeds, and Huddersfield, large audiences attended his course of ten lectures on slavery and emancipation.[45] William Craft, who with his wife, Ellen, was a founding member of the London Emancipation Society, spent most of the war years as a businessman and schoolteacher in Dahomey. Before leaving for Africa, however, he toured Scotland as an agent of the society's predecessor, the London Emancipation Committee, lecturing on slavery and raising money for the cause.[46]

Much of the work of promoting American abolition in Britain had fallen to Craft and other African Americans in the months prior to the firing on Fort Sumter. There were two exceptions: George Cheever and the tireless George Thompson, who as agent of the American Anti Slavery Society un-

43. *Index*, 19 November 1863. The Reverend J. Page Hopps dismissed the spectacle of Jackson lecturing on "his master and mistress" as sheer vulgarity and warned the Sheffield Emancipation Society that "parading the ex-coachman" in public could work to their disadvantage. Such warnings were more an expression of concern by a Confederate supporter that Jackson's involvement in the public debate strengthened the Union's cause. *Inquirer*, 24 January 1863.

44. *Guardian* (Manchester), 29 June 1861; *Review* (Nottingham), 17 October, 28 November 1862; *Advertiser* (Newark), 15 October, 26 November 1862. Quotation in *Chronicle* (Burton), 28 November 1861.

45. *Newcastle Daily Chronicle and Northern Counties Advertiser*, 5, 10, 12 April, 2 September, 22 October 1862.

46. *Advertiser* (Hawick), 25 May 1861; *Advertiser* (Dundee), 28 June, 1, 19, 20, 23, 31 July 1861.

dertook a grueling tour in 1860, delivering no fewer than fifty lectures in the first six months of 1860, a feat he would repeat with equal success the following year. It was the sort of itinerary that would tax the strength of a much younger person. It was not unusual for Thompson to suspend a series of lectures, as he did in Manchester in January 1862, journey to Bath to give two lectures, and then return to Manchester to complete his engagement.[47] His message was the same wherever he went. He usually opened with a history of the United States, emphasizing the lengths to which the country had gone to paper over divisions caused by slavery. The war had put paid to any further compromises, but Lincoln, a strict constitutionalist and pragmatist, was still limited in his ability to interfere with slavery. To abolish slavery at that time ran the risk of alienating the border states and subverting all chances of reunion. Thompson was convinced, however, that Lincoln could and soon would use the powers invested in the presidency during war to declare the slaves free. He also predicted that slaves would flee their masters as Union armies advanced into the slaveholding states, thus increasing the pressure for emancipation. Critical of Lincoln's refusal to enroll blacks in the army, Thompson saw hopeful signs of a country moving toward emancipation, although he feared that it would not get there before Southern intransigence produced widespread slave insurrections. Given these developments, Thompson maintained that lovers of freedom had to remain vigilant, give their critical support to the government in Washington, and resist all calls for recognition of the Confederacy.[48]

The basic features of the competing agencies were well established by the time the organized effort to influence public opinion moved into high gear in the fall of 1862. The efforts of Spence, Grimshaw, and others to win Lancashire textile workers' support for the Confederacy, although initially unsuccessful, set in place the machinery that Confederate supporters would utilize in 1863. The approach employed by friends of the Union looked remarkably similar. It rested, as has been shown, on national organizations, each of which spawned local affiliates, the tendrils of political agitation to borrow a term from F. K. Prochaska. National organizations and their affiliates were responsi-

47. Thompson to Garrison, London, 14 August 1860, and minutes of the executive committee of the American Anti Slavery Society, AASS Papers; *Anti Slavery Advocate*, 1 May 1860; *Examiner and Times* (Manchester), 18 December 1861, 14, 22, 29 January 1862; *Guardian* (Manchester), 19 December 1861, 25, 29 January 1862; *Gazette* (Bath and Cheltenham), 8 January 1862.

48. *Stockport and Cheshire County News*, 2 November 1861.

ble for hiring agents, publishing pamphlets, preparing fact sheets for distribution to the press, organizing meetings, and circulating petitions. Much of the money to finance these activities came from wealthy members. Thomas Bayley Potter, president of the UES, contributed £5,000 to the society's coffers, while the Manchester Southern Club was reputed to have raised £4,000 from sympathetic manufacturers. Money also came from American sources. In spite of his public denials, Hotze earmarked £1,000 for Grimshaw's and Aitken's efforts in April 1862, and he and Lord Wharncliffe were major contributors to the campaign for the Peace Address in 1864. There is even some suggestion that a portion of the money raised by the Confederate Cotton Loan found its way into the campaign. Adams gave some support to the efforts of the LES above and beyond the substantial sums provided by the American consuls Freeman Morse in London and Thomas Dudley in Liverpool. Near the end of the war Dudley reported that Thomas Nelson, an Edinburgh publisher, had contributed an unspecified amount of money to the cause.[49] Both sides also relied on unpaid supporters who volunteered their time in the interest of the cause. John C. Edwards, secretary of the UES, recalled that "gentlemen of independent position" had done a great deal of traveling on behalf of the society without charge.[50]

In the wake of the preliminary proclamation of emancipation, a great deal of time, money, and effort was spent shoring up relatively inactive societies and establishing new ones as a prelude to launching a public campaign. In London, supporters of the Union gave new life to the LES. Working through Sinclair and Morse, the LES decided on a strategy that included holding frequent public meetings throughout the capital and in the surrounding counties. Success in this area, they calculated, would have considerable influence on the way the agitation unfolded in other parts of the country. Following its reorganization in November 1862, the LES held at least a dozen meetings in and around London, which were addressed by an

49. Prochaska, *Women and Philanthropy*, 24; Stange, *British Unitarians against American Slavery*, 207; Temperley, *British Antislavery*, 255; Chamerovzow to Brougham, London, 9 December 1863, Brougham Papers; Hotze to Secretary of State, London, 24 April 1862, Hotze to Kershaw, London, 27 August 1864, both in Hotze Papers; *Examiner and Times* (Manchester), 7 May 1862; Kershaw to Wharncliffe, Manchester, 23 August 1864, Wharncliffe Muniments; Dudley to Seward, Liverpool, 27 February 1865, Despatches from U.S. Consuls in Liverpool, 1790–1906; Adams to Seward, London, 29 November 1862, Despatches from U.S. Ministers to Great Britain, 1791–1906; Morse to Seward, London, 6 February 1863, Despatches from U.S. Consuls in London, 1790–1906; Adams, *Great Britain and the American Civil War*, 2: 155–56.
50. *Stockport and Cheshire County News*, 14 January 1865.

impressive list of speakers including Thompson, Newman Hall, Jackson, Baptist Noel, and John Gorrie. Wherever a chapel or schoolroom could be obtained or a hall rented, the LES later reported, they "arranged for the delivery of a lecture, or the holding of a public meeting." The crowds that turned out, such as the one numbering three thousand at Lambeth in December, were impressive.[51]

There was little that was spontaneous about any of this: resting on a firm foundation of national and local societies, the agitation was organized, well financed, and aimed to reach the broadest audience possible. Beginning in the fall of 1862, both sides made every effort to organize national societies with branches scattered throughout the country. Not surprisingly, a substantial number of the local societies were established in areas that, because of economic distress, were considered most vital to the success of the cause. Lancashire, Cheshire, and Derbyshire were cases in point. In many instances, branches were formed to counter local societies formed by the opposition. The establishment of a Rawtenstall branch of the UES in August 1863, for example, was followed in a matter of days by the formation of an auxiliary of the SIA. Although this pattern does not hold true for all of Lancashire and Cheshire, its replication in many areas suggests that the success of the agitation rested in large measure on the existence of these local societies. There were some notable exceptions. In Bury, for instance, where there is no evidence that the local branches of the LES and UES were very active, pro-Union organization of public meetings and lectures rested almost entirely on the shoulders of David Thomas. And there also, where there was no one comparable to Thomas in the Confederate camp, the first prorecognition meeting was not held until June 1863, and only seven such meetings and lectures were held during the entire course of the war, the last in February 1864. Pro-Union forces in comparison organized twenty-two meetings and lectures between February 1863 and December 1864. And in Bacup and surrounding towns, where there was no one of Thomas's stature on either side, most meetings were organized before the formation of local UES and SIA branches in September 1863.

While the reasons for Bacup's uniqueness remain elusive, the evidence suggests that the existence of local branches and/or the activities of point men such as Thomas ensured greater public interest. The Sheffield branch of the

---

51. Morse to Seward, London, 21 November, 2 December 1862, Despatches from U.S. Consuls in London, 1790–1906; *Morning Star*, 17, 27 November, 2, 12, 13, 16 December 1862; *Anti Slavery Reporter*, 1 March 1864.

LES was responsible for the organization of ten meetings and lectures between late December 1862 and March 1863. Its efforts were supported by J. W. Burns, a workingman who through frequent letters to the press kept Confederate proponents on the defensive. With the exception of the massive May 1863 public meeting at which John Roebuck spoke in favor of recognition and the much smaller affair attended by about one hundred and organized by the relatively ineffective Yorkshire Association for the Recognition of the Confederacy, friends of the Confederacy in Sheffield suffered from the absence of both an active local society and an energetic proponent. In Bristol, where local societies were not very active, Handel Cossham promoted the cause of the Union through a constant stream of letters to local newspapers—one almost every three weeks, plus an annual Fourth of July letter praising progress in America and predicting eventual abolition—and the organization of frequent meetings. Even in areas not immediately affected by the war, the existence of an active society and/or the leadership of committed individuals ensured that the message was heard. In Hereford, for example, the local society and Joseph Jones, a bookseller, were responsible for initiating an address to President Lincoln in September 1863. The same was true in the small Scottish town of Newmilns.[52] Friends of the Confederacy were not always as successful in developing this critical combination. Where societies were relatively inactive, few local supporters emerged to take up the cudgels. An officer of the Oldham branch of the SIA, a town many considered more pro-Confederate than any in Britain, J. L. Quarmby was the most visible proponent of the cause, making fourteen public appearances between April and September 1863. Then for some inexplicable reason he dropped from sight in October 1863. Edward Verity played a comparable role in and around Burnley, but then was largely lost to the local movement when he became a national agent in July 1863. Even if Verity had stayed at home, his effectiveness would have been compromised by his knack for alienating potential supporters with his uncompromising rejection of the principles of the Manchester school. Only William Aitken in Ashton and Stalybridge seemed to have achieved a status comparable to Thomas or Cossham among local supporters.

There was no surer way of canvassing public sentiment about the war than

52. For Sheffield see issues of the *Independent* (Sheffield and Rotherham) for the period December 1862 to June 1863. For a sample of Burnes's letters see *Telegraph* (Sheffield), 6 October 1863. Cossham's activities are recorded in *Daily Post* (Bristol), 4 July, 4, 18, 19, 24, 26 December 1862, 5 July 1864; *Times* (Hereford), 26 September 1863; *Morning Star*, 10 October 1863; *Advertiser* (Ayr), 22 December 1864.

through public meetings. While it is impossible to measure Morse's hopeful calculation that regular meetings in support of the Union in London would affect the way the country (and ultimately the government) viewed the war, it is clear that meetings were considered by both Confederate and Union supporters the most reliable indicator of public opinion. Although knowledgeable about conditions across the Atlantic, the public still had to be courted by those who knew the situation firsthand and coaxed into declaring their support for one side or the other. Such appeals by their very nature were calculated and targeted to achieve specific ends. Nothing was left to chance, and every effort was made by both sides to employ the most effective messengers. That is why Spence could hardly contain his delight at word that Confederate sympathizers in Manchester had employed the services of Barker. But it was an achievement that could not be replicated. No one else of Barker's stature, with the possible exception of Verity, would join the Confederate agency. The Union cause, in contrast, was replete with talent, so much so that it could afford to employ teams of agents. Jackson and Thompson were pivotal to these efforts in 1863. Jackson had his first exposure to British audiences in partnership with Thompson in London, the Potteries, and the west country and in Sheffield, where they held five meetings in one month. Jackson also worked on different occasions with Denison, Ernest Jones, James Cooper, J. C. Edwards, John Rowlinson, and E. O. Greening.[53] There were many other such teams including that of Thompson and Cossham in the west country, Washington Wilkes and Martin in Northampton, and Conway and Martin in London. On only a handful of occasions did Confederate agents work in teams.

"It is a singular feature of this struggle in America," Charles F. Adams observed at the close of 1863, "that its merits should be debated at popular meetings held all over this kingdom. The association of sympathizers with the Insurgents have of late been assiduously engaged in sending paid agents to deliver lectures in behalf of their cause at various places. This has given occasion to counter efforts. Frequently discussions are held by representatives of both sides. I very much doubt whether anything precisely similar ever took place before."[54]

53. For reports of meetings held by these teams see *Times* (Blackburn), 21 March 1863; *Guardian* (Bolton), 21 February, 4 April, 2 May, 27 June 1863; *Review* (Bradford), 27 August 1863; *Advertiser* (Burnley), 8 August 1863; *Examiner and Times* (Manchester), 24 February 1863; *Independent* (Sheffield and Rotherham), 8, 10, 20, 24 January 1863.

54. Adams to Seward, London, 17 December 1863, Despatches from U.S. Ministers to Great Britain, 1791–1906.

Although it is impossible to determine with any exactness the number of public meetings held during the war, it is clear that they numbered in the hundreds. In early 1865 the UES reported that it had organized more that 350 public meetings "besides one hundred and forty other meetings for general and specific business." To these should be added the scores organized by the LES in London and the Home Counties. There are no comparable figures for the SIA, but it is clear that at the height of the agitation in 1863, it organized as many meetings as did the opposition in Lancashire and Cheshire.[55]

If public gatherings can be used to measure levels of activity and support, then over the country as a whole the Confederacy was at a distinct disadvantage. Between November 1861 and January 1864, when Thompson departed for America, pro-Union forces organized close to 100 meetings and lectures in London and the south of England. They ranged from the annual series of lectures at the LES rooms and more select meetings at the Whittington Club to massive public meetings, such as the one organized in January 1863 by the LES in Exeter Hall to commemorate the Emancipation Proclamation. The attendance was so large that a satellite meeting had to be arranged in another hall. When that could not accommodate all who wanted to participate, an impromptu open-air meeting was organized, blocking all traffic in the Strand.[56] It was arranged to coincide with a similarly large gathering in Bradford and a smaller one in Stroud. Over the next few weeks, meetings celebrating the proclamation were held throughout the country.[57] If Morse's estimation is right about the potential of London meetings to influence public opinion, it is surprising that supporters of the Confederacy made no attempt to engage the opposition in the capital city. Yancey and Mann held a desultory meeting at Fishmongers' Hall in November 1861, and according to Thompson, there were two other meetings in the city: one addressed by a Colonel Fuller, the other held "up a pair of stairs in Devonshire Street."[58] Confederate supporters also shied away from any public appearances in Manchester, the country's second city and mercantile center of the textile industry. Taunted by the opposi-

55. "Summary of the Third Report of the Executive of the Union and Emancipation Society," enclosed Dudley to Seward, Liverpool, 4 March 1865, Despatches from U.S. Consuls in Liverpool, 1790–1906; *Liberator*, 15 April 1864, 24 March 1865; Adams, *Great Britain and the American Civil War*, 2: 223; Hernon, *Celts, Catholics, and Copperheads*, 102–103 states there were only four public meetings in Ireland, all in favor of the Union.

56. *Morning Star*, 29, 30 January 1863; *Bee Hive*, 31 January 1863.

57. Meetings were also held in cities such as Bath, Bristol, Coventry, Edinburgh, Glasgow, Halifax, Leeds, Newcastle, Carlisle, and Kendal.

58. *Morning Star*, 21 October 1863.

tion for its lack of activity, the Manchester Southern Club announced plans for a meeting at Free Trade Hall at which Spence would be the main speaker. Spence demurred, arguing that the time was not right. It was clear, however, that he did not have the stomach for a bruising, rowdy welcome from the opposition. In the end the meeting was postponed, according to Spence because of "adverse news—the Polish question, and the state of the cotton question at the moment." Later, Thomas Barker would take pride in the fact that friends of the Confederacy considered Manchester hostile territory. "One of their least scrupulous champions [Joseph Barker]," he wrote Garrison, "tried a lecture, admission by paid ticket, in our Mechanics Institution, but he was so taken aback by the feeling of his audience that he did not repeat the experiment there. He made another similar experiment in our Corn Exchange but met with a more decided rebuff there so that he had to content himself by selling a few copies of his lecture in print, instead of delivering it to those who had paid their money for admission to the Hall."[59]

Confederate supporters, however, were more actively engaged in other parts of the country, particularly in Lancashire and Cheshire, counties that had taken the brunt of the Cotton Famine and whose public was actively targeted by the UES and the SIA. Here and elsewhere, as in Sheffield and Glasgow, advocates of recognition were able to attract large crowds to their meetings. In Ashton six thousand came out to hear plans for dealing with the Cotton Famine and, as has been shown, might have voted in favor of recognition. More than eight thousand were at Sheffield to hear Roebuck, and nearly four thousand attended Spence's Glasgow meeting.[60] Yet, in the aggregate, pro-Union meetings and lectures far surpassed those of their opponents, even in those areas of Lancashire where, in Ellison's estimation, the effects of the Cotton Famine should have produced votes in favor of the Confederacy.[61] What was true of Ashton and Stalybridge held for the rest of Lancashire. Not

59. Spence to Mason, Liverpool, 3, 6 August 1863, Mason Papers; Barker to Garrison, Manchester, 27 August 1864, AASS Papers.

60. Lord to Seward, Manchester, 1 May 1862, Despatches from U.S. Consuls in Manchester, 1847–1906; *Reporter* (Ashton and Stalybridge), 3 May 1862; *Independent* (Sheffield and Rotherham), 27 May 1863; *Daily Herald* (Glasgow), 27 November 1863.

61. This conclusion comes from an examination of local newspapers in the following towns: Ashton and Stalybridge; Bacup; Blackburn; Bolton; Burnley; Bury; Liverpool; Manchester; Oldham; Preston; Rochdale; and Stockport. The survey also included meetings and lectures held in smaller towns and villages surrounding these major centers. So, for example, meetings held in Mossley and Lees are included in the figures for Oldham. Nearly twice as many pro-Union meetings and lectures were organized: 231 to 115.

even in Oldham did the activities of Quarmby and the local SIA surpass those of the opposition. The same was true of Preston over the course of the war, although in 1863 pro-Confederate forces did hold a very slight advantage. Liverpool, home of many Southern families and Spence's base, was surprisingly quiet in its public expressions of support for the South considering its extensive trading connections with the Confederacy. The local Southern Club spent most of its time in social rather than political activities, organizing only a few public meetings to which entry was limited by ticket. Its most visible public engagement was the successful three-day bazaar in October 1864 that raised money for the relief of Confederate prisoners.

Pro-Union forces had similar successes in other parts of the country that were unaffected by the economic crisis. The Cotton Famine had no discernable effects on the economy of Halifax, second only to Bradford as a center of the worsted trade. If anything, Lancashire's troubles were a boon to Halifax. The city also had a long tradition of antislavery activity dating back thirty years. The local movement, which included the Halifax Ladies Anti Slavery Society formed in 1856, continued to be active during the war. It was dominated by members of the Carpenter family, particularly Russell Lant, a Unitarian minister who moved there from Warrington sometime in 1862. Over the course of the war, friends of the Union organized forty meetings and lectures. Interestingly, none of the lecturers and speakers were residents of Halifax. These included Marmaduke Miller of Darlington, Newman Hall of London, John Rowlinson of Bury, Ernest Jones of Manchester, Henry Vincent of London, the Americans Archibald Mackenzie and Crammond Kennedy, and the African Americans Isaac Davison, Edward Irving, and Jacob Green. The opposition managed just four meetings and lectures, the first by Joseph Barker late in August 1863. All three of the pro-Confederate lecturers, Barker, Spence, and Balme, were also outsiders. Such a level of domination by pro-Union forces might have been unusual, but the fact remains that in Halifax, as in other cities, supporters of the Confederacy were bested. The range and consistency of the activities also speak to the continued interest of the people of Halifax and elsewhere during the war. Following the lecture by Kennedy, a local editor expressed surprise at the large attendance "considering," as he observed, "how often the American question has been publicly dealt with in Halifax."[62]

62. Kathleen Tiller, "Working Class Attitudes and Organisations in Three Industrial Towns, 1850–1875" (Ph.D. diss., University of Birmingham, 1975), 46–47; Midgley, *Women against Slavery*, 207; Stange, *British Unitarians against American Slavery*, 127–28; *Courier* (Halifax),

If meetings were expressions of shared community views, their frequency and unanimity had, as Brian Harrison has argued in another context, "the ancillary advantage of assuring those present of the strength and righteousness of their cause."[63] To attain public endorsement, these meetings had to be carefully organized. They had to be advertised through posters and placards; a chairman, usually a prominent local figure, had to be found; if held indoors, sympathetic platform guests had to be assured; resolutions had to be drafted and individuals who would submit them identified; and if trouble was brewing, as it usually was, every effort had to be made to ensure that the hall was packed with supporters, or if that was not possible, that sufficient policemen would be present to ensure some degree of order. Control was critical to the success of these "interactive relationships" between speakers and audiences.[64] With well-informed audiences for whom the war had become a metaphor for domestic politics, these relationships could and frequently did become sticky. Speakers were regularly disrupted and constantly heckled by audiences that had raised barracking to a high art form. Without careful organization, one could and often did lose control of meetings.

Sometime in early July 1863 a Blackburn organization of overlookers began making plans for a pro-Confederate meeting to be held at the end of the month. Colonel R. Rayford Jackson and other prominent local supporters of secession had agreed to participate, and outside agents of the cause, including Barker and W. E. Stutter of Manchester, were slated to speak. On the day of the meeting, mills owned by Confederate sympathizers closed early so millhands could attend and pack the hall. Placards were posted throughout the town, one of them depicting the way Negroes had been treated by mobs during the recent New York Draft Riots. Opponents countered by getting many of their supporters into the hall long before the proceedings began. The organizers seemed to have been surprised by the appearance of Ernest Jones. What followed was sheer theater. Some audience members attempted to hoist Benjamin Hornbury, a mechanic and an opponent of the Confederacy, onto the stage but met resistance. According to a reporter, "Hornbury's body was seen elevated, his toes on the platform, while his friends were pushing to place him where he had a right to be. At last they succeeded in putting

---

18 May 1861, 5 April, 20 September 1862, 2, 21 February, 29 August, 9 September, 14 November, 1863, 22 October, 3 December 1864, 7 January 1865; Guardian (Halifax), 3 December 1864.

63. Hewitt, The Emergence of Stability, 286; Harrison, Drink and the Victorians, 227.

64. Pickering, Chartism and the Chartists, 165.

Mr. Hornbury up, and the conclusion of the business was the signal for a loud and hearty cheer." Latecomers jostled to gain entrance from the rear of the hall, while at the front, Union supporters who were being disruptive were threatened with expulsion. William Andrew Jackson appeared in the middle of Stutter's speech and was passed from the back to the front over the heads of the audience, a section of which struck up a chorus of "Rule Britannia." The choice of song might have been meant to convey patriotic revulsion against slaveholding, symbolically apt as Jackson arrived, but just as likely it was in-tended to disrupt the meeting still further. During Colonel Jackson's speech, a portion of the crowd broke into a rendition of "Hard Times, Come Again No More," a chorus of which was repeated as Barker rose to speak. The end of Barker's speech was greeted with another strain of "Rule Britannia." Barker had run up against similar treatment at the Free Trade Hall in Manchester two months earlier when he was prevented from speaking by opponents who sang "Rule Britannia" and "Old Joe Barker, Oh." Repeated loud and discordant singing frustrated the best of speakers, but it was also symbolically a statement of collective action. Many years later, James Odgen recalled that crowds gath-ered in the streets of Bacup welcomed the news of the Emancipation Proclama-tion by singing "John Brown's Body." The tribute to the martyr of Harpers Ferry became the anthem (if not the hymn) of the pro-Union movement and would maintain its currency throughout the struggle for political reform in Britain.[65]

If songs frustrated the best of speakers, so did strange noises emanating from the audience. In the midst of Colonel Jackson's speech, someone started crowing, while others shouted, "Aye; thou'rt a plucked one." Speakers op-posed to the Confederacy went relatively unscathed. In the end, pro-Unionists achieved their objective. While the first resolution decrying the fact that the war was hurting both those in America and Lancashire was

65. *Times* (Blackburn), 1 August 1863; *Advertiser* (Heywood), 13 June 1863; Ogden, "Fifty Years of Bacup Life"; William Farish, *Autobiography of William Farish: The Struggle of a Handloom Weaver* (n.p., 1892), 116. Supporters of the Confederacy never crafted a comparable anthem. Hotze hired a London barrel organist to play "The Bonnie Blue Flag," a Confederate anthem, but there is no evidence that it had any popular appeal. Jordon and Pratt, *Europe and the American Civil War*, 184–85. "Southerns Hear, Your Country Calls You," composed by the Reverend Woodville Woodman, a Confederate supporter from Stoneclough, near Bolton, had only limited local appeal. Brook, "Confederate Sympathies in North East Lancashire," 215; Biagini, *Liberty, Retrenchment, and Reform*, 38, explores the relation between music and political action; so does Epstein, *Radical Expression*, 151; Vernon, *Politics and the People*, 123. See also Walter L. Arnstein, "The Murphy Riots: A Victorian Dilemma," *Victorian Studies* 19 (September 1975), who points out that "John Brown's Body" was sung by mobs that attacked Irish homes in Birmingham.

passed, it appears that Jones's amendment calling for continued British neutrality was also accepted. The vote on the amendment led Confederate supporters to call for a recount, at which point many of them rushed the platform holding up both hands so the chairman could not see how those behind them in the audience were voting—a fitting end to a closely contested meeting, which was unusual only in the inconclusiveness of the resolutions adopted.[66]

The Blackburn meeting was indeed typical. Very few assemblages were uncontested, in spite of the best efforts of organizers to arrange for the presence of sympathetic audiences. All features, from the organization to the program to the proposed resolutions, were challenged. Placards, posters, and handbills announcing the meeting and summoning the faithful to attend were, like those posted by the Clarks in Butleigh, large and colorful—Kershaw called them "flaming." In their details they anticipated the debate that would engage audiences' interests. The sheer size of the placards that denounced Seward on the streets of Manchester surprised Henry Lord, the American consul there. They were in excess of one yard square. In Stockport, John Hindle put up myriad posters calling on Union supporters to attend a pro-Confederate meeting "in their thousands and shout for freedom." Placards were also sometimes used as a form of protest. Julia Griffiths Crofts recalled one at the Halifax train station that had "printed in ominously large letters 'Withdrawal of General Fremont by the Government,'" a criticism of Lincoln's reversal of the popular general's order emancipating slaves in his military district. Similarly, when James Mason left a meeting of the Confederate States Aid Society in London, he was met in the streets by a group of men carrying a placard showing a slave in torn clothes wearing an iron collar.[67] Handbills were usually more informational. In their efforts to dissuade Irish immigrants from settling in the North, Confederate agents distributed two thousand handbills at churches and boarding houses, warning that immigrants would be conscripted and sent to fight in the "Swamps of the Carolinas." In an effort to counter Confederate propaganda, the American consul in Dublin circulated several hundred copies

66. *Times* (Blackburn), 1 August 1863.

67. *Standard* (Oldham), 16 May 1863; Lord to Seward, Manchester, 20 September 1864, Despatches from U.S. Consuls in Manchester, 1847–1906; *Advertiser* (Stockport), 6 November 1863; *Douglass Monthly*, January 1862; Thompson to Garrison, London, 5 December 1862, AASS Papers. Prior to Roebuck's motion, Hotze plastered London with placards. See Jordon and Pratt, *Europe and the American Civil War*, 184–85. Posters were vital to the success of any meeting. One local reporter attributed the sparse attendence at a Kendal meeting to the fact that the posters were too small and not widely distributed. *Mercury* (Kendal), 13 May 1865.

of a handbill titled "No Excuse For Rebellion," which contained an extract from Alexander Stephens's by then well-known speech warning against seces-sion.[68] As supplements to public meetings and as sources of information, plac-ards, posters, and handbills—"street literature"—were also contested. Once they got wind of the true intentions of the organizers of the Ashton meeting in May 1862, opponents, as has been shown, produced a very effective and de-tailed placard that condemned any effort to break the blockade or otherwise support the Confederacy. One day after the appearance of the SIA poster in Manchester, Lord reported that the UES had countered with a placard of equal dimensions.[69]

The poster wars were but one more reflection of the contested nature of the public debate. All organizers of meetings could hope for was to limit the strength of the opposition. Open-air meetings were more difficult to control for they generally attracted much larger crowds. Not always able to hear the speakers, those farthest from the platform were also the ones most likely to en-gage in banter. Organizers deployed flags, buntings, and banners as symbolic devices to reach those in the crowd who could not hear the speakers. These rarely worked. Among the eight thousand who gathered at the marketplace in Ashton, one reporter recorded, "a good bit of pleasant banter was indulged in, but all seemed quite willing to crack and give and take a joke with the great-est good humour." At another open-air meeting in Ashton attended by an es-timated twelve thousand, three carts were brought in to provide the podia and act as symbolic stages: one representing the North; a second, the South; and the third, neutral territory. Before Joseph Barker could begin speaking, oppo-nents on the Union cart began to throw out handbills and seemed intent on upsetting the Southern cart. Barker and his supporters were forced to retreat to a spot opposite the town hall. Before Barker had finished his address, his supporters stole the Northern cart and so prevented the opposition from mak-ing any speeches. On another occasion, Union supporters, among whom was William A. Jackson, drew up a cart in the croft, an open space opposite the Stamford Arms in Mossley, next to another on which sat the organizers of a pro-Confederate meeting. Jackson and his supporters promptly began making

68. James Capston to Benjamin, Queenstown, 24 August 1864, John Bannon to Benjamin, Dublin, 15 December 1864, both in Records of the Confederate States of America; West to Seward, Dublin, 29 October 1864, Despatches from U.S. Consuls in Dublin, 1790–1906.

69. Vernon, *Politics and the People,* 132; *Reporter* (Ashton and Stalybridge), 3 May 1862. The central office of the SIA in Manchester plastered the walls of Bury with posters condemning an upcoming UES meeting. *Times* (Bury), 15 May 1863; Lord to Seward, Manchester, 24 September 1864, Despatches from U.S. Consuls in Manchester, 1847–1906.

a nuisance of themselves. They soon left, drawing off about six hundred of the crowd to hold a meeting at another location, the cart driven, as if to effect some curious symbolism, by Jackson, the former coachman of Jefferson Davis. One reporter could not resist the irony: "They beat a hasty retreat, the coachman for once being metamorphosed into a jolly wagoner, his ivories indicating that he liked the ride as well as the 'respectable' passengers who accompanied him in his inglorious ride round the croft."[70]

The situation was only slightly different at indoor meetings. Early in the proceedings of an Oldham meeting called to endorse Lincoln's emancipation edict, sections of the crowd began swaying backward and forward and laughing loudly. Before long they had carved out a space for themselves in the middle of the hall "and kept pushing one another about in it." Above the noise and hubbub of an Edward Verity meeting in Wigan "could be heard the deep wail of a squeaking doll in the possession of some individual in the room, and which was a source of great amusement." In an effort to rile Verity, opponents regularly offered cheers for John Bright whom, as all knew, Verity despised. At a Smallbridge meeting addressed by T. B. Kershaw, an opponent brandished a ticket and insisted that he be seated on the platform. Once on the platform he began to act out a pantomime while Kershaw spoke, offered to deliver a lecture on his three fingers, rose to his feet when Kershaw mentioned slavery to show how he would fight the slaveholders to the death, and, when policemen were called, offered them seats on the platform. In exasperation Kershaw dismissed his tormentor as an ass, but the damage was done. At a pro-Confederate meeting in Burslem, speakers were alternately cheered and jeered, which, a reporter recorded, was only "a preliminary exercise to the extraordinary performance which ensued . . . which embraced every variety of sound capable of being produced by human organs."[71] There is no evidence that the noises emanated only from organs above the neck.

Efforts to control the opposition at indoor meetings by issuing tickets was only marginally successful. The Blackburn Southern Club, for example, gave the majority of the tickets available for a Barker lecture to supporters free of charge, sold some to other known supporters, and issued very few to opponents. Charles Denison charged an entry fee of six pence for those wishing to

70. *Reporter* (Ashton and Stalybridge), 3 May 1862, 18 July 1863; *Standard* (Oldham), 11, 18 July 1863.

71. *Chronicle* (Oldham), 21 February 1863; *Observer* (Wigan), 22 January 1864; *Observer* (Rochdale), 30 January, 13 February 1864; *Spectator* (Rochdale), 30 January 1864; *Staffordshire Sentinel*, 19 November 1864.

sit on the platform or in the reserve seats of his Bury meeting; there was no charge for sitting in the body of the hall or in the gallery. When they lost control of their first meeting in Todmorden, Peter Sinclair and William Jackson organized a second to which admission was charged. Although attendance at the second meeting was smaller, "good order was kept the whole of the time." There were times when the opposition managed to subvert these efforts at control. Tickets to a Bristol pro-Union meeting, according to the local U.S. consul, were "bought by wealthy cotton aristocrats" and distributed free of charge to a group who disrupted the proceedings.[72]

Even when organizers packed meetings with their supporters, the opposition found ways to express its views. Subverting such controls became something of a dare, akin to a sporting event. Opponents sometimes positioned themselves at the back of the hall or in the gallery, where they could not be easily reached and ejected, and from there lobbed questions at the speaker or made their own speeches in the middle of the proceedings. More difficult to handle were the groups that were paid to attend and disrupt meetings, for inherent in this form of protest was the increased likelihood of violence. One sympathetic reporter recorded that at a pro-Union Rawtenstall meeting, a number of men from "Burnley, Bacup, and other places opposed to the North, and youth composed a large portion of the audience and served the purpose for which they were met, viz. giving the most unseemly opposition to the speakers." One of the leaders of the group was William Cunliffe, a workingman from Burnley who the night before had challenged Sinclair during a meeting in that town. Following a Preston meeting, a Union supporter wrote lamenting the fact that "certain employers who sympathise with the South had their workpeople organised and drilled by the overlookers for the purpose of attending the meeting; and they were ordered to leave the mills at a very early hour for the purpose of getting and keeping possession of the place of meeting. Secondly, that the people were paid a quart of beer each for their services. Thirdly, that a number of notorious fellows who are the dread of peaceable people at an election time were imported into the meeting for the purpose of overawing the free expression of opinion." Areas of the country far removed from the economic pressures and political passions brought on by the Cotton Famine employed similar devices. At a Hereford meeting, for exam-

72. *Guardian* (Preston), 1 August 1863; *Times* (Bury), 21, 28 March 1863; *Times* (Todmorden), 6 June, 12 September 1863; Eastman to Seward, Bristol, 5 February 1863, Despatches from U.S. Consuls in Bristol, 1792–1906.

ple, "several gentlemen" who were from another town entered the hall without paying and began disrupting the proceedings.[73]

Although the Hereford group left peacefully, these confrontations always ran the risk of turning violent, particularly in those parts of the country ravaged by the Cotton Famine. In the fall of 1861 Stephen Bourne, anxious to promote the interests of the Jamaica Cotton Company, warned that the potential for violence was as great as in the time when, not so long before, crowds gathered to welcome back "Orator" Hunt from exile. "The money market felt it no less than the cotton spinners. The bankers all over the country, tradesmen and manufacturers of every class, members of Parliament, peers as well as commoners, statesmen, judges, the Crown itself, were in fear of the results of an agitation, grounded in the distress of the people."[74] Bourne might have exaggerated the chances of violence for his own ends, but the fear was nonetheless real. Throughout Lancashire, meetings were held to denounce the demeaning methods for relief devised by local and national committees, and these sometimes turned testy. Both sides of the political divide, as well as working-class leaders, pleaded with the unemployed not to resort to violence. For many, vigorous but peaceful protest against the relief system demonstrated the level of political sophistication workingmen had achieved, a level sufficient, they insisted, to warrant being given the right to vote. Although there was not massive social upheaval as was feared, here and there in some of the most affected areas protests against the relief system sometimes turned violent. The most damaging occurred in Stalybridge in March of 1863. A reduction in the already meager relief provided by two competing local committees and the decision to issue tickets that could be redeemed at stores rather than to continue to give aid in cash sparked the trouble. A mob destroyed machinery at mills, stoned the police and the homes of relief committee members, and attacked bread shops. The military was called out, the Riot Act read, and almost thirty rioters were sent to trial.[75]

The flour and bacon brought over from New York and Philadelphia by the *George Griswold* was gratefully acknowledged by the unemployed and was a

---

73. *Times* (Bury), 18 April 1863; *Guardian* (Bury), 25 April 1863. Preston comments quoted in Auger, "The Cotton Famine," 254; *Times* (Hereford), 9 September 1863.

74. *Newcastle Daily Chronicle and Northern Counties Advertiser*, 7 September 1861.

75. Lock, "The Role of Local Clergy and Ministers in the Stalybridge Riots," 83–84; Rose, "Rochdale Man and the Stalybridge Riot," 195; *Reporter* (Ashton and Stalybridge), 21, 28 March 1863. There were also disturbances in Chorley and Preston in April 1863. Longmate, *The Hungry Mills*, 202.

propaganda bonanza for the Union. Even among such critics of the Federal administration as George Reynolds, the *Griswold*'s cargo was a "republican gift to a starving and aristocratic-ridden people [that] has no equal in anything recorded of the generosity of princes."[76] In the months after the ship's arrival, its "chaplain," Charles Denison, teamed up with George Thompson, Jackson, and sometimes Sinclair at a series of large meetings in Lancashire and Cheshire that warmly acknowledged the gift as an act of true benevolence. The gift won the Union considerable goodwill. Distribution of the goods fell to local relief committees and as such were subjected to traditional restrictions: only the truly destitute, those unable to find any form of work, were deemed eligible. The parsimony and insensitivity of some local officials threatened to turn what was a public-relations bonanza for the Union into a disaster. When some relief committees, such as the one in Glossop, Derbyshire, decided to sell their allotment, there was almost a riot. Merchants were verbally abused, there was pushing and jostling, and stones were thrown; but the police managed to maintain control. When the auctioneer declined to start the sale of the flour for fear of being attacked, some in the crowd broke the barrels, spilling their contents into the street and occasioning a free-for-all. Women were "down upon their knees," a reporter observed, "ladling the flour as best they could into their aprons, lads filling their caps, and others cramming it in any available place they might have about their person." Flour was scattered all over the streets, covering people who "presented the appearance of having been in a heavy snow storm."[77] A potentially more volatile situation developed at a meeting in Stevenson Square, Manchester. Supporters of Garibaldi and the Italian independence movement, most of whom were advocates of the Union, attempted to use the occasion of the distribution of bread made from the flour brought over by the *Griswold* to organize a group in favor of Italian independence. Two floats, one carrying a replica of the *Griswold*, the other a pirate ship meant to be the *Alabama*, the Confederate privateer that had ravaged Union shipping, were driven into the square. The organizers had planned to make a number of pro-Union speeches, then lead a march to the moors outside the city, where those on relief were usually taken to break rocks and pick oakum, to distribute the bread. Many in the square thought such theatrics

76. *Reynolds's Newspaper*, 15 February 1863.

77. *Reporter* (Ashton and Stalybridge), 7 March 1863. Verity reported that the Manchester committee had plans to sell bacon at three pence per pound. *Bee Hive*, 31 January 1863.

much too contrived and exploitative. Near pandemonium ensued, and some of the organizers were pelted with loaves of bread.[78]

Much of the violence at Stalybridge, Glossop, and Manchester was blamed on the Irish (and Irish women in particular) and so could be dismissed as not attributable to English workers. The fact remains, however, that such upheavals troubled those involved in the public debate over the war. Reporters were impressed by the banter, the heckling, and the give-and-take that occurred at these meetings, but turning "the proceedings into a shindy," as a group opposed to the Confederacy allegedly did in Rochdale, always ran the risk of getting out of hand. Throughout an open-air pro-Confederate meeting in Ashton, "numerous fights occurred in different parts of the Market Place, but nothing serious took place, with the exception of one or two parties being locked up. Altogether," a reporter wrote, "the proceedings were uproarious, and many people seemed to enjoy the affair more as a joke than anything else."[79] The reporter might have had a keen eye for the lighter side of things, but those who eleven months earlier had threatened to throw John Matthews into a nearby canal if he attempted to prevent Jacob Green, a fugitive slave, from holding his street-corner meeting were deadly serious.[80]

That such actions and the frequent fisticuffs that broke out rarely degenerated into full-scale violence testifies to the levels of control organizers were able to maintain and to the recognition by the majority of the audiences that to allow banter and heckling to slip into violence was politically unwise. By 1863 most of those who attended meetings in Lancashire had concluded that the economic crisis was the result of greed by speculators and merchants eager to profit from the war, not the work of employers. Working-class leaders, aware that violence could deflect the movement for political reform, also preached moderation. Patrick Joyce and others see in this absence of widespread vio-

78. *Examiner and Times* (Manchester), 11, 17 March 1863; *Guardian* (Manchester), 12 March 1863; *Inquirer*, 11, 18, 25 April, 2 May 1863.

79. M. Brennan, "The Cotton Famine in Rochdale, 1861–1865, with Special Reference to the Role of John Bright" (master's thesis, Leeds University, 1990), 16; *Reporter* (Ashton and Stalybridge), 18 July 1863.

80. *Reporter* (Ashton and Stalybridge), 16 August 1862. For examples of other acts of violence during meetings see *Guardian* (Bolton), 28 February 1863; *News* (Bacup and Rawenstall), 26 September 1863; *Examiner* (Huddersfield), 28 February 1863; *Chronicle* (Huddersfield), 28 March, 4 April 1863; *Examiner and Times* (Manchesters), 4, 22 June, 16 July 1863; *Guardian* (Manchester), 4, 22 June 1863; *Barker's Review*, 13 June 1863; Spence to Mason, Liverpool, 6 June 1863, Mason Papers; Conway, *Autobiography*, 1: 376.

lence increasing deference on the part of workers to their employers. Yet the fear of violence and the periodic outbursts of riotous behavior in Lancashire and other parts of the country suggest a far more unpredictable and complex situation.[81] The organizers of the Bristol meeting to congratulate Lincoln on his reelection were surprised by the furor of what Handel Cossham described as a "half-drunk" mob. Unable to explain the mob's passion, Cossham resorted to the traditional dismissal that it was spurred on by an excess of drink; however, all the indications are that it had its origins in a recent bitterly contested municipal election won by Cossham. His opponent in the election, H. Melson, a Confederate supporter, took revenge by organizing the group to disrupt the meeting. At least three hundred of Melson's supporters paid the price of admittance; and, as one reporter observed, "like the 'Mountain' party in the assembly during the French Revolution, appeared to be most obnoxious to anything like order." They burst into song even before the proceedings began. "We won't go home till morning, till daylight does appear," an old bacchanalian song, stymied all efforts to elect a chairman and was followed by cheers for Jefferson Davis, Stonewall Jackson, and Robert E. Lee. The stage was then rushed and cleared of Lincoln sympathizers. With the opposition in retreat, the mob took control of the meeting, and someone in the gallery burst into a "parody of John Brown's body—the burden of which was that they would 'hang Abe Lincoln to a sour apple tree,' and the chorus, which was heartily joined in, 'Glory, glory, hallelujah.'"[82]

Rare as it was, such violence, or more correctly its likelihood, was part and parcel of the public contest. The attack may have been premeditated and the work of the "scum of Bristol," a group of "small shot, peas, and penny whistles,"[83] as one supporter of Cossham insisted, but it temporarily put paid to the efforts of Union sympathizers to use the occasion to declare the city's support for Lincoln's policies. But even when the capture of meetings denied organizers the opportunity to declare that the public supported their view of the war, they found other ways to assert their position. In the weeks after the fiasco in Bristol, Cossham used a more controlled setting, a meeting of the Bristol Emancipation Society, to have the "Address to Lincoln" endorsed. Even here

81. Joyce, *Work, Society, and Politics*, 99; Kirk, *The Growth of Working-Class Reformism*, 108. See *News* (Hinkley), 9 May 1863 for a report of a disturbance at the workhouse when the board of guardians, who were in charge of relief, tried to increase the numbers of hours that had to be worked at stone breaking before the unemployed could qualify for relief.

82. *Western Daily Press*, 2, 3 December 1864; *Daily Post* (Bristol), 1, 2 December 1864.

83. *Daily Post* (Bristol), 5 December 1864.

he ran into opposition from about sixty "drunken men," but in the end what mattered most to those engaged in the public debate in Bristol and elsewhere was that their position (in this case the "Address to Lincoln") had been voted on favorably. What was once rejected, or more correctly, prevented, was now declared to be the will of the people of Bristol. Cossham found refuge in a rather interesting method of measuring public opinion. As the preamble to the address stated, the Bristol Emancipation Society claimed to be speaking in the "name of a large number of our fellow-citizens, who, in meeting assembled, on several occasions, and invariably by a large number of votes, have adopted resolutions in agreement with the tenor of the address."[84] By this slight of hand, Cossham and the society had been elevated to the rank of tribune of the people.

There is a logic, however, to Cossham's argument: one negative result should not be the only indicator of the way the people viewed the war. If, as he argues—and the evidence supports his claim—previous meetings had voted in support of the Union, then those accumulated votes should be considered a reliable indicator of the public's position. It was these votes, in the form of resolutions, that for organizers of meetings became the most effective means of measuring the public's support. Lincoln was so concerned that these resolutions express the right sentiment that he crafted and had sent to Charles Sumner for transmission to John Bright a set of resolutions that could be adopted by public meetings in Britain. Resolutions, like everything else in this public debate, were contested. In spite of their ultimate objective, Melson's men had come prepared with a series of amendments to counter the address. Had the opportunity presented itself and had it looked likely that they could carry the day, these amendments would have been an effective method of subversion.[85] Nor were resolutions "spontaneous expressions of goodwill," as Charles Francis Adams and some historians believed. Both resolutions and amendments were prepared well in advance, and certain people were assigned to submit them. Prior to a meeting in Manchester, George Thompson pleaded with a local organizer to "arrange for the passing of a resolution before and after" his lecture. The effects of such a resolution, he insisted, "would be good," both for the cause in Britain and for those fighting against the Confederacy in America.[86]

84. *Western Daily Press*, 27 January 1865.

85. Roy P. Basler, et. al., eds., *The Collected Works of Abraham Lincoln* (New Brunswick, 1953), 6: 176–77. Conway makes mention of Lincoln's resolution, but there is no evidence that it was ever used at a public meeting. Conway, *Autobiography*, 1: 366–67; *Daily Post* (Bristol), 2 December 1864.

86. Adams to Rev. Edwin Davis, London, 18 October 1862, letterbook, Adams Papers; Thompson to Wilson, London, 11 January 1862, Wilson Papers.

Carefully worded resolutions and carefully crafted challenges in the form of amendments prepared well in advance were part and parcel of meetings in every part of the country, both in areas devastated by the Cotton Famine and in those experiencing no ill effects from the shortage of cotton. There were few occasions when either resolutions or amendments were put together in the heat of a meeting. Although organizers of public meetings made every effort to ensure that the opposition was kept to a minimum and that resolutions of support were adopted, the best laid plans sometimes went awry. At the end of one of Verity's meetings in Bury, for instance, the chair declared that a resolution in support of the Confederacy had been carried when it appeared that an amendment had been adopted. Verity and the chairman left the room rather than face a recount, at which time the opposition took control of the meeting. Before a new vote could be taken, however, Verity's supporters had the gas turned off. A few months earlier Joseph Barker had tried unsuccessfully to speak at a meeting that was called to hear Thompson and the Reverend J. W. Massie, a Congregationalist minister. Following Thompson and Massie's departure, Barker organized a rump meeting that adopted a resolution calling on the government to use its influence to end the war.[87] The contest in Bury was fairly typical, although rarely did lecturers have to flee. If, however, the adoption of resolutions are reasonably accurate indicators of levels of support, then it appears that Ellison has exaggerated the degree to which meetings in Lancashire voted in support of the Confederacy. Southern supporters seem to have had their greatest success in Oldham, Accrington, Burnley, and Padiham. The North had majorities in Blackburn, Bolton, Bury, and Rochdale. Votes in Ashton and Stalybridge and in Bacup and Rawtenstall were evenly split. Southern supporters did have more success hijacking meetings. They did so once each in Blackburn and Burnley and twice in Bacup. Union supporters returned the favor once in Mossley. But such defeats were almost immediately countered by meetings that adopted resolutions of support. In response to the defeat in Burnley, for instance, pro-Union forces orga-

87. *Times* (Bury), 6 February 1864, 9 May 1863; *Guardian* (Bury), 5 May 1863.

88. Using simply the number of resolutions passed without looking at the meetings at which they were adopted can distort the picture. If, for example, one simply counted the number of resolutions adopted, then one could conclude that in Heywood support was evenly split. But the reality was that resolutions in support of the Union were passed at a large Sinclair/Jackson meeting, while those in support of the Confederacy were adopted at a much smaller Kershaw meeting. *Advertiser* (Heywood), 13, 27 June 1863; *Free Press* (Burnley), 4 April, 9, 16 May 1863; *Advertiser* (Burnley), 18 April, 6, 20 June 1863; *Barker's Review*, 18 April 1863; *Chronicle* (Oldham), 6 February 1864.

nized a series of meetings within a matter of weeks.[88] Whereas in Lancashire the opposing forces seemed to be equally divided, the rest of the country voted overwhelmingly in favor of the Union. In the first three months of 1863 Charles Francis Adams received close to three dozen pro-Union resolutions from all parts of Britain.[89]

By any measurement it seems obvious that the friends of the Union carried the day. They swamped the opposition in London and the Home Counties. While Union supporters ran into stiff opposition in Lancashire and Cheshire, in the end they could exult with Thomas Barker that the opposition was no longer effective. Earlier in 1864 Spence had confirmed this assessment when he wrote Wharncliffe that he considered Manchester "very unsafe." Sheffield was no safer, and Spence declined an offer to lecture there.[90] Spence's uncharacteristic expression of enthusiasm when Manchester friends of the Confederacy engaged Barker as their agent may have hidden a deeper concern over the strength of the Union agency. A few local figures, such as J. L. Quarmby in Oldham and W. E. Stutter in Manchester, provided sterling service, but much of the burden of getting the message across fell to Barker, Kershaw, and Verity. The agency of John Smith, the English emigrant to the United States and former slaveholder, was a disaster for the cause. Aware that without Barker the effect of the Confederate agency would be severely curtailed, his opponents did everything they could to discredit him. They followed him wherever he went, challenging him every step of the way and accusing him of being a renegade for abandoning his former friends in the abolitionist movement. African Americans such as William Andrew Jackson and Edward Irving intervened during his meetings to question the veracity of his statements. W. W. Broom of Manchester and S. Payton McDowall of Preston dogged him in the summer of 1863. In August, McDowall issued a handbill containing Barker's 1856 letter to American abolitionists in which he denounced slavery and the South and dared him to explain his reversal. The letter added weight to the accusation that Barker was a political chameleon, someone who was willing to abandon old associates for what Broom called blood money. By October, Barker had retired from the fray, and the Confederacy had lost its most effective spokesman.[91]

89. See Adams's letters to Seward in this period in Despatches from U. S. Ministers to Great Britain, 1790–1906.

90. Barker to Garrison, Manchester, 27 August 1864, AASS Papers; Spence to Wharncliffe, Liverpool, 15 January 1864, Wharncliffe Muniments.

91. *Chronicle* (Preston), 25 July, 1, 29 August, 5 September 1863; *Herald* (Preston), 3 October 1863; *Times* (Huddersfield), 1 November 1863; *Albion* (Middleton), 10 October 1863; *Boston Commonwealth*, 23 October 1863; *Observer* 14 August 1863.

The strength and reach and near monopoly of its agency, especially after the departure of Barker, may be largely responsible for the success of the Union's cause, but equally as critical was the fact that Northern supporters engaged a public very knowledgeable about America and generally partial to the cause of union and emancipation. It was, nevertheless, a public that had to be persuaded that its interest lay in maintaining the union of American states, clearly a much more difficult task in Lancashire and Cheshire, where the shortage of cotton had devastated the lives of textile workers and their families. All the indications are, however, that even in Lancashire, where Spence and his coworkers had hoped to exploit the crisis to rally support for the Confederacy, the friends of the Union carried the day.

6

The Assassination of President Lincoln

Every son of toil, whether cast in ivory or in ebon mould, knew too well that when the earth was piled o'er the bloody corpse of honest, good Lincoln, he had lost a friend, and Humanity and Right one of the firmest and stateliest buttresses.

—Bacup *Times,* 13 May 1865

Few in the Bacup audience that had gathered to hear Mark Price of Manchester promote the interests of the National Reform Union would have questioned the speaker's portrayal of Lincoln's significance to the struggle for political reform in Britain and emancipation and equality in America. Supporters of the Union had been emphasizing and opponents had been downplaying that link between the two countries since the beginning of the war. Much of the debate about the merits of the contending sides and of the war's impact on Britain was centered on the person of the president. To some he was the fulfillment of America's democratic promise; to others he represented all that was wrong with a system that insisted on giving every citizen the vote. As the war drew to a close, it seemed that Lincoln had worked his magic, remaining firm in his commitment to the maintenance of the Union at all cost, offering a reconciling hand to the secessionists, while insisting that the slaves had to be freed. More importantly, for those in Britain committed to political reform, his reelection in the midst of the war spoke to the resiliency of democratic institutions. Depressingly, just when it appeared all the promises of the conflict would be attained came word of Lincoln's assassination.

The politics of scale is crucial to an understanding of the deep sense of shock, loss, and even betrayal that greeted the news of Lincoln's murder. From its commencement, the war had generated widespread popular interest. In the months leading up to the Confederate surrender at Appomattox, for example, supporters had taken every opportunity to celebrate publicly each successive Union victory. Supporters in Perth, Scotland, welcomed news of the fall of Atlanta by firing a brace of cannons and flying the American flag. The cannons and flag were on display again two months later following Lincoln's reelection. The nearby town of Crieff chose to toll its church bells to honor the president on his reelection. When Petersburg was captured, supporters in Ashton unfurled six flags. The Stars and Stripes was flown from a hotel in Aberdare, Wales, and over the mills of Brighouse, Yorkshire, following the Confederate evacuation of Richmond. The fall of the Confederate capital was the topic of conversation in "the clubs, newsrooms, coffee-houses, and public promenades" of Edinburgh. In Hollinwood and in Compton, near Oldham, Lee's surrender became the topic of discussion in all the local inns, Union supporters boasting that Lee and Davis had been (or ought to be) hanged, their opponents hoping that the Confederate leaders had escaped to Europe.[1]

Out of this local interest in the war came the first stirrings of public grief over Lincoln's murder. In Huddersfield, Union supporters who had hoisted the American flag over their warehouses in celebration of the fall of Richmond lowered them to half staff on hearing of the president's death. Crowds gathered, one reporter recorded, "to converse briefly on the sad event, and on the countenances of all there seemed to be something like an expression as if some dreadful calamity had happened in the world."[2] Elsewhere the reaction was the same. At the close of work in Halifax, millhands gathered in groups "earnestly and sadly discussing the news." From south Staffordshire came word that miners, forgemen, furnacemen, artisans, and "the lesser group of sable

1. *Weekly Herald Mercury and News*, 24 September, 26 November 1864; *Reporter* (Ashton and Stalybridge), 22 April 1865; *Times* (Cardiff) 28 April 1865; *Caledonia Mercury*, 17 April 1865; *Guardian* (Halifax), 29 April 1865; *Courier* (Halifax), 29 April 1865; *Times* (Bury), 29 April 1865; *Chronicle* (Oldham), 29 April 1865; *Standard* (Oldham), 29 April 1865; *Staffordshire Advertiser*, 29 April 1865.

2. *Examiner* (Huddersfield), 29 April 1865; *Chronicle* (Huddersfield), 6 May 1865.

workmen" collected in groups at factory doors, forge gates, and coal pits to express their "abhorrence at that dark deed of blood" and their sympathy with "the bereaved and suffering nation." Large crowds also gathered at local telegraph and newspaper offices, where the particulars of the assassination were posted.[3]

Given the passions unleashed by the debate over the war and the prompt and almost universal public expressions of grief over the assassination, Confederate supporters found themselves in a quandary. They could remain silent, as most chose to do, or they could add their voices to the public expressions of grief and condolences, as a handful did. Few opted to follow the lead of the small group of Confederate supporters in Nantwich, Cheshire, who greeted the news with "expressions of delight." Rather, like Joseph Barker, they chose to keep their views to themselves. Lincoln's death, Barker recorded in his diary, was "the due reward of his deeds." Although expressing sorrow that the president had been killed and worried that Lincoln's assassination would enhance the image of the North and destroy that of the South, Barker felt "as if something would have been working in the Universe if Lincoln had been allowed to die a natural death."[4] But Barker kept his views to himself, and as far as is known he was in the minority. Publicly, there was a genuine sense of horror as people tried to come to terms with the death of the president. Assassinations were usually associated with countries such as France and Italy in times of revolutions, not with a country, one speaker in Huddersfield insisted, of "kindred race" with similar institutions. The people of Britain and America, the Reverend Newman Hall observed, were of common Anglo-Saxon stock, spoke the same language, worshiped the same God, were both driven by the search for liberty, and were linked by immigrant ties. Neither people had a tradition of resolving political differences by assassination. Even among radicals who were willing to entertain tyrannicide as a legitimate political act in Europe there was no stomach for assassination. Quoting Walter Savage Landor, W. E. Adams differentiated between tyrannicide, "the highest of virtues," and assassination, "the basest of crimes."[5] The almost frenetic attempt to understand what could have prompted John Wilkes Booth to commit such an act

3. *Guardian* (Halifax), 29 April 1865; *Daily Post* (Liverpool), 27 April 1865; *Daily Post* (Birmingham), 8 May 1865; *Guardian* (Preston), 29 April 1865.

4. *Record* (Chester), 6 May 1865; Diaries: 1865–1875, Vol.1, 12 May 1865 through 29 October 1869, Joseph Barker Papers, Nebraska Historical Society, Lincoln.

5. *Chronicle* (Huddersfield), 6 May 1865; Newman Hall, *A Sermon on the Assassination of Abraham Lincoln Preached at Surrey Chapel, London, Sunday, May 14, 1865* (Boston, 1865), 5; Adams, *Memoirs of a Social Atom*, 364.

underscored the sense of disbelief that a crime of this sort could have occurred in a country whose political traditions led back to Britain. Some insisted that, like his father who had lived and worked as a japanner in Wolverhampton and Birmingham before migrating to America and who was described as an "eccentric character," Booth suffered from bouts of insanity. He might even have been a frustrated abolitionist of the "Johnson and Butler school," a handful of Southern supporters in Liverpool speculated.[6]

Public expressions of grief regardless of affiliation provided much needed solace for Union and Confederate sympathizers alike. They also opened the door to reconciliation between those who had been at political loggerheads for four years. The Reverend Joseph Binns expressed the hope that the "great calamity was already soothing the asperity with which different parties viewed the strife in America." Englishmen of "all sects, all parties, and all classes," the chairman of a Huddersfield meeting declared, were united in their revulsion. Even among those who had taken no part in the public debate over the war, there seemed to be a need for public catharsis. Of those who participated in the public mourning in Nottingham, for instance, only J. S. Gilpin had been involved in the dispute over the war.[7]

Within hours of the telegraph offices' confirmation that Lincoln had been murdered, requisitions were being circulated for local authorities to hold meetings at which the public could express their sympathy with America. Within a matter of days, close to forty meetings had been held in response to these requisitions. Another seventeen were the work of local Union supporters, as in Colchester, or as in Manchester, which were organized by pro-Union organizations. When Bury's commissioners refused to respond to a requisition, local pro-Unionists acted unilaterally. In addition, six meetings were held for the purpose of allowing workers to express their opinions. Few areas were untouched by these gatherings. Major cities such as Manchester and Birmingham held more than one; smaller towns such as Hawick, Scotland, and Merthyr Tydfil, Wales, made their feelings known, as did even smaller towns such as Frockheim, near Forfar, Scotland, and Heckmondwicke, Yorkshire. Surprisingly, Bolton and Burnley, two important centers in the public agitation over the war, chose to remain silent. From these gatherings came close to three hundred addresses of condolence to Mrs. Lincoln and to the family of William Seward, the secretary of state who was also a target for assassination. Expressions of support were sent

6. *Spirit and Times* (Wolverhampton), 6 May 1865; *Chronicle* (Liverpool), 29 April 1865.
7. *Reporter* (Ashton and Stalybridge), 6 May 1865; *Examiner* (Huddersfield), 6 May 1865; *Review* (Nottingham), 5 May 1865.

to the new government under Andrew Johnson. Not all the addresses sent to the American legation in London came from public meetings. Bristol sent five, one each from the Working Men's Club, the teachers at the Ragged School, members of city government, members of the Reform Club, and a public meeting. The Chamber of Commerce, the local branch of the Union and Emancipation Society, the city government, and the Merchants House of Glasgow adopted separate addresses. The address from the teachers, superintendents, and representatives of the Stockport Sunday School Union was fairly typical.[8]

Large audiences also gathered at churches and halls to hear sermons and lectures about Lincoln and the meaning of his death. The Reverend J. Gregory of Bradford, for example, took for his sermon Psalm 97:2, "Clouds and darkness are round about him, righteousness and judgement are the habitation of his throne." In Merthyr Tydfil the Reverend Charles White followed a blistering attack on the Confederacy at a public meeting with a sermon at his chapel on the theme "He had served his own generation."[9] At Leigh, Lancashire, the Reverend T. Mills lectured on "Abraham Lincoln and the American War." The Reverend J. B. Spring spoke on the same topic in Bristol, as did the Reverend J. C. Street, a member of the executive council of the Union and Emancipation Society, at Dudley Colliery near Newcastle. At the end of Mills's lecture, motions were adopted expressing sympathy with the president's family and the people of the United States. The assassination, the audience declared, was the "culminating point" of slavery's attempt to keep millions of Africans in bondage. Members of the Working Men's Institute in Swansea and in Hull and the Fifteenth Durham Rifle Volunteers adopted similar resolutions of sympathy.[10] Most unusual of all was the massive funeral procession held by the Ashton branch of the Union and Emancipation Society.

8. The tabulations draw on letters from Adams to Hunter, London, 25 May, 2, 8, 15, 22 June, 13 July 1865; Moran to Seward, London, 28 April 1865, Despatches from United States Ministers to Great Britain, 1791–1906; *Morning Journal* (Glasgow), 3, 4 May 1865; *Stockport and Cheshire County News*, 20 May 1865, and other sources. E. D. Adams claims that the legation received more than four hundred addresses within two weeks. Adams, *Great Britain and the American Civil War*, 263.

9. *Observer* (Bradford), 4 May 1865; *Telegraph* (Merthyr), 13, 20 May 1865. For other examples see *Observer* (Heywood), 13 May 1865 and *Courier* (Halifax), 6 May 1865. For an analysis of sermons preached in America see Jay Monaghan, "An Analysis of Lincoln's Funeral Sermons," *Indiana Magazine of History* 41 (March 1945).

10. *Chronicle* (Leigh), 27 May 1865; *Post* (Bristol), 18 May 1865; *Chronicle* (Newcastle) 13, 27 May 1865; *Herald* (Swansea and Glamorgan), 13 May 1865; *Mercury* (Leeds), 28 April 1865; *Herald* (York), 20 May 1865.

Some in the crowd wore "mourning costumes," and the blinds in homes and public buildings along the route were drawn as if, one reporter observed, "some great and good man of our own land was about to be interred." The Town Hall was draped with "broad cloth" and the platform covered with the Union Jack, the Cross of Saint George, and the Stars and Stripes. An estimated seven thousand were unable to gain entrance to the building to hear the Reverend S. A. Steinthal's lecture.[11]

Requisitions calling for meetings of sympathy were usually signed by the town's "most influential inhabitants." In Hull, for example, "bankers, merchants, traders, and other inhabitants" requested a meeting, while in Belfast "the wealthy and influential people" of the city attended the gathering. In Rochdale the mayor and the "principal inhabitants of the town" joined members of the local emancipation society in expressions of sorrow.[12] The promptness with which these requisitions were made reflected a genuine sense of shock at the assassination. But while most were stunned by Lincoln's murder, not all were willing or able to forget the deep divisions caused by the war. Few of those who attended the public meetings could claim not to have taken sides in the war. One was either for or against the secessionists. The frequency with which chairmen and speakers at public meetings called for suspending political differences in the interest of speaking with a united voice is testament to the deep fissures caused by the war. The asperity to which the Reverend Binns alluded was real. For many participants, especially those who had been critical of the Union or who had privately harbored support for the Confederacy, ways had to be found to depoliticize these expressions of public grief. But try as Confederate supporters might, this was not always possible. In Preston, for instance, those signing the requisition to the mayor were all active supporters of the Union. In Colchester, Essex, pro-Unionists called their own meeting rather than go through the usual channel of requisitioning the mayor. In Paisley, Scotland, Unionists planned to exclude supporters of the Confederacy, but later relented, insisting, however, on conditions that opponents found so onerous that they stayed away. In the adjoining town of Barrhead, Unionists refused to give ground and called a "social meeting" limited to friends of the North.[13]

11. *Reporter* (Ashton and Stalybridge), 13 May 1865. A similar if smaller procession was held in nearby Mossley. *Chronicle* (Oldham), 6 May 1865.

12. *Banner of Ulster*, 4 May 1865; *Advertiser* (Advertiser), 29 April 1865; *Observer* (Rochdale), 6 May 1865; John Young to Hunter, Belfast, 10 May 1865, Despatches from United States Consuls in Belfast, 1796–1906.

13. *Guardian* (Preston), 3 May 1865; *Essex and West Suffolk Gazette*, 5 May 1865; *Herald* (Paisley), 6 May 1865; *Paisley and Renfrewshire Gazette*, 6 May 1865.

The calls for reconciliation, for presenting a united front in the face of assassination, were genuine. To carry conviction, however, these expressions of sympathy had of necessity to be the collective voice of the British people. Some narrowing of differences over the war had already occurred in the work to aid the freedmen in the South. Freedmen's aid brought back into the fold abolitionists such as Wilson Armistead of Leeds, Charles Buxton, and many leading figures of the British and Foreign Anti Slavery Society who for one reason or another had refused to endorse Union policy or had supported the Confederacy. Aid for the freedmen, seen as a traditional philanthropic activity, and consequently free of any political baggage, attracted a wide cross section of the public. There was a deep foreboding among Unionists when Buxton declared his support for the South in 1862 and an equal sense of relief when he agreed to serve as president of the Freedmen's Aid Society the following year. Armistead's return was greeted similarly. The Reverend George Scott of Newcastle spoke for many when he insisted that the work of aiding the freedmen could only be accomplished if it were nonsectarian. By appealing to all, "the titled, the famous, and the powerful," as well as workingmen, Christine Bolt has argued, freedmen societies broke through some of the alliances formed during the war.[14]

It is this cooperative effort that some of the requisitioners had in mind when they called on local authorities to organize public meetings of sympathy. A town that spoke with one voice about the assassination stood a fair chance of also muting differences created over the previous three years. But the approach was not always successful. In spite of their best efforts, "leading inhabitants" could not always control the tenor of the resolutions adopted nor, for that matter, what was said from the platform. In many respects these meetings tended to revisit some of the same divisive issues that dominated earlier encounters. Part of the difficulty is illustrated by the way the press reacted to Lincoln's murder. Many quickly condemned the assassination without in any way altering their views of the president. In Newcastle, for instance, a Conservative editor, citing what he thought was ample precedent, insisted that "Republicans are infamously notorious for deeds of assassination; and doubtless the disciples of Mazzini, in this town and elsewhere, will approve this law-

14. For the most extensive discussion of British freedmen aid see Christine Bolt, *The Anti-Slavery Movement and Reconstruction: A Study of Anglo-American Co-operation, 1833–1877* (London, 1969). *Morning Star*, 7 November 1862, 2 December 2 1864; *Chronicle* (Newcastle), 18, 25 March 1865; *Mercury* (Leeds), 25 March 1865; *Review* (Nottingham), 14 April 1865; *Reporter* (Ashton and Stalybridge), 25 March 1865; *Daily Post* (Birmingham), 25 January 1865.

less fearful act of the two Confederates" for it accorded with the "theory of the dagger which is associated with Mazzinianism." Radicals countered that the "English champions of the South," feigning surprise, were using the assassination to wash "their hands of the whole concern, and of confessing that they have been all along deceived in the character of their *protéges*." But these expressions of surprise at "the atrocious scoundralism of the Confederates" could only be pardoned, this editor concluded, "at the expense of their intellects." Taking the middle ground, a Liberal editor, eager to promote reconciliation, expressed the hope that differences would be overlooked and that the town would speak with one voice. Honest men could differ about the merits of the war, but all that now had to be shelved in the face of such a disaster. Balance, he insisted, had to be found, for the "political oratory of this town is too much confined to one little clique, some members of which are about as deficient in good taste and prudence as in culture; and we all know to our cost what it is to endure a shower of *their* superlatives."[15]

Editors, like others involved in the public debate over the war, especially those who had been critical of Union policy, faced a ticklish problem in April 1865: how to express abhorrence of the president's assassination without sounding as if they were retreating from a position they had done a great deal to foster. Thomas Keiser's conclusion that the "great majority of English editors of all classes viewed the assassination with satisfaction and malice" is wide of the mark. Editors at the *Times*, recognizing that the Union was on the brink of victory, threw in the towel in the wake of the assassination, as did those at *Punch*. Long vilified by these editors, the president was now considered to be judicious and prescient. Such changes of heart drove one speaker to reach for a religious analogy. The British press, he declared, had a tendency to "keep a man in purgatory during his life, and [send] him to Paradise when he had gone off."[16] Not all editors were willing to elevate the dead president to such heights. While trying to make sense of the assassination, and to strike a balanced tone, a number refused to give political ground. Nothing, not even the fall of Sebastopol, one editor observed, had so stirred the "public heart" as had the murder of the president. A week after a blistering editorial predicted that

15. *Journal* (Newcastle), 27 April 1865; *Chronicle* (Newcastle), 29 April 1865; *Express* (Newcastle), 4 May 1865.

16. Keiser, "The English Press and the American Civil War," 411. See Gabor S. Boritt, "*Punch*'s Lincoln: Some Thoughts on Cartoons in the British Magazine," *Journal of the Abraham Lincoln Association* 15 (winter 1994), for a discussion of the image of Lincoln in the leading satirical magazine; *Gazette and Daily Telegraph* (Shields), 3 May 1865.

the Confederates would fight on even after the fall of Richmond, this editor observed that the death of Lincoln had taken "hold upon our kindly sympathies . . . because [of] his moderation, humanity, shrewdness, and honour of heart." But these were "elements," the editor was careful to point out, that pertained to the man, not to the system he represented. While showing respect for the dead, others found nothing good to say about the man or the political system that produced him.[17] A few editors continued to hold to positions first enunciated at the outbreak of the war. The war was the result of forty years of injustice, a "revolt of free-trading communities against the oppressive and iniquitous enactments of a band of monopolists—such a revolt as Yorkshire and Lancashire might have raised had the landed aristocracy of this country obstinately and insolently persisted in maintaining the bread tax and other duties on the importation of food from abroad." Lincoln, who had drawn the sword to conduct "the most ruthless, cruel, and devastating warfare ever known within the pale of civilization," had not surprisingly perished by the sword.[18]

One editor dismissed such views as a disgrace to the Fourth Estate. Never had the world witnessed such a "wicked, cowardly and brutal act committed (with one exception—the crucifixion of Christ, and even that took the course of law) as the assassination of Abraham Lincoln." Many in England might have supported the South because it was the underdog, but most were driven "in no small degree from a feeling of envy, and lust for power and gain on the part of the aristocratical and the money-critical portion of the English community." Others had little interest in the sources of English support for the Confederacy and chose instead to devote their editorial comments to the nature of the man who had led America through trying times. "The brave, honest, President, the friend of all men, especially of the outcast poor, hurried into eternity, before God's good time—with his large heart even then welling up with kindness to his very foes, and with his tongue, on which no lies had ever lain, speaking only the words of reconciliation and peace."[19]

Part of the problem facing those anxious to effect reconciliation lay in the fact that in life, as in death, the president had become a metaphor for British politics. For some he was the embodiment of all that was wrong with Ameri-

17. *Observer* (Bradford), 20, 27 April 1865; *Guardian* (Preston), 6 May 1865; *Independent* (Sheffield and Rotherham), 29 April 1865.

18. *Chronicle and Mercury* (Leicester), 6 May 1865; *Westmorland Gazette and Kendal Advertiser*, 6 May 1865; *Guardian* (Brighton), 3 May 1865.

19. *Free Press* (Hartlepool), 6 May 1865; *Mercury* (Kendal), 29 April 1865.

can democracy; for others his rise from rural poverty to the presidency demonstrated the system's capacity to accommodate all within its political ambit. From the very beginning of the war, the contending groups had appealed to competing heroes and villains in an effort to influence the public debate. Confederate supporters had placed their hopes initially in Jefferson Davis, and when his image failed to take root, in General Lee and in Stonewall Jackson, particularly after his death. Lectures and articles about Davis painted him as "a refined, educated, patriotic Southern aristocrat." Alexander Beresford-Hope described him as a man of "British descent, of a British name, who spoke and wrote so nobly the British language." Despite such accolades, Davis never achieved the popularity Confederate supporters hoped for. Bland, with little to excite the imagination, he lacked either the charisma or the quirkiness traditionally associated with heroic figures. More tellingly, his image was tarnished at the most critical juncture of the public debate by the work of his former slave and coachman, William Andrew Jackson, who joined the lecture circuit in late 1862. Articulate and commanding, with a wry sense of humor, Jackson in freedom was a visible refutation of all that was destructive in the slave system. He never tired of reminding his audiences that his former master was the greatest enemy of the slave, that he had "never met anyone who had worked more zealously to keep his race and the poor 'white-trash' in bondage." The Reverend J. Sella Martin, another former slave, also did his share to tarnish Davis's image. He painted the Confederate president as the prototype of Milton's Satan in "Paradise Lost." Like Satan, Davis had raised an impious war so that he might be able "to gratify the aspiration of his inordinate ambition, that he might keep for ever those that believed in his sway behind his triumphal car of sin and death."[20]

If Confederate supporters epitomized Yankees as "Butler, Brag, and Beastliness," they elevated to heroic stature Robert E. Lee and Stonewall Jackson, the pride, as they saw it, of the aristocratic South. The marquis of Lothian thought Lee the best general since Wellington, and Lord Wolseley considered him "a splendid specimen of an English gentleman, with one of the most rarely handsome faces I ever saw." The Reverend George Gilfillan, a Dundee

20. *Times* (Cardiff), 24 October 1862; Botsford, "Scotland and the American Civil War," 606–607; *Telegraph* (Maidstone), 24 January 1863; *Record* (Chester), 25 April 1863; *Guardian* (Preston), 5 September 1863. Moncure Conway regularly compared Lincoln and Davis. The Union leader had "toiled up with his own right arm splitting rails, and was not ashamed of it," while Davis was a "soft and gentle president who had always somebody to fan him when asleep, and when he waked up to tremble at his word." *Leicestershire Mercury*, 19 December 1863.

Congregationalist divine who, although critical of the Union, never lent his support to the Confederacy, found an apt description of Lee in celestial imagery: he was the "Orion of the South—majestic, heroic, a warrior armed for battle, glorious in his apparel, and travelling in the greatness of his strength." Members of the Oldham branch of the Southern Independence Association toasted Lee as "the greatest hero of the age."[21] In death Stonewall Jackson, the eccentric professor who seemed to be driven by religious demons—the antithesis of everything one normally associates with the cavalier tradition—became a hero. Beresford-Hope considered him the Garibaldi of the cause. "He looks the hero he is," Lord Wolseley reported after a visit to Jackson in the field, and "his thin compressed lips and calm glance, which meets yours unflinchingly, give evidence of that firmness and decision of character for which he is famous." While Lee was the "infallible Jove, a man to be reverenced," Jackson was "loved and adored with all that child-like and trustful affection which the ancients are said to have lavished upon the particular deity presiding over their affairs." The Reverend Edward R. Verity believed that it was because Jackson was in the habit of praying three times a day and reading his Bible to his men that they followed him as "children follow a father."[22]

If the Confederate supporters had heroes, they also had villains, the most notorious of which was General Benjamin Butler, who during the Federal occupation of New Orleans had issued an order threatening to treat white women who continued to disrespect Federal soldiers as women of "the town plying their avocation." In condemning the order, the London *Times* found an historical parallel in the French Revolution's Reign of Terror. Others wept publicly for the honor of those "witty women and patriotic Southerners" who were exposed to the barbarity of the "arch-scoundrel and enslaver of New Orleans." Benjamin Moran at the American legation reported that on Guy Fawkes night 1862—a night when the British publicly ridicule their most famous traitor—a group of men and boys paraded the streets with a "gigantic Guy in military dress, with a gallows at its side" labeled "The Brute Butler." A few Union supporters came to the defense of Butler. After all, they said, the actions of the New Orleans women raised serious questions about whether they could reasonably be con-

21. Van Auken, "English Sympathy for the Southern Confederacy," 64–66; *Proceedings of the Massachusetts Historical Society*, October 1913, 17; Rowland, "English Friends of the Confederacy," 200; *Northern Warder*, 9 May 1865; *Chronicle* (Oldham), 20 August 1864.

22. *Telegraph* (Maidstone), 24 January 1863; *Advertiser* (Stockport), 29 May 1863; *Proceedings of the Massachusetts Historical Society*, October 1913, 19; *Reporter* (Ashton and Stalybridge), 30 January 1864; Thomas, *The Confederate Nation*, 224.

sidered ladies. Butler was a "wise and brave commander," the Reverend Baptist Noel insisted, one who brought order to a rebellious city. The Reverend J. R. Little of Nottingham thought it touching "how tender some people can be in their *fears* for the white ladies, and how callous concerning the *facts* of the black ones." Whatever the merits of the case, Butler's order was a public relations bonanza for the Confederacy just at a time, as Brian Jenkins has argued, when the capture of the Crescent City should have worked in favor of the Union.[23]

If there was a true hero and martyr to the cause of the Union and the slave prior to 1865, it was John Brown, whose raid on the federal arsenal at Harpers Ferry in October 1859 and whose summary execution weeks later, many believed, were the first shots fired in the Civil War. The man of violence seems out of place among those who believed in moral suasion as the only legitimate route to emancipation. In death, however, his life and work quickly became a staple of abolitionist lectures. Frederick Douglass, who had been forced to flee to Britain after being implicated in the raid, lectured frequently on Brown's plan for freeing the slaves. So, too, did Sarah Parker Remond and George Thompson.[24] While the outbreak of hostilities, with the attendant fear of slave rebellions, should have tempered the image of Brown as the victim of a barbarous slave system and a hero of the oppressed slave, he in fact emerged by the second year of the war as a Moses leading his people to freedom. Like the biblical patriarch, argued Manchester unionist Thomas Barker, Brown was "equally justified in the sight of God and just men for his brave, patriotic, and generous efforts to liberate the slaves of Virginia." If he had succeeded, all Christians would have "applauded the heroism of the brave old Christian," as they did "Garibaldi's not more righteous or patriotic deeds." Barker refused to concede that the raid had been a failure, insisting that it should be seen as "a grand moral success . . . a needful prelude to the more stupendous, but not more heroic efforts of the freemen of the North."[25]

23. For analyses of the impact of Butler's order on New Orleans see John D. Winters, *The Civil War in Louisiana* (Baton Rouge, 1963), 132, and Chester G. Hearn, *When the Devil Came down to Dixie: Benjamin Butler in New Orleans* (Baton Rouge, 1997), 101–07; *Times* (London), 29 December 1862; *Observer* (Bradford), 12 June 1862; *Express* (Nottingham), 27, 30 January 1863; *Independent* (Sheffield and Rotherham), 19 March 1863; Wallace and Gillespie, eds., *The Journal of Benjamin Moran*, 2: 1087; Jenkins, *Britain and the War of the Union*, 2: 54.

24. For Thompson's lectures see *Anti Slavery Advocate*, 1 March, 2 April 1860. Much of the following analysis leans heavily on Drescher, "Servile Insurrection and John Brown's Body in Europe."

25. Thomas H. Barker, *Union and Emancipation: A Reply to the "Christian News" Article on Emancipation and War* (Manchester, England, n.d.), 14.

When Brown was hanged, William Andrew Jackson told a Bury audience that the slaves said "his spirit would walk about in Virginia until there was not a slave to be found." Thompson saw Brown as a "saint and martyr" and looked forward to the day "when he would be permitted to stand on the spot where John Brown suffered, and sing the song of jubilee."[26] This transformation of Brown from a man of violence into an "apostle and martyr," to use Seymour Drescher's phrase, had its fullest expression in the December 1863 meeting organized by the London Emancipation Society to commemorate his execution. Held on December 2—the twelfth anniversary of the garroting of French liberty, the day Napoleon III "planted his foot on the neck of the French people," as Moncure Conway put it—the meeting brought together abolitionists and former slaves such as J. Sella Martin, symbolizing Brown's vision of America's future. "It was for the weak that he interfered," Conway, the son of a prominent Virginia slaveholding family, declared, "not the strong; for the poor, not the rich; for the negro, not whites." His death, Martin observed, "touched and awakened the religious heart of white America and revived the dying hopes of the black race." Brown was, in W. T. Malleson's view, "the martyr of negro freedom."[27]

If Brown had shown the way, it was Lincoln who had committed the country to emancipation. The death of both acted as symbolic brackets of martyrdom with which unionists encased the war. The rebellion was inaugurated, Robert Cochran of Paisley declared, "by the blood of honest John Brown, and it was sealed by the blood of Abraham Lincoln."[28] Only in death, however, did Lincoln come to achieve such universal acclaim among Union supporters; in life some had considered him as enigmatic, temporizing, and much too concerned about keeping the Union together. Enemies were even less flattering. The Union had gotten the political and military leadership it deserved, friends of the Confederacy believed. "Lincoln was a buffoon," according to the Reverend W. Croke Squire, "jesting while his fellow-creatures were dying, like Nero fiddled while Rome burned." The difference in talent between Confederate and Union leaders, "Conservative of Birmingham" pointed out,

26. *Times* (Bury), 21 February, 21 March 1863.

27. Drescher, "Servile Insurrection and John Brown's Body in Europe," 516–17; *The Martyrdom of John Brown: The Proceedings of a Public Meeting Held in London on the 2nd December, 1863, to Commemorate the Fourth Anniversary of John Brown's Death* (London, 1864), 5, 7, 13, 19.

28. *Telegraph* (Essex), 9 May 1865; *Herald* (Paisley), 6 May 1865. Similar parallels were drawn elsewhere. See, for example, *Mercury* (Kendal), 6 May 1865; *Western Express*, 6 May 1865: and *Midland Free Press*, 6 May 1865.

was like "Hyperion to a satyr."[29] How, one editor asked, could any country elect as leader "a man unlettered, undignified, unable, uneverything, but uncommon." Only the American political system could throw up someone like Lincoln, Beresford-Hope agreed; no one in Britain, "clever as he might be at rail-splitting, at navigating a barge, or at an attorney's desk, would, with no other qualifications, ever become Prime Minister of England, let alone County Court Judge." James Spence dismissed Lincoln as a "Sancho Panza," someone who turned to humor when reason failed, and Lord Wharncliffe thought Americans ought to hang their collective heads in shame for electing a man such as Lincoln, "with the grammar he wrote and the nonsense he talked."[30]

Although friends of the Union did not always make their views public, many were quite acerbic about the president. Richard Cobden, for instance, spoke to friends such as John Bright about his concern that Union leadership was not equal to the task. Lincoln might have "a certain moral dignity," but he was "intellectually inferior" and had surrounded himself with "mediocre men." According to Benjamin Moran, Samuel Lucas, editor of the *Morning Star,* was only less brusque: "He thinks we select our Presidents as Catholics do their Pope—for their imbecility."[31] Other critics were not as reticent about making their views publicly known. Some thought the president had lost his bearings because of his reverence for the Union, a reverence that bordered on the obsessive. When Lincoln told New York *Tribune* editor Horace Greeley that his principal concern was to save the Union at all costs, many believed the obsession had affected the president's ability to reason. As far as Lucas was concerned, a man of loftier vision would have seen that emancipation and the preservation of the Union were inextricably linked; the "two things being right, the one could not need to be put in abeyance to the other." George Reynolds dismissed Lincoln's insistence on maintaining the Union as befuddled and feebleminded and called for British intervention. Another Radical

29. *Guardian* (Preston), 27 June 1863; *Daily Gazette* (Birmingham), 22 January 1863. See also *Reporter* (Ashton and Stalybridge), 25 June 1864, for similar views of the shortcomings of Union leadership.

30. *Chronicle* (Bath), 26 February 1863; *Telegraph* (Maidstone), 24 January 1863; Beresford-Hope, *The American Disruption,* 19; *Times* (London), 29 August 1862; *Examiner and Times* (Manchester), 6 October 1863. See *Blackwood's Magazine,* January 1862, for similar views. One editor even believed that Lincoln was certifiably insane. *Express* (Nottingham), 23 December 1862.

31. Cobden to Bright, Edinburgh, 7 October 1862, Cobden Papers; Wallace and Gillespie, eds., *The Journal of Benjamin Moran,* 2: 1075.

editor north of the border in Glasgow was even less uncompromising: "We have no wish to draw too plain a parallel between President Lincoln and the despots who have rendered hateful the houses of the Hapsburgs and Romanoffs, but the federal chief has not yet been able to free himself from such unscrupulous advisers as have found their way to power through the generalship of turbulent demagogues and plundering placehunters."[32] Lincoln's policies during the first year of the war caused friends of the Union considerable discomfort. His response to Greeley seemed all of a piece with his reversals of Fremont's and Hunter's proclamations freeing the slaves in their military districts. Lincoln could claim with some justification that emancipation was outside the purview of field commanders, but his refusal to articulate clearly a policy for freeing the slaves did the Union cause considerable harm and set in place an image of the president as a temporizer, an image he would find very hard to shake even after he had issued the Emancipation Proclamation. The best Union supporters could do was to insist that the president's hands were tied by constitutional restrictions. But such arguments struck many as unnecessarily arcane, especially so when by his public declarations and actions Lincoln seemed averse to freeing the slaves. Even among those who were willing to concede that the president had no power to move against slavery, there was a genuine sense of disbelief when his proposals to colonize free blacks in Central America and elsewhere were made public. One friendly editor dismissed the plan as impractical, chimerical, and as feasible as trying to "send off the Norman, or Saxon, or Celtic element of English society." James Watkins, a fugitive slave, issued a blistering condemnation of this attempt to deny black Americans "their rights as citizens of America—a right that was conceded to them when their valour and blood was needed, and shed in gaining the independence of that Union over which Mr. Lincoln now presides." It was galling, undignified, demeaning, and totally impractical. "Men who were born free, and others who have gained their emancipation, toiled and elbowed their way into position, some of ease and comfort, some of affluence, and most of them to respectability, must break up their homes, sever the dearest ties, throw their business to the winds, and go and meet a dark and ominous future on some remote and desolate highway between the Caribbean Sea and Pacific Ocean."[33] The London *Times* took particular pleasure in deriding

32. *Morning Star*, 9 September 1862; *Reynolds's Newspaper*, 2 August 1863. Reynolds's views are also analyzed by Lillibridge, *Beacon of Freedom*, 111–17; *Sentinel* (Glasgow), 28 June 1862. For similar views see *Bee Hive*, 5 March 1864, and *Advertiser* (Dundee), 25 April 1863.

33. *Newcastle Daily Chronicle and Northern Counties Advertiser*, 2 September, 22 October

this "scheme of philanthropic expatriation." The logic of the president was "the old logic of the inquisitor who stretched his captive upon the rack, and then told him that it was entirely his own fault that he was in pain, because if he would change his religion he would be immediately released."[34]

Lincoln's colonization scheme provided additional political fodder for the opposition. Colonization was only the most recent manifestation of the country's profound antipathy for its free black population and a reflection of its unwillingness (even some in the Confederate camp were emboldened to argue) to confront the issue of slavery openly. As a result, the pro-Confederate claim that the Union mistreated its free black population carried considerable weight in the public debate about the war. One did not have to look far to find ample evidence of open discrimination against free blacks in the North. State laws, such as those of Indiana and Illinois that prohibited black settlement, were regularly quoted to prove the point. Former immigrants to the United States, who had seen firsthand the way blacks were treated, frequently made life difficult for pro-Unionists at public meetings and in letters to their local newspapers. Visiting African Americans, at least in the early years of the war, also added their voices to the chorus of protest against discrimination in the North. The Reverend J. W. C. Pennington, a former slave and the recipient of an honorary doctorate from the University of Heidelberg, spoke of school segregation, of discrimination on public transport, and of the refusal of white ministers to exchange pews with him. "If the black man had not a well-balanced mind, and a great amount of common sense, he ran the risk of being driven out of his mind by the persecutions to which he was subjected."[35]

The Union's cause was at its most vulnerable on this score even after the Emancipation Proclamation and Lincoln's decision to enlist blacks into the armed forces. Opponents continued to ridicule the North's attempts to address the issue. Events such as the New York Draft Riots in July 1863 and the refusal of states such as Indiana to end discriminatory practices gave the lie to

---

1862. The *Leicestershire Mercury*, 27 September 1862, condemned the plan to consign Negroes to the "coal-pit in Central America."

34. *Times* (London), 2 September 1862.

35. See Emma Lou Thornbrough, *Indiana in the Civil War Era, 1850–1880* (Indianapolis, 1965), and V. Jacque Voegeli, *Free But Not Equal: The Midwest and the Negro during the Civil War* (Chicago, 1967), for a discussion of the treatment of free blacks in the Midwest. The *Chronicle* (Huddersfield), 2 July 1864, and *Guardian* (Bury), 21 January 1865 contain English eyewitnesses' accounts of racial discrimination. *Albion* (Middleton), 22 February 1862. See also *Recorder* (Rhyl), 16 January 1862, for a similar statement by Pennington.

the argument by Union supporters that the country was moving in the right direction. Opponents even tried to turn the courageous and bloody charge by black soldiers against Fort Wagner to their advantage. The Reverend Verity and others saw this as another example of Union callousness. Black soldiers, Verity insisted, were being used as cannon fodder. While white soldiers were "skulking and sheltering their bodies from the enemy's bullets," black soldiers were ordered to make a suicidal assault on a well-fortified stronghold.[36] Such actions, the products of discrimination, were a deterrent, Verity believed, to emancipation; no conscientious slaveholder would consign his charges to the mercies of such unscrupulous people. Such was the message of a purported conversation about freedom between the characters Sambo, a Southern slave, and Uncle Sam, a Northern free black, which was published in the pages of a Bury newspaper. Conducted in dialect, the conversation was steeped in the traditions of minstrelsy. In it Sambo is about to get his freedom and fifty acres of land. All his friend Uncle Sam has to show for his liberty is the right to be used as cannon fodder in the Union army, to be refused access to public trans-port, and to be excluded from worship with whites. Northern liberty, it devel-ops, is the right of blacks to be hanged from lampposts. It is no wonder that Sambo ends the conversation with the rousing line, "I wish I was in Dixie, hi ho."[37]

Proponents of the Union were forced to spend an inordinate amount of time and energy refuting such allegations. Much of the work fell to visiting Americans, particularly to African Americans such as Remond, Martin, and Jackson, whose experience gave their views some weight and authenticity. Remond defined discrimination as an "institutional apparatus" created by slavery to protect itself. Destroy slavery, she implied, and discrimination would die with it. Jackson acknowledged the existence of discrimination but insisted that the situation had improved significantly in some states. Where it had not, he said, it was because Irish immigrants were afraid that "if the slaves obtained their freedom they would do the work which the Irish had been ac-customed to do." Jackson's experience of life in the North was limited to a brief stay in New York on his way to England. One also wonders about the wisdom of playing the anti-Irish card in Lancashire towns, where there was a significant Irish presence. Martin spoke to the issue with greater conviction and experience of conditions in the North, where he had lived since his es-

36. *Observer* (Wigan), 22 January 1864; *Chronicle* (Oldham), 21 February 1863.
37. *Times* (Blackburn), 18 April 1863; *Guardian* (Bury), 19 September 1863.

cape from slavery in 1856. He admitted that there were proslavery supporters in the North, but they were fossils of the past, "men who like the Bourbons, never got a new idea, and never forgot an old one." Yet these fossils were unable to stop progress, for the "negro car and negro pews were all but abolished, and now in the whole of New England there did not exist a law which prevented a coloured man from filling the highest office in the state." Discrimination was clearly receding, at least in New England, but even if the Negro was still being unfairly treated in the North, such treatment in regard to political rights was "against the spirit of Northern law and the protest of a large part of the Northern people." In the South, Martin argued, the Negro's "social, political, and even religious rights are trampled under foot . . . according to law, and with the unanimous consent of its inhabitants."[38]

Lincoln's preliminary proclamation of emancipation in September 1862 changed the terms of the debate. In spite of the predictions of servile insurrections, it appeared that the reluctant emancipator had finally taken the leap for which Union supporters had long been clamoring. The president's ungainly political dance with emancipation, with its tentative steps toward freedom followed by steps away in the direction of expatriation, had finally gained some form—and, some would say, dignity—in this declaration of freedom. Yet there were Union supporters who were critical of its limited reach and who chafed at what they considered its nakedly political nature. One year later Professor Francis Newman continued to marvel at the notion that one could ignore morality and instead claim emancipation to be a military necessity. It was that absence of morality, he insisted, that made it possible for Lincoln and his representatives to appease the enemy in conquered portions of the South by setting such minimal standards for readmission to the Union, by turning a blind eye to the continual denial of the rights of freedman, and by insisting, as General Banks did in Louisiana, that former slaves return to the plantations under conditions just short of slavery. "A pure morality must be enunciated by your Chief Magistrate," Newman wrote Garrison, "and sternly applied, before you can purge your civil and military administration of virtual traitors.

38. *National Anti Slavery Standard*, 11 May 1861; *Times* (Bury), 21 February 1863; *Chronicle* (Oldham), 11 April 1863; *Liberator*, 28 November 1862; *Independent* (Kentish), 28 March 1863; *Morning Star*, 4 June 1863. "A Working Man" of Birmingham arrived at the same conclusions, insisting that at least in the North the Negro is not enslaved and equating their treatment in the North to "precisely that which is extended to the Irishman in England." *Daily Post* (Birmingham), 3 July 1863. See also Conway, *Testimonies concerning Slavery*, 98–100, for comparable arguments.

Everyone in Europe who has any political thought knows that your Union can have no future, unless your stupid and base legislating about the colour of a man's skin be now, once for all, extirpated and renounced."[39] Others, such as Thomas Hughes, were more understanding. Even Harriet Martineau, who had broken with fellow abolitionists over Union policy on free trade early in the war, dismissed Newman's criticism as baseless. It was the result, she boldly asserted, of mental lapses. "Mr. Newman's eccentricities have created a void round him; and his enormous vanity impels him into incessant controversy, in which society now refuses to gratify him."[40]

Martineau might have allowed her tendency to be dismissive to get the better of her judgment, but about one thing she was right: Newman spoke for few. By and large, the proclamation won Lincoln (if not always the Union) considerable praise and confirmed for those already partial to the cause the strength and merits of democratic systems of government. To John Turner, secretary of the Ashton Union and Emancipation Society, Lincoln epitomized the potential of the man of "humble birth," who through hard work and application had risen to the highest office in a political system that, he predicted, would soon be adopted by Europe. David Thomas of Bury "gloried in him, because he was a man of the people, who had by his own strength of intellect and honest purpose raised himself from the lowest ranks to hold the highest possible position in a country peopled by millions." John Donald of the Newmilns Anti Slavery Society, who had been active in Scottish Radical politics since the 1830s, considered the president a "man from the people, with the people, and for the people."[41]

In the midst of war Lincoln came to embody all the perceived strengths and weaknesses of American democracy. To opponents he was at best a reluctant emancipator, who was brought kicking and screaming to abolition, all the while insisting that his proclamation was driven almost entirely by military necessity. He was antiblack, recommending expatriation and doing nothing to stop his home state's policy of expelling blacks. He was antidemocratic, prosecuting opponents, curtailing press freedom, and suspending habeas cor-

39. *Liberator*, 1 July 1864; Newman to Garrison, London, 14 October 1864, AASS Papers. For reactions to Newman and comments on Banks's policies see *Liberator*, 15 July, 23, 30 September, 23 December 1864; *Boston Commonwealth*, 25 March, 29 April, 3 June 1864.

40. Hughes to Garrison, London, 9 September 1864; Martineau to Garrison, Ambleside, 8 October 1864, AASS Papers.

41. *Reporter* (Ashton and Stalybridge), 28 February 1863; *Times* (Bury), 13 February 1864; *Advertiser* (Ayr), 22 December 1864.

pus. Exasperated, some even dismissed him as a dimwit, always ready with a cache of folksy anecdotes. But John Donald spoke for many: Lincoln was a son of the soil, the emblem of working-class potential in a society freed from political restrictions. It was the president who had taken the bold initiative in the face of considerable opposition and, at the risk of alienating slaveholders in the border states, had declared the slaves free. Aware of the difficulties British abolitionists had faced in the 1830s, supporters of the president appealed for understanding and the recognition that decisions of this sort were always pragmatic and rarely based exclusively on principle.

The conflicting images of the president reflected the deep divisions created by the war. Even as it appeared that the Confederacy was about to succumb, there were those who refused to give ground. Few were willing to move appreciably from positions held during the war, yet Lincoln's murder was transformative. Even Thomas Dudley, who had been a mainstay of the Union's attempt to limit Confederate support, had to admit that the "public mind" had been greatly moved by the assassination. It seemed odd to Dudley that "he who has been so reviled, abused and grossly misrepresented throughout the length and breadth of this land, in the Newspapers and in their public assemblies of the people, by the Church and the State . . . called an idle jester, a man without refinement and education, a low vulgar individual, a tyrant, cruel, malignant and base," could by "martyrdom" be transformed into "a Saint." The change of heart, however, did not last long. As early as May, Dudley thought he saw a return to the old ways. Francis Newman agreed. While all, even "our worst men and parties" were sincere in their execration of the crime, he predicted that soon "the dog will return to his vomit."[42]

Both Dudley and Newman might have underestimated the genuineness of the reaction to the assassination, but whether or not people were sincere in their declarations of horror over Lincoln's death, reconciliation under such circumstances proved difficult. It would require, at least as far as Union supporters were concerned, public expressions of grief and some degree of remorse from friends of the Confederacy. Few pro-Southerners, however, were willing to endure or participate in such public displays. Spence was away from Liver-

---

42. Dudley to Seward, Liverpool, 2, 17 May 1865, Despatches From United States Consuls in Liverpool, 1790–1906; Newman to Sargent, London, 3 May 1865. AASS Papers. Benjamin Moran thought he saw a change of heart at the Saint James Hall, London, meeting, a meeting that, he confided to his diary, made him "inwardly vow that hereafter I would think better of the feelings entertained towards us by Englishmen than ever before." Wallace and Gillespie, eds., *The Journal of Benjamin Moran*, 2: 1419.

pool at the time of the assassination meeting there, but it is very likely that he would have declined an invitation to participate. None of the major figures in the local Southern Club, with the exception of Edward Lawrence, who as mayor was obligated to attend requisitioned meetings, participated in either of the two public gatherings. Spence wrote the organizers of the meeting, insisting that the assassination had cast an unwarranted slur on the South's noble struggle for independence. S. R. Graves, a fellow Liverpudlian, agreed: so chivalrous a people could never have stooped to such action.[43] Other Confederate supporters, such as the Reverend W. Croke Squire of Preston and the Reverend J. Page Hopps of Dukenfield, did see the need to participate in the public expressions of grief. Croke, who had publicly demanded that the South be allowed to establish a separate state, felt an obligation, he said, to join in the public mourning for the president in the hope that America would see that England from "the Queen to the peasant" was united in its condemnation of the murder. Hopps insisted that his views of Lincoln had been undergoing significant changes as the president moved to reincorporate conquered sections of the South. "Some of us may have been wrong in our estimation of the man throughout," he admitted at a Dukenfield meeting. "Perhaps, the thoughts, the aims, the aspirations, and the clear policy, which seem to us of later growth, were, in reality, his own from the first; perhaps we did not think sufficiently of the awful difficulties of his position; but history will be just where we have been hasty, and time will only serve to bring to light whatever was wise in the statesman, and whatever was virtuous in the man."[44]

Few supporters of the Confederacy were willing to indulge in such public expressions of remorse as Hopps. Their opponents, however, demanded exactly that. George B. Browne hoped Halifax opponents of the Union would see that "it was time to alter their views." Similarly, William Brooke insisted that meetings "throughout the length and breath of the land" called up "a sort of spontaneous feeling" that after all the country did "sympathise with their brethren in the calamitous war."[45] Confederate proponents, or those who insisted on bridging differences, hoped the public meetings did not convey such sentiments. What the British ought to do, they insisted, was speak with a united voice against murder, express condolences with the Lincoln family, and in so doing send a message to all Americans that it was time to put differ-

43. *Post* (Liverpool), 29 April 1865; *Courier* (Liverpool), 28 April 1865.
44. *Guardian* (Preston), 6 May 1865; *Inquirer*, 29 April 1865.
45. *Courier* (Halifax), 5 May 1865.

ences over this bloody war behind them. While supporters of the Union were willing to join with others in expressions of grief and condolences, they were determined to control the medium through which the message was expressed and the means of its articulation. While reports of meetings stressed that, as in the case of Leeds, "men of all parties" participated, it is clear that Union supporters generally were in control and were responsible for the wording and the submission of resolutions. In Bury, for instance, all of the resolutions were submitted by supporters of the North. Of the thirteen speakers, five were clearly identified with the Union. One, William Pickstone, was just back from America and spoke highly of the Union, and none of the others had any record of support for the Confederacy. The same was generally true of the two meetings in Liverpool. The first was chaired by the mayor, Edward Lawrence, a wealthy brewer, Tory politician, and pro-Southerner who had invested heavily in blockade runners. Of the eight speakers at the meeting, half were known supporters of the Union, none of the Confederacy. The same divisions generally held at the second meeting. In Leeds, none of the ten speakers was identified with the Confederacy, while six were known supporters of the Union.[46] In Colchester and Paisley, little attempt was made to accommodate the wishes of Confederate supporters, and not surprisingly, few were willing to attend the meeting in Manchester organized by the Union and Emancipation Society.[47]

There were some exceptions to this pattern. Some degree of reconciliation seemed to have been effected in Bradford, where D. G. Wright argues that the assassination meeting brought together Tories and Radicals for the first time on the same platform to discuss aspects of the war. But Bradford was unique in another interesting respect: none of those who had been publicly active in the pro-Union movement, with the exception of the Reverend J. P. Chown, a Radical Baptist minister, seemed to have been present at the meeting.[48] Some elements of reconciliation were also attained in Leicester, a city that in late 1862 had agonized over the merits of forming a pro-Union society. Reports of the meeting recognized the presence of supporters from both sides on the plat-

46. *Guardian* (Bury), 13 May 1865; *Times* (Bury), 13 May 1865; *Chronicle* (Liverpool), 29 April 1865; *Daily Courier* (Liverpool), 28 April 1865; *Mercury* (Leeds), 2 May 1865.

47. *Telegraph* (Essex), 9 May 1865; *Essex Standard and Eastern Counties Advertiser*, 5 May 1865; *Paisley and Renfrewshire Gazette*, 6 May 1865; *Examiner and Times* (Manchester), 29 April 1865.

48. D. G. Wright, "Bradford and the American Civil War," *Journal of British Studies* 8 (May 1969): 82.

form and commented on the fact that resolutions had been "judiciously prepared." The presence of Church of England ministers here and in places such as Gateshead, Carlisle, Merthyr Tydfil, and Sunderland reflects the lengths to which some organizers went to try to involve all shades of opinion.[49] With a few notable exceptions, such as the Reverend P. Hains, the incumbent at Saint George's, Wigan, Church of England ministers had supported the secessionists. The major driving force for reconciliation in Leicester was the Reverend James Phillipo Mursell, a Radical Baptist minister who had done everything he could to ensure that the city and his denomination remained neutral during the war. That Leicester established local branches of the two major pro-Union national organizations and a more ephemeral auxiliary of the Southern Independence Association speaks to the significance of the war in the political life of the country. Mursell had greater success in the Baptist Union, where in 1864 he used his influence as president to thwart an attempt to adopt a pro-Union address to the Baptists of America. In his address to the meeting, Mursell condemned the assassination and expressed the hope that British feelings of revulsion would be seen as a measure of the country's friendship toward America. Yet even here, where every attempt was made to involve supporters of the Confederacy, it is clear that pro-Unionists were the most visible.[50] Pro-Union domination of these meetings is exactly what friends of the Confederacy feared and why, as in Sheffield, they declined all invitations to participate in them. Organizers reported that they were anxious to involve all shades of opinion but that their efforts were rebuffed. Not one of the town's prominent Confederate supporters was willing to sign the requisition or to move or second resolutions. Their worst fears were confirmed when Isaac Ironside, a driving force in the Foreign Affairs Committee, which laid the blame for most of the world's problems at the doorstep of the Russians, first suggested that the Russians were trying to foment a war between Britain and the United States. When these curious views met with the disapproval of the meeting, Ironside shifted his condemnatory gaze to the Confederacy and its local supporters. Others who were less concerned about the Russian threat also focused their attention solely on the South. Although the leaders of the Confederacy might not condone the assassination, the Reverend David Loxton was convinced that the act "originated in Southern sentiment," which

49. For the involvement of Church of England ministers in public meetings see *Observer* (Gateshead), 6 May 1865; *Examiner* (Carlisle), 20 May 1865; *Telegraph* (Merthyr), 13 May 1865; *Times* (Sunderland), 2 May 1865.

50. *Chronicle and Mercury* (Leicester), 6 May 1865; *Midland Free Press*, 30 April 1864.

Congressman in House of Representatives

had previously approved such acts as Senator Brooks's brutal attack on Senator Sumner on the floor of the Senate.[51] Even in situations where it appeared some agreement had been reached to keep the tone of the meeting neutral, as was the case in Edinburgh, Confederate supporters were discomforted by the tone of the speeches. In differing, if not always subtle ways, Union supporters took the opportunity, as they did in Merthyr Tydfil, to launch conventional attacks on the Confederacy and its friends in Britain. When C. H. Jones drifted into an anti-Confederate tirade, the chairman of the Merthyr Tydfil meeting tried to steer him back on course, but was met by howls of protest from the audience. When the Reverend C. White declared that the South "sought to exterminate . . . Liberty, justice, freedom—freedom for the negro slave as well as for the white man," the chair accused him of moving the meeting into the political arena and complained that he had been induced to take the chair under false pretenses. The Reverend J. Griffith, a local rector, insisted that he had agreed to attend a meeting that was organized to express condolences, not a political rally. When Titus Lewis of Carmarthen rose in support of Griffith, he was shouted down. Those who agreed with Lewis and Griffith could do nothing but lament that the meeting had been coopted, as one of them said, by Chartists.[52]

For all intents and purposes these meetings were intensely political. Try as they might, those who insisted that this was not the time or the place for the expression of political views generally failed to impress participants who thought otherwise. In vain, chairmen pleaded with speakers to refrain from making political speeches. Some consented, only to launch blistering attacks on the Confederacy and its British friends. Edward Jones of Liverpool, for example, had little time for those who once dismissed Lincoln as the "American Joe Miller," but who now praised him for his political wisdom. Their change of heart, he declared, was driven by "a consideration of pence, shillings and pounds."[53] Nothing seemed more political to some than the decision to hold meetings at times when workingmen were unable to attend. John Wilson complained that the decision by the provost to hold Dundee's meeting at noon was a deliberate attempt to limit working-class participation. Wilson's complaints were echoed in Edinburgh, Hull, and elsewhere. Even when meetings were organized to attract a broad cross section of the population, there

51. *Independent* (Sheffield and Rotherham), 2, 6 May 1865.
52. *Caledonian Mercury*, 4 May 1865; *Telegraph* (Merthyr), 13 May 1865.
53. See for example *Express* (Wakefield), 6 May 1865; *Guardian* (Preston), 6 May 1865; *Examiner and Times* (Manchester), 5 May 1865; *Courier* (Liverpool), 28 April 1865.

were complaints that members of the working class were not invited to sit on the platform. A "Working Man" of Leicester was critical of the exclusion, for workingmen, he observed, had been "true to the noble martyr . . . and to the cause of freedom for which he has so earnestly contended."[54]

In most instances, the working class participated in the meetings called by requisition or in those organized by supporters of the Union. Where this was not possible, or where local authorities were unwilling to call a meeting, as was the case in Wigan, workingmen organized their own meetings. While the Keighley meeting was not called by the working class, it was the result of pressure from that quarter. In some cases, as in Merthyr Tydfil, the audience was made up almost exclusively of workingmen. In all, there were six meetings that could be classified as working class. The Birmingham meeting was the work of W. Radford and a group of artisan supporters of the Union. Radford was critical of the speed with which the "representative" meeting had been arranged and the time at which it was held. An afternoon meeting, he suspected, was meant to exclude the working class, who would have protested the resolutions that failed to address pertinent and pressing domestic issues. Determined to express their own views on the meaning and significance of Lincoln's presidency for the British working classes, Radford, John Oxford, and others, all local advocates of political reform, wrote some of the city's trade societies suggesting the need for a separate working-class gathering. The resulting meeting encountered some opposition, if attempts from the floor to amend resolutions congratulating the North on the suppression of the rebellion and the destruction of slavery are anything to go by. The speeches made and the resolutions passed at this meeting went far beyond simple expressions of sympathy and condolence. They had come together, J. Arthur Partridge observed, to express their horror at the assassination of the leader of the "first Republic the world ever saw"; to rejoice at the destruction of the "worst oligarchy the world ever saw"; and to promote those principles of democracy that governed political life in the United States in Britain. Those principles were based on democratic equality and on the inclusion of "the whole of the national manhood." They were the principles of "the rights of labour against capital, when labour came into general conflict with capital, and of representation and constitutional majorities." Had the Confederacy, which stood for everything that was anathema to democracy, succeeded in establishing its in-

---

54. *Advertiser* (Dundee), 2 May 1865; *Scotsman*, 3 May 1865; *Advertiser* (Hull), 3 May 1865; *Midland Free Press*, 6 May 1865.

dependence, it would have impeded the growth of democracy everywhere, for "it would have been a Republic in distinct negation of everything that promoted the welfare of man, the honor of women, and the power of the State." It was this effort to impede the march of democratic institutions in Britain that had led many opponents of political reform to support the Confederacy.[55]

Other working-class meetings also stressed the links between support for the Union and political reform. The Brighton meeting adopted resolutions that observed that Lincoln was the first from the working class to be elected president and praised him for carrying out the struggle against slavery and for consolidating the Union in which all were able to vote. The meeting in Bradford was, as D. G. Wright has shown, "partly a political affair," all of the speakers being members of the Bradford Political Union. The meeting in Wigan, a city that had been only marginally involved in the public debate about the war, was the most politically charged. The assassination, the resolutions declared, was the work of those who wished to establish slavery, and the success of the Union was a refutation of those who insisted American institutions were a failure. Such views were not meant to be simply a condemnation of assassination, schoolteacher John Davies insisted; instead they covered "far higher and holier ground." If American institutions were a failure, Davies looked forward to the day when English politics would adopt such failures. One observer was stunned by the way in which a meeting that was advertised to express sympathy for Mrs. Lincoln and America was "deliberately perverted . . . into a grand exhibition of party feeling, and magnificent tirade against all and everything English, and a mighty burst of plaudits for all and everything American and democratic."[56]

It seems apparent, as Valerie Beadsmore has speculated, that those who pressed most for reconciliation, for presenting a united front in the face of the assassination, were anxious "to cut the ground from under the feet of those who hoped to exploit Lincoln's death in the cause of franchise reform."[57] Even before Lincoln's murder, Radicals had come to view the impending collapse of the Confederacy as freighted with domestic political messages. Mag-

55. *Daily Post* (Birmingham), 4, 18, 20 May 1865.

56. *Guardian* (Brighton), 10 May 1865; Wright, "Bradford and the American Civil War," 82; *Observer* (Bradford), 4 May 1865; *Examiner* (Wigan), 19 May 1865; *Observer* (Wigan), 26 May 1865.

57. Valerie Beardsmore, "Moses, Martyr, and Messiah: Abraham Lincoln and Black Emancipation: A Study of Popular Development and Political Uses of Myth, with Special Reference to the Years from 1860–1870" (Ph.D. diss., University of Kent, 1980), 368.

nus C. Rendell of Leith saw the fall of Richmond as "emblematic of the down-fall of all despotic and corrupt systems in the Old World—of the French despotism, of our own Tory oligarchy, of the Plutocracy of the iron and cotton masters; and generally as the beginning of a new and glorious era for the world—an era not equalled since the memorable French Revolution of 1789." Rendell's vision of revolutionary connections might have been a bit over-drawn, but it nonetheless captured, if in admittedly more picturesque prose, the hopes of J. Arthur Partridge and the organizers of the Birmingham meet-ing to honor Lincoln. The election of Thomas Bayley Potter, president of the Union and Emancipation Society, to Parliament to fill the position caused by Richard Cobden's death early in April 1865 seemed to confirm the links be-tween the war and British domestic politics.[58] It is these very same connec-tions, which some considered attempts to Americanize British institutions, that had worried Tories and Whigs ever since the outbreak of hostilities. They were convinced that proponents of political reform had been blinded by the promises of America and were even willing to ignore all the signs of imminent collapse of the system. "In the middle is true safety—in hastening slowly is true progress," one editor cautioned.[59] But it was a long-held article of faith among reformers that political reforms in one country strengthened the hands of those working for similar changes everywhere. "If Italy gained its liberty there was the same chance of liberty for the Englishman," Peter Taylor told his Leicester constituents, "if there was a chance for the blacks of America, there was a chance for the Englishman at home." T. Perronet Thompson put it more graphically early in the war: emancipation was contagious. "If the dig-ger of the soil in America is to cease to see his daughter sold for prostitution to the best bidder, it will have its effect in making the operative and middle classes in England revolt against the degradation they are subjected to by being obliged to make known how each man votes, that he may be kicked ac-cordingly."[60]

A country that had twice elected a man of Lincoln's background to the highest political office, the second time in the midst of a war, provided inspi-

58. *Caledonian Mercury*, 18, 19 April 1865.

59. *Weekly Scotsman*, 4 January 1862. There were those who thought that the war had the positive effect of silencing the call for reform. *Examiner* (Glasgow), 24 October 1863.

60. *Chronicle* (Leicester), 24 January 1863; *Advertiser* (Bradford), 2 November 1861. Ernest Jones emphasized a similar connection during a speech in Rochdale in 1864: "I trust that we shall find that in establishing liberty universally throughout the American continent we shall be plac-ing the crowning pinnacle on the edifice of freedom here as well." Quoted in John Saville, *Ernest Jones: Chartists* (London, 1952), 78.

ration to all those committed to political reform. The links between reform and support for union and emancipation were clearly definable. In both instances the alliance was composed mainly of political Radicals, Dissenting ministers, and politically active workers and artisans. Opposed to it was a coalition that drew its support largely from those averse to political reform. In fact, the sides people took in the war determined to a measurable degree their commitment to political reform. In many parts of Scotland, in Leith and Edinburgh, for example, support for the Confederacy and opposition to an extension of the franchise seemed to go together. The same held true in other parts of the country. In Ashton, for instance, the creation of the local Workingmen's Conservative Association was the inspiration of a group of individuals all of whom were friends of the Confederacy. This is not to suggest that an identical composition of the Union alliance in Scotland was replicated elsewhere. Middle-class Radicals in London, for example, were much more successful in forging a working relationship with trade unionists over the war, one that worked to their advantage in the resurgent movement for political reform beginning in 1865, than were their counterparts in Glasgow.[61] But the London alliance held together in the face of strong opposition from trade unionists such as T. J. Dunning; while in Bradford, Wright has argued, trade unionists remained above the fray. The picture is further complicated by the fact that some staunch supporters of the Union, such as J. W. Burns of Sheffield, were adamantly opposed to any form of unionization, while the Reverend E. W. Verity, a strong proponent of the Confederacy, was one of the leading lights in the trade union movement. Nor should it be assumed that members of the Union alliance spoke with one voice about the nature of political reform. David Thomas and Ernest Jones, for example, both members of the Union and Emancipation Society, worked together for reform but differed over the form it should take: Thomas supported household suffrage, Jones the more expansive manhood suffrage.[62]

In spite of these qualifiers, the links between support for the Union and political reform are indisputable. Philip John Auger has found that of the fifty-

61. Lillibridge, *Beacon of Freedom*, 87; Botsford, "Scotland and the American Civil War," 854; W. Hamish Fraser, "'A Newspaper For Its Generation': The Glasgow *Sentinel*, 1850–1877," *Journal of the Scottish Labour History Society* 4 (July 1971): 27. D. G. Wright identifies similar connections in Bradford between "middle class Radicals and the labour aristocracy, between Positivists and trade unionists, between radical Dissenters and freethinkers" that were forged during the war. Wright, "Politics and Opinion in Nineteenth-Century Bradford," 512–13; *Reporter* (Ashton and Stalybridge), 7 January 1865.

62. *Times* (Bury), 29 April 1865. See also *Nottingham and Midland Counties Daily Express*, 4 May 1865, for similar differences among those who were friends of the Union.

six vice-presidents of the Union and Emancipation Society who were from Lancashire, twenty-nine held similar positions in the National Reform Union and "a further eleven were known reformers." Of the sixty-one Lancastrians who were vice-presidents of the Reform Union, thirty-two were pro-Union, while only a handful supported the Confederacy. The same was true of the leadership of the National Reform League: of its fifty-four vice-presidents, seventeen can be identified as members of either the London Emancipation Society or the Union and Emancipation Society. Of the more than two hundred representatives who attended the Reform Union's meeting in Manchester in May 1865, almost one-quarter can be identified as members of pro-Union organizations. None was known to support the Confederacy.[63]

It was clear to contemporaries that the assassination meetings were crucial links between pro-Union activity and political reform. The recognition of this fact gave added urgency to the efforts of those who tried to depoliticize the meetings by limiting the speeches and resolutions to expression of condolence. In this they were largely unsuccessful. Pro-Unionists gave little ground. It was "a privileged class" who had supported the secessionists and their "hellish compact," a leader of the London glassmakers union insisted, and only the opposition of the "working classes who had always stood firm for freedom" had saved the country from disaster. Edmund Beales, president of the Reform League, agreed: It was largely the action of the working classes that stymied an influential minority's attempt to have the South recognized. That class had to now step forward to see that justice was done at home by insisting on the reform of Parliament. Aware of the connection between the war and reform, Nottingham workingmen distributed handbills at the assassination meeting calling for reform.[64]

The assassination meetings were also a celebration of democracy's strength and of the man who at its center was the personification of working-class potential and democracy's promise. Lincoln was, Newman Hall told his congregation, "a combination of honesty, sagacity, magnanimity, and gentleness, such as few rulers have ever manifested." W. Smith of Keighley insisted the late president was the "embodiment of liberty and freedom." Lincoln was frequently compared to the recently deceased Richard Cobden. Like "our Richard Cobden," Lincoln was a self-made man, a man from "the backwoods

63. Auger, "The Cotton Famine," 333–34; membership list, Reform League Mss., and minute book, April 1865 to November 1866, Howell Collection; *Examiner and Times* (Manchester), 10 May 1865.

64. *Bee Hive*, 6 May 1865; *Morning Star*, 5 May 1865; *Review* (Nottingham), 5 May 1865.

of America, without any parentage or pedigree of importance, without any distinguished patronage, without any of the adventitious circumstances that help men to rise, with scarcely any education but the education of circumstances," the Reverend Robert Bruce observed.[65] The assassin and the system that produced him had in murdering the president tried to kill the democratic dream. The act was in keeping with the character of the "life-long and inhuman disregard of every human right," the Reverend G. W. Conder lamented, and is "in perfect accord with all its brutality and outraging of all decent humanity." It was the same disregard for life and liberty that was evident in Sumner's beating, "which hung the hero John Brown, which murdered the negroes at Ft. Pillow, which tried to burn New York," which was behind the murder of "the only rightful king of working men in all the world."[66]

This image of the martyred president did not go uncontested. Even if critics were forced to admit that Lincoln had been making every effort to reconcile the South, they continued to insist that his murder was the logical outcome of his war of destruction and the product of what "Anti Jacobin" of Dundee called "the levelling Republic."[67] If good taste and popular opinion had forced Union opponents to temper their criticism of the murdered leader, there was nothing standing in the way of transferring their dislike of the political system to his successor. As if to confirm their views of American politics, Andrew Johnson seemed to be cut from the same cloth as Lincoln. He was widely condemned as a drunken sot, another example of American democracy's tendency to choose its leaders from among people of little talent. Lincoln, the rail splitter, had been replaced by Johnson, the tailor. Some, such as the editor of the *Dundee Advertiser*, pleaded with British commentators to be "more cautious, somewhat more scrupulous, and somewhat more truthful in their remarks on the public men of the United States." But the plea went largely unheeded in the Confederate alliance, for the relevance of the American democracy's shortcomings was too germane to the debate over political reform to ignore such issues as the inadequacy of its leadership. Pro-Unionists did everything they could to paint Johnson in the most favorable light. The assassination meeting in Merthyr Tydfil, for instance, adopted a resolution praising Johnson's commitment to the Union and "his pledges to

65. Hall, *Sermon on the Assassination of Abraham Lincoln*, 6; *News* (Keighley), 6 May 1865; *Examiner* (Huddersfield), 6 May 1865; *Examiner and Times* (Manchester), 29 April 1865.

66. *Examiner and Times* (Manchester), 29 April 1865; *Advertiser* (Dundee), 1 May 1865.

67. *Evening Courant*, 28 April 1865; *Northern Warder*, 5 May 1865. See also the editorial in *Advertiser* (Hull), 29 April 1865.

maintain the great principles of human liberty." The meeting expressed confidence in his commitment to follow Lincoln's wise policies. Johnson was a man of the people, declared the Reverend Charles White, neither a "drunkard nor a driveller," and a man who had demonstrated his commitment to emancipation by freeing his own slaves.[68]

The assassination meetings were in many respects a celebration of the success of democracy over tyranny, an affirmation of the wisdom and courage of the man who had led the country through a bloody war, and a recognition of the commitment and labor of those who had sustained the Union alliance in Britain. What kept the alliance together was a conviction that America's best chances of fulfilling its democratic promise rested on the survival of the Union and the freedom of the slaves. In death, if not in life, Lincoln came to embody that promise. He had by his policies defied the prediction of opponents who insisted that emancipation was incompatible with national unity. He had also shown the way to emancipation and reconciliation. Most importantly for an alliance committed also to political reform at home, the defeat of the Confederacy and the freedom of the slaves seemed to lead the way to the enfranchisement of the freedman. "A Working Man" of Ashton saw the connection between the vote for the freedman and franchise reform in Britain: "We have a general impression amongst us that the once despised and enthralled African will not only be set free, but enfranchised, and in spite of his master; and when the slave ceases to be, and becomes enfranchised free men, that then the British workman's claim may be listened to."[69] The public debate over the war became an important testing ground for those committed to political reform. That fact and the symbolic significance of Lincoln to the struggle explain why prints of the president's image became common in artisan homes and why by the end of the century, as Eugenio Biagini has shown, honest Abe was a staple of democratic literature.[70]

68. *Advertiser* (Dundee), 5 May 1865; *Telegraph* (Merthyr), 15 May 1865. C. F. Adams was struck by the fact that eulogies for Lincoln were mingled "with the alloy of unworthy aspersions of the Vice President." Adams to Seward, London, 28 April 1865. Despatches from United States Ministers to Great Britain, 1791–1906.

69. *Reporter* (Ashton and Stalybridge), 21 January 1865. See also *Review* (Nottingham), 10 February 1865, for an expression of similar connections.

70. Biagini, *Liberty, Retrenchment, and Reform,* 79–80.

Bibliography

Bibliographical note: Much of this study is based on the mining of newspapers for the years 1861–1865. In many of the large cities there were competing dailies, usually with distinct political inclinations; generally, smaller towns were covered by weeklies. Close to 125 newspapers were examined in roughly forty cities and towns covering all areas of Britain and ranging in size from London and Manchester to Hinkley and Todmorden. Finally, newspapers that catered to specialized groups of readers were also consulted, including such working-class papers as the *Bee Hive* and *Reynolds's Newspaper* and abolitionist periodicals such as the *Liberator*. A sample of the range of newspapers consulted can be gleaned from the footnotes.

CONTEMPORARY MATERIALS

Manuscript Sources

Birmingham Central Library, Birmingham, England
  Birmingham and Edgbaston Debating Society. Minutes.
  Birmingham Sunday Evening Debating Society. Minutes.
Bishopgate Institute, London
  Howell, George. Collection.
Boston Public Library, Boston
  American Anti Slavery Society. Papers.
British Library, London
  Bright, John. Papers.
  Cobden, Richard. Papers.
Cornell University, Ithaca, N.Y.
  May, Samuel. Papers.
  Smith, Godwin. Papers.

Glasgow Public Library, Glasgow, Scotland
    Smeal Collection.
Huntington Library, Pasadena, Calif.
    Dudley, Thomas H. Collection.
    Lieber, Francis. Collection.
Library of Congress, Washington, D.C.
    Hotze, Henry. Papers.
    Mason, James. Papers.
    Maury, Matthew. Papers.
Manchester Public Library, Manchester, England
    Wilson, George. Papers.
Massachusetts Historical Society, Boston
    Adams Family. Papers.
Merseyside Maritime Museum, Liverpool
    Trenholme, Fraser. Collection.
Nebraska State Historical Society, Lincoln
    Barker, Joseph, Collection.
Newcastle Public Library, Newcastle-upon-Tyne
    Cowen, Joseph. Collection.
Rhodes House Library, Oxford University, Oxford
    British and Foreign Anti Slavery Society. Papers.
John Rylands Library, Manchester, England
    English, Raymond. Deposit.
Sheffield Archives, Sheffield, England
    Lord Wharncliffe. Muniments.
University College, London
    Lord Brougham. Papers.
University of Nottingham, Nottingham, England
    Duke of Newcastle. Collection.
University of Rochester, Rochester, N.Y.
    Seward, William. Papers.
    Weed, Thurlow. Papers.

Government Documents

United Kingdom. House of Commons: *Reports of the Select Committee on Public Petitions*. 1861, 1862, 1863, 1864.
United States State Department
    General Records of the Department of State, RG 59, National Archives, Washington, D.C.
    Despatches from U.S. Minister to Great Britain, 1791–1906.
    Despatches from U.S. Consuls in:

London, England, 1790–1906.
Belfast, Ireland, 1796–1906.
Bristol, England, 1792–1906.
Cardiff, Wales, 1861–1906.
Cork, Ireland, 1800–1906.
Dublin, Ireland, 1790–1906.
Dundee, Scotland, 1834–1906.
Glasgow, Scotland, 1801–1906.
Leeds-upon-Hull, England, 1797–1906.
Liverpool, England, 1790–1906.
Manchester, England, 1847–1906.

Books, Pamphlets, and Articles

Adams, W. E. *Memoirs of a Social Atom*, 2 vols. 1903. Reprint, New York, 1968.

———. *The Slaveholders' War: An Argument for the North and the Negro*. London, 1863.

Aitken, William. *Journey up the Mississippi River from its Mouth to Nauvoo, the City of the Latter Day Saints*. Ashton-under-Lyne, England, 1845.

Armstrong, Richard Acland. *Henry William Crosskey: His Life and Work*. Birmingham, England, 1895.

Ashmore, O. "The Diary of James Garnett of Low Moor, Clitheroe, 1858–1865": Parts 1 and 2. *Transactions of the Historic Society of Lancashire and Cheshire* 121 (1969): 77–98; 123 (1971): 105–43.

Balme, Joshua R. *American States, Churches, and the War*. London, 1865.

———. *Letters on the American Republic; or, Common Fallacies and Monstrous Errors Refuted and Exposed*. London, 1865.

Bancroft, George. *In Memoriam of Abraham Lincoln, the Martyr President of the United States: Oration of the Hon. George Bancroft, the Historian, at the Request of Both Houses of Congress . . . , on Monday February 12, 1866*. Washington, D.C., 1866.

Banks, Thomas. *A Short Sketch of the Cotton Trade of Preston: The Last 67 Years*. n.p., 1888.

Barker, Joseph. *The Life of Joseph Barker*. London, 1880.

Barker, Thomas H. *Union and Emancipation: A Reply to the "Christian News" Article on Emancipation and War*. Manchester, England, n.d.

Barlee, Ellen. *A Visit to Lancashire in December 1862*. London, 1863.

Bayley, M. *Lancashire Homes: And What Ails Them*. London, 1863.

Baxter, William E. *America and the Americans*. London, 1855.

Beresford-Hope, A. J. B. *The American Disruption: In Three Lectures Delivered by Request before the Maidstone Literary and Mechanical Institution*. London, 1862.

Bigelow, John. *Lest We Forget: Gladstone, Morley, and the Confederate Loan of 1863: A Rectification*. New York, 1905.

Blanc, Louis. *Letters on England*, 2 vols. London, 1866.

Boase, Frederic, ed., *Modern English Biography*, 6 vols. 1892. Reprint, London, 1965.

Brigg, Mary. "Life in East Lancashire, 1856–1860: A Newly Discovered Diary of John O'Neil (John Ward), Weaver, of Clitheroe." *Transactions of the Historic Society of Lancashire and Cheshire* 120 (1968): 87–133.

Bright, John. *Speeches of John Bright, M.P., on the American Question*. Boston, 1865. Reprint, New York, 1970.

Bulloch, James D. *The Secret Service of the Confederate States in Europe: or, How the Confederate Cruisers Were Equipped*, 2 vols. 1883. Reprint, London, 1959.

Cairnes, John E. *The Slave Power: Its Character, Career, and Probable Designs*. 1863. Reprint, Newton Abbot, 1968.

Chirgwin, George. *Chirgwin's Chirrup: Being the Life and Reminiscences of George Chirgwin*. London, 1912.

Cobb, Frances Power. *The Red Flag in John Bull's Eyes*. London, 1863.

Collings, Jesse and John L. Green. *Life of the Right Hon. Jesse Collings*. London, 1920.

Conway, Moncure D. *Testimonies Concerning Slavery*. London, 1864.

———. *Autobiography, Memories, and Experiences of Moncure D. Conway*, 2 vols. London, 1904.

Corsan, W. C. *Two Months in the Confederate States: An Englishman's Travels through the South*. 1863. Reprint, Benjamin H. Trask, ed., Baton Rouge, 1996.

Crawford, Martin, ed. *William Howard Russell's Civil War Private Diary and Letters, 1861–1862*. Athens, Ga., 1992.

Crimes, Tom. *Edward Owen Greening: A Maker of Modern Co-operation*. Manchester, 1923.

Curti, Merle, ed. *The Learned Blacksmith: The Letters and Journals of Elihu Burritt*. New York, 1937.

Davidson, Samuel. *The Autobiography and Diary*. Edinburgh, 1899.

De Leon, Edwin. *Thirty Years of My Life on Three Continents*, 2 vols. London, 1890.

Dicey, Edward. *Six Months in the Federal States*. 1863. Reprint, Herbert Mitgang, ed., *Spectator of America*. Athens, Ga., 1971.

Dudley, Thomas H. "Three Critical Periods in Our Diplomatic Relations with England during the Late War." *Pennsylvania Magazine of History and Biography* 17 (1893): 34–54.

Dundee Ladies' Anti-Slavery Association. *Tenth Annual Report of the Dundee Ladies' Anti-Slavery Association*. Dundee, 1862.

Epps, John. *Diary of the Late John Epps, M.D.* Edited by Mrs. Epps. London, n.d.

Fairbanks, Charles. *The American Conflict as Seen from a European Point of View*. Boston, 1863.

Ford, Worthington Chauncey, ed. *A Cycle of Adams Letters, 1861–1865*, 2 vols. Boston, 1920.

France, R. Sharpe. "The Diary of John Ward of Clitheroe, Weaver, 1860–1864." *Transactions of the Historic Society of Lancashire and Cheshire* 105 (1953): 137–85.

Frost, Thomas. *Forty Years' Recollections, Literary and Political*. London, 1880.

Fyfe, Janet, ed. *Autobiography of John McAdam (1806–1883)*. Edinburgh, 1980.

Goddard, Samuel A. *The American Rebellion: Letters on the American Rebellion by Samuel A. Goddard, 1860–1865*. London, 1870.

Gourley, William. *History of the Distress in Blackburn, 1861–1865, and the Means Adopted for its Relief*. Blackburn, 1865.

Grattan, Thomas Colley. *England and the Disunited States of America*. London, 1861.

Greg, Percy. *History of the United States from the Foundation of Virginia to the Reconstruction of the Union*, 2 vols. London, 1887.

Hall, Newman. *The American War: A Lecture to Working Men, Delivered in London, October 20, 1862*. London, 1862.

———. *A Sermon on the Assassination of Abraham Lincoln Preached at Surrey Chapel, London, Sunday, May 14, 1865*. Boston, 1865.

Hall, Robert G. and Stephen Roberts, eds. *William Aitken: The Writings of a Nineteenth-Century Working Man*. Tameside, England, 1996.

Harland, John, comp. *Ballads and Songs of Lancashire, Ancient and Modern*. London, 1882.

Harrison, Frederic. *Autobiographical Memoirs*, 2 vols. London, 1911.

Hinton, John. *English Radical Leaders*. New York, 1875.

Hopley, Catherine C. [Sarah L. Jones]. *"Stonewall" Jackson, Late General of the Confederate States Army: A Biographical Sketch, and an Outline of His Virginia Campaigns*. London, 1863.

Hopps, John Page. *Southern Independence: A Lecture*. London, 1865.

Hughes, Sarah Forbes, ed. *John Murray Forbes: Letters and Recollections*, 2 vols. Boston, 1899.

Jacobs, Harriet A. *The Deeper Wrong; or, Incidents in the Life of a Slave Girl*. London, 1862.

Jones, Ernest. *Democracy Vindicated: A Lecture Delivered to the Edinburgh Working Men's Institute on the 4th January 1867 in Reply to Professor Blackie's Lecture on Democracy, Delivered on the Previous Evening*. London, 1867.

———. *The Slaveholders' War: A Lecture Delivered in the Town Hall, Ashton-under-Lyne . . . on November 16th, 1863*. Ashton-under-Lyne, England, 1863.

Kemble, Frances Anne. *Journal of a Residence on a Georgia Plantation in 1838–1839*. n.p., 1863. Reprint, Athens, Ga., 1984.

Kershaw, T. Bentley. *The Truth of the American Question: Being a Reply to the Prize Essay of Mr. Rowan*. Manchester, 1864.

Knight, William Angus. *Memoir of John Nichol*. Glasgow, 1896.

Leader, Robert Eadon. *Life and Letters of John Arthur Roebuck*. London, 1897.

Leng, William C. *The American War: The Aims, Antecedents, and Principles of the Belligerents: A Lecture Delivered on the 10th December 1862 in Castle Street Church*. Dundee, 1863.

Leno, John Bedford. *The Aftermath, with Autobiography of the Author*. London, 1892.

Lewis, A. S., ed. *My Dear Parents: An Englishman's Letters Home from the American Civil War*. London, 1982.

Mackie, J. B. *The Life and Work of Duncan McLaren*, 2 vols. London, 1888.

Maitland, Frederic William. *The Life and Letters of Leslie Stephens*. London, 1906.

Malet, William Wyndham. *An Errand to the South in the Summer of 1862*. London, 1863.

Marles, H. *The Life and Labours of the Reverend Jabez Tunnicliffe, Minister of the Gospel at Call Lane Chapel, Leeds, and Founder of the Band of Hope in England*. London, 1865.

Martin, Sella. *The Cotton Question: Free versus Slave Labour*. Glasgow, 1865.

Martyrdom of John Brown, The: The Proceedings of a Public Meeting Held in London on the 2nd December, 1863, to Commemorate the Fourth Anniversary of John Brown's Death. London, 1864.

Marx, Karl and Frederick Engles. *The Civil War In the United States*, 3d ed. New York, 1961.

Mason, Virginia. *The Public Life and Diplomatic Correspondence of James M. Mason*. Roanoke, Va., 1903.

Mills, John. *Vox Humana Poems*. London, 1897.

Morgan, James Morris. *Recollections of a Rebel Reefer*. Boston, 1917.

"One of the Ruck." *The Cotton Famine: An Attempt to Discover Its Cause, with Suggestions for Its Future Prevention*. London, n.d.

Palmer, Beverley Wilson, ed. *The Selected Letters of Charles Sumner*, 2 vols. Boston, 1990.

Parker, Joseph. *American War and American Slavery: A Speech Delivered in the Free Trade Hall, Manchester on Wednesday, June 3, 1863*. Manchester, 1863.

―――. *For Peace in America: A Report from Mr. Joseph Parker of Manchester, to Sir Henry De Hogton, Bart., on His Mission as Bearer of the Peace Address from the People of Great Britain and Ireland to the People of the United States of America*. n.p., 1865.

―――. *A Preacher's Life: An Autobiography and an Album*. London, 1899.

Pennington, J. W. C., ed. *A Narrative of Events in the Life of J. H. Banks, an Escaped Slave, from the Cotton State of Alabama, in America*. Liverpool, 1861.

Ramsbottom, Joseph. *Phases of Distress: Lancashire Rhymes*. Manchester, 1864.

Rathbone, Eleanor F. *William Rathbone: A Memoir*. London, 1905.

Reynolds, Harry. *Minstrel Memories: The Story of Burnt Cork Minstrelsy in Great Britain from 1836 to 1927*. London, 1928.

Richardson, James D., ed. *A Compilation of the Messages and Papers of the Confederacy including the Diplomatic Correspondence, 1861–1865*, 2 vols. Nashville, Tenn., 1905.

Rogers, J. Guiness. *An Autobiography*. London, 1903.

Sieveking, Isabel Giberne. *Memoir and Letters of Francis W. Newman*. London, 1909.

Sinclair, Peter. *Freedom and Slavery in the United States: Being Facts and Testimonies for the Consideration of the British People*. London, 1863.

Smith, Goldwin. *The Civil War in America: An Address Read to the Last Meeting of the Manchester Union and Emancipation Society.* London, 1866.

———. *Does the Bible Sanction American Slavery?* Cambridge, England, 1863.

———. *England and America: A Lecture Read before the Boston Fraternity.* Boston, 1865.

Solly, Henry. *"These Eighty Years;" or, The Story of an Unfinished Life,* 2 vols. London, 1893.

Spence, James. *The American Union: Its Effect on National Character and Policy, with an Inquiry into Secession as a Constitutional Right and the Causes of the Disruption.* London, 1862.

———. *Southern Independence: An Address Delivered at a Public Meeting in the City Hall, Glasgow, 26th November 1863.* London, 1863.

Stoddard, A. F. *Slavery and Freedom in America, or the Issue of the War: A Lecture Delivered in Paisley, January 28, 1863.* Glasgow, 1863.

Stephens, Leslie. *The "Times" on the American War: A Historical Study.* London, 1865.

Green, J. D. "Narrative of the Life of J. D. Green, A Runaway Slave From Kentucky, Containing an Account of His Three Escapes, in 1839, 1846, and 1848." 1864. Reprint in *I Was Born a Slave: An Anthology of Classic Slave Narratives,* 2 vols., edited by Yuval Taylor. Chicago, 1999.

Trollope, Anthony. *North America,* 2 vols. 1862. Reprint, London, 1968.

Troup, George Elmslie. *Life of George Troup, Journalist.* Edinburgh, 1881.

Wallace, Sarah Agnes and Frances Elma Gillespie, eds. *The Journal of Benjamin Moran, 1857–1865,* 2 vols. Chicago, 1949.

Waugh, Edwin. *Home-life of the Lancashire Factory Folk during the Cotton Famine.* London, 1867.

Wilson, John. *Memories of A Labour Leader: The Autobiography of John Wilson.* London, 1910.

SECONDARY MATERIALS

Books and Articles

Abbot, Martin. "Southern Reaction to Lincoln's Assassination." *Abraham Lincoln Quarterly* 7 (1952): 111–27.

Adams, Ephraim Douglass. *Great Britain and the American Civil War,* 2 vols. 1925. Reprint, 1 vol., New York, 1958.

Armytage, W. H. G. *A. J. Mundella, 1825–1897: The Liberal Background to the Labour Movement.* London, 1951.

Arnstein, Walter L. "The Murphy Riots: A Victorian Dilemma." *Victorian Studies* 19 (September 1975): 51–71.

Ashmore, Owen and Trevor Bolton. "Hugh Mason and the Oxford Mills and Community, Ashton-under-Lyne." *Transactions of the Lancashire and Cheshire Antiquarian Society* 78 (1975): 38–50.

Ashton, Owen. W. E. Adams: Chartist, Radical, and Journalist (1832–1906), "An Honour to the Fourth Estate." Tyne and Wear, England, 1991.

————. "W. E. Adams and Working-Class Opposition to Empire, 1878–1880: Cyprus and Afghanistan." North East Labour History 27 (1993): 49–74.

Aspen, Chris. Mr. Pilling's Short Cut to China and Other Stories of Rossendale Enterprise. Helmshore, England, 1983.

Baylen, Joseph O. and Norbert J. Grossman, eds. Biographical Dictionary of Modern British Radicals, 2 vols. Brighton, 1979–1984.

Bellamy, J. and J. Saville, eds. Dictionary of Labour Biography, 9 vols. London, 1972–1993.

Bellows, Donald. "A Study of British Conservative Reaction to the American Civil War." Journal of Southern History 51 (November 1985): 505–26.

Beloff, Max. "Great Britain and the American Civil War. " History 37 (1952): 40–48.

Benson, Lee. "An Approach to the Scientific Study of Past Public Opinion." Public Opinion Quarterly 31 (winter 1967–1968): 522–67.

Berger, Max. "American Slavery as Seen By British Visitors, 1836–1860." Journal of Negro History 30 (1945): 181–202.

————. The British Traveller in America, 1830–1860. 1943. Reprint, Gloucester, Mass., 1964.

Berwanger, Eugene H. The British Foreign Service and the American Civil War. Lexington, 1994.

Biagini, Eugenio F. Liberty, Retrenchment, and Reform: Popular Radicalism in the Age of Gladstone, 1860–1880. New York, 1992.

———— and Alistair Reid, eds. Currents of Radicalism: Popular Radicalism, Organised Labour, and Party Politics in Britain, 1850–1914. Cambridge, England, 1991.

Birch, A. H. Small-Town Politics: A Study of Political Life in Glossop. London, 1959.

Bolt, Christine. The Anti-Slavery Movement and Reconstruction: A Study of Anglo-American Co-operation, 1833–1877. London, 1969.

———— and Seymour Drescher, eds. Anti-Slavery, Religion, and Reform: Essays in Memory of Roger Anstey. Folkestone, England, 1980.

Boston, Ray. British Chartists in America, 1839–1900. Manchester, England, 1971.

Brady, Eugene A. "A Reconsideration of the Lancashire 'Cotton Famine.'" Agricultural History 37–38 (1963–1964): 156–62.

Brauer, Kinley J. "The Slavery Problem in the Diplomacy of the American Civil War." Pacific Historical Review 46 (1977): 439–69.

————, ed., Chartist Studies. London, 1959.

Brock, Peter. "Polish Democrats and English Radicals, 1832–1862: A Chapter in the History of Anglo-Polish Relations." Journal of Modern History 25 (1953): 139–56.

Brock, William. "The Image of England and American Nationalism." Journal of American Studies 5 (December 1971): 225–45.

Brode, Patrick. The Odyssey of John Anderson. Toronto, Canada, 1989.

Brook, Michael. "Confederate Sympathies in North East Lancashire, 1862–1864." *Transactions of the Lancashire and Cheshire Antiquarian Society* 75 and 76 (1965–1966): 211–17.

Carrie, David C. "Dundee and the American Civil War, 1861–1865." *Abertay Historical Society Publication* 1 (1953): 5–24.

Challinor, Raymond. "Chartism and Cooperation in the North-East." *North East Labour History* 16 (1982): 34–39.

Chaloner, W. H. "Letters from Lancashire Lads in America during the Civil War, 1863–1865." *Transactions of the Lancashire and Cheshire Antiquarian Society* 77 (1967): 137–51.

Chambers-Schiller, Lee. "'A Good Work Among the People': The Political Culture of the Boston Antislavery Fair." In *The Abolitionist Sisterhood: Women's Political Culture in Antebellum America*, edited by Jean Fagan Yellin and John C. Van Horn. Ithaca, N.Y., 1994.

Choate, Joseph H. *Abraham Lincoln and Other Addresses in England*. New York, 1910.

Claeys, Gregory. "Mazzini, Kossuth, and British Radicalism, 1848–1854." *Journal of British Studies* 28 (1989): 225–61.

Clausen, Martin. "Peace Factors in Anglo-American Relations, 1861–1865." *Mississippi Valley Historical Review* 36 (1940): 511–22.

Colley, Linda. *Britons: Forging the Nation, 1707–1837*. New Haven, Conn., 1992.

Collins, Kathleen. "The Scourged Back." *History of Photography* 9 (January–March 1985): 43–45.

Coltham, Stephen. "The 'Bee-Hive' Newspaper: Its Origins and Early Struggles." In *Essays in Labour History*, edited by Asa Briggs and John Saville. London, 1960.

Crawford, Martin. *The Anglo-American Crisis of the Mid–Nineteenth Century: The Times and America, 1850–1862*. Athens, Ga., 1987.

———. "British Travelers and the Anglo-American Relationship in the 1850s." *Journal of American Studies* 12 (August 1978): 203–19.

Crook, D. P. "Portents of War: English Opinion on Secession." *Journal of American Studies* 4 (1971): 163–79.

Cruikshank, A. F. "J. A. Roebuck, M.P.: A Re-Appraisal of Liberalism in Sheffield, 1849–1879." *Northern History* 16 (1980): 196–214.

Cullop, Charles P. *Confederate Propaganda in Europe, 1861–1865*. Coral Gables, Fla., 1969.

———. "English Reaction to Stonewall Jackson's Death." *West Virginia History* 29 (October 1967–July 1968): 1–5.

———. "An Unequal Duel: Union Recruiting in Ireland, 1863–1864." *Civil War History* 13 (1967): 101–13.

Cunningham, Hugh. "The Language of Patriotism." In *Patriotism: The Making and Unmaking of British National Identity*, edited by Raphael Samuel, 3 vols. London, 1989.

Cunliffe, Marcus. "America at the Great Exhibition of 1851." *American Quarterly* 3 (summer 1951): 115–26.

———. *Chattel Slavery and Wage Slavery: The Anglo-American Context, 1830–1860.* Athens, Ga., 1979.

Curtin, Philip D. *The Image of Africa: British Ideas and Action, 1780–1850.* Madison, Wis., 1964.

Darrah, William C. *Cartes de Viste in Nineteenth-Century Photography.* Gettysburg, Pa., 1981.

Davidoff, Leonore and Catherine Hall. *Family Fortunes: Men and Women of the English Middle Class, 1780–1850.* Chicago, 1987.

Davis, Charles S. *Colin J. McRae: Confederate Financial Agent.* Tuscaloosa, Ala., 1961.

Davis, William C. *Jefferson Davis: The Man and His Hour.* New York, 1991.

d'Entremont, John. *Southern Emancipator: Moncure Conway, the American Years, 1832–1865.* New York, 1987.

Drescher, Seymour. *Capitalism and Antislavery: British Mobilization in Comparative Perspective.* New York, 1987.

———. "Cart Whip and Billy Roller: Antislavery and Reform Symbolism in Industralizing Britain." *Journal of Social History* 15 (1981): 3–24.

———. "Public Opinion and the Destruction of British Colonial Slavery." In *Slavery and British Society, 1776–1846,* edited by James Walvin. London, 1982.

———. "Servile Insurrection and John Brown's Body in Europe." *Journal of American History* 80 (1993): 499–524.

Duberman, Martin. *Charles Francis Adams, 1807–1886.* Stanford, 1968.

Dutton, H. I. and J. E. King. *"Ten Percent and No Surrender": The Preston Strike, 1853–1854.* New York, 1981.

Edsall, Nicolas C. *Richard Cobden: Independent Radical.* Cambridge, Mass., 1986.

Ellison, Mary. *Support For Secession: Lancashire and the American Civil War.* Chicago, 1972.

Epstein, James and Dorothy Thompson, eds. *The Chartist Experience: Studies in Working-Class Radicalism and Culture, 1830–1860.* London, 1982.

Farnie, D. A. *The English Cotton Industry and the World Market, 1815–1896.* Oxford, 1979.

Ferris, Norman. *The Trent Affair: A Diplomatic Crisis.* Knoxville, Tenn., 1977.

Fielden, Samuel. "Autobiography of Samuel Fielden." In *The Autobiographies of the Haymarket Martyrs,* edited by Philip S. Foner, New York, 1969.

Finn, Margot C. *After Chartism: Class and Nation in English Radical Politics, 1848–1874.* New York, 1993.

Fladeland, Betty. *Abolitionists and Working-Class Problems in the Age of Industrialization.* Baton Rouge, 1984.

———. "Compensated Emancipation: A Rejected Alternative." *Journal of Southern History* 42 (1976): 169–86.

———. *Men and Brothers: Anglo-American Antislavery Cooperation.* Urbana, Ill., 1972.

Foner, Philip S. *British Labor and the American Civil War*. New York, 1981.

Foster, John. *Class Struggle and the Industrial Revolution: Early Industrial Capitalism in Three English Towns*. New York, 1974.

Fox, J. H. "The Victorian Entrepreneur in Lancashire." In *Victorian Lancashire*, edited by S. P. Bell. Newton Abbot, England, 1974.

Franklin, John Hope. *The Emancipation Proclamation*. New York, 1963.

Fraser, W. Hamish. "'A Newspaper For Its Generation': The Glasgow *Sentinel*, 1850–1877." *Journal of the Scottish Labour History Society*, 4 (July 1971): 18–30.

Freidel, Frank. "The Loyal Publication Society: A Pro-Union Propaganda Agency." *Mississippi Valley Historical Review*, 26 (December 1939): 359–76.

Gillespie, Frances E. *Labor and Politics in England, 1850–1867*. Durham, N.C., 1927.

Glicksberg, Charles I. "Henry Adams Reports on a Trades-Union Meeting." *The New England Quarterly* 15(1942): 724–28.

Glickstein, Jonathan A. "Poverty is Not Slavery: American Abolitionists and the Comparative Labor Market." In *Anti Slavery Reconsidered: New Perspectives on the Abolitionists*, edited by Lewis Perry and Michael Fellman. Baton Rouge, 1979.

Goodyear, Irene E. "Wilson Armistead and the Leeds Antislavery Movement." *Thoresby Society Publication* 54 (1974): 113–29.

Gordon, Beverley. *Bazaars and Fair Ladies: The History of the American Fundraising Fair*. Knoxville, Tenn., 1998.

Gray, Robert Q. *The Labour Aristocracy in Victorian Edinburgh*. Oxford, 1976.

Greenleaf, Richard. "British Labor Against American Slavery." *Science and Society*, 17 (1953): 42–58.

Hall, Catherine. "Rethinking Imperial Histories: The Reform Act of 1867." *New Left Review* 208 (1994): 3–29.

Hall, Robert G. "Chartism Remembered: William Aitken, Liberalism, and the Politics of Memory." *Journal of British Studies* 38 (October 1999): 445–70.

Harrison, Brian. *Drink and the Victorians: The Temperance Question in England, 1815–1872*. Pittsburgh, 1971.

———. "Philanthropy and the Victorians." *Victorian Studies* 9 (1966): 353–76.

———. "Religion and Recreation in Nineteenth-Century England." *Past and Present* 38 (1967): 98–125.

Harrison, Roydon. *Before the Socialists: Studies in Labour and Politics, 1861–1881*. London, 1965.

——— "British Labour and American Slavery." *Science and Society* 25 (December 1961): 291–319.

———. "British Labour and the Confederacy." *International Review of Social History* 2, Pt. 1 (1957): 78–105.

———. "Professor Beesly and the Working-Class Movement." In *Essays in Labour History*, edited by Asa Briggs and John Saville, 205–49. London, 1960.

Harrison, Roydon. *Before the Socialists: Studies in Labour and Politics, 1861–1881*. London, 1965.

Haynes, Ian. *Mossley Textile Mills*. Radcliffe, England, 1996.

Henderson, W. O. "The Cotton Famine in Scotland and the Relief of Distress, 1862–1864." *Scottish Historical Review* 30 (October 1951): 154–64.

Hernon, Joseph M., Jr. "British Sympathies in the American Civil War: A Reconsideration." *Journal of Southern History* 33 (1967): 356–67.

———. *Celts, Catholics, and Copperheads: Ireland Views the American Civil War*. Columbus, Ohio, 1968.

———. "Irish Religious Opinion on the American Civil War." *Catholic Historical Review* 49 (1964): 508–23.

Hewitt, Martin. *The Emergence of Stability in the Industrial City: Manchester, 1832–1867*. Aldershot, England, 1996.

Holcroft, Fred. *A Terrible Nightmare: The Lancashire Cotton Famine around Wigan*. Wigan, England, 1992.

Holland, John. "Hugh Mason, Cotton Master and Father Figure." In *Victorian Ashton*, edited by Sylvia A. Harrop and E. A. Rose. Tameside, England, 1974.

Holt, Thomas C. *The Problem of Freedom: Race, Labor, and Politics in Jamaica and Britain, 1832–1938*. Kingston, Jamaica, 1992.

Honour, Hugh. *The Image of the Black in Western Art*, 4 vols. Cambridge, Mass., 1989.

Horsman, Reginald. "Origins of Racial Anglo-Saxonism in Great Britain before 1850." *Journal of the History of Ideas* 37 (1976): 387–410.

Hubbard, Charles M. *The Burden of Confederate Diplomacy*. Knoxville, Tenn., 1998.

Ittmann, Karl. *Work, Gender, and Family in Victorian England*. New York, 1995.

Jameson, J. F. "The London Expenditure of the Confederate Secret Service." *American Historical Review* 25 (1930): 811–24.

Jenkins, Brian. *Britain and the War of the Union*, 2 vols. Montreal, 1980.

———. "Frank Lawley and the Confederacy." *Civil War History* 23 (1977): 144–60.

———. *Sir William Gregory of Coole: The Biography of an Anglo-Irishman*. Gerrards Cross, England, 1986.

———. "William Gregory: Champion of the Confederacy." *History Today* 28 (1978): 322–30.

Jones, Gareth Stedman. *Languages of Class: Studies in English Working-Class History, 1832–1982*. Cambridge, England, 1983.

Jones, Howard. *Union in Peril: The Crisis over British Intervention in the Civil War*. Chapel Hill, N.C., 1992.

Jones, Robert Huhn. "Anglo-American Relations, 1861–1865, Reconsidered." *Mid America* 44–45 (1962–1963): 36–49.

Jones, Wilbur Devereux. "Blyden, Gladstone, and the War." *Journal of Negro History* 49 (1964): 56–61.

————. "The British Conservatives and the American Civil War." *American Historical Review* 58 (1953): 527–43.

Jordon, Donaldson and Edwin J. Pratt. *Europe and the American Civil War.* Boston, New York, 1931.

Joyce, Patrick. *Work, Society, and Politics: The Culture of the Factory in Late Victorian England.* New Brunswick, N.J., 1980.

Kelly, John. "The End of the Famine: The Manchester Cotton Trade, 1864–1867—A Merchant's Eye View." In *Textile History and Economic History,* edited by H. B. Harte and K. G. Ponting. Manchester, England, 1973.

Kertzer, David I. *Ritual, Politics, and Power.* New Haven, Conn., 1988.

Kirk, Neville. *The Growth of Working-Class Reformism in Mid–Victorian England.* Urbana, Ill., 1985.

Kutolowski, J. F. "Victorian Provincial Businessmen and Foreign Affairs: The Case of the Polish Insurrection, 1863–1864." *Northern History* 21 (1985): 236–58.

Lancaster, Bill. *Radicalism, Cooperation, and Socialism: Leicester Working-Class Politics, 1860–1906.* Leicester, England, 1987.

Leventhal, F. M. *Respectable Radical: George Howell and Victorian Working-Class Politics.* New York, 1971.

Leys, Colin. "Petitioning in the Nineteenth and Twentieth Centuries." *Political Studies* 3 (February 1955): 59.

Lillibridge, G. D. *Beacon of Freedom: The Impact of American Democracy upon Great Britain, 1830–1870.* Philadelphia, 1955.

Lock, Alice. "The Role of Local Clergy and Ministers in the Stalybridge Riots of 1863." In *Looking Back at Stalybridge,* edited by Alice Lock. Tameside, England, 1989.

Logan, Frenese A. "India—Britain's Substitute for American Cotton, 1861–1865." *Journal of Southern History* 24 (1958): 472–80.

Longmate, Norman. *The Hungry Mills.* London, 1978.

Lonn, Ella. *Foreigners in the Confederacy.* Chapel Hill, N.C., 1940.

Lorimer, Douglas A. *Colour, Class, and the Victorians: English Attitudes to the Negro in the Mid–Nineteenth Century.* New York, 1978.

————. "The Role of Anti-Slavery Sentiment in English Reactions to the American Civil War." *The Historical Journal* 19 (1976): 405–20.

Lowe, J. C. "The Tory Triumph of 1868 in Blackburn and in Lancashire." *The Historical Journal* 16 (1973): 733–48.

Lowe, W. J. "Lancashire Fenianism, 1864–1871." *Transactions of the Historic Society of Lancashire and Cheshire* 126 (1974): 156–85.

Marriner, Sheila. *Rathbones of Liverpool, 1845–1873.* Liverpool, 1961.

Maurer, Oscar. "*Punch* on Slavery and the Civil War in America, 1861–1865." *Victorian Studies* 1 (September 1957): 5–28.

Maynard, Douglas. "Civil War 'Care': The Mission of the *George Griswold.*" *New England Quarterly* 34 (September 1961): 291–310.

Merli, Frank J. *Great Britain and the Confederate Navy, 1861–1865.* Bloomington, Ind., 1965.

—— and Theodore A. Wilson. "The British Cabinet and the Confederacy: Autumn 1862." *Maryland Historical Magazine* 65 (1970): 239–62.

Midgley, Clare. "Slave Sugar Boycotts, Female Activism, and the Domestic Base of British Anti-Slavery Cultures." *Slavery and Abolition* 17 (1996): 137–62.

——. *Women against Slavery: The British Campaigns, 1780–1870.* London, 1992.

Milner, D. M. "J. P. Chown, 1821–1886." *The Baptist Quarterly* 25 (1973): 15–40.

Moffatt, Frederick C. *Errant Bronzes: George Grey Barnard's Statues of Abraham Lincoln.* Newark, N.J., 1998.

Monaghan, Jay. "An Analysis of Lincoln's Funeral Sermons." *Indiana Magazine of History* 41 (March 1945): 31–44.

Morgan, James M., Jr., *The Jackson-Hope and the Society of the Cincinnati Medals of the Virginia Military Institute.* Verona, Va., 1979.

Neely, Mark E. *The Fate of Liberty: Abraham Lincoln and Civil Liberties.* New York, 1991.

Oates, Stephen B. "Henry Hotze: Confederate Agent Abroad." *Historian* 27 (1965): 131–54.

Oldfield, J. R. *Popular Politics and British Antislavery: The Mobilisation of Public Opinion against the Slave Trade.* Manchester, England, 1995.

Owsley, Frank Lawrence. *King Cotton Diplomacy: Foreign Relations of the Confederate States of America.* 1939. Reprint, Chicago, 1969.

Owsley, Harriet Chappell. "Henry Shelton Sanford and Federal Surveillance Abroad, 1861–1865." *Mississippi Valley Historical Review* 48 (September 1961): 211–28.

Park, Joseph H. "The English Workingmen and the American Civil War." *Political Science Quarterly* 39 (1924): 432–57.

Parry, Jonathan. *The Rise and Fall of Liberal Government in Victorian Britain.* New Haven, Conn., 1993.

Paterson, R. M. "Newmilns Weavers and the American Civil War." *Ayrshire Archeological Natural History Collection,* 2d ser., 1 (1949): 98–105.

Patterson, A. Temple. *Radical Leicester: A History of Leicester, 1780–1850.* Leicester, England, 1954.

Pelling, Henry. *America and the British Left from Bright to Bevan.* New York, 1957.

Phillips, Paul T. *The Sectarian Spirit: Sectarianism, Society, and Politics in Victorian Cotton Towns.* Toronto, 1982.

Pickering, Paul A. *Chartism and the Chartists in Manchester and Salford.* New York, 1995.

Pole, J. R. *Abraham Lincoln and the Working Classes of Britain.* London, 1959.

Pollard, Sidney. *A History of Labour in Sheffield.* Liverpool, 1959.

——. "Nineteenth-Century Co-operation: From Community Building to Shop-keeping." in Briggs and Saville, *Essays in Labour History,* 74–112.

Prochaska, F. K. *Women and Philanthropy in Nineteenth-Century England.* Oxford, 1980.

Pugh, P. D. Gordon. *Staffordshire Portrait Figures and Allied Subjects of the Victorian Era.* London, 1970.

Rainger, Ronald. "Race, Politics, and Science: The Anthropological Society of London in the 1860s." *Victorian Studies* 22 (autumn 1978): 51–70.

Randall, J. G. *Lincoln, the Liberal Statesman.* New York, 1947.

Rayback, Joseph G. "The American Workingman and the Antislavery Crusade." *Journal of Economic History* 3 (1943): 152–63.

Read, Donald. *Cobden and Bright: A Victorian Political Partnership.* London, 1967.

Reader, W. J. *Professional Men: The Rise of the Professional Classes in Nineteenth-Century England.* New York, 1966.

Rehin, George F. "The Black Image: American Negro Minstrelsy through the Historian's Lens." *Journal of American Studies* 9 (1975): 365–73.

―――. "Harlequin Jim Crow: Continuity and Convergence in Blackface Clowning." *Journal of Popular Culture* 9 (winter 1975): 682–701.

Reinders, R. C. "Anglo-Canadian Abolitionism: The John Anderson Case, 1860–1861." *Renaissance and Modern Studies* 19 (1975): 82–94.

Riach, Douglas C. "Blacks and Blackface on the Irish Stage, 1830–1860." *Journal of American Studies* 7 (December 1973): 231–41.

Rice, C. Duncan. *The Scots Abolitionists, 1833–1861.* Baton Rouge, 1981.

Roberts, Stephen. "Joseph Barker and the Radical Cause, 1848–1851." *Miscellany,* Thoresby Society, 2d ser., 1 (1990): 59–73.

Robertson, A. J. "The Decline of the Scottish Cotton Industry, 1860–1914." *Business History* 12 (1970): 116–28.

Rose, Michael. "Rochdale Man and the Stalybridge Riot: The Relief and Control of the Unemployed during the Lancashire Cotton Famine." In *Social Control in Nineteenth-Century Britain,* edited by A. P. Donajgrodzki. London, 1977.

Ross, Ishbel. *Rebel Rose: Life of Rose O'Neal Greenhow, Confederate Spy.* New York, 1954.

Rowland, Kate Mason. "English Friends of the Confederacy." *Confederate Veteran* 25 (May 1917): 198–202.

Royle, Edward. *Victorian Infidels: The Origins of the British Secularist Movement, 1791–1866.* Manchester, England, 1974.

Runkle, Gerald. "Karl Marx and the American Civil War." *Comparative Studies in Society and History* 6 (1964): 117–41.

Saville, John. *Ernest Jones: Chartist.* London, 1952.

Schwartz, Barry. "Mourning and the Making of a Sacred Symbol: Durkheim and the Lincoln Assassination." *Social Forces* 70 (1991): 343–64.

―――. "The Reconstruction of Abraham Lincoln." In *Collective Remembering,* edited by David Middleton and Derick Edwards. London, 1990.

Sears, L. M. "A Confederate Diplomat at the Court of Napoleon III." *American Historical Review* 27 (January 1921): 255–81.

Semmel, Bernard. *Democracy versus Empire: The Jamaica Riots of 1865 and the Governor Eyre Controversy.* Garden City, N.J., 1969.

Shaine, Charles E. "The English Novelists and the American Civil War." *American Quarterly* 14 (fall 1962): 399–421.

Shapiro, Herbert. "Labor and Antislavery: Reflections on the Literature." *Nature, Society, and Thought* 2 (1989): 471–90.

Shepperson, Wilbur S. *Emigration and Disenchantment: Portraits of Englishmen Repatriated from the United States.* Norman, Okla., 1965.

Silver, Arthur W. "Henry Adams' 'Diary of a Visit to Manchester.'" *American Historical Review* 50 (1945): 74–89.

———. *Manchester Men and Indian Cotton, 1847–1872.* Manchester, England, 1966.

Sirett, K. F. and K. J. Williams. "Liverpool and the American Civil War: A Confederate Heritage in England." *Journal of Confederate History* 4 (1989): 113–29.

Stange, Douglas Charles. *British Unitarians against American Slavery, 1833–1865.* Rutherford, N.J., 1984.

Stock, Leo Francis. "Catholic Participation in the Diplomacy of the Southern Confederacy." *Catholic Historical Review* 16 (1930): 1–18.

Storch, Robert D. "The Problem of Working-Class Leisure: Some Roots of Middle-Class Moral Reform in the Industrial North: 1825–50." In *Social Control in Nineteenth-Century Britain*, edited by A. P. Donajgrodzki. London, 1977.

Stuart, Denis, ed. *People of the Potteries: A Dictionary of Local Biography.* Keele, England, 1985.

Taylor, Amos. "Walker's Financial Mission to London on Behalf of the North, 1863–1864." *Journal of Economic and Business History* 3 (1931): 296–320.

Taylor, Miles. *The Decline of British Radicalism, 1847–1860.* Oxford, 1995.

Taylor, Peter. *Popular Politics in Early Industrial Britain: Bolton, 1825–1850.* Keele, England, 1995.

Temperley, Howard. *British Antislavery, 1833–1870.* Columbia, S.C., 1972.

———. "Capitalism, Slavery, and Ideology." *Past and Present* 75 (1977): 94–118.

Thomas, Emory. *The Confederate Nation, 1861–1865.* New York, 1979.

Thompson, Alvin O. "'Happy—Happy Slaves!': Slavery as a Superior State of Freedom." *Journal of Caribbean History* 29 (1995): 93–119.

Thornbrough, Emma Lou. *Indiana in the Civil War Era, 1850–1880.* Indianapolis, 1965.

Todd, Nigel. "Black-on-Tyne: The Black Presence on Tyneside in the 1860s." *North East Labour History* 21 (1987).

———. *"The Militant Democracy": Joseph Cowen and Victorian Radicalism.* Tyne and Wear, England, 1991.

Toole, Janet. "Workers and Slaves: Class Relations in a South Lancashire Town in the Time of the Cotton Famine." *Labour History Review* 63 (1998): 160–81.

Trevelyan, George M. *The Life of John Bright.* Boston, 1913.

Tucker, Philip. "Confederate Secret Agent in Ireland: Father John B. Bannon and the Irish Mission, 1863–1864." *Journal of Confederate History* 5 (1990): 55–85.

Turner, Thomas Reed. *Beware the People Weeping: Public Opinion and the Assassination of Abraham Lincoln.* Baton Rouge, 1982.

Van Brockhoven, Deborah. "'Better than a Clay Club': The Organization of Women's Antislavery Fairs, 1835–1860." *Slavery and Abolition* 19 (1998): 24–45.

Van Deusen, Glyndon G. *Thurlow Weed, Wizard of the Lobby.* Boston, 1947.

Verity, T. E. A. "Edward Arundel Verity, Vicar of Habergham: An Anglican Parson of the Industrial Revolution." *Transactions of the Lancashire and Cheshire Antiquarian Society* 9 (1977): 73–94.

Vernon, James. *Politics and the People. A Study in English Political Culture, c. 1815–1867.* New York, 1993.

Villiers, Brougham and W. H. Chesson. *Anglo-American Relations, 1861–1865.* 1919. Reprint, Port Washington, N.Y., 1972.

Voegeli, V. Jacque. *Free But Not Equal: The Midwest and the Negro during the Civil War.* Chicago, 1967.

Waller, John O. "Charles Kingsley and the American Civil War." *Studies in Philology* 60 (1963): 554–68.

Waller, P. J. *Democracy and Sectarianism: A Political and Social History of Liverpool, 1868–1939.* Liverpool, 1981.

Ward, J. T. "Revolutionary Tory: The Life of Joseph Rayner Stephens of Ashton-under-Lyne (1805–1879)." *Transactions of the Lancashire and Cheshire Antiquarian Society* 68 (1958): 93–116.

Ware, Edith W. "Committees of Public Information, 1863–1866." *The Historical Outlook* 10 (1919): 65–67.

Webb, R. K. *Harriet Martineau: A Radical Victorian.* London, 1960.

Webster, Eric. "Edward Akroyd (1810–1887): Also a Brief History of James Akroyd and Son." *Transactions of the Halifax Antiquarian Society* (1987): 19–45.

Weisser, Henry. "Chartist Internationalism, 1845–1848." *The Historical Journal* 14 (1971): 49–66.

Weller, David. "Northampton and the American Civil War." *Northampton Past and Present* 8 (1990): 137–53.

Whiteridge, Arnold. "British Liberals and the American Civil War." *History Today* 12 (1962): 688–95.

Wiener, Martin J. *English Culture and the Decline of the Industrial Spirit, 1850–1980.* New York, 1981.

Williams, Frances Leigh. *Matthew Fontain Maury: Scientist of the Sea.* New Brunswick, N.J., 1963.

Wilson, Alexander. *The Chartist Movement in Scotland.* Manchester, England, 1970.

Wilson, Keith. "Chartism in Sunderland." *North East Labour History* 16 (1982): 13–18.

Wise, Stephen R. *Lifeline of the Confederacy: Blockade Running during the Civil War.* Columbia, S.C., 1988.

Wright, D. G. "Bradford and the American Civil War." *The Journal of British Studies* 8 (May 1969): 69–85.

――――. "Leeds Politics and the American Civil War." *Northern History* 9 (1974): 96–122.

―――― and J. A. Jowitt, eds. *Victorian Bradford.* Bradford, England, 1982.

Young, Robert W. *Senator James Murray Mason: Defender of the Old South.* Knoxville, Tenn., 1998.

Ziegler, Valerie H. *The Advocates of Peace in Antebellum America.* Bloomington, Ind., 1992.

Theses and Dissertations

Anderton, Paul. "The Liberal Party of Stoke-on-Trent and Parliamentary Elections, 1862–1880: A Case Study in Liberal-Labour Relations." Master's thesis, University of Keele, 1974.

Auger, Philip John. "The Cotton Famine, 1861–1865: A Study of the Principal Cotton Towns During the American Civil War." Ph.D. dissertation, Cambridge University, 1979.

Beardsmore, Valerie. "Moses, Martyr, and Messiah: Abraham Lincoln and Black Emancipation: A Study in the Popular Development and Political Use of Myth, with Special Reference to the Years from 1860–1870." Ph.D. dissertation, University of Kent at Canterbury, 1980.

Bingham, Robert LeBaron. "The Glasgow Emancipation Society, 1833–76." M.Litt. thesis, University of Glasgow, 1973.

Botsford, Robert. "Scotland and the American Civil War." Ph.D. dissertation, Edinburgh University, 1955.

Brennan, M. "The Cotton Famine in Rochdale, 1861–1865, with Particular Reference to the Role of John Bright." Master's thesis, Leeds University, 1990.

Clayton, Caroline. "Black Face Power: The Construction of Black Face Performance in England and Their Contribution to Attitudes to Race, 1832–1867." Master's thesis, University of Warwick, 1991.

Corke, Margaret Wendy. "Birmingham and the American Civil War." Master's thesis, University of Liverpool, 1963.

Eckersley, T. P. "The Growth of the Cotton Industry in Mossley, with Special Reference to the Mayalls." Master's thesis, Manchester Polytechnic, 1991.

Fielden, Kenneth. "Richard Cobden and America." Ph.D. dissertation, Cambridge University, 1965.

Gunn, Simon. "The Manchester Middle Class, 1850–1880." Ph.D. dissertation, University of Manchester, 1992.

Hall, Robert G. "Work, Class, and Politics in Ashton-under-Lyne, 1830–1860." Ph.D. dissertation, Vanderbilt University, 1991.

Harrison, Gillian E. "A Study of the Effects of the Cotton Famine in Blackburn, 1861–1865: Its Effects and Consequences." Bachelor's thesis, University of Lancaster, 1985.

Hooper, H. F. "Mid-Victorian Radicalism: Community and Class in Birmingham, 1850–1880." Ph.D. dissertation, University of London, 1979.

Hughes, Frank. "Liverpool and the Confederate States." M.Phil. thesis, Keele University, 1998.

Keiser, Thomas J. "The English Press and the American Civil War." Ph.D. dissertation, University of Reading, 1971.

Kenworthy, F. "The Industrial Development of Mossley, Lancashire." Honors thesis, history, University of Manchester, 1928.

Lancaster, William. "Radicalism to Socialism: The Leicester Working Class, 1860–1906." Ph.D. dissertation, Warwick University, 1982.

Mair, Miriam. "Black Rhythm and British Reserve: Interpretation of Black Musicality in British Racist Ideology since 1750." Ph.D. dissertation, University of London, 1987.

Morgan, Henry Nigel Barre. "Social and Political Leadership in Preston, 1820–1860." M.Litt. thesis, University of Lancaster, 1980.

Owen, Gwynne E. "Welsh Anti-Slavery Sentiments, 1790–1865: A Survey of Public Opinion." Master's thesis, University College of Aberystwyth, 1964.

Parker, Brian. "The Effect of the American Civil War on Britain, with Specific Reference to the Cotton Industry in Nottinghamshire, 1861–1865." Master's thesis, University of Nottingham, n.d.

Peers, P. M. "The Cotton Famine in Ashton-under-Lyne, 1861–1865." n.d., University of Manchester, 1970.

Peters, Lorraine. "Scotland and the American Civil War: A Local Perspective." Ph.D. dissertation, University of Edinburgh, 1999.

Ratcliffe, Peter. "A Consideration of the Lancashire Cotton Famine, 1861–1865, and the Exceptional Case of Bolton." Bachelor's thesis, Liverpool University, 1985.

Reid, Carol Anne Naomie. "The Chartist Movement in Stockport." Master's thesis, University of Hull, 1974.

Sweeney, Irene Elizabeth. "The Municipal Administration of Glasgow, 1833–1912: Public Service and the Scottish Civil Identity." Ph.D. dissertation, University of Strathclyde, 1990.

Tiller, Kathleen. "Working Class Attitudes and Organisations in Three Industrial Towns, 1850–1875." Ph.D. dissertation, University of Birmingham, 1975.

Van Auken, Sheldon. "English Sympathy for the Southern Confederacy: The Glittering Illusion." Bachelor's thesis, Oxford University, 1957.

Wright, D. G. "Politics and Opinion in Nineteenth-Century Bradford, 1832–1880." Ph.D. dissertation, University of Leeds, 1966.

Unpublished

Birley, C. B. "The Pedigree of the Birley Family of Lancashire and Other Branches." Typescript, 1930, Manchester Public Library.

Flatman, Janella. "Goodacre's America: A Weekly Letter from America to the Citizens of Nottingham." Prepared for Dr. Reinders's tutorial, University of Nottingham, n.d.

Hill, Joanne. "The Special Case of Bolton During the Lancashire Cotton Famine." Prepared for Dr. Reinders's tutorial, University of Nottingham, n.d.

Pearson, Richard. "The Effects of the Cotton Famine Caused by the American Civil War upon the Domestic Life of Preston." Typescript, 1966, Preston Public Library.

Smith, Charles. "Stockport in the Age of Reform, 1822–1870; or, History from a Newspaper File." Typescript, 1938, Stockport Public Library.

Index